Native American Women

A Biographical Dictionary

Garland Reference Library of the Social Sciences (Vol. 649)
Biographical Dictionaries of Minority Women, Volume 1

Biographical Dictionaries of Minority Women

Native American Women
A Biographical Dictionary

Gretchen M. Bataille
editor

African American Women
A Biographical Dictionary

Dorothy C. Salem
editor

Angela Howard Zophy
Series Editor

Native
American
Women

A Biographical Dictionary

Gretchen M. Bataille
editor

Laurie Lisa
editorial assistant

Garland Publishing
New York & London
1993

Library of Congress Cataloging-in-Publication Data

Bataille, Gretchen M. 1944–
    Native American women : a biographical dictionary /
Gretchen M. Bataille, editor.
        p.   cm. — (Garland reference library of social
science : v. 649) (Biographical dictionaries of minority
women : v. 1)
    ISBN 0-8240-5267-6
Includes bibliographical references and index.
    1. Indians of North America—Women. 2. Indians of
North America—Biography—Dictionaries. 3. Women—
North America—Biography—Dictionaries. I. Title.
II. Series. III. Series: Biographical dictionaries of
minority women : v. 1.
E98.W8B38   1993
920.72'08997—dc20
[B]   92-19990
                                                             CIP

Printed on acid-free, 250-year-life paper
Manufactured in the United States of America

Contents

Preface

As series editor for *Garland's Biographical Dictionaries of Minority Women*, I have had the privilege to work with many outstanding colleagues in the field of women's history whose scholarship has already expanded the scope of women's history to include and acknowledge the presence and contributions of all women in the pluralistic society of this nation. Each volume in this series focuses upon the biographic and bibliographic sources available to inform both lay and professional researchers from many academic disciplines about women within a particular ethnic group.

I first confronted the paucity and inadequacy of basic reference sources on minority women when I began to edit the *Handbook of American Women's History* in the late 1980s. My contributors and I had to use our best and most determined research techniques to track down biographical information and bibliographical sources for women who were significant historical participants, yet whose names appeared in general historical monographs in a few places like UFO blips on a radar screen. When I lamented this appalling lack of collections of minimal facts and works on minority women to my editor at Garland, Kennie Lyman offered me the opportunity to coordinate the collection of such basic historical and historiographical data on these neglected women.

Gretchen Bataille was one of the first to accept my invitation to edit one of our volumes. We are very fortunate that she agreed to undertake this ambitious but long overdue effort to restore to the historical record the names and contributions of Native American women whose lives influenced the development of the history of the United States. I am very proud to be associated with this much needed reference work that is the result of the indefatigable efforts of its editor and her contributors. I applaud her execution of our mission to render accessible fundamental information and research sources for this significant group of American women.

I thank Professor Bataille for allowing her commitment to her field to overrule the wisdom of all previous editorial experience which decrees that "no good deed goes unpunished," and welcome her into my informal support group of editors of reference works in Women's Studies who accept the challenge of the almost impossible task of restoring to public awareness all women whose lives have earned them the honor of being remembered by generations to come. Despite our knowledge that inevitably a few significant women still would not be found among the entries within each volume, we nonetheless strive to offer comprehensive coverage of minority women within this series.

Angela Howard Zophy
Series Editor
Associate Professor of History
University of Houston—Clear Lake

Acknowledgments

From the first telephone call I received from Angela Zophy, I knew this project would involve many, many people. Her own book, *Handbook of American Women's History*, was a monumental undertaking and, while I knew that I would be focusing only on one group, I also knew that it would take the cooperation of many others to make this dictionary a reality. In the end, there are sixty-one contributors, ranging from known scholars who took the time to prepare brief entries on women about whom they have written lengthy manuscripts to graduate students who took on the task of researching often obscure Native women of history and sometimes myth. Throughout the project, contributors continued to send in additional names for inclusion, and the project grew even larger. There is no way to acknowledge the many voices which contributed to making the final collection possible.

To Laurie Lisa, my research assistant who became the editorial assistant for this book, I am immensely grateful. Without Laurie's diligence, good sense, and excellent writing and editing abilities, this book could not have been completed. For her always cheerful approach to an immense typing task, I am grateful to Kathy Sidlik. Kathy's keen eye often noticed discrepancies both Laurie and I missed. Roxana Martin ably prepared the final manuscript for publication and worked overtime to complete the task.

I appreciate the institutional support of Arizona State University and the academic climate which makes possible research projects such as this. The College of Liberal Arts and Sciences supported a research assistant throughout the life of the project and supported the preparation of the final manuscript. The staff at Interlibrary Loan at the Hayden Library at Arizona State University was prompt and helpful as we tried to locate obscure sources to verify entries.

To all those who contributed and to those about whom this book is written, I am indebted.

Gretchen M. Bataille
Arizona State University

Introduction

Although the lives of Native American women have generally been ignored by many historians, and Indian women have been stereotyped as "squaws" and "princesses" in children's books and many textbooks, ongoing research continues to establish the importance of their roles in both traditional and contemporary cultures. Many factors have combined to produce inaccurate images of American Indian women in today's society. Historically, cultural determinants and the diversity of Indian cultures established the traditional roles and positions of women within their tribes, but political mandates, educational reforms, and religious fervor often eroded tribal organization and women's roles, a contradiction which continues to define the lives of American Indian women. The histories of Native women from the past such as Pocahontas, Sacagawea, Lozen, or Dahteste resonate with fabulous tales of sacrifice or exploits, achieving for Native women explorer or warrior status, but much of what has been published perpetuates myths which have been repeated by scholars for so long that the complete truth will probably always remain hidden.

From the earliest journals, Native women's lives have been described by outsiders unfamiliar with the cultures or the women's roles within those cultures. In his earliest journals, Christopher Columbus praises the "gentle" people he encountered, but he quickly replaces his admiration with scorn when it becomes clear to him that he must subdue these people to achieve any recognition as a hero for his ambitious journeys to a "new world." Amerigo Vespucci, after whom two continents are named, observes in his letters that Indian men and women are "dirty and shameless" with "no modesty." Of the women, he writes, "They are very fertile women, and in their pregnancies avoid no toil." This view was resurrected by later writers and moviemakers who consistently have shown Native women disappearing briefly into the trees to give birth and then returning to hoe the fields or tan hides without seeming to have suffered either pain or exhaustion. He also writes that Native women are "heartless and cruel" and go about "utterly naked," certainly a contrast to the heavily robed women of his contemporary Europe and therefore unacceptable to European tastes.[1] These descriptions by male outsiders with ethnocentric expectations began a pattern of description of Native American women which continues to influence biography, fiction, and visual images.

Later historians were influenced by such written accounts as well as by early woodcuts which portrayed Native women in ambiguous ways. While decrying the nakedness and cruelty of these women, early writers also referred to their generosity and attractiveness. John Smith, in his accounts of Pocahontas, portrays the girl-child as gentle and eager to please the white settlers. Many woodcuts showed Native women as representing America itself, usually depicted as a semi-naked woman in a bucolic setting. The image appeared frequently on seventeenth century maps of the New World.

For the past forty years scholars have attempted to develop and communicate realistic portrayals of Native American women, but much of their work has been fragmentary and undocumented. In spite of these efforts, many writers have been hampered by the inaccuracies and misconceptions of previous work. Carolyn Foreman, in *Indian Women Chiefs* (1954), relies on many earlier sources of dubious authenticity in an attempt to provide documentation of the lives of Indian women who had power within their tribes. Repeatedly, she generalizes and perpetuates inaccurate data and terminology. For instance, Foreman calls Sarah Winnemucca (Hopkins) a "chief." Although Winnemucca was influential in her tribe, she never carried the title of "chief." Just as the terms "princess" and "queen" had been misused by Europeans who did not understand Indian tribal organization, Foreman erroneously uses "chief" to designate women leaders who held positions of power and influence. Ten years later, Lela and Rufus Waltrip published *Indian Women*, a collection of thirteen embellished narratives about Indian women. The authors provided speeches for Pocahontas and Sacagawea, attempting to recreate the world of the 1600s and 1700s. Although they provide a bibliography, it is incomplete and often inaccurate. As a scholarly source, the book fails to provide accurate or even convincing information. These two books were followed in 1974 by Marion E. Gridley's *American Indian Women*. Gridley borrows heavily from the Waltrips' book in her generalizations about Indian women. She includes Pocahontas and Sacagawea along with seventeen other Indian women from Wetamoo to contemporary figures such as Wilma Victor and Annie Dodge Wauneka, providing readable but often undocumented biographies.

It finally took the efforts of Indian women themselves to present an accurate account of Native women's histories and lives. Rayna Green's essay in *Signs* (1980), followed by her work with the Ohoyo Resource Center and then her bibliography *Native American Women: A Contextual Bibliography* in 1983, offers a substantial body of reliable historical, biographical, and ethnographic information on Indian women in traditional and contemporary tribal cultures. More recently, the feminist work of Paula Gunn Allen in *The Sacred Hoop* (1986) reinterprets Indian women's history within a contemporary framework which relies on sacred myth as well as Indian women's personal testimonies. Writers such as Louise Erdrich, Leslie Marmon Silko, Linda Hogan, Joy Harjo, Lee

Maracle, Beverly Hungry Wolf, Wendy Rose, and others continue to contribute to a revisionist view of American Indian women's experiences. Many of these women use their bi-cultural training to communicate both the scholarly and the personal to define female experience within tribal communities threatened by external factors.

The lives of legendary and historical figures as well as contemporary American Indian women presented in this dictionary reflect cultural continuities and changes. Information on the historical figures included herein was drawn from existing sources, some of which remain ambiguous and contradictory. Some women might have several names in their lifetime, and those names often have been spelled or translated differently in various sources, making the task of compiling accurate information more difficult. The biographies of contemporary women were often edited by the women themselves, providing verification and credibility to the entries.

These biographies represent many American Indian women with diverse roles within their cultures. Every effort has been made through networking and research to present a broad cross-section of Native women's experiences in both historical and contemporary contexts. Their roles reflect the historical times within which they lived, the degree of acculturation, or the level of education. The variety of gender roles and degrees of power experienced by Native American women is not easily represented in the pre-contact or early colonial periods in a collection such as this because so little is known about individual lives. Nevertheless, we have enough information to conclude that in agricultural societies such as the Iroquois or the Navajo, women were accorded more status than they received in the primarily hunting societies of the Great Plains. Women's status among the Iroquois has been a subject of much interest, yet little is known about specific Iroquois women in history except such exceptional figures as Kateri of the Mohawks or Molly Brant. The Iroquois organized their kinship groups into matrilineal clans whose members traced their descent from a common female ancestor. Iroquois women owned the longhouses in which they lived and passed them on to their descendants. They also had a great deal of power because they controlled the agricultural life of the tribes by managing the farming activities. They are but one example of Native women whose roles and responsibilities gave them significant power in traditional tribal societies, a power which is still evident in some contemporary accounts.

Prior to white contact, women also had a great deal of power among the Cherokee in the South. Women had the right to speak in village councils, and some accompanied the men when the tribe went to war. Cherokee tribal chairwoman Wilma Mankiller is a contemporary example of the strength of Cherokee women which exists yet today. Women of the Southwest continue to exist in matrilocal and matrilineal societies where their roles in agriculture, female puberty ceremonies, and tribal government remain prominent. Myths of

Spider Woman, Changing Woman, and Yellow Woman reinforce the position of women in these tribal societies.

Between 1790 and 1840 missionaries and government agents urged Native Americans to value individual ownership of land, European gender roles, and the patriarchal family. The traditional base of women's power among groups such as the Iroquois and the Cherokee was eroded by the imposition of Judeo-Christian values, the influence of which only abated with the passage of the American Indian Religious Freedom Act of 1978. The Act guaranteed legal recognition of sacred places such as Taos Blue Lake, sacred plants, and ceremonies such as the Sun Dance, and in doing so often reaffirmed the traditional roles of women in these societies.

Many of the negative images of Indian women developed as a result of contact with Euro-American society, and the assault on traditional practices took many forms. Fur trappers and traders changed the material culture of the tribes by introducing and developing a demand for iron, glass beads, cloth, and dyes. The missionaries judged Indian women by traditional Judeo-Christian views that denigrated the power women held in some tribes in favor of European-style patriarchy. Often Native women were judged on the basis of how helpful they could be to whites. Pocahontas, who saved Captain John Smith in 1607 and married John Rolfe, a leader of the English colony in Virginia, is one famous example of an Indian woman valued by whites. Sacagawea of the Shoshone, who traveled with the Lewis and Clark expedition between 1804 and 1806, gained a significant place in history for purportedly leading explorers across the country.

Efforts to assimilate Native women into Euro-American society through education also changed the status of women. Schools run by missionaries and the Bureau of Indian Affairs established curricula along stereotypical lines, training women in homemaking skills while punishing them for speaking their native languages or wearing traditional clothing. In the twentieth century Indian women have been victims of medical practices that resulted in mass sterilizations and dubious experimentation with depoprovera, a hormonal shot given to mentally retarded Indian women, leading to accusations of genocide. Such spokespersons as Connie Uri and groups such as Women of All Red Nations (WARN) have brought media attention to these practices, and regulations governing sterilization were issued by HEW in 1979. The United States court system has interfered with tribal laws regarding child custody and hunting and fishing practices, and civil rights laws, although passed in support of minority rights, have actually conflicted with some tribal powers and traditions.

There has been some redress for grievances in recent times, and much of the pressure has been brought to bear by Indian women. Groups such as WARN and Ohoyo and women within the National Indian Education Association have argued for women's issues to receive attention from educators, the government, and tribes. The Indian Child Welfare Act of 1978, which mandated preference for placement of Indian children with Indian families and recognized tribal rights in adoption and placement of foster children, brought attention to one of contemporary Indian women's greatest concerns: the future of their children.

Today the rate of infant mortality of Indians exceeds that of the national rate of all races, the rate of Fetal Alcohol Syndrome (FAS) is three to six times higher than the national average, and Indian children suffer disproportionately from otitis media (middle ear disease), probably the leading cause of learning deficiencies among these children. Native American children with handicapping conditions are less likely to receive services than other American children. Until the passage of the Indian Child Welfare Act, preservation of the Indian family was not considered a priority by government agencies, and many Indian children were placed in non-Indian foster care and adoptive homes or boarding schools without consultation with the families or tribes involved.

All of the factors which have affected Indian peoples have impacted upon the women. These external influences are reflected in the choices they have made in their lives and in their ability to endure and to succeed. Many contemporary women have spoken out and have written their own stories, tribal histories, fiction, and poetry. Beth Brant has spoken for many of these women: "What good is this pen, this yellow paper, if I can't fashion them into tools or weapons to change our lives?" [2] These brief accounts cannot possibly provide all the details of these women's lives; however, the words are indeed "weapons" to change the popular impression that Indian women have no viable history and no recognizable present.

Accurate biographies, even if they are brief, are an effective means of gaining a true picture of the variety of experiences and of the powers and endurance of Indian women. This collection provides information which is missing from general biographical dictionaries of women, books which include sketches of only the most obvious and well-known figures. The European views which incorporated both fascination and repugnance obscured accurate depictions, and even the most well-intentioned scholarship has often been flawed. This volume begins a series of biographical dictionaries which will fill in the missing figures in history, the women of color who are as much a part of America's past and present as their lighter-skinned sisters and brothers.

From an original list of fewer than one hundred names, this project grew as each contributor became engaged in the process of adding new names. The list was made available to all contributors and, throughout the United States, Canada, and Europe, interested scholars corrected inaccurate data and provided alternate spellings for individual names, set the record straight on misinformation, and suggested additions or deletions. There are sure to be women who should have been included and were not, perhaps because of insufficient information or because contributors who volunteered to prepare certain entries were unable to complete the material. Every attempt was made to verify information; however, there are sure to be errors because of the difficulty of verifying the realities of women's lives. The involvement of many women in their own biographies is a beginning, however, and gives assurance that future accounts might be more accurate.

1. *Amerigo Vespucci: Letter to Piero Soderini Gonfaloniere.* Translated and edited by George Tyler Northup. Princeton: Princeton University Press, 1916, 7–10.
2. *Food and Spirits: Stories by Beth Brant.* Ithaca: Firebrand Books, 1991.

Selected Bibliography

Albers, Patricia, and Beatrice Medicine, eds. *The Hidden Half: Studies of Plains Indian Women.* Washington, DC: University Press of America, 1983.

> Essays on Plains tribal women covering such topics as slaves, male/female roles, work division, women's production of ceremonial objects, women's political roles, and the changing status of Plains women.

Allen, Paula Gunn. *The Sacred Hoop: Recovering the Feminine in American Indian Traditions.* Boston: Beacon Press, 1986.

> Analysis of the gynocentric character of pre-contact Pueblo culture and the erosion of women's power through imposition of European patriarchal systems. Discussion of the role of American Indian women writers within the context of contemporary Indian women's cultures.

Anderson, Owanah, ed. *Ohoyo One Thousand: A Resource Guide of American Indian/Alaska Native Women, 1982.* Wichita Falls, TX: Ohoyo Resource Center, 1982.

> Biographical sketches of over 1000 American Indian/Alaskan Native women indexed according to area of expertise.

Axford, Roger W. *Native Americans: 23 Indian Biographies.* Indiana, PA: A.G. Halldin, 1980.

> Includes interviews with and statements by Ida Carmen, Betsy Kellas, Clara Sue Kidwell, Veronica L. Murdock, Joanne Linder, Vivian Ayoungman, Yvonne Talachy, Gay Lawrence, Carol Allen Weston, and Roxie Woods.

Bataille, Gretchen M., and Kathleen M. Sands. *American Indian Women: A Guide to Research.* New York: Garland, 1991.

> A comprehensive bibliography of over 1500 annotated entries including bibliographies, reference works, ethnography, cultural history, social roles, politics, law, health, education, employment, visual and performing arts, literature and criticism, autobiography, biography, interviews, film, and video.

―――. *American Indian Women Telling Their Lives.* Lincoln: University of Nebraska Press, 1984.

> Examination of American Indian women's personal narratives and the centrality of women in tribal cultures. Focuses on eight autobiographical texts and speculates on emerging forms of autobiography by American Indian women.

Dockstader, Frederick J. *Great North American Indians; Profiles in Life and Leadership*. New York: Van Nostrand Reinhold, 1977.
>   An extensive compilation of 300 biographies; includes photographs and biographies of many Indian women.

Foreman, Carolyn. *Indian Women Chiefs*. 1954. Reprint. Washington, DC: Zenger, 1976.
>   Foreman summarizes the roles of women in several tribes and discusses well-known Indian women such as Nancy Ward and Sarah Winnemucca as well as lesser-known figures.

Green, Rayna. *Native American Women: A Contextual Bibliography*. Bloomington: Indiana University Press, 1983.
>   A briefly annotated bibliography of over 600 entries covering political, social, cultural, and biological issues.

———. "Native American Women: Review Essay." *Signs* 6 (Winter 1980): 248–67.
>   Discussion of the scholarship and popular literature written about American Indian women since the seventeenth century.

Gridley, Marion E. *American Indian Women*. New York: Hawthorn Books, 1974.
>   General introduction and chapters summarizing the lives of nineteen American Indian women.

Medicine, Beatrice. *The Native American Woman: A Perspective*. Austin, TX: National Educational Laboratory Publishers, 1978.
>   A contemporary perspective by a Lakota woman who has been a spokeswoman for Indian women's rights and who is also an anthropologist.

Niethammer, Carolyn. *Daughters of the Earth: The Lives and Legends of American Indian Women*. New York: Collier Books, 1977.
>   The cycle of life for women in traditional Indian cultures is described and analyzed. Childbirth, childhood, courtship, marriage, homemaking, power roles, arts, religious practices, aging, and death are described for several cultures of North America.

Ohoyo Resource Center. *Words of Today's American Indian Women: Ohoyo Makachi*. Wichita Falls, TX: Ohoyo Resource Center, 1982.
>   Collection of conference proceedings and speeches by American Indian and Alaska Native women who attended a major conference in Tahlequah, Oklahoma, in 1981.

Secretary of State of Canada. *Speaking Together: Canada's Native Women*. Ottawa: Hunter Rose, 1975.
>   Published in conjunction with the celebration of International Women's Year. Includes brief biographical sketches, personal statements, and photographs of twenty-nine Canadian Indian women.

Terrell, John Upton, and Donna M. Terrell. *Indian Women of the Western Morning: Their Life in Early America*. New York: Dial Press, 1974.

Descriptions of the various roles of American Indian women with examples from different culture areas. Includes many pan-Indian generalizations.

Waltrip, Lela, and Rufus Waltrip. *Indian Women: Thirteen Who Played a Part in the History of America from the Earliest Days to Now*. New York: David McKay, 1964.

Biographical sketches of thirteen Indian women from 1535 to the 1960s.

ABEITA, LOUISE [E-YEH-SHURE', BLUE CORN] (b. 1926) is the author of *I Am a Pueblo Indian Girl*, a limited edition book prepared under the sponsorship of the National Gallery of the American Indian. She was born in Isleta Pueblo, New Mexico. When her father realized her natural talent as a poet, he had the inspiration to bring together Indian artists, Navaho, Apache, and Pueblo, in a cooperative endeavor to make the first truly Indian book.

Abeita describes her way of life in both prose and poetry and includes interesting insights into the Pueblo traditions. The illustrators present a stirringly beautiful picture of the surviving Pueblo culture. The book was printed when she was thirteen years old.

Abeita is a member of one of the strong families of the Isleta Pueblo who wish to hold onto the good things of their culture and the ancient religion. Her publication was part of an effort to unite the traditional words and implied ideas with illustrations to make Pueblo life understood in the simplest way possible. This was a first tentative step to make their artistry understood by the English speaking public.

—Joyce Ann Kievit

Reference

Abeita, Louise. *I Am a Pueblo Indian Girl*. New York: William Morrow, 1939.

ACKERMAN, MARIA JOSEPH [LDANEIT] (b. 1927), a Tlingit, was born in Juneau, Alaska, and is a member of the Raven tribe in the Cohoe Clan. During her childhood, she lived with her maternal grandparents, who earned their living from traditional arts. Her grandmother did beadwork and made moccasins and spruce root baskets; her grandfather carved totem poles. Ackerman attended school for four years at the Pius X Mission School in Skagway, Alaska, living with her aunt, Jessie Jacobs, during that time. From her, Ackerman learned sewing and heard the traditional Tlingit stories. These oral stories that had been handed down from one generation to the next are recorded in Ackerman's *Tlingit Stories*, a compilation of thirteen tales, including "The Girl and Woodworm," "May the Best Animal Win," and "The Trapper and the Kooshd'aa K'aas."

Ackerman is the mother of five children and has worked as a resource Native artist for the Anchorage Borough School District Indian Education Program. She maintains a great interest in Tlingit arts and crafts and has given courses on skin sewing and beadwork.

—Laurie Lisa

Reference

Ackerman, Maria. *Tlingit Stories*. Anchorage: Alaska Methodist University Press, 1975.

AHENAKEW, FREDA (b. 1921), Plains Cree linguist and university professor, comes from Atâhkakohp (also known as Sandy Lake), Saskatchewan. She resumed her interrupted high school education in 1968 and attended classes with nine of her twelve children. She became a Cree language teacher under the guidance of the late Ida MacLeod, received a BEd from the University of Saskatchewan in 1979, and took an MA in Cree linguistics at the University of Manitoba in 1984. Director of the Saskatchewan Indian Languages Institute at Saskatoon from 1985 to 1989, she is now associate professor and head of Native Studies at the University of Manitoba. She is widely recognized as a leader in the movement to retain the indigenous linguistic and literary heritage of Canada.

In addition to articles on Cree language teaching and linguistics, children's story books, and an introductory grammar book, *Cree Language Structures: A Cree Approach*, she has published several volumes of Cree texts. In recent years, she has devoted much of her time and energy to the careful transcription, analysis, and translation of traditional stories and autobiographical accounts (especially women's life experiences), preparing them for publication in Cree (in both syllabic and roman orthographies) and exactly as they were told in Cree.

—John D. Nichols

References

Ahenakew, Freda. *Cree Language Structures: A Cree Approach*. Winnipeg: Pemmican Publications, 1987.

Ahenakew, Freda, ed. *kiskinahamawâkan-âcimowinisa/Student Stories Written by Cree-Speaking Students*. Algonquian and Iroquoian Linguistics Memoir 2, 1986.

———. *wâskahikaniwiyiniw-âcimowina/Stories of the House People*. Told by Peter Vandall and Joe Doquette. Publications of the Algonquian Text Society. Winnipeg: University of Manitoba Press, 1987.

Tootoosis, Kevin, ed. *Profiles: Professional Aboriginal Peoples of Saskatchewan*. Saskatoon: Saskatchewan Indian Cultural Centre, 1990.

AINSE, SALLY [SALLY MONTOUR, SARA MONTOUR, HANDS, HAINS, WILLSON] (c. 1728–1823), Oneida fur trader, land owner, and diplomat, was probably born in 1728 and raised in the Susquehanna River region. At age seventeen she married Andrew Montour, Indian interpreter for the British government, by whom she had several children. According to her own words, after several years of marriage she was left with her people, the Oneidas. This

probably occurred between 1757 and 1758. From the Oneidas she acquired a deed to certain lands in the Fort Stanwix (Rome, New York) area. Records indicate that by this time Ainse had begun her career as a trader. Sometime after the commencement of the American Revolution, she abandoned her New York lands and removed to the British-controlled Detroit District. Known until then as Sally or Sara Montour, in the Detroit region she became best known as Sally Ainse, although there are references to her as Hands, Hains, or Willson. By the spring of 1775, Ainse was doing business in the region trading cider and other goods to the Indians for furs, and in 1778 she bought a house and lot in Detroit with the profits from that business. According to the 1779 Detroit census records, she continued to prosper. Her holdings at that time were four slaves, three cows, four horses, and one hundred pounds of flour.

Ainse also became well known as a woodland diplomat and intermediary. After the 1794 defeat of the allied Indian tribes by United States forces commanded by General Anthony Wayne at the Battle of Fallen Timbers, Ainse participated in the peace negotiations between these warring nations. She also acted on behalf of Chief Joseph Brant, transmitting messages and speeches between the various Indian tribes and the British government.

In 1783 Ainse acquired, through a Chippewa deed, land along the north shore of the Thames River at present-day Chatham, Ontario. By 1787 she had sold her land in Detroit and permanently settled on her Chatham lands. Her holdings there were extensive, and at any one time she was in possession of three improved farms, an orchard, and a "mansion" house. The formal purchase from the Chippewas of the lands in this region by the British Crown in 1790 (the McKee Purchase) marked the beginning of what became a twenty-three year legal struggle by Ainse to retain possession of her Chatham lands. The British Land Board charged with the subsequent sale and distribution of these lands refused to recognize her Chippewa deed. Ainse's claim rested not only on her Chippewa deed, but also on a specific exemption of her property from the McKee Purchase. She was supported in her claim by seven Chippewa chiefs, who in 1791 signed a statement affirming that indeed their "sister's" lands had been exempted. Other prominent Indians and Europeans came to her defense: the influential Mohawk Chief Joseph Brant, Lieutenant Governor Simcoe, and the powerful head of Indian Affairs, Sir John Johnson. But, in the end, not even these personages could secure Ainse's claim against the rising tide of white settlers to the region. In 1813 Ainse relinquished the fight for her lands. Sometime after 1806 Ainse is said to have moved to Amherstburg, Ontario, where she resided until her death in 1823.

—Faren R. Siminoff

References

Hamil, F.C. *The Valley of the Lower Thames, 1640–1850*. Toronto: University of Toronto Press, 1951.

————. *Sally Ainse, Fur Trader*. Detroit: The Algonquin Society, 1939.

Kelsay, Isabel Thompson. *Joseph Brant 1743–1807: Man of Two Worlds*. Syracuse, NY: Syracuse University Press, 1984.

Surtees, Robert J. "Indian Land Cessions in Ontario, 1763–1862: The Evolution of a System." PhD diss., Carleton University, Ottawa, 1983.

Tanner, Helen Hornbeck, ed. *Atlas of Great Lakes Indian History*. Norman: University of Oklahoma Press, 1986.

ALBERTY, ELIZA MISSOURI BUSHYHEAD

ALBERTY, ELIZA MISSOURI BUSHYHEAD (1839–1919), Cherokee educator and businesswoman, was the seventh child of Rev. Jesse Bushyhead (also called Unaduti), a Cherokee and Baptist minister, and Eliza Wilkinson (also spelled Wilkerson by some descendants), of mixed white and Cherokee blood. Her father established a Baptist mission, originally known as "Bread Town" because of the rations given to the immigrants who passed through it, near present-day Westville, Arkansas. Alberty attended school at the Baptist mission until 1854, when she enrolled in the Cherokee Female Seminary at Park Hill, Cherokee Nation, where she graduated in 1856. She then taught at the Post Oak Grove and Vann's Valley schools (two of the Cherokee Nation's public schools) until 1859. In 1858 she married David Rowe Vann, a mixed-blood Cherokee. Three years after his death in 1870, she married Bluford West Alberty, also a mixed-blood.

Soon after their marriage, the Albertys were appointed stewards of the Cherokee Insane Asylum (they named their homestead "Belleview"). In 1885 they purchased a hotel in Tahlequah—the capital of the Cherokee Nation—and named it "National Hotel." After her husband's death in 1889, Alberty managed the hotel, making it one of the most successful hotels in Indian Territory. Eliza Alberty was active in the Baptist church and because of the seminarians' affection for her was also known as "Aunt Eliza." Her brother, Dennis Wolfe Bushyhead, served as Principal Chief of the Cherokee Nation from 1879 to 1888.

—Devon A. Mihesuah

References

Foreman, Carolyn Thomas. "Aunt Eliza of Tahlequah." *Chronicles of Oklahoma* 9 (March 1931): 43–55.

Miner, H. Craig. "Dennis Bushyhead." In *American Indian Leaders: A Study in Diversity*, edited by R. David Edmunds, 192–205. Lincoln: University of Nebraska Press, 1980.

West, Clarence William. *Tahlequah and the Cherokee Nation: 1841–1941*. Muskogee, OK: Muskogee Publishing, 1978.

ALLEN, ELSIE (1899–1990), tribal scholar, cultural consultant, and re-nowned Pomo weaver, was born in a hop field outside Santa Rosa, California, to George (Ukiah Pomo) and Annie Comanche (Cloverdale Pomo). George died when Allen was a young girl; her mother married Richard Burke (half Pomo), with whom she had a boy and girl.

Allen, who spoke only Pomo as a youth, learned to read and write English between ages thirteen and sixteen. She spent her teens working as a field hand. At eighteen, she went to San Francisco, where she worked as a housekeeper, then secured a job at Saint Joseph's Hospital. In 1919 she married Arthur Allen (Pinoleville Pomo), with whom she had three children.

Allen was active in the Pomo Women's Club (established in 1940 and disbanded in 1957), through which Native American women provided "social and financial support for their people." She helped with club fundraisers and headed up the basket committee. In the 1940s the club supported a successful lawsuit by Steven Knight against a Ukiah theater that denied Indians the right to sit on its lower floor. To avoid future lawsuits, other Ukiah business owners ended their "No Indians Allowed" policies as a result. Later, Allen was active in the similar Hintil Women's Club, which did charitable work and gave educa-tional scholarships to local Indians.

Allen's mother, Annie Burke, broke with Pomo tradition on her deathbed when she begged Allen to keep the family's baskets rather than burying them with Burke. Burke told Allen the baskets would take Allen travelling, bring people enjoyment, and create an understanding the Pomo weren't "dumb." These baskets and others from the Allen collection are now on loan to the Mendocino County Museum in Willets.

At age sixty-two, Allen found time to take up the Pomo basketmaking she had learned in her youth, a tradition she demonstrated to a wide audience. In 1972 Allen's book, *Pomo Basketry: A Supreme Art for the Weaver*, brought widespread recognition of Pomo basketry to a contemporary audience. From 1979–81, Allen was also a primary consultant for the Warm Springs Cultural Resources Study, which detailed the history and culture of the Dry Creek and Cloverdale Pomo. Because of her cultural work, Allen received an honorary Doctorate of Divinity as "Pomo Sage."

Allen's most enduring contribution was in becoming the first Pomo weaver to teach Pomo basketry to people outside her family, including non-Indians, against all tradition. According to Kathleen Smith (Bodega Miwok/Dry Creek Pomo), "Elsie Allen felt this urge that if she didn't share what she knew, it would die. She didn't want it to die, so she broke with the real strong tradition of not teaching to those outside your family. She got a lot of flack, but the time was right for people to listen to her." According to her grandniece, Susan Billie (Hopland Pomo), who is carrying on Allen's basketmaking tradition, "Elsie just loved people. She didn't care about money and material things. She cared about people."

—Bev Ortiz

References

Allen, Elsie. *Pomo Basketmaking: A Supreme Art for the Weaver.* Edited by Vinson Brown. Healdsburg, CA: Naturegraph Publishers, 1972.
Eisenberg, Bonnie, and Marylynne Slayen. "An Interview with Kathleen Smith." *Women's Voices* 6 (March 1981): 16–17.
Frederickson, Vera Mae, ed. "School Days in Northern California: The Accounts of Six Pomo Women." *News from Native California* 4 (Fall 1989): 40–45.
McGill, Marsha Ann. "California Indian Women's Clubs: Past and Present." *News from Native California* 4 (Spring 1990): 22–23.
Ortiz, Bev. Personal Communication with Elsie Allen, 1986.
———. Personal Communication with Susan Billie, 1990.
———. Personal Communication with Kathleen Smith, 1990.

ALLEN, MINERVA (b. 1943) is an Assiniboine poet and short story writer from Lodgepole on the Fort Belknap Reservation on the high line in northern Montana. She was educated at a private high school in Flandreau, North Dakota, then went on to Central Michigan University. She holds two graduate degrees, an MA in Career Guidance from Northern Montana College and an MAT from Weber State College in Utah.

She has eight children and has worked as administrator for the Hays-Lodgepole Schools in Fort Belknap, Montana. She says, "I write poetry concerning my tribe to keep our heritage and culture."

—Renae Moore Bredin

References

Allen, Minerva. *Like Spirits of the Past Trying to Break Out and Walk to the West.* Albuquerque, NM: Wopai, 1974.
———. *Spirits Rest.* Los Angeles: By the author, 1981.
Hobson, Geary. *The Remembered Earth.* Albuquerque: University of New Mexico Press, 1980.
Kittredge, William, and Annick Smith, eds. *The Last Best Place: A Montana Anthology.* Seattle: University of Washington Press, 1988.
Lourie, Dick, ed. *Come to Power.* Trumansburg, NY: The Crossing Press, 1974.
Scholer, Bo. "Minerva Allen: A Few Good Words." *Wicazo Sa Review* 3 (Spring 1987): 1–7.

ALLEN, PAULA GUNN (b. 1939) was born at Cubero, New Mexico, to a Lebanese-American father and a Laguna-Sioux-Scotch mother, both of whom were native New Mexicans. She is divorced and a mother of three children. In 1966 she received her BA from the University of Oregon, Eugene; in 1968 an

MFA from the same university; and in 1975 a PhD in American Studies from the University of New Mexico, Albuquerque.

She taught at San Francisco State University in 1975–76; at the University of New Mexico in 1977–78; at Fort Lewis College, Durango, Colorado, in 1978–79; and at the University of California, Berkeley, in 1982–86. Currently, she teaches English at UCLA.

Her research and writing fellowships include a NEA Fellow, Creative Writing, 1977–78; a Research Fellow, Institute of the Americas—American Indian Center for Research, UCLA, 1981–82; and a National Research Council Senior Post Doctoral Fellow for Minority Scholars, 1984–85.

She has been awarded with a Kappa Kappa Gamma Prize for Poetry, University of New Mexico, 1964; a Julia Burgess Prize for Poetry, University of Oregon, 1967; a Creative Writing Award, National Endowment for the Arts, 1977–78; a nomination for the Pushcart Poetry Prize, 1981 and 1979; and for *The Woman Who Owned the Shadows*, a 1983 citation from the San Francisco Board of Supervisors for contributions to the San Francisco Native American community.

Paula Gunn Allen is one of the most important American Indian intellectuals and artists. She is an avowed feminist and very active in women's movements as well as in antiwar and antinuclear organizations. A prolific writer, she has written seven collections of poems, a novel, and a huge body of critical essays. As a poet, she uses a remarkable range of techniques and language through which she conveys to the reader the basic thematic elements of her poetry, juxtaposing her Pueblo reality against white dominant culture, to the role of women in the traditional Indian world view, the sense and meaning of her own Indianness, and the powerful mythic imagery as a means of resistance, regeneration, and survival. Her novel, *The Woman Who Owned the Shadows*, is a stream-of-consciousness narrative of an Indian woman caught between cultures and her quest to become whole, surrounded by the shadows of her tribal and personal past. Innovative in its structure and influenced by writers such as Gertrude Stein and Virginia Woolf, the novel still remains distinctly Native American; its thematic interaction between past and present, the Pueblo ceremonial life and culture, and the storytelling tradition play a fundamental role in shaping the main character's new identity.

Allen's outstanding work as a critic centers on American thought and on American history from a minority perspective, a comprehensive introduction to Indian spiritual beliefs, a mythopoetic approach to American Indian literature, and the theme of alienation in Indian prose and poetry. *Studies in American Indian Literature*, which she edited in 1983 for the Modern Language Association, is a standard work in the cross-disciplinary field. *The Sacred Hoop: Recovering the Feminine in American Indian Traditions* is a collection of seventeen essays dealing with cultural history, ethnic feminism, literary criticism, and the spirituality of traditional tribes and their use of the feminine.

She has also edited one of the most praised anthologies, *Spider Woman's Granddaughters: Short Stories by American Indian Women*, a collection of short fiction, along with stories from the oral tradition and excerpts from autobiographies.

—Laura Coltelli

References

Allen, Paula Gunn. *The Blind Lion*. Berkeley, CA: Thorp Springs Press, 1974.
———. *A Cannon Between My Knees*. New York: Strawberry Press, 1983.
———. *Coyote's Daylight Trip*. Albuquerque: La Confluencia, 1978.
———. "The Grace That Remains: American Indian Women's Literature." *Book Forum* 5 (1981): 376–82.
———. "The Sacred Hoop: A Contemporary Indian Perception of American Indian Literature." In *Literature of the American Indians: Views and Interpretations*, edited by Abraham Chapman, 111–35. New York: New American Library, 1975.
———. *The Sacred Hoop: Recovering the Feminine in American Indian Traditions*. Boston: Beacon Press, 1986.
———. *Shadow Country*. Los Angeles: American Indian Studies Center Series, 1982.
———. *Skins and Bones*. San Francisco: West End Press, 1988.
———, ed. "Special Issue: Native Women of New Mexico." *A: A Journal of Contemporary Literature* 3 (Fall 1978).
———, ed. *Spider Woman's Granddaughters: Traditional Tales and Contemporary Writing by Native American Women*. Boston: Beacon Press, 1989.
———. *Star Child*. Marvin, SD: Blue Cloud Quarterly Press, 1981.
———. "A Stranger in My Own Life: Alienation in Native American Prose and Poetry." *ASAIL Newsletter* 3 (Spring 1979): 16–23. Reprint. *MELUS* 7 (1980): 3–19.
———, ed. *Studies in American Indian Literature: Critical Essays and Course Designs*. New York: MLA, 1983.
———. "Where I Came From Is Like This." In *Rereading America: Cultural Contexts for Critical Thinking and Writing*, edited by Gary Colombo, Robert Cullen, and Bonnie Lisle, 273–81. New York: St. Martin's Press, 1990.
———. *The Woman Who Owned the Shadows*. San Francisco: Spinster's Ink, 1983.

ANAUTA [ANAUTA FORD BLACKMORE, A STICK FOR BEATING SNOW FROM YOUR CLOTHES] (b.?), an Inuit, was born on Baffin Island, the third child and first daughter of Yorgke (George Ford) and Alea. She does not know the exact date of her birth, but she does know that her birth occurred during a blizzard when a respected hunter was lost. She was named Anauta after him, expected to follow in his footsteps and expected to excel. Consequently, her mother allowed the hunter Anauta's mother, Oomiálik, to raise Anauta.

Anauta dressed as a male for the first years of her life and learned the skills of hunting and trapping. Later, she wore women's clothing and learned the sewing and domestic skills of her people. She had the traditional arranged wedding to Uille, a man who respected her abilities as a hunter and trapper. They had two daughters; a third was born after Uille's drowning. Anauta then travelled to Labrador, then through Canada, finally settling in Indianapolis. Anauta married Blackmore, and it was a union that produced one daughter and that was later amicably ended.

Anauta's autobiography details her difficulties in adjusting to a new culture, the problems she had with money, her struggle to learn English, and the illnesses of her family. She worked for five years in a factory before finding a career as a lecturer of Baffin Island culture and way of life. She spoke at churches and schools throughout the Midwest.

At the request of the Reverend E.J. Peck in Toronto, Anauta translated the Psalms and the Lord's Prayer into her Native language. The task was difficult because the English words often had no Eskimo equivalent; she worked on this project for several years. Anauta is also the co-author, with Heluiz Washburne, of three books. *Land of Good Shadows* is her autobiography, *Wild Like the Foxes* is based on the childhood of Anauta's mother, Alea, and *Children of the Blizzard* is a collection of stories depicting the life of Eskimo children.

—Laurie Lisa

References

Washburne, Heluiz, and Anauta. *Children of the Blizzard.* London: Dennis Dobson, 1960.

———. *Land of Good Shadows: The Life Story of Anauta, an Eskimo Woman.* New York: John Day, 1940.

———. *Wild Like the Foxes: The True Story of an Eskimo Girl.* New York: John Day, 1956.

ANDERSON, MABEL WASHBOURNE (1863–1949), a writer and teacher, descended from two well-known families in Cherokee affairs. Her maternal grandfather was John Ridge, a leader of the Treaty Party, and her paternal grandfather was Cephus Washburn (Anderson's father changed the spelling), an early missionary and founder of Dwight Mission among the Cherokee. Although she was born in Arkansas, Anderson lived from early childhood onward in the Cherokee Nation, later Oklahoma. She was educated in the Cherokee public school system, graduating from the Cherokee Female Seminary in 1883 and later becoming a teacher at Vinita.

After her marriage to John Carlton Anderson in 1891, she continued to teach and began to write. She wrote for the local newspaper concerning education and school systems. She was also a member of the local Sequoyah Literary Society, writing and reading presentations of Cherokee history and lore and contributing articles and poems on such topics to local and out-of-territory newspapers. In 1904 the Andersons moved to Pryor Creek, where Mabel continued to write biographies, histories, and articles about folklore, art, and literature, for the most part concerning American Indians, and she taught English in the local high school. She was also active in civic affairs, the Christian church, and the United Daughters of the Confederacy (UDC).

In relation to the latter, it was one of her life's goals to have a monument erected to the memory of the Cherokee general, Stand Watie, her grandfather's cousin. In 1913 she organized a UDC chapter in his name and in 1915 published a short biography to promote interest in his memory. She revised and republished the work in 1931.

After the Andersons moved to Tulsa in 1930, she wrote little and dropped from public view. When she died, she was described by a local newspaper as a "colorful pioneer," and no emphasis was placed on the distinguished Cherokee family from which she descended.

—Daniel F. Littlefield, Jr.

References

Anderson, Mabel Washbourne. *The Life of General Stand Watie, the Only Indian General of the Confederate Army and the Last General to Surrender.* Pryor, OK: Mayes County Republican, 1915. 2nd rev. ed. Pryor, OK: By the author, 1931.
Boren, Lyle H., and Dale Boren. *Who Is Who in Oklahoma.* Guthrie, OK: Co-operative Publishing, 1935.
Littlefield, Daniel F., Jr., and James W. Parins. *A Biobibliography of Native American Writers, 1772–1924.* Metuchen, NJ: Scarecrow Press, 1986.
Pryor Jeffersonian [Pryor OK] 22 September 1949: 8.
"Sketch of Mrs. Mabel W. Anderson." *Twin Territories* 3 (June 1901): 99.
Vinita Weekly Chieftain [Vinita, Cherokee Nation] 5 March 1903: 8.

ANDERSON, OWANAH (b. 1926), editor, author, administrator, was

born to Choctaw parents in Choctaw County, Oklahoma. A priority in Anderson's career has been helping to advance the status of American Indian/ Alaska Native women. Pursuing this goal, she founded and directed the Ohoyo (Choctaw for "woman") Resource Center in 1979 and served as its director. Anderson's other leadership roles include serving as chairperson of the National Committee on Indian Work in 1979–80 and as the co-chairperson of the Texas delegation during the Houston Women's Conference in 1977. She also sat on President Carter's Advisory Committee on Women from 1978 to 1981 and was the only American Indian appointment to the Commission on Security and Cooperation held in Madrid, Spain, in 1980. In 1981 Anderson received the Anne Roe Award from the Harvard University Graduate School of Education.

in the late 1980s as part of SITES (Smithsonian Institution Traveling Exhibits Series). She has also been series editor for a collection of tribal catalogs.

—Cynthia Kasee

References

Anderson, Owanah, ed. *Ohoyo One Thousand: A Resource Guide of American Indian/Alaska Native Women, 1982.* Wichita Falls, TX: Ohoyo Resource Center, 1982.

Fixico, Michelene, comp. *Resource Directory of American Indian Professionals.* Milwaukee: University of Wisconsin Press, 1987.

Who's Who Among the Sioux. Vermillion: University of South Dakota Institute of Indian Studies, 1988.

ARMSTRONG, JEANNETTE (b. 1948) was born on the Okanagan

Reserve near Penticton, British Columbia, where she grew up receiving instruction from her parents and traditional elders, as well as attending the local school system. She is a grandniece of Hum-Ishu-Ma (Mourning Dove, 1888–1936), the author of an early Native American novel by a woman, *Cogewea: The Half-Blood* (1927).

Jeannette Armstrong earned a diploma of fine arts from Okanagan College and later a BFA in creative writing from the University of Victoria. An active member of the political and cultural life of her Okanagan Nation, she has worked in various capacities in the curriculum development and cultural programs of her people. Two books of juvenile fiction came out of this involvement: *Enwhisteetkwa: Walk on Water* and *Neekna and Chemai.*

Jeannette Armstrong was an elected council member of the Penticton Band. Since 1978 she has been working with the Okanagan people's En'Owkin Cultural Center, serving as its director since 1985. The En'Owkin Center also houses Theytus Books, the first Native owned and operated publishing house in Canada. In 1985 Jeannette Armstrong's first novel (for young and adult readers), *Slash*, was published by Theytus Books. The novel combines historiography (of the American Indian Movement and related Native struggles in Canada) with the fictional biography of a young Okanagan man, Thomas Kelasket, who moves from a very traditional upbringing on the reserve, through skid row, addiction, crime and prison, towards political awakening and active involvement in the Red Power Movement. Kelasket finally comes to realize that unless he observes, follows, and practices a traditional Indian way even in a modern setting, there is no Indian identity and no survival worth struggling for, so that the people may continue.

Besides her internationally acclaimed novel, Jeannette Armstrong has published poetry and short fiction, winning artistic achievement prizes like the Mungo Martin Award (1974), the Helen Pitt Memorial Award (1978), and the

Vancouver Foundation Graduate Award (1978). A brilliant orator, she has addressed Native and non-Native audiences across North America on issues of cultural self-determination, ethnic pride, Native voice, and Indian self-expression through the arts, especially literature.

She initiated the establishment of the En'Owkin School of International Writing, the first creative writing program designed and operated by Native people, affiliated with the University of Victoria. Since September 4, 1989, when the En'Owkin School first started to operate, she has been the director of that program, which attracts increasing numbers of students and published its first journal, entitled *Gatherings*, in the fall of 1990.

—Hartmut Lutz

References

Armstrong, Jeannette. *Enwhisteetkwa: Walk on Water*. Cloverdale, MB: Friesen Printers, 1982.
———. *Neekna and Chemai*. Penticton, BC: Theytus Books, 1984.
———. "Rights on Paper: An Interview by Victoria Freeman." *Fuse* (March/April 1988): 36–38.
———. *Slash*. Penticton, BC: Theytus Books, 1985. Rev. ed. 1988.
Currie, Noel Elizabeth. "Jeannette Armstrong and the Colonial Legacy." *Canadian Literature* 124–25 (Spring/Summer 1990): 138–52.
Fee, Margery. "Upsetting Fake Ideas: Jeannette Armstrong's 'Slash' and Beatrice Culleton's 'April Raintree.'" *Canadian Literature* 124–25 (Spring/Summer 1990): 168–80.
"Jeannette Armstrong [interview]." In *Contemporary Challenges: Conversations with Canadian Native Authors*, edited by Hartmut Lutz, 13–32. Saskatoon, SK: Fifth House, 1991.

ARTHUR, CLAUDEEN BATES (b. 1942), Navajo attorney, was born in Ganado, Arizona. After graduating with her JD degree from Arizona State University in 1974, Arthur worked for two years at Navajo Legal Services in the reservation town of Shiprock, New Mexico. In 1978, following the establishment of her private practice, Arthur gained the distinction of becoming the only Indian woman lawyer to attain the rank of Field Solicitor for the United States Department of the Interior. She served with the USDI for four years.

Because of her career accomplishments and her strong belief in the ability of the Navajo woman, Arthur is seen as a role model for Indian women considering a career in law. Concerned also with the entire Navajo Nation, Arthur recognizes the need for Navajos, male and female, to make careful decisions about their future. To insure the self-determination of her people, Arthur stresses the need for education to combat the poverty and unemployment that the Nation faces.

—Steven R. Price

References

Anderson, Owanah, ed. *Ohoyo One Thousand: A Resource Guide of American Indian/Alaska Native Women, 1982.* Wichita Falls, TX: Ohoyo Resource Center, 1982.

Wood, Beth, and Tom Barry. "The Story of Three Navajo Women." *Integrateducation* 16 (March/April 1978): 33–35.

ASHEVAK, KENOJUAK [KENOYUAK, KINOAJUAK] (b. 1927) was born at Ikarasak near Cape Dorset in Arctic Canada. After her father died, Kenojuak and her younger brother were raised by her maternal grandmother, Quisa. In 1949 she married Johnniebo, an artist and hunter with whom she reared sixteen children (five of them adopted). Probably the best known woman Inuit printmaker, Kenojuak resides at Cape Dorset.

In the late 1950s Canadian artist and author James A. Houston, serving as a civil administrator for the Department of Northern Affairs and National Resources, introduced drawing and printmaking to the Inuit people of Cape Dorset. Although not residing in Cape Dorset at the time (but in a nearby fishing village), Kenojuak, encouraged by Houston, began drawing in the late 1950s. By the time Kenojuak and Johnniebo moved to Cape Dorset around 1967, printmaking was a well-established way to earn a living. Kenojuak's graphic designs have appeared in almost every collection of Inuit art since 1959. Since that time her work has been exhibited, collected, and sold internationally.

As early as 1961 the National Film Board of Canada produced a film about Kenojuak's life and environment entitled: *Eskimo Artist—Kenojuak.* Like other Cape Dorset artists, Kenojuak depicts scenes from seasonal activities and figures from Inuit myths. Her images are memorable—filled with grace and spirit. In 1967 (one source says 1970) Kenojuak received the Order of Canada, the nation's highest civilian honor, for her artistic contribution to Canada. Frequently, she creates bird and sun designs for which she is well known. Her most renowned piece is a stone-cut, entitled "The Enchanted Owl," which appeared in the 1960 collection of Inuit art. In 1970 this dazzling bird was used as the design for the six-cent Canadian postage stamp which commemorated the Centennial of the Northwest Territories. Often Kenojuak and Johnniebo collaborated on prints. Together they created a 96–foot square plaster mural (a carved wall panel) which was displayed at the Canadian Pavilion at Expo '70 in Osaka, Japan. In 1974 Kenojuak became a member of the Royal Canadian Academy.

In addition to museum curators and art collectors, Kenojuak's designs have been sought by religious and commercial organizations; the Roman Catholic church used one of her designs in their Sunday Missal Book (1976), while the retail store Northern Images used a Kenojuak design for their logo (1978). In 1980 her 1961 print, "Return of the Sun," was made into a seventeen-cent Canadian stamp. Two years later she was appointed a Companion to the Order of Canada. After Johnniebo's death, Kenojuak remarried. She continues her work as a graphic artist, occasionally producing stone-cuts and engravings.

—Hertha D. Wong

References

Barz, Sandra B., comp. *Inuit Artists Print Workbook*. New York: Arts and Cultures of the North, 1981.
Blodgett, Jean. *Graphic Masterworks of the Inuit: Kenojuak*. Toronto: Mintmark, 1981.
Dorset 79: The Twentieth Annual Cape Dorset Graphics Collection. Toronto: M.F. Feheley, 1979.
Furneaux, Patrick. "Evolution and Development of the Eskimo Print." In *Arts of the Eskimo: Prints*, edited by Ernst Roch, 9–16. Barre, MA: Barre, 1975.
Rosshandler, Leo. "The Eskimo Print, an Appreciation." In *Arts of the Eskimo: Prints*, edited by Ernst Roch, 17–19. Barre, MA: Barre, 1975.
Schuldberg, Jane. "Kenojuak Ashevak." Seattle: Snow Goose Associates, n.d.

ASHOONA, PITSEOLAK (1904–1983) was born on Nottingham Island in Hudson's Strait in Arctic Canada. As a child, Pitseolak lived with her father, Ottochie, and her mother, Timangiak, near Frobisher Bay and Cape Dorset and later on Akudluk Island. One of the best-known Inuit printmakers, she spent much of her adult life at Cape Dorset and is referred to as a Cape Dorset artist. Since in Inuit societies, surnames are not traditional and since there are various spellings of names, there is sometimes considerable confusion about individuals and their relationship to others with the same name. Although Pitseolak is a fairly common name, Pitseolak Ashoona is widely known simply as Pitseolak. Following in her footsteps, Pitseolak's children are also Cape Dorset artists. Her four sons, Ottochie, Kumwartok (variant Koomwartok), Kaka, and Kiawak, are sculptors and her daughter Nawpachee (sometimes spelled Nawpashee, Napachee, Napatchie, or Napassie) is a printmaker.

When in the late 1950s Canadian artist and author James A. Houston, serving as a civil administrator for the Department of Northern Affairs and National Resources, introduced drawing and printmaking to the Inuit people of Cape Dorset, Pitseolak Ashoona was among the first to learn. A widow trying to support her children, Pitseolak began drawing to supplement the income she made from sewing. According to some sources, she produced over seven thousand original drawings, only some of which have been made into prints.

Pitseolak's graphic designs appeared in every one of the annual Cape Dorset print collections from 1960–84. Her prints have been exhibited internationally and some of them are housed at the National Gallery of Canada. Like other Inuit artists, the subject matter of Pitseolak's drawings often includes animals, birds, mythical figures, and seasonal activities, such as hunting, kayaking, or tanning hides. According to Leo Rosshandler, Pitseolak combines "imagination and recollection in well-organized patterns," and her prints convey movement and spirit.

In 1971 she traveled to Ottawa for the formal presentation of the book about her life, *Pitseolak: Pictures Out of My Life*, to the National Library by the Honorable Jean Chretien. Later that year she traveled to Montreal to attend the opening of a solo exhibition of her work at the Canadian Guild of Crafts. Elected a member of the Royal Canadian Academy of Arts in 1974, Pitseolak received a Canada Council Senior Arts Grant in 1975. That same year the International Cinemedia Centre Ltd. made two films about her work: *The Way We Live Today* and *Spirits and Monsters*. In recognition of her contribution to Canadian art, in 1977 she received the Order of Canada, Canada's highest civilian honor. "To make prints is not easy," Pitseolak once explained, "but I am happy doing prints. . . . If I can, I'll make them even after I am dead." Even when ill, Pitseolak continued to draw. She died on May 28, 1983.

—Hertha D. Wong

References

Barz, Sandra B., comp. *Inuit Artists Print Workbook*. New York: Arts and Cultures of the North, 1981.
Dorset 79: The Twentieth Annual Cape Dorset Graphics Collection. Toronto: M.F. Feheley, 1979.
Eber, Dorothy, ed. *Pitseolak: Pictures Out of My Life*. Toronto: Oxford University Press, 1971.
Furneaux, Patrick. "Evolution and Development of the Eskimo Print." In *Arts of the Eskimo: Prints*, edited by Ernst Roch, 9–16. Barre, MA: Barre, 1975.
Katz, Jane B. *This Song Remembers: Self-Portraits of Native Americans in the Arts*. Boston: Houghton Mifflin, 1980.
Rosshandler, Leo. "The Eskimo Print, an Appreciation." In *Arts of the Eskimo: Prints*, edited by Ernst Roch, 17–19. Barre, MA: Barre, 1975.
Schuldberg, Jane. "The Matriarchs." *Snow Goose Flyer* 102 (January/ February 1987).
———. "Pitseolak Ashoona." Seattle: Snow Goose Associates, n.d.

AWASHONKS [THE QUEEN] (b. ?) was one of at least three women chieftains in New England during King Philip's War (1675–76). Her husband Tolony is believed to have died before this period because she was already the squaw sachem of the Saconnet (or Sakonnet) band in the vicinity of present-day Little Compton, Rhode Island, succeeding her brother after his death. Her band was originally part of the Wampanoag confederacy. Unlike two other women chieftains of the period, Weetamoo and Magnus, Awashonks agreed in 1671 to a non-aggression pact with the colonial officials. She allied her tribe with the white settlers (c. 1876), committing some of her warriors to the English advances against King Philip and his confederates. In this way, Awashonks was able to preserve the integrity of her tribe during this time, and during the fighting, she also led her band to the settlement of Sandwich, Massachusetts.

—Laurie Lisa

References

Mathes, Valerie Sherer. "Native American Women in Medicine and the Military." *Journal of the West* 21 (April 1982): 41–48.
Waldman, Carl. *Who Was Who in Native History: Indians and Non-Indians from Early Contacts through 1900.* New York: Facts on File, 1990.

AWIAKTA, MARILOU (b. 1936) is an Eastern Cherokee poet whose unique mixing of themes from Cherokee mythology and antinuclear messages reflects the milieu in which she was raised. In the foothills of the Smoky Mountains, not far from the Cherokee Reservation of Qualla, lies Oak Ridge, the site of nuclear experimentation, key to the success of the Manhattan Project in World War II. Still a leading research area in nuclear energy, Oak Ridge is also federal land, what Awiakta describes as "a reservation for atoms, not Indians."

Graduating magna cum laude with a BA in English from the University of Tennessee in 1958, Awiakta went on to a distinguished career as a poet, lecturer, and folklorist. In 1986 her books, *Abiding Appalachia: Where Mountain and Atom Meet* and *Rising Fawn and the Fire Mystery* (St. Luke's Press, 1978 and 1983, respectively) were chosen by the United States Information Agency's global tour, entitled *Women in the Contemporary World.* She was the only American to have her work featured at the Ceremony for the Survival of the World in Le Havre, France (the poem was "Out of Ashes, Peace Will Rise").

In 1986 Tennessee celebrated Homecoming '86 Literary Festival in Nashville, and once again, Awiakta was honored for her unique contributions to the preservation of traditional culture and its incorporation with atomic age issues. From the works read at this event, Awiakta's "Motheroot" was chosen by Alice Walker to begin a section of her book, *In Search of Our Mothers' Gardens.*

Marilou Awiakta has appeared in PBS programs, such as "Natchez Trace Parkway: A Microcosm of America" (1988) and "American Indian Stories" (1989). She has lectured in such venues as Boston University, the Memphis Arts-in-the-Schools Program, and Tufts University's Conference to Develop a New Model for American Studies, Using Black, Ethnic and Feminist Perspectives. Numerous commissioned articles have appeared in such journals and periodicals as *Southern Exposure, Mandala, Fireweed,* and *The Tennessee Conservationist.*

Marilou Awiakta's latest release is *Selu; Spirit of Survival* (Tradery House, 1991), another commingling of Cherokee stories and modern conservationist themes. She lives in Memphis, Tennessee, with her husband, Paul Thompson, and their three children.

—Cynthia Kasee

References

Cherokee Nation of Oklahoma, ed. *Proceedings of the National Women's Symposium, Tahlequah, OK, 1989.* Tahlequah: Cherokee Nation of Oklahoma, 1990.

Radford University, comp. *Appalachian Studies Conference Proceedings, 1985.* Radford, VA: Radford University, 1985.

Tennessee Arts Commission. *Homewords '86: An Anthology of State Writers.* Knoxville: University of Tennessee Press, 1986.

Walker, Alice. *In Search of Our Mothers' Gardens.* New York: Harcourt Brace Jovanovich, 1983.

AYOUNGMAN, VIVIAN (b. 1947) was born into the Siksika (Blackfoot) Indian Nation, east of Calgary, Alberta, Canada. She attended the "Old Sun" Anglican boarding school until the seventh grade when she was transferred to the public school system due to a Department of Indian Affairs "integration initiative." Encouragement from her family and her own desire to learn helped her to graduate near the top of her class. After graduating from Western Canada High School in Calgary in 1966, she attended the University of Calgary where she majored in secondary education with an emphasis in second languages, graduating in 1970 with a BEd degree. Following college, she worked for three years as a teacher at the Ermineskin Morley Indian Schools before returning to the University of Calgary where she served as a counselor in the Indian Student University Program, which she helped to establish. In 1974 she was elected to the board of directors of Old Sun Community College, later serving as academic vice president. She received her MA and PhD degrees from Arizona State University. She now serves as the director of education for the Treaty Seven Tribal Council in Calgary, Canada. While engaged in her doctoral studies, she was the principal writer for the Sisiai'powashin Curriculum Project of the Siksika Curriculum Committee.

Vivian Ayoungman's interest in education goes beyond the classroom to include the community itself. At the University of Calgary, her interest in cultural diversity led her to join the International Students' Association where she was exposed to different peoples and lifestyles. Her association with the campus Civil Liberties organization increased her awareness of problems within the community, particularly the negative image of American Indians found in textbooks and the media. She worked to dispel this image through speaking engagements at various community and educational organizations as well as the school classroom. Her selection as "Indian Princess of Canada" in 1968 gave her the opportunity to travel throughout Canada speaking in a more official capacity. Personal knowledge of the social and financial hardships faced by the Native American community has served to strengthen her commitment to education.

Throughout her life, Ayoungman has maintained strong ties with her family and community. As part of a family that ranched on the Siksika Nation, she attended the rodeos, pow wows, and ceremonies, including the Sun Dance, that were a part of community life. When away at school, she retained her ties with the Reserve by returning on weekends and spending vacations at home with her family. She attributes much of her success as an educator to her ability to blend formal education with traditional Indian values and cultural traits.

—Arlon Benson

References

Axford, Roger W. "Vivian Ayoungman: Canadian Blackfoot Counselor." In *Native Americans: 23 Indian Biographies.* Indiana, PA: A.G. Halldin, 1980.

Benson, Arlon. Personal communication with Vivian Ayoungman, 20 March 1992.

B

BAHE, LIZ SOHAPPY [OM-NA-MA, CHESHUTS] (b. 1948), a Yakima poet, was born and spent her childhood near Topperish, Washington. In 1969, at the age of twenty-one, she was assigned her Native American name, On-na-ma. According to Bahe, this was a crucial moment in her experience: "My Indian name has made a great difference in my life," she relates. "I really felt like a floating body until I received my name."

Before studying art for a time in Portland, Oregon, Bahe attended the renowned Institute of American Indian Arts in Santa Fe, New Mexico, where, in addition to poetry, she was schooled in painting, sculpture, weaving, ceramics, music, and drama. She returned to the Institute in the summer of 1970 to study in a post-graduate poetry workshop.

Bahe's poetry has been anthologized several times and has appeared in *Suntracks* and *The South Dakota Review*. Her verse, while drawing its form from modern western poetry, conveys a concern for the poet's Native American heritage through subject matter ranging from a tribal parade to a Blackfoot ration card to a cornhusk bag. As Kenneth Lincoln has suggested, the significance of her work, and that of the other young poets from the Institute of American Indian Arts, is that it "mark(s) the beginning of artists fusing old tribal names, new tongues, and adopted literary forms." Bahe currently resides in Topperish with her husband.

—Eric Severson

References

Allen, Terry, and Mae Durham, eds. *The Whispering Wind: Poetry by Young American Indians*. Garden City, NJ: Doubleday, 1972.

Blicksilver, Edith. *The Ethnic American Woman: Problems, Protests, Lifestyle*. Dubuque, IA: Kendall/Hunt, 1978. Expanded printing. 1989.

Jacobson, Angeline, comp. *Contemporary Native American Literature: A Selected and Partially Annotated Bibliography*. Metuchen, NJ: Scarecrow Press, 1977.

Lincoln, Kenneth. *Native American Renaissance*. Berkeley: University of California Press, 1983.

Milton, John R., comp. *The American Indian Speaks*. Vermillion: University of South Dakota Press, 1969.

Niatum, Duane, ed. *Carriers of the Dream Wheel*. New York: Harper and Row, 1975.

BENNETT, KAY CURLEY [KAIBAH] (b. 1922), a Navajo artist, author, and dollmaker, was born in a hogan at Sheepsprings Trading Post, New Mexico. Her father was Keedah, a silversmith, and her mother was Mary (Chahiilbahi) Chischillie. She attended Toadlena Boarding School in Toadlena, New Mexico, where she was later employed as a dormitory attendant (1945–46). From 1946–52 she served as a teacher-interpreter at Phoenix Indian School. In addition, Bennett lived in Afghanistan during 1958–60 and has traveled in the Far East, Middle East, and Europe.

Bennett's autobiography and first book, *Kaibah: Recollections of a Navajo Girlhood*, covers the period 1928–35 and chronicles the everyday life of her New Mexico childhood and girlhood. In the introduction, Bennett states that this is a true story, one that gives the history of her people by recording everyday family life as it was lived during that period. Bennett also illustrates the chapter heading of each vignette. Her second novel, *A Navajo Saga*, written with her husband, Russell Bennett, is another family chronicle spanning the years 1845–68. The central figure is Shebah, based on Bennett's grandmother, and the fictional form focuses on the Bosque Redondo experience and The Long Walk back. Bennett writes, she says, with the purpose of preserving part of Navajo history and culture.

Bennett was a member of the New Mexico Human Rights Commission from 1969–73 and a member of the Inter-Tribal Indian Ceremonial Association. She has also won numerous prizes for her dolls at state fairs in Arizona and New Mexico, as well as at the Navajo Tribal Fair. In 1968 Bennett was chosen as New Mexico's Mother of the Year.

—Laurie Lisa

References

Bennett, Kay. *Kaibah: Recollections of a Navajo Girlhood.* Los Angeles: Westernlore Press, 1964.
———. "Letter to the Editor." In *The American Indian Speaks*, edited by John R. Milton, 171–72. Vermillion: University of South Dakota Press, 1969.
———, and Russ Bennett. *A Navajo Saga.* San Antonio: Naylor, 1969.
Kinsman, Clare, ed. *Contemporary Authors.* First Revision Series, vol. 17–20, 68–69. Detroit: Gale Research, 1976.
Stensland, Anna Lee. *Literature by and about the American Indian: An Annotated Bibliography.* 2nd ed. Urbana, IL: National Council of Teachers of English, 1979.

BIG EYES [TATTOOED WOMAN] (c. 1520–?), a woman of the Wichitas Indians, was captured around 1535 by the Tejas Indians near the Red River in what is today east Texas. The Wichitas women had a custom of decorating their faces, and Big Eyes had two lines tattooed just under her eyes that accentuated her high cheekbones. The Tejas later sold her to the Tiguex Indians in Arizona as a slave. Big Eyes remained with the Tiguex until the summer of 1540, when the Spanish explorer Francisco Vasquez de Coronado made contact with the Natives. A battle ensued between the Spanish and the Tiguex, and Big Eyes was taken captive and became the possession of Juan de Zaldivar, a captain under Coronado.

Coronado's expedition headed north and then east, following the Pecos and then the Red River in search of the Seven Cities of Cibola and gold. In the spring of 1541, the explorer reached what is now the panhandle of Texas. Big Eyes recognized the country and slipped away from Zaldivar. When Big Eyes arrived in her Wichitas village, she told the people of the Spanish explorers and the strange foods, sights, and sounds she had experienced.

In the summer of 1542, members of Hernando de Soto's Florida expedition arrived in the Mississippi valley. The Natives told them of a Wichitas woman who had travelled westward and back and had seen the great Coronado. Luis de Moscovo located Big Eyes and asked for news of the Coronado expedition. She told him that she had fled the other Spaniards about a year earlier from a location nine days distant and was able to name the captains in Coronado's camp. When the Spanish pressed her for more information, she sketched a crude map in the dirt that illustrated the route Coronado had followed from the Rio Grande and the route she had followed after she had left the Spaniards on the plains near Tule Canyon. One of Moscovo's men copied her crude map on a piece of parchment paper, and in time that map reached Europe and the map makers of the world.

The chronology of Big Eyes's story has raised some questions among historians concerning discrepancies in times, dates, and places. However, Big Eyes, because of her flight across Texas, was a personal link between the exploration of Coronado from the west and the men of de Soto in the east. The two expeditions had spanned the continent and for the first time the width of North America could be estimated.

—Joyce Ann Kievit

References

Bolton, Herbert E. *Coronado, Knight of the Pueblos and Plains*. Albuquerque: University of New Mexico Press, 1949.

Coronado, Francisco Vasquez de. *The Journey of Coronado 1540–1542 from the City of Mexico to the Grand Canyon of the Colorado and the Buffalo Plains of Texas, Kansas and Nebraska*. Edited and translated by George Parker Winship. New York: A.S. Barnes, 1904.

Waltrip, Lela, and Rufus Waltrip. *Indian Women: Thirteen Who Played a Part in the History of America from the Earliest Days to Now*. New York: David McKay, 1964.

BIGHORSE, TIANA (b. 1917), Navajo weaver and writer, is a member of the Deer Spring Clan and was born to the Bitterwater Clan north of Tuba City, Arizona. She learned weaving at the age of seven from her mother, who taught her not only the skills but also the pride of weaving. Although Bighorse's married name is Butler, she uses the last name of Bighorse to honor her father. He was of the Rock Gap Clan, and his father was Edgewater Clan. The mother of seven children, Tiana Bighorse has spent her life in the western part of the Navajo Reservation.

In 1971, with Noel Bennett, she published *Working with the Wool*, an introduction to the art and technique of Navajo weaving. In 1990 Noel Bennett edited Tiana Bighorse's letters and recollections about her father into *Bighorse the Warrior*. His life spanned the Long Walk period of the 1860s and the stock reduction period of the 1930s. From his memory of finding his parents murdered when he was just sixteen to his account of the white-clad figure of death, Tiana Bighorse tells her father's story in his own voice with the subtlety, precision, and artistry characteristic of a people for whom memory is a vital means of valuing life. "I don't want to throw away what he told us," says Tiana Bighorse in *Bighorse the Warrior*, "Right now the young generation knows nothing. . . . I want the world to know that the Navajo warriors were heroes. . . . I want everyone to remember how the Navajo got this big reservation. They will tell their grandchildren, and our warriors will not be forgotten."

—Rhoda Carroll

References

Bennett, Noel, and Tiana Bighorse. *Working with the Wool: How to Weave a Navajo Rug.* Flagstaff, AZ: Northland Press, 1971.
Bighorse, Tiana. *Bighorse the Warrior.* Edited by Noel Bennett. Tucson: University of Arizona Press, 1990.

BILLIE, SUSIE (c. 1900) is a renowned and highly respected medicine woman of the Seminole people in Florida. She was born in Collier County at the turn of the century and now lives on the Big Cypress Reservation. She is a matriarch of the large Panther Clan, which has traditionally provided most of the medicine men for the Seminole and Miccosukee tribes in Florida. She learned the medicine from her father, uncles, and grandfather; her brother, Buffalo Jim, is one of the oldest living medicine men.

Susie Billie practices "healing medicine," which is a combination of an extensive knowledge of herbs and their medicinal properties, as well as the songs and rituals which give the preparations their power. This is distinct from the spiritual "big medicine" practiced during the Green Corn Dance, which is strictly secret and limited to males. Her life has spanned one of the most tumultuous periods in the history of her people; within a century the Seminoles moved from a hunting-trapping society to modern tribal government and highly prosperous business enterprises. To assure that the old ways are not lost in an age of rapid transition, she is actively transmitting her knowledge of herbal medicine and rituals to her children and grandchildren. In 1984 the Florida Folklife Program, the Florida Endowment for the Humanities, and the National Endowment for the Humanities collaborated to produce a video documentary for public television entitled "Four Corners of Earth," which featured Susie Billie and the women of her family. Its focus was the woman's role in ensuring cultural continuity in Indian life. In 1985 she was designated as an official Florida Folk Artist by the Florida Department of State.

—Harry A. Kersey, Jr.

References

Florida Department of State. "Florida Folk Artists and Apprentices 1984–1985." Tallahassee: Florida Folklife Program, 1985.
"Four Corners of Earth." Florida Folklife Program/WFSU-TV. 30 min. 1984. Documentary.
Kersey, Harry A., Jr. *The Florida Seminoles and the New Deal, 1933–1942.* Gainesville: University Presses of Florida, 1989.
———. Interview with Susie Billie (translation), 6 May 1984. Tape recording SEM 187A, University of Florida Oral History Archives, Gainesville.

BIRD, GAIL (b. 1949) is a contemporary jeweler of Laguna/Santo Domingo descent. Born in California, she attended the University of California at Berkeley and the University of Colorado in Boulder before settling in New Mexico. She currently lives in Ojo Caliente with her partner and collaborator, Yazzie Johnson (Navajo).

Bird designs and Johnson fabricates contemporary jewelry characterized by the use of over seventy different types of stones and gems, including Coyomito white agate, iolite, Ceylon blue moonstone, hematite, Chinese turquoise, snowflake obsidian, psilomelene, covelite, coral, dinosaur bone, banded onyx, Deschutes and Wild Horse jasper, crysocholla, charoite, and multiple varieties of pearls.

A consummate artist, Bird sketches out all of her designs in great detail, creating intricate patterns for both the front and the back of her primarily 14k gold pins, necklaces, earrings, and bracelets. The images chosen for the underlay or overlay designs on the backs of the various metal casings of buckles, pendants, and clasps include Pueblo pottery designs, Southwest petroglyphs, animals and birds, textile patterns, shooting stars, and elegant abstract designs.

Her necklaces are characterized by their versatility in use. Because of her unusual clasp designs, a single necklace may be worn in three distinct ways.

Often, the clasp is removable to be worn as a pin. Asymmetry is another stylistic device used to great advantage. Bracelets, for example, are designed with stones slightly off center so they may be stacked in multiples.

Each year, she and Johnson concentrate their major creative effort in designing and making one or two concha belts that reflect their ideas and experiences in a given period. The belts have a single theme carried out by the design and choice of stones.

In 1981 Bird and Johnson won the Best of Show, Best of Class, and Best of Division awards at the prestigious and juried Santa Fe Indian Market sponsored by the Southwest Association on Indian Affairs. Their work has been widely collected by corporations, individuals, and museums, including the Museum of Man (San Diego), the Wheelwright (Santa Fe), the Millicent Rogers (Taos), the Museum of New Mexico, and the Indian Arts and Crafts Board in Washington, DC.

Besides her talent as a designer, Bird is also a prominent spokesperson on American Indian art and culture. She lectures widely on historic and contemporary jewelry and is a consultant to various New Mexico arts organizations, such as the Eight Northern Pueblos, Museum of New Mexico, Laboratory of Anthropology, and the Southwestern Association on Indian Affairs.

She is currently a member of the board of trustees of the Institute of American Indian and Alaska Native Arts and Culture Development, a position to which she was appointed by the President of the United States, and the board of the Wheelwright Museum of the American Indian, both in Santa Fe. For five years she was on the board of the Southwestern Association on Indian Affairs.

—Dexter Fisher Cirillo

References

Jacka, Jerry, and Lois Essary Jacka. *Beyond Tradition: Contemporary Indian Art and Its Evolution.* Flagstaff, AZ: Northland, 1988.

Mather, Christine. *Native America.* New York: Clarkson Potter, 1990.

McGrew, Kate. "Partners in Art and Life: Gail Bird and Yazzie Johnson: Master Jewelers." *New Mexico Magazine* 67 (August 1989): 60–65.

BIRD, JoANNE (b. 1945) was born JoAnne Maestas in Oakland, California. Before her first birthday, her mother took her to Sisseton, South Dakota, to live with her maternal grandparents, Mr. and Mrs. Charles White. She remembers her childhood with them with great pleasure.

Her education began with the first grade in Wahpeton, North Dakota. Her next six years were spent in the Sisseton public school, but she finished elementary school in the Pierre Indian Boarding School. Her high school years were spent at the Flandreau Indian School from which she graduated in 1964. In

1965 she attended the Institute of American Indian Art in Santa Fe, New Mexico. She returned to Sisseton before finishing school, however, and married Gordon Bird in 1965. From 1967–70, she worked at the 3M Corporation in Minneapolis as a design artist.

After working as an independent artist in Sisseton, she left in 1972 to attend Macalester College in St. Paul to study art. In 1974 she transferred to Dakota State College in Madison, South Dakota, where her husband was a counselor. She left there in 1976.

During these years she continued to paint and to sculpt, and her reputation as an artist grew. Her subjects are the old Sioux culture, focusing on the horse and warrior as main objects. She has had exhibitions of her work in many of the major cities in the United States, as well as in Canada and Europe. Her paintings are in galleries in Arizona, the Midwest, and New York. She has had numerous commissions, including some for bronze busts of Chief Gall for Manitoba, Wabasha for the Minnesota Historical Society, and Winnetou for the city of Bad Segeberg in Germany.

Disgusted with her painting in 1987, she took a brush and threw paint at her canvas. She was astonished at what she saw. She has developed this action into a new technique and style that have caused her work of recent years to be in demand in art galleries.

Although she had won awards earlier, they have multiplied since 1987. She won first place in traditional painting in Sioux Falls in 1988, Best of Show in painting in Minneapolis, in Bartelsville, Oklahoma, and in Sioux Falls at the Center for Western Studies, all in 1990. She received an honorable mention at the Northern Plains Tribal Art Show in Sioux Falls in 1990 and also received a Special Merit Award at the Tulsa Indian Art Show in 1990.

She and her husband and children reside in the village of Bushnell, South Dakota, where they have established a studio, which they call Featherstone. Throughout the year, they travel to art exhibitions in all parts of the country.

—Jack Marken

References

Bird, JoAnne. "Plains Warrior Representing July." *Wounded Knee Commemorative Sioux Art Calendar 1990*. St. Joseph's Indian School, Chamberlain, SD: Tipi Press, 1990.

Grauvogl, Ann. "Art Show changed Bird's Career." *Argus Leader* [Sioux Falls] 22 September 1989: 38.

BLACKGOAT, ROBERTA (c. 1920), of the Big Mountain Diné (Navajo) Bitter Water Clan, was born on Big Mountain land where her great grandmother, her grandmother, her mother, and later, her own child, are buried. Blackgoat was

married in 1941. She has six living children. Her husband, Benny Blackgoat, died in 1966.

Blackgoat is a traditional Navajo woman in that she raises sheep and goats and weaves rugs from her sheep's wool. She is somewhat non-traditional in that she has, along with other Big Mountain elders, taken a very vocal and sometimes militant stand in opposing the forced relocation of Diné from their homeland.

Natural resource companies, such as Peabody Coal, interested in the large deposits of oil, natural gas, uranium, and coal on the reservation, promoted a so-called "Navajo-Hopi Land Dispute," which then prompted the passing of Public Law 93–531 in 1974. Under this law, the Joint Use Area of Navajo-Hopi reservation land was "divided" by a barbed wire fence, a line that sometimes went between a family's house and corral. Grazing lands, and sacred shrines and grave sites along the way, were bulldozed and dragged with customized ship anchor chains to remove trees and plants. Approximately one hundred Hopi and ten thousand Navajo caught on the "wrong side of the fence" were told they had to relocate.

The Big Mountain Diné resisted fencing and defended their homes. Traditional Diné have also taken their protest to Washington, DC. Pauline Whitesinger, an elder and a leader of the Big Mountain resistance, has said, "There is no word for relocation in the Navajo language; to relocate is to disappear and never be seen again." Roberta Blackgoat says that, "The Creator is the only one who can relocate me."

As is typical of many of the relocatees, Blackgoat's children, most of whom did choose to relocate, are having a hard time adjusting to life off the reservation. One daughter has lost her relocation home, and a son has returned to Big Mountain in order to heal the scars his relocation experiences have brought to him. Blackgoat wants her children and grandchildren to return to their ancestral land.

In the 1930s Blackgoat experienced a government stock reduction program that was designed to reduce Navajo self-sufficiency and to open up more land to mining interests. The program destroyed about one-third of all Navajo livestock. In this latest relocation effort, the government has again ordered sheep to be taken away, thereby attempting to force the traditional Navajo to make a "starve or move choice." Roberta Blackgoat and other Big Mountain Diné have refused to move or to give up their way of life.

—Elizabeth A. McNeil

References

Florio, Maria, and Victoria Mudd. *Broken Rainbow.* 1985. Distributed by Earthworks Films.

LaDuke, Winona. "Interview with Roberta Blackgoat, a Diné Elder." *Woman of Power* 4 (Fall 1986): 29–31.

———. "Words from the Indigenous Women's Network Meeting." *Akwesasne Notes* 17 (Winter 1985): 8–10.

BLACKSTONE, TSIANINA REDFEATHER [FLORENCE TSIANINA

EVANS] (1882?-1985) was born into a large Creek family in Indian Territory (later Oklahoma). Listed on the Creek tribal rolls as Florence Evans, she was known to family and friends by her Creek name, Tsianina, which she used in a long and distinguished career as a professional singer and entertainer. In her professional life, she often identified herself as Cherokee and Creek. She attended public primary school near Muskogee, Oklahoma, and a federal Indian school in Eufaula, Oklahoma. Encouraged by her piano teacher, and with the assistance of Alice Robertson, Oklahoma's first congresswoman, Tsianina traveled as a young woman to Denver, Colorado, to study voice and piano.

In Denver, she met Charles Wakefield Cadman, an "Indianist" composer inspired by Native American melodies; his best known work was *From the Land of the Sky Blue Water*. He toured the country presenting his "Indian Music Talk" lecture and recital; the Talk reached its greatest popularity when Tsianina became the principal soloist in 1913. Cadman's third opera, *Shanewis: The Robin Woman*, was based on Tsianina's life, although quite loosely, as Cadman himself admitted her life was colorful, but not dramatic enough for opera. *Shanewis* was the first American opera with a modern setting to be produced in two consecutive seasons (1918 and 1919) at the Metropolitan Opera in New York City. Tsianina sang the title role in 1926 when the opera was staged at the Hollywood Bowl, Los Angeles. Critical reviews in contemporary papers did not comment so much on the fineness of her mezzo soprano voice as on the forcefulness of her personality.

In addition to her tours with Cadman, Tsianina was invited to sing in the Santa Fe Fiesta Program by the program's organizer, Edgar Hewett, noted anthropologist and founder of the School of American Research and Museum of New Mexico. Tsianina left the Cadman tour in 1918 to answer General Jack Pershing's call for volunteer entertainers; she sailed to England and Europe, arriving in Paris shortly before the Armistice was signed. She rejoined Cadman late in 1919 for another national tour highlighted by her appearance at the Greek Theater in Berkeley, California.

Her marriage to Albert Blackstone (French-Indian?) ended in separation due to his alcoholism, and she went on tour yet again. Tsianina was plagued by illness after her European tour in World War I, and she turned to Christian Science. She retired from her singing career in the 1930s and devoted her energies to religious activities in her home in southern California, as well as to political work. She was an active fund raiser for the Republican Party for many years. She also took a vital interest in Indian issues, organizing a group of friends in Los Angeles to establish the Foundation for American Indian Education, as well as serving on the board of managers of the School of American Research from 1933 to 1963. Tsianina passed away in San Diego on January 10, 1985.

—K. Tsianina Lomawaima

References

Blackstone, Tsianina. *Where Trails Have Led Me*. Santa Fe, NM: Vergara Printing, 1968.

Index to and the Final Rolls of Citizens and Freedmen of the Five Civilized Tribes in Indian Territory. Census card #1117, November 11, 1899. Federal Records Center, Fort Worth, TX.

Lomawaima, K. Tsianina. Personal Communication with Marjorie F. Lambert, 4 January 1991.

———. Personal Communication with Martha Noss, 4 January 1991.

Maddox, Brent. Review of PhD Dissertation *Charles Wakefield Cadman: His Life and Works* by Harry Perison. *Inter-American Music Review* 4 (1982): 100–103.

Perison, Harry D. "The 'Indian' Operas of Charles Wakefield Cadman." *College Music Symposium* 22 (Fall 1982): 20–48.

Who's Who of American Women. 4th ed. Chicago: A.N. Marquis, 1966–1967.

BLUE LEGS [ALICE NEW HOLY] (b. 1925) was born on July 25 at Grass Creek on the Pine Ridge Reservation, the daughter of Julia and Joseph New Holy. She has lived all her life in the house of her birth near Oglala, South Dakota. She was educated in the Oglala Community School through the twelfth grade.

Her mother died when she was very young. Blue Legs remembers that both her mother and grandmother used porcupine quills in decorating skins and cloth and in making medallions and other objects. As a girl, she found that no one was doing this kind of artistry. She believed that the process should be resurrected, but there was no one to teach her except her father. He gave her as much instruction as he could remember, but he would not touch the quills because he believed that was women's work.

Through trial and error Blue Legs has succeeded in resurrecting the lost art of quilling. With the help of her husband, Emil Blue Legs, and her daughters, she prepares the quills by collecting them, boiling them, dyeing them, and drying them carefully before use. When using them in decorations, she softens them in her mouth, as her predecessors did. Softening them in water does not work, she says, because the additives and minerals in water dry them too much.

She does most of her work at night because then everyone is asleep, there is no noise, and it is calm. Her artistry and skill have earned her many awards, the chief one being a cash award from the National Endowment for the Arts in 1985. She was the only Indian artist from South Dakota to win such an award that year. In that year she and her daughters and husband were the subject of a film by Nauman Productions of Rapid City. Entitled *Lakota Quill Work*, it pictures them preparing the quills at her house.

In recent years she has traveled near and far to teach Indian youth how to use quills because she thinks the art is in danger of being lost. She goes to museums and schools and workshops to give demonstrations. She has traveled as far west as the Hopi Reservation and as far east as New York and New England for this purpose. She has had exhibits of her work in these places, as well as at Anadarko, Indianapolis, and St. Louis.

Two of her daughters, Bernadine and Catherine, have learned the art from their mother and have their own traveling exhibits. They live near their mother in Oglala, where they can be found in the evenings quilling when they are not traveling.

—Jack Marken

Reference

Lakota Quill Work. 16mm, 27 min. 1985. Distributed by Nauman Productions, Rapid City, SD.

BONNIN, GERTRUDE SIMMONS [ZITKALA ŜA, RED BIRD]
(1876–1938) has been called the most important figure in reform Pan-Indianism during the twenties. Not only a highly visible Indian rights activist, she was also an important early Native American writer, publishing essays and short stories and a volume of Indian legends. She was also an award-winning orator.

Born a Sioux at the Yankton Agency in South Dakota in 1876, she was taken at age seven to a Quaker school in Wabash, Indiana. Although her initial experiences there were traumatic, she remained for the full three-year course before returning to the reservation for four years. She then returned and completed another three-year course, and in 1895, at the age of nineteen, she entered Earlham College at Richmond, Indiana, where she distinguished herself as a skillful orator, winning a state-wide speech contest.

After she left Earlham in 1897, she obtained a teaching job at the government's showpiece Indian school at Carlisle, Pennsylvania. While at Carlisle, Bonnin began cultivating literary contacts and published essays and short stories under the Sioux name Zitkala Ŝa, or Red Bird, in such prestigious publications as the *Atlantic Monthly* and *Harper's*.

After two difficult years at Carlisle, she resigned her position to study the violin at the New England Conservatory of Music in Boston. She treasured her life in Boston, studying music, writing, and moving in literary circles, but felt a great sense of responsibility to her people. She resolved to spend at least a year at the Yankton Agency, gathering material for her stories and caring for her mother. This contributed to the end of her engagement to Dr. Carlos Montezuma, whom she had met at Carlisle and who was reluctant to give up his Chicago medical practice to accept a position as a reservation doctor, as Bonnin wished him to do.

Her plans to stay in South Dakota changed, however, when in 1902 she met and married Raymond T. Bonnin, also a Yankton Sioux, who had accepted a Bureau of Indian Affairs clerk position on the Uintah and Ouray Reservation in

Utah. Once there, Gertrude Bonnin became involved with the Society of American Indians and performed community center work under its auspices. In 1916 she was elected secretary of the organization, and shortly thereafter, the Bonnins moved to Washington, DC, where Gertrude assumed the duties of secretary from 1916 until 1919. She was also editor of the society's *American Indian Magazine* and wrote numerous editorials for that publication. In Washington, she allied herself with other important Indian rights organizations, including John Collier's American Indian Defense Association and the Indian Rights Association of Philadelphia.

Bonnin was instrumental in the creation of an Indian welfare committee within the General Federation of Women's Clubs of America, and as its research agent participated in a 1923 investigation which exposed the wide-spread corruption associated with white guardianships of Indian properties and oil leases in Oklahoma. In 1922 and 1923 she made a speaking tour of the Midwest and South, addressing women's clubs in order to crystalize public opinion in favor of Indian citizenship.

In addition to their association with these formal organizations, Gertrude and Raymond Bonnin also devoted considerable time to lobbying governmental departments and congressional committees on behalf of a wide variety of Indian individuals and tribes. The Bonnins testified before congressional committees promoting peyote suppression, Indian citizenship, Indian education reforms, and Native land claims. Although often at odds with him, Gertrude Bonnin also served as an informal advisor to John Collier after he became the head of the Bureau of Indian Affairs under Franklin D. Roosevelt.

In 1926 Bonnin and her husband organized the National Congress of American Indians (NCAI). For the twelve years it existed, it was the only nationally organized reform group with exclusively Native American membership. The Bonnins tirelessly traveled the United States, combining speaking tours with visits to reservations to organize NCAI chapters and enroll members. Her work came to an end in 1938, when she died in Washington, DC. She is buried in the Arlington National Cemetery.

—Catherine Udall

References

Bonnin, Gertrude [Zitkala Ŝa]. *American Indian Stories.* 1921. Reprint. Lincoln: University of Nebraska Press, 1985.

———. *Old Indian Legends.* 1901. Reprint. Lincoln: University of Nebraska Press, 1985.

Fisher, Dexter. "Zitkala-Ŝa: The Evolution of a Writer." *American Indian Quarterly* 5 (August 1979): 229–38.

The Gertrude Simmons and Raymond T. Bonnin Papers. University Archives, Brigham Young University, Provo, Utah.

Johnson, David L., and Raymond Wilson. "Gertrude Simmons Bonnin, 1876–
1938: 'Americanize the First Americans.'" *American Indian Quarterly* 12
(Winter 1988): 27–40.

Welch, Deborah. "Zitkala Ŝa: An American Indian Leader, 1876–1938." PhD
diss., University of Wyoming, 1985.

Willard, William. "Zitkala Ŝa: A Woman Who Would Be Heard." *Wicazo Sa
Review* 1 (Spring 1985): 11–16.

Williams, Walter L. "Twentieth Century Indian Leaders: Brokers and Providers."
Journal of the West 23 (July 1984): 3–6.

Zitkala-Ŝa [Gertrude Bonnin]. "America, Home of the Red Man." *The American
Indian Magazine* 6 (Winter 1919): 165–67.

———. "Why I Am a Pagen." *Atlantic Monthly* 90 (December 1902): 802–3.

———. "A Year's Experience in Community Service Work Among the Ute
Tribes of Indians." *The American Indian Magazine* 4 (October/December 1916):
307–10.

———, Charles N. Fabens, and Matthew K. Sniffen. *Oklahoma's Poor Rich
Indians: An Orgy of Graft and Exploitation of the Five Civilized Tribes—Legalized
Robbery*. Publication of the Indian Rights Association, 2nd Series, no. 127.
Philadelphia: Indian Rights Association, 1924.

BORDEAUX, SHIRLEY (b. 1950), a business analyst with the University
of South Dakota Business Opportunity Center, works with a variety of organizations and businesses to promote economic development for Native Americans.
Bordeaux serves on the boards of South Dakotans for the Arts, the South Dakota
Community Foundation, and the Lakota Development Council, while working
toward an MA in business administration at USD.

Born at Valentine, Nebraska, Bordeaux grew up near Mission, South Dakota,
on the Rosebud Reservation. Her parents, Catherine Robinson, a Chocktaw from
Oklahoma, and Ralph Carlson Bordeaux, a Sicangu, worked at the Old Rosebud
Boarding School; the family lived there when Bordeaux was a child. She was sent
to St. Mary's School for Indian Girls, an Episcopal boarding school, from the
seventh through ninth grades. She then attended Todd County High School,
graduating in 1968.

After her daughter, Ann, was born in 1970, Bordeaux enrolled in Black Hills
State College, graduating with a BS in social sciences in 1974. She then worked
as an information officer for Sinte Gleska College until 1976.

She spent the following two years in Arcata, California, at Humboldt State
University where she worked in natural resource planning and interpretation for
the California State Parks. She would have begun work as a forest ranger in the
fall of 1978, but when Proposition 13 passed, the state had a hiring freeze.
Bordeaux returned to the Dakotas.

In the late 1970s she served as director of public information for United Tribes
Technical College in Bismarck, North Dakota, and continues to serve as a

consultant, writing grants, promotional materials, and conference newsletters and planning programs for the college.

She left Bismarck in 1980 and returned to Rosebud to be an information officer for the Rosebud tribe for the following two years. Then from 1982 through 1984, she was regional editor of the *Lakota Times*. Still at Rosebud, she worked for the next three years for First Computer Concepts, and she continues to work as a consultant for this firm.

From the fall of 1986 through the spring of 1987, she was managing editor of the *Lakota Times*. She wrote editorials and news articles for the newspaper during this period.

In 1987 she moved to Sioux Falls to work with American Indian Services as the first director of the Northern Plains Tribal Arts Project. Working with a diverse, cross-cultural group of art enthusiasts, Bordeaux helped to plan and implement a market for Native American visual artists from North and South Dakota, Montana, Nebraska, Wyoming, and Canada. The show has grown from seventy-one artists exhibiting in 1988 to over one hundred today. Working with USD's Small Business Development Center, Bordeaux continues to work in the long-range development of the Project.

Having served on the first South Dakota Reconciliation Council in 1990–91, Bordeaux continues to work interculturally for better access to and implementation of economic resources necessary for the benefit of Native American people.

Looking back on her own life, Bordeaux is glad that her daughter, Ann, never had to endure the boarding school experience. She works with the vision of a better life for her granddaughter, Vanessa McDaniel, and future generations.

—Norma C. Wilson

Reference

Giago, Doris. "Many find road to city paved with hardship." *Sioux Falls Argus Leader* 21 August 1988: 1A.

BRANT, BETH [DEGONWADONTI] (b. 1941) was born in Melvindale, Michigan. She is a Mohawk of the Bay of Quinte who began writing at the age of forty because of an encounter with a bald eagle. She first gained national recognition as the editor of *A Gathering of Spirit*, the first anthology of contemporary Indian women's art and literature. *A Gathering*, now in its fourth printing, continues to be an important collection of Indian women's writing. In order to assemble a representative sampling of Indian women's work, Brant not only contacted established writers, but she also ran ads in tribal newspapers and contacted women's prisons with large Indian inmate populations. Some of the correspondence from her experience as editor and collector is included in the volume.

In her first book, *Mohawk Trail*, Brant draws on memories of her grandparents, her family, and her own experiences of being a mixed-blood, a lesbian, and a feminist to seed new ground in Native literature. Brant is not in possession of degrees—in fact, she did not complete high school—but she has a tremendous education in living, writing, and reading. Her "education" has led her to form creative writing workshops for Indian women and Indian high school students. For Brant, the power of writing can be the act that frees Indian people from institutionalized racism and internalized self-hatred they have been taught to inflict on themselves. Indian writers are in a constant state of translation—from oral to written—and it is this act of translation that gives such power to the works of Indian artists.

Her work reflects the many identifications that come from being Mohawk, and she feels that being a feminist is a natural reflection of her own matrilineal and matriarchal heritage. Her latest work includes *Food & Spirits*, a collection of short fiction.

She has been an active speaker and lecturer on Indian literature and against the appropriation, by non-Indians, of Native belief systems and religions. She has written several essays on Native women who are considered "traitors" to their people—such as Pocahontas, Nancy Ward, and Malinche—and has brought new understanding to the motives of these women. "Grandmothers of a New World" is one such essay, widely reprinted in scholarly journals, Native magazines, and feminist anthologies. In addition to writing full-time, Brant has served as mentor to many emerging Native writers and has conducted writing workshops for women in prison. She is also an activist for People with AIDS (PWA) and has given AIDS education workshops in the Indian community. She has lectured and given readings at many universities and Indian cultural centers and has received grants from the Michigan Council for the Arts, the Ontario Arts Council, Money for Women, and the National Endowment for the Arts.

—Kathryn W. Shanley

References

Brant, Beth. *Food & Spirits*. Ithaca, NY: Firebrand Books, 1991.

———. *A Gathering of Spirit*. Special issue of *Sinister Wisdom* 22/23 (July 1983). Reprint. Ithaca, NY: Firebrand Books, 1988.

———. "Grandmothers of a New World." *Women of Power* 16 (Spring 1990): 40–47.

———. *Mohawk Trail*. Ithaca, NY: Firebrand Books, 1985.

Bruchac, Carol, Linda Hogan, and Judith McDaniel. *The Stories We Hold Secret: Tales of Women's Spiritual Development*. Greenfield Center, NY: Greenfield Review Press, 1986.

Bruchac, Joseph, ed. *Songs from this Earth on Turtle's Back: Contemporary American Indian Poetry*. Greenfield Center, NY: Greenfield Review Press, 1983.

Cochran, Jo, et al., eds. "Bearing Witness/Sobreviviendo: An Anthology of Native American/Latina Art and Literature." Special Issue of *Calyx: A Journal of Art and Literature by Women* 8 (1984).

Roscoe, Will, comp. *Living the Spirit: A Gay American Indian Anthology.* New York: St. Martin's Press, 1988.

BRANT, MOLLY [MARY BRANT, GONWATSIJAYENNI] (1736?-1796) was the most influential Iroquois woman on the New York frontier from 1759 to 1776. In part her power flowed from the traditionally influential position of women in the matrilineal society of the Iroquois, but Molly Brant parlayed her opportunities to the highest advantage. As a young woman of twenty-three, she became the mistress of William Johnson, the powerful official in charge of the British Indian Department's Northern District. She relished this role and fulfilled it so effectively for fifteen years that she was not only the mother of several children with Johnson, but also his political consort as well as the hostess of his estate.

Since the women of Iroquois villages brokered power by influencing the nomination of sachems, as well as decisions favoring war or peace, Molly Brant proved an invaluable asset to William Johnson's forest diplomacy. British visitors were so impressed by her hospitality that she was sent gifts and mentioned by name in notes of thanks. In her position of influence she could see to it that her younger brother Joseph Brant, or Thayendanegea, was one of the young Mohawks chosen to attend a missionary school in Connecticut. Indeed, she had no qualms about ordering her brother home when she thought the threat of frontier warfare threatened his safety. Thus she repeatedly advanced the ends of her husband, her brother, and her Mohawk people. She was generous in using credit at local merchants to satisfy the needs of relatives and friends who came to her seeking largess. When she had to leave her husband's baronial home after his death in 1774, she took with her numerous expensive dresses and luxury items. Invaders who drove her from her village during the American Revolution reportedly dug up several barrels of dresses from the backyard of her abandoned home. Prior to her flight into exile, when American representatives sought means to neutralize the power of the Iroquois in 1775 and 1776, it was understood by frontier diplomats that Molly Brant was the *deus ex machina*. One observer impressed by her political prowess concluded, "Women govern the Politics of Savages as well as the refined part of the world." Even after she was driven from her homeland, she encouraged Iroquois support of the British. She was instrumental in inspiring continued loyalty to the English king by her people; as one official noted, one word from Molly Brant was far more persuasive than a thousand words from a British official. Indeed, Molly Brant's effectiveness during her term as William Johnson's lady had established sufficient connections with British officialdom that she would be supported financially for the rest of her life. Her claims for damages of £1206 and her yearly pension of £100 exceeded even those of her brother Joseph Brant, the faithful Mohawk war captain. Forced by the fortunes of war to remain away from her homeland, she eventually settled in Kingston, Ontario, where she died in 1796.

—James H. O'Donnell III

References

Green, Gretchen. "Molly Brant, Catharine Brant, and Their Daughters: A Study in Colonial Acculturation." *Ontario History* 81 (1989): 235–50.
Gundy, H. Pearson. "Molly Brant—Loyalist." *Ontario History* 14 (1953): 97–108.
Hamilton, Milton W. *Sir William Johnson: Colonial American, 1715–1763.* Port Washington, NY: National University, 1976.
Kelsay, Isabel T. *Joseph Brant, 1743–1807: Man of Two Worlds.* Syracuse, NY: Syracuse University Press, 1984.
Seymour, Flora Warren. *Women of Trail and Wigwam.* New York: Woman's Press, 1930.

BRASS, ELEANOR (b. 1905),

the daughter of Frederick Charles Dieter (Cree, German) and Marybelle Cote (Saultaux, French), was born on May 1 on the Peepeekisis Reserve in the Balcarrer District, east of Regina, Saskatchewan. She is the direct descendent of two signataries to Treaty No. Four (Fort Qu'Apelle, 1874), Cree Chief Okanese (her father's grandfather) and Saultaux Chief Gabriel Cote (her mother's grandfather). She attended the Presbyterian File Hills Indian Boarding School and later went to high school in Kenora, Saskatchewan, leaving after grade ten in 1921. On January 12, 1925, she married her childhood friend Hector Brass, with whom she farmed on the File Hills Colony on the Peepeekisis Reserve until 1949. At the same time she started writing articles on Native issues and Native/non-Native relations for the *Regina Leader Post* and other newspapers and magazines in Saskatchewan. After having left the reserve for the city, Eleanor and Hector Brass both worked in Regina in various capacities, ranging from menial to secretarial work. In the city, Eleanor Brass became increasingly involved in human rights issues pertaining to Native people. Through the YWCA, her employer for many years, she organized social events for urban Natives, founded the Regina Native Society, and in 1960, together with four other activists including her husband, she established the Regina Indian Friendship Center. Her increasing involvement in Native affairs, and her dedication to re-educate uninformed and prejudiced non-Natives, led to further publishing and CBC broadcasting for public schools, including the retelling of Cree legends from the oral tradition.

In 1965 she was hired by the Provincial Government as an information writer for the Department of Agriculture. This engagement coincided with the tragic death of her husband on October 17, 1965. The widow soon transferred to the Provincial Government's Indian and Métis branch, where she did counseling work and served as placement officer, checking the quota of Native employees in government institutions and finding employment opportunities for Native youth in the private sector. In 1970 she transferred to Saskatoon, from where she officially retired in 1971.

After her "retirement," Eleanor Brass started a fourth career, working as executive director of the Sagitawa Indian Friendship Center until 1975, when the Alberta Native Communications Society hired her as a news correspondent for the Peace River region, where she also helped establish an Indian Friendship Center. All the while, Eleanor Brass was actively engaged in campaigning for a better understanding between Native and non-Native people, addressing school children, the inmates of correctional institutions, and the public at large via publications and broadcasts. This included the 1978 publication of her collection of Cree narratives, *Medicine Boy and Other Cree Tales*. In 1982 she addressed the World Assembly of First Nations in Regina. Failing health forced her to retire in 1985.

Since April 27 of that year, Eleanor Brass has been living in Regina as a retired but far from inactive elder, using her time to write her autobiography, *I Walk in Two Worlds*, and continuing to serve the Native community as a speaker and writer campaigning for a deconstruction of the barriers of mistrust and ignorance which keep many non-Natives from respecting her and her people as humans and equals. Publishing Cree tales from the oral tradition in English and writing down her own life's experiences, she sees as an extension of the traditionally didactic function of storytelling: teaching coming generations how to act properly and which mistakes to avoid, and strengthening identity and pride in one's heritage.

Besides her two published books, Eleanor Brass has countless articles and essays to her name. She also wrote a play (unpublished), *Strangers in Their Own Land*, which was performed by the Fort Qu'Apelle Drama Group.

—Hartmut Lutz

References

Brass, Eleanor. "Eleanor Brass." In *Speaking Together: Canada's Native Women*, 42–43. Ottawa: The Secretary of State, 1975.
———. *I Walk in Two Worlds*. Calgary: Glenbow Museum, 1987.
———. *Medicine Boy and Other Cree Tales*. 1982. Reprint. Calgary: Glenbow Museum, 1978.
Livingston, Donna. "She Walks in Two Worlds." *Glenbow* 8 (Spring 1988): 8–9.

BRIGHAM, BESMILR MOORE (b. 1913), the daughter of Monroe I. and
Bessie May Emmons Moore, was born near Pace, Mississippi. She lived in this
area and in Jonesboro, Arkansas, for ten years before moving to Donna, Texas,
where she finished high school. Later she attended Mary Harden Baylor Women's
College in Belton, Texas, from which she graduated in 1935 with a BA degree in
journalism. There she met Roy Brigham, who was working for a local printer.
They married in 1936 and spent the next few years moving from place to place
in Texas, Oklahoma, and Mississippi. During these years Roy worked as a
typesetter while Brigham wrote copy for local newspapers.

In the early 1940s they moved to New York City where Brigham studied for
two years at the New School for Social Research, about which she says, "There
is no school like it." Her major teachers there were Horace Gregory and Sidney
Alexander. She took courses in poetry and fiction and tried "to get as far away
from journalism as possible," writing her works without punctuation or capitals.
She also became interested in the theater, particularly mime, and she left
journalism forever.

Always restless, she and Roy traveled frequently, going to Mexico, Central
America, and to Europe. Brigham was fascinated by her father's trips to work with
the Meskito Indians in Nicaragua and succeeded in tracing the same routes he
had followed there. These trips and their experiences among the Indians in the
Americas and Mexico provided material for the increasing amount of writing
Brigham was doing. Her own ancestry (her mother's father was half Choctaw)
strongly influenced her. During the 1940s and 1950s, she thought of herself as a
writer, and she continued to fill notebooks with poems, essays, and stories which
Roy helped her with by collaborating, editing and typing.

Her first work was published in 1965 when her poem "Yaqui Deer" was
accepted for publication by *Como Emplumada* in Mexico City. Since then her
work has been included in numerous anthologies, including *31 New American
Poets* (Hill and Wang, 1969), *From the Belly of the Shark* (Vintage Books, 1973),
and *New Generation: Poetry* (Ann Arbor Review, 1971). She is included in
Dorothy Abbot's *Mississippi Writers* (University Press of Mississippi, 1985), and
her work has been included in most of the literary magazines in this country, from
The Atlantic to the *Southern Review*, from *American and Canadian Poetry* to *West
Coast Review*. Her stories have also been listed in Martha Foley's *Best Short Stories
of 1972*, *Best Short Stories of 1973* and in *Best Short Stories for 1983*.

Brigham is an interesting speaker whose observations and reminiscences have
fascinated audiences for many years. Her readings and conversations have been
recorded at Southwest Minnesota State University, the University of Wisconsin
at LaCrosse and Green Bay, and at the Library of Congress. She and Roy have
lived for years in a small house in the country near Horatio, Arkansas, where they
continue preparing Brigham's works.

—Jack Marken

References

Brigham, Besmilr. *Agony Dance: Death of the Dancing Dolls*. Portland, OR: Prensa de Lagar/Wine Press, 1969.

————. *Heaved from the Earth*. New York: Alfred A. Knopf, 1971.

Kopp, Karl, and Jane Kopp, eds. *Southwest: A Contemporary Anthology*. Albuquerque: Red Earth, 1977.

BRINK, JEANNE (b. 1944) was born in Montpelier, Vermont, of the Abenaki Nation of Missisquoi. Known throughout Vermont for her expertise in Abenaki culture and language, Brink published *Alnôbaôdwa: A Western Abenaki Language Guide* in conjunction with the Franklin Northwest Supervisory Union Title V Indian Education Office in Swanton, Vermont. *Alnôbaôdwa* consists of twenty Abenaki language lessons and accompanying audiotape.

Currently adjunct faculty in the Department of Humanities at Johnson State College in Johnson, Vermont, Jeanne Brink co-teaches Introduction to Native American Culture. She serves as a consultant to the Vermont Council on the Humanities on matters of Abenaki culture and traditions and directs the Abenaki Research Project of Wobanaki (part of the Material Heritage of Vermont project of the Vermont Council on the Humanities). She is a resource agent on the Vermont Abenaki for the Vermont Department of Education, a part-time coordinator for the Abenaki Cultural Center of the Sovereign Abenaki Nation of Missisquoi in Swanton, Vermont, and a consultant for the Vermont Department of Libraries.

Brink is committed to the preservation of Abenaki language and tradition. She remembers watching her grandmother Elvine Obomsawin Royce and her great-aunt Marion Obomsawin make baskets of ash splint and sweetgrass at Thomson's Point in Charlotte, Vermont. Marion Obomsawin's baskets are part of the permanent Native American Basket Collection at Dartmouth College in Hanover, New Hampshire. The Historical Society of Charlotte, Vermont, displays Marion Obomsawin's baskets, a cedar lawn chair made by Brink's great uncle William Obomsawin, and a miniature birch bark canoe made by his father, Simon Obomsawin. Marion Obomsawin's baskets are described in *Always in Season*, Vermont Folklife Center director Jane Beck's text featuring Vermont craftspeople. Continuing the family tradition, Brink makes and sells baskets of ash splint and sweetgrass.

Jeanne Brink completed an MA in Native American Studies at Vermont College of Norwich University in May, 1991; she is the first Norwich University student to receive a degree in Native American Studies. She holds a BA in Liberal Studies (1989) and an AS in Executive Administrative Assistance (1986), both from Vermont College.

The mother of three children, Brink resides in Barre, Vermont, with her husband Douglas.

—Rhoda Carroll

Reference

Brink, Jeanne, and Gordon M. Day. *Alnôbaôdwa: A Western Abenaki Language Guide*. Swanton, VT: Franklin Northwest Supervisory Union, Title V Indian Education Office, 1990.

BROKER, IGNATIA (1919–1987) was concerned with bridging generation gaps for the Ojibway. She was born and raised on the White Earth Reservation in Minnesota. Broker attended Indian boarding school at Wahpeton Indian Boarding School in North Dakota until she broke her hip at age fourteen. After she recovered, Broker attended Haskell Institute in Lawrence, Kansas, for three years. For her senior year, she transferred to a Park Rapids, Minnesota, public school, withdrawing due to the prejudices of the white students. She completed her high school degree and took a college level business course at the all-girls North Star College in Warren, Minnesota.

During World War II Broker worked for a defense plant and took night classes in journalism. After the war she married a veteran and moved to the River Flats district of St. Paul, which had a significant Indian population. However, she was only able to get day work cleaning houses for middle-class whites. In 1953, she attended the Minnesota School of Business in Minneapolis. She was unable to find a position utilizing her business training because of discriminatory hiring practices. However, she did volunteer work for Indian organizations concerned with Indian's rights issues, such as American Indians Incorporated, Service to American Indian Resident Students, Indian Upward Bound, halfway houses, and the Minority Task Force of the Minneapolis Public Schools. After her husband was killed in Korea, she moved back to Minneapolis and was finally able to land her first clerical job in a health clinic.

As a member of Concerned Indian Citizens, Broker led a study of welfare abuses on Indians. It was common policy that if Indians requested welfare support, they were given a bus ticket back to the reservations. Through the combined efforts of the Concerned Indian Citizens and the United Church Committee, the study was successful in changing attitudes about the productivity of Indians, and consequently, the bus ticket policy was rescinded, securing welfare rights for Indians.

Broker was a founder and active member of the Upper Midwest American Indian Center of Minneapolis, where she headed a research staff that collected data in order to educate public officials on understanding Indians and to improve social services to Indians. She was also a founder and member of the American

Indian Center, the Urban American Indian Federation of the State of Minnesota, the Department of Indian Work of the United Church Committee, and the Minnesota Indian Historical Society.

Ignatia Broker made contributions to education by producing films and stories on Ojibway culture for the Minneapolis Public Schools Indian Elementary Curriculum Project and the Indian Education Program at Cass Lake in northern Minnesota.

In 1982, Broker retired and moved with her mother to Bemidji, Minnesota, near the White Earth Reservation. However, she continued to be active, participating in the Minnesota Indian Council on Aging and local senior citizens' organizations.

In 1982 Broker published a biography of her great-great grandmother, *Night Flying Woman*. Her goals were to instruct the younger generation of the life style of earlier generations of Ojibway, create a sense of identity for the contemporary generation, ensure the continuity of the Ojibway tribal customs, and dispel stereotypes of Indians. In *Night Flying Woman*, Broker explains that telling these stories to her grandchildren ensured the continuity not only of the customs but also of the Ojibway people themselves. She believed her grandchildren's generation would close the circle of five generations that began with Night Flying Woman's generation. According to Ojibway traditions, this closure would return the Ojibway to their traditional ways.

Ignatia Broker was honored in 1984, when she was awarded the National Wonder Woman Award for her efforts in furthering equality and peace.

—Pattiann Frinzi

References

Broker, Ignatia. *Ahmik Nishgahdahzee, the Story of an Angry Beaver*. Minneapolis: Minneapolis Public Schools, Indian Elementary Curriculum Project. Filmstrip and Poster Story.

———. *Night Flying Woman, an Ojibway Narrative*. St. Paul: Minnesota Historical Society Press, 1983.

———. *Our People*. Cass Lake, MN: Indian Education Program. Film series, booklets and teachers' guides.

———. *Weegwahsimitig, the Story of a Birch Tree*. Minneapolis: Minneapolis Public Schools, Indian Elementary Curriculum Project.

BRONSON, RUTH MUSKRAT [RUTH MARGARET MUSKRAT]
(1897–1982) was born in the Delaware district of the Cherokee Nation, Indian Territory. By the time she reached high school age, Cherokee schools, like the Nation itself, had suffered from a successful Oklahoma Statehood movement. To pursue a college preparatory education, fourteen-year-old Ruth Muskrat left

home for Tonkawa, Oklahoma, in 1911. After graduating in 1919, she spent one year at the University of Oklahoma, one year on a partial scholarship at the University of Kansas, and in 1923 she entered Mount Holyoke College in Massachusetts with advanced standing and in possession of a full scholarship. She became the first Indian woman to attend and graduate from that institution in 1925.

Ruth M. Bronson received national attention when she became the first American Indian representative at the World's Student Christian Federation annual conference held in Beijing in 1922. The following year she spoke again on behalf of Indian students at the so-called Committee of 100 Meeting, a group of national leaders who met in Washington, DC, to offer their advice on Indian Affairs. After a summer as Dean of Women at Northeastern State Teachers College in Tahlequah, Oklahoma, Bronson accepted a teaching position at Haskell Indian Boarding School in Lawrence, Kansas. She began a career in the field of Indian education that would never stray far from her underlying commitment to developing Indian leadership.

In 1930 Bronson benefitted from a reform movement within the Bureau of Indian Affairs (BIA) Education Division when she accepted an offer to fill the newly created Guidance and Placement Officer position. From her office first in Kansas City and later in Washington, DC, she dispensed educational loans and promoted Indian student success in post-secondary educational institutions for the next thirteen years. In the interim she married John F. Bronson, and they adopted a two-year-old Laguna girl named Delores. In 1944, Bronson wrote and published her only book-length manuscript *Indians Are People Too*.

Having lived and worked in Washington, DC, since 1936, Bronson possessed the type of experience the National Congress of American Indians (NCAI) hoped to benefit from when they asked her to open up a Washington bureau for their organization in 1945. Over the next decade Bronson not only established an effective Washington bureau, she also acted as NCAI's executive director, editor of its *Washington Bulletin*, treasurer, delegation coordinator, lobbyist, and general problem solver. More often than not, she did so on a volunteer basis. In 1949, Bronson also became one of the three original trustees of NCAI's first nonprofit educational affiliate, an organization that became known as Arrow, Inc. (Americans for the Restitution and Righting of Old Wrongs).

By the time Bronson left Washington in 1957, she had fought many battles in the war against termination legislation, initiatives that had repeatedly threatened tribal sovereignty around the nation. She left national politics to become a health education specialist for the United States Indian Health Service (IHS) on the San Carlos Apache Indian Reservation in eastern Arizona. Bronson's interest in leadership development at the community level had begun much earlier, but accepting this position marked the first time she went beyond supporting grassroots activities from afar to become a community activist in her own right.

Bronson used her position as health educator to encourage a fundamental type of adult education that went beyond preventive health to the nurturing of community leadership. During her five years at San Carlos, she especially encouraged the women there to get more involved in determining the health of their community. She helped them regain their right to make fundamental community health decisions, one that had been assumed for far too long by government employees and medical professionals stationed on or near the reservation. For her community development efforts at San Carlos, Bronson received the Department of Health, Education and Welfare's Superior Service and Oveta Cult Hobby Awards in 1962. When she and her husband retired to Tucson shortly thereafter, she remained supportive of community development programs in the region, until ill health in the 1970s finally made activism impossible.

—Gretchen G. Harvey

References

Bernstein, Alison. "A Mixed Record: The Political Enfranchisement of American Indian Women During the Indian New Deal." *Journal of the West* 23 (July 1984): 13–20.

Bronson, Ruth Muskrat. Clipping File, Mount Holyoke College Library/Archives, Holyoke, MA.

———. *Indians Are People Too*. New York: Friendship Press, 1944.

———. "San Carlos Apache Community Development." In *Indian Communities in Action*, edited by Broderick H. Johnson, 132–54. Tempe: Bureau of Publications, Arizona State University, 1967.

BROWN, CATHARINE (1800–1823) of Creek Path was one of the first Cherokee converts to Christianity. She and her brother John, children of James Brown, one of the headmen of the Creek Path community, entered the school established at Brainard Mission in the Cherokee Nation by the American Board of Commissioners for Foreign Missions in 1818. Although she was described as "proud and haughty" when she first arrived, she was later described as "modest and amiable." She showed signs of Christian conversion and was received into the mission church established at Brainard in November of 1818.

The following year, her father called her home because he wanted to move his family to the Arkansas Territory west of the Mississippi River. Although Brown considered leaving "more bitter than death," she dutifully followed her father's wishes. However, four months later her family still had not moved, and her parents gave her permission to return to the school and remain even after they moved. Brown attributed her father's change of heart to "the special providence of God," and to her own "fervent believing prayer." Her father evidently did not emigrate to Arkansas. In January 1820 Brown and her brother David went to Creek Path to visit him because he was sick. David, who had also converted to Christianity, read the Bible to his father and exhorted him to repent of his sins. Upon his recovery, James Brown wrote to the American Board in February, asking for a school to be established in his community. Several missionaries from Brainard went to Creek Path, and the school commenced in March 1820. By June, it was full, and a second school was proposed. Catharine Brown offered to teach a school for girls if the community would erect a building for it. Her offer was accepted, and in May she left Brainard to return to Creek Path and commence her teaching career. She became ill with tuberculosis and finally went to a physician in Limestone County, Alabama, for treatment. She died at his home on July 18, 1823. Her passing was mourned by the missionaries. Because she was one of the earliest Cherokee converts and served as a pious example to her students, her life was glorified by the American Board in a number of pamphlets and school books used in American Board mission schools. Choctaw children read about her in *Chahta Holisso a tukla, or the Second Chahta Book*, written by Alfred Wright and Cyrus Byington.

—Clara Sue Kidwell

References

American Board of Commissioners for Foreign Missions. *First Ten Annual Reports of the American Board of Commissioners for Foreign Missions, with Other Documents of the Board.* Boston: Crocker and Brewster, 1834.
Missionary Herald 19 (October 1823): 336.
Tracy, Joseph. "History of the American Board of Commissioners for Foreign Missions. Compiled Chiefly from the Published and Unpublished Documents of the Board." *History of American Missions to the Heathen from their Commencement to the Present Time.* Worcester, MA: Spooner & Howland, 1840.
Wright, Alfred, and Cyrus Byington. *Chahta Holisso a tukla, or the Second Chahta Book: Containing Translations of Portions of the Scriptures, Biographical Notices of Henry Obokiah and Catharine Brown, a Catechism, and Dissertations on Religious Subjects.* Cincinnati, OH: Morgan, Lodge and Fisher, 1827.

BROWN, EMILY IVANOFF [TICASUK] (1904–1982) was born in Unalakleet, Alaska, and died in Fairbanks, Alaska. She was the granddaughter of Sergei Ivanoff, a Russian immigrant to Alaska and his Yupik Eskimo wife Chikuk, the daughter of Stephan Ivanoff and his wife Malquay. She began school at the village of Shaktoolik, which her father helped to establish in 1907. After graduating from high school, she obtained a provisional teaching certificate and became a grade school teacher and an advocate of bilingual education. She enrolled at the University of Alaska in 1959 to obtain a formal college degree

because she felt that her provisional credentials had never been fully accepted by fellow teachers, and she ultimately received two BA degrees from the University of Alaska. Her master's thesis at the University of Alaska was published as a book, *Grandfather of Unalakleet*, in 1974. She ultimately revised the book, and it was republished in 1981 as *The Roots of Ticasuk: An Eskimo Woman's Family Story.* She was widely recognized by Alaska Native people as an educator and writer of articles about Eskimo cultures and education. Among her many honors were a Presidential Commendation from Richard M. Nixon for exceptional service, and recognition by the Alaskan Legislature and the National Federation of Press Women. Her death came two weeks before she was to receive an honorary doctorate from the University of Alaska.

—Clara Sue Kidwell

Reference

Ticasuk [Emily Ivanoff Brown]. *The Roots of Ticasuk: An Eskimo Woman's Family Story.* Anchorage: Alaska Northwest Publishing, 1981.

BUFFALO BIRD WOMAN [MAXIDIWIAC, WAHEENEE] (1839?-1932), a Hidatsa who experienced the traditional life of her people in what is now North Dakota, is known through the work of Gilbert Wilson, who first interviewed her in 1906 and who wrote two books about her life: *Waheenee* and *Buffalo Bird Woman's Garden.* Additional information can be found in Wilson's book about her son, *Goodbird the Indian*, and in Gilman and Schneider's *The Way to Independence*, a chronicle of her family's life from 1840–1920.

During a series of interviews over a period of twelve years, Buffalo Bird Woman told Wilson of the history of the Hidatsa that had been transmitted to her through the oral tradition, and she described her own experience and the lives and work of women in Hidatsa culture. She spoke only the Hidatsa language, and her accounts were translated into English by her son.

In 1837 a smallpox epidemic had killed over half the Hidatsas. Buffalo Bird Woman told Wilson that she was "born in an earth lodge by the mouth of the Knife River, in what is now North Dakota, three years after the smallpox winter." She was with the Hidatsa and Mandan tribes in 1845 when they relocated and built Like-a-Fishhook Village overlooking the Missouri River, upstream from their traditional homeland.

Her mother, Weahtee, was one of four sisters—all wives of Small Ankle—and the three aunts were like mothers to her. When she was six, Weahtee died; thereafter, her primary caretaker was her grandmother, Turtle, who taught her proper values and behavior. Her grandfather, Missouri River, a medicine man, taught her of the spirits.

The family's earth lodge was also the community meeting place and church. Kept within it were the holy objects of their clan, the Midipadi or Waterbusters. Missouri River had brought these holy objects, the Maa-duush, from the Knife River villages.

When she was ten, a naming ceremony was held for her and she was given the name, "Good Way." But later her father, Small Ankle, gave her the name, Maxidiwiac, meaning Buffalo Bird Woman, in the effort to help her recover from sickness.

She learned and practiced all the traditional skills of Hidatsa women—gardening, the preparation of foods, earth lodge building, the weaving of mats and baskets, and many others. Her Aunt Sage honored Buffalo Bird Woman with the gift of a woman's belt as a reward for tanning hundreds of hides.

When she was fourteen Buffalo Bird Woman joined the Skunk Society. Among the activities of this group of girls was dancing and singing in celebration upon the return of a successful war party.

At sixteen, Buffalo Bird Woman was married in the traditional way, with an exchange of gifts. She and her half sister agreed to marry Magpie, the stepson of a Crow man named Hanging Stone, who also lived in Like-a-Fishhook Village. After the ceremonial gifts had been given, Magpie went to live with the two young women in their lodge, according to the matrilocal Hidatsa custom. Buffalo Bird Woman lived with Magpie for the next thirteen years, until he died of tuberculosis.

Her second marriage, to Son of a Star, was to last the rest of her life. In the autumn of 1869, when she was thirty, she gave birth to their son, her first and only child, Tskaka-sakis, Goodbird. Life at Like-a-Fishhook Village continued until 1885, when Hidatsa, Mandan, and Arikara families began to spread out on allotments along the Missouri River, usually settling according to tribal affiliation on land that became the Fort Berthold Reservation.

Buffalo Bird Woman held to the traditional ways of her culture and generously and tirelessly transmitted them. Her information is valuable for its detailed description of the lifestyle her people had developed to sustain themselves in balance with nature. As important as her explanation of how to garden in the traditional Hidatsa manner is her transmission of the philosophical view of her people in statements such as these: "We thought that the corn plants had souls as children have souls," and "We thought an earth lodge was alive and had a spirit like a human body, and its front was like a face, with the door for mouth."

—Norma C. Wilson

References

Gilman, Carolyn, and Mary Jane Schneider. *The Way to Independence*. St. Paul: Minnesota Historical Society Press, 1987.

Goodbird, Edward. *Goodbird the Indian: His Story, Told by Himself to Gilbert L. Wilson*. New York: Fleming H. Revell, 1914.

Jensen, Joan M. *With These Hands: Women Working the Land*. Old Westbury, NY: The Feminist Press, 1981.

Wilson, Gilbert L. *Agriculture of the Hidatsa Indians: An Indian Interpretation*. Minneapolis: University of Minnesota Studies in the Social Sciences, no. 9, 1917.

————. *Buffalo Bird Woman's Garden: Agriculture of the Hidatsa Indians*. St. Paul: Minnesota Historical Society Press, 1987.

————. *Waheenee: An Indian Girl's Story Told by Herself to Gilbert L. Wilson*. Lincoln: University of Nebraska Press, 1987.

Wilson, Norma C. Personal Communication with Arnie Goodbird, 27 February 1991.

BURNS, DIANE M. (b. 1957), poet and artist, was born in California to a Chemehuevi father and an Anishinabe/Chippewa (Ojibwa) mother; she was educated at the Sherman Institute, the Institute of American Indian Arts (where she was awarded the Congressional Medal of Merit for artistic and academic excellence), an alternative school in Scarsdale, New York, and Barnard College of Columbia University (class of 1978), where she majored in political science. A painter and illustrator who has written book reviews for the Council on Interracial Books for Children and has taught a course in poetry at St. Marks Poetry Project in New York, she is a member of the Poet's Overland Expeditionary Troupe (POET), the Third World Writers Association, and the Feminist Writers Guild. She has read her poetry throughout the country and has been published in such places as *Greenfield Review*, *Blue Cloud Quarterly*, *White Pine Journal*, *Hard Press*, *Sunbury*, *New York Waterways*, and *Contact/II*.

Her first volume of poetry, *Riding the One-Eyed Ford* (1981; Reprint, 1982), nominated for the William Carlos Williams Award, marked Burns as one of the most important contemporary Indian poets. This collection of narrative verse, examining issues of conformity and nonconformity from a particularly urban and female Indian perspective, is strongly influenced by popular culture and performance theory. Her poetry is also distinctly rhythmic, shaped by both contemporary and traditional music, for her a primal force, a reflection of Native ceremony and the storytelling tradition. She believes that women, particularly, have "tapped into a more creative and individual persona. They've got their own voice, only more so. They're more on the cutting edge, more avant-garde," especially Native women, who have a heritage of power and creativity. Recognizing the possibility of paradox in her dual emphasis on individuality and community, she asserts that "creativity is the force that propels everything. That's the energy of the universe."

Long a resident of New York, the setting of much of her work, she is completing another volume of poetry and a science fiction novel about conquest from Jupiter, for, as she says, "I like the irony of the second invasion."

—Rodney Simard

References

Bruchac, Joseph, ed. *Songs from this Earth on Turtle's Back: Contemporary American Indian Poetry.* Greenfield Center, NY: Greenfield Review Press, 1983.

———."That Beat, That Pulse: An Interview with Diane Burns." In *Survival This Way: Interviews with American Indian Poets,* 42–56. Sun Tracks, vol. 15. Tucson: University of Arizona Press, 1987.

Burns, Diane M. *Riding the One-Eyed Ford.* 1981. Reprint. Brooklyn, NY: Strawberry Press, 1982.

Green, Rayna, ed. *That's What She Said: Contemporary Poetry and Fiction by Native American Women.* Bloomington: Indiana University Press, 1984.

BURTON, JIMALEE CHITWOOD [HO-CHEE-NEE] (b. 1920) was

born in eastern Oklahoma. A Cherokee, she came to prominence with her collected poetry, prose, and traditional stories entitled *Indian Heritage, Indian Pride: Stories That Touched My Life.* Her most prolific period was from 1967 to 1974, during which she authored several well-received poems in addition to *Indian Heritage, Indian Pride.* Aside from her poetry and prose, Jimalee Burton is also known as a graphic artist who melded traditional motifs with contemporary themes and media. She served as editor of the intertribal newspaper, *The Native Voice,* for fifteen years.

—Cynthia Kasee

References

Brumble, David H., III. *An Annotated Bibliography of American Indian and Eskimo Autobiography.* Lincoln: University of Nebraska Press, 1981.

Burton, Jimalee. *Indian Heritage, Indian Pride: Stories That Touched My Life.* Norman: University of Oklahoma Press, 1974.

Green, Rayna, ed. *That's What She Said: An Anthology of Contemporary Native American Women.* Bloomington: Indiana University Press, 1984.

C

CALLAHAN, SOPHIA ALICE

CALLAHAN, SOPHIA ALICE (1868-1894), a teacher and writer in the Creek Nation, was a member of a family that was prominent in Creek national political affairs. Qualified to teach grammar, arithmetic, geography, history, and physics, in 1892-93 she taught at Wealaka Mission School and during the fall of 1893 at Harrell Institute, a Methodist school at Muskogee. At the time of her death in January 1894, she was also serving in a minor official capacity in the Indian Mission Conference of the ME Church, South.

Although Callahan wrote verse, her most ambitious literary effort was *Wynema: A Child of the Forest*, a loosely constructed novel, which she published at age twenty-three. She dedicated the work to the oppressed Indian tribes of North America with the hope that it would help to bring about an era of goodwill and justice for the American Indian. Thin, and sometimes highly improbable, plots are woven through themes concerning the importance of Christianity and education in English, fraud in Indian administration, allotment, temperance, the Ghost Dance movement, and atrocities committed upon the Sioux at Wounded Knee. Though her novel is extremely flawed, Callahan stands as the first Indian woman known to have written a novel.

—Daniel F. Littlefield, Jr.

References

Butler, M. L. "In Memorium." *Our Brother in Red*, 11 January 1894.
Callahan, S. Alice. *Wynema: A Child of the Forest*. Chicago: H. J. Smith, 1891.
Foreman, Carolyn Thomas. "S. Alice Callahan: Author of *Wynema: A Child of the Forest*." *Chronicles of Oklahoma* 33 (Autumn 1955): 306-14.

CAMPBELL, MARIA

CAMPBELL, MARIA (b. 1940), a Métis born in Saskatchewan, is best known for her autobiography *Halfbreed*, published in 1973. She is a generative influence on the current group of Native Canadian writers. The autobiography is a loving, bitter, and comic portrait of a cultural and individual life during a transitional period in Métis culture. Campbell recalls the happy family times and close community ties. Among the most influential people in her early life was her great-grandmother Cheechum, who taught her traditional Métis ways and who served as a conscience for the community by encouraging Métis political activism against the racism of the Canadian government. Upon the death of Campbell's mother, the family became Maria's responsibility, even as they were forced into extreme poverty. Eventually, the younger children were removed from the home by a misguided social welfare system, and Campbell married an Euro-Canadian in an effort to reclaim the children. At the same time as Campbell was relating her descent into self-destructive behavior, including alcoholism, drug abuse, prostitution, and drug smuggling, the parallel disintegration of Métis cultural life was occurring through the loss of traditional Métis hunting and trapping lands and the demoralizing effect of a paternalistic welfare system. Eventually, Campbell realized that "if I was to know peace I would have to search within myself," and she embarked on a career of political activism based upon traditional Métis spiritual values.

Sometimes referred to as "the mother of us all," Campbell's political concerns since the publication of *Halfbreed* have been for the welfare of Métis women and children. She has also conducted numerous workshops for young Native writers. In an effort to teach young Métis about their history, she has written three children's books: *People of the Buffalo* (Douglas & McIntyre, 1976), *Little Badger and the Fire Spirit* (1977), and *Riel's People* (Douglas & McIntyre, 1978). A play based upon *Halfbreed, Jessica: A Transformation*, was performed by the Great Canadian Theatre Company of Toronto in October, 1986. The play was then published in *The Book of Jessica* in 1989 by Campbell and her collaborator, Linda Griffiths. Most recently, she has worked on a television film, *The Road Allowance People*.

—Kathleen Donovan

References

Bataille, Gretchen M., and Kathleen M. Sands. *American Indian Women Telling Their Lives*, 113–26. Lincoln: University of Nebraska Press, 1984.

Campbell, Maria. *Halfbreed*. Toronto: McClelland and Stewart, 1973. Reprint. Lincoln: University at Nebraska Press, 1982.

Godard, Barbara. "The Politics of Representation: Some Native Canadian Women Writers." *Canadian Literature* 124-25 (Spring/Summer 1990): 183-225.

Grant, Agnes. "Contemporary Native Women's Voices in Literature." *Canadian Literature* 124-25 (Spring/Summer 1990): 124-32.

"Indian Feminine Identity." *American Indian Culture and Research Journal* 12 (1988): 1-37.

"Maria Campbell [Interview]." In *Contemporary Challenges: Conversations with Native Canadian Writers*, edited by Hartmut Lutz. Saskatoon: Fifth House, 1991.

Petrone, Penny. *Native Literature in Canada: From the Oral Tradition to the Present*. Toronto: Oxford University Press, 1990.

CARDIFF, GLADYS (b. 1942), a prolific poet, is an Eastern Cherokee who was born in the area of Browning, Montana. She studied English, literature, and creative writing at the University of Washington, where she is currently finishing her graduate program. A frequent participant in seminars, workshops, and conferences in the Pacific Northwest, she reads her poetry (much of it devoted to themes from her tribal legends) and teaches others about creative writing through venues such as the Poetry in the Schools Program, an official program of the State of Washington.

Her first book, *To Frighten a Storm*, received the Governor's Writers Award for a First Book after its publication by Copper Canyon Press. She won several other state-sponsored writing awards, as well as independent literary awards, such as the Louisa Kern Award and the Nelson Bentley Award for Poetry (both in 1988).

Working almost exclusively in the format of poetry, Cardiff's works have appeared in journals, periodicals, and anthologies, ranging from *Songs from this Earth on Turtle's Back*, *That's What She Said: An Anthology of Contemporary Native American Women*, and *Dancing on the Rim of the World*. Gladys Cardiff is currently writing a play in dramatic verse based on the creation story and modern myths of the Eastern Cherokee. She makes her home in Seattle, Washington.

—Cynthia Kasee

References

Bruchac, Joseph, ed. *Songs from this Earth on Turtle's Back*. Greenfield Center, NY: Greenfield Review Press, 1983.

Cardiff, Gladys. *To Frighten a Storm*. Port Townsend, WA: Copper Canyon Press, 1976.

Green, Rayna, ed. *That's What She Said: An Anthology of Contemporary Native American Women*. Bloomington: Indiana University Press, 1984.

Lerner, Andrea, ed. *Dancing on the Rim of the World: An Anthology of Contemporary Northwest Native American Writing*. Tucson: University of Arizona Press, 1990.

Niatum, Duane, ed. *Carriers of the Dream Wheel: Contemporary Native American Poets of the Twentieth Century*. New York: Harper and Row, 1975.

CARIUS, HELEN SLWOOKO (c. 1935), a Sevukakmet Inuit Eskimo, was born at camp Noosak on Boxer Bay in Alaska. For the first few years of her life, she thought that her family members were the only people on earth. Life changed for her around 1940 when her father became ill and the family moved to Gambell to get aid from the missionaries.

When Carius was about ten years old, she contracted polio. She was given therapy at the Indian Hospital in Tacoma, Washington, and in Mt. Edgecumbe, Alaska. After high school she married an airman, and they left Alaska in 1954.

For the next twenty-three years, she lived in California, Arizona, and Missouri. She made and sold leather art work, such as Eskimo dolls, slippers, and hassocks decorated with whale, walrus, and polar bears. She gave a series of lectures in the Kansas City schools about the Sevukakmet way of life on St. Lawrence Island. In 1976 at the Chicago National Council of Teachers of English Convention, she lectured on her life as one of the Sevukakmet and illustrated this discussion with slides of the drawings she had made.

In 1977 she returned to Alaska, and she now lives in Anchorage. She works as a resource person in the Anchorage public schools. She has also helped direct and was technical advisor for a television show on Eskimo heritage. She has two sons and one daughter.

In 1979 Helen wrote and illustrated *Sevukakmet*, a book that describes the way of life of the Siberian Eskimo. For the last fifteen years, she has dedicated her life to preserving the knowledge and heritage of the St. Lawrence Island Eskimos.

—Joyce Ann Kievit

Reference

Carius, Helen Slwooko. *Sevukakmet*. Anchorage: Alaska Pacific University Press, 1979.

CARLO, POLDINE DEMOSKI (b. 1920), Yukon Athabascan author,

was born at Nulato, Alaska, the daughter of Priscilla Stickman and James Demoski. Her father drowned while crossing the Yukon in a canoe. Priscilla, however, remarried and had two more daughters, Anna and Florence. When Carlo's mother died in 1928, she and her sisters were raised by their grandparents, Joseph and Anna Stickman (Otzosia and K'Oghotaaineek), two of the most powerful medicine people in the Yukon. Baptized at Nulato, Carlo was named after Sister Mary Leopoldine, the Superior of the St. Ann Order of Nuns of Alaska. although she attended the Catholic school at Nulato and spent a short time at the high school in Eklutna, much of her knowledge came from her grandparents. On March 19, 1940, she moved to Tanana, Alaska, where she met and married Bill Carlo. The couple had eight children, five boys and three girls, and have lived throughout Alaska in Ruby, Galena, Rampart, and Fairbanks.

Carlo's accomplishments include serving as a charter member of the Fairbanks Native Association, a board member of the State of Alaska Bicentennial Commission, and as a consultant for the Tanana Chiefs Conference. She dedicates her book, *Nulato: An Indian Life on the Yukon*, to her son Stewart Allen, who died in a 1975 auto accident. Praised by Alaskan Senator John C. Sackett for recording "the vital elements of the Yukon Indian culture," the book shows a society steeped in tradition, yet still living with the modern influences of gold mining, fur trading, and missionaries. Divided into chapters on Growing Up, Beliefs and Remedies, Work, Celebration, and Old Ways and New, with a helpful index, the biography provides an insightful examination of the Athabascan Indian way of life in Nulato, Alaska.

—Steven R. Price

Reference

Carlo, Poldine. *Nulato: An Indian Life on the Yukon*. Caldwell, ID: Caxton
    Publishers, 1978.

CHONA, MARIA (1845?-1936) was born at Mesquite Root village in the
Spanish province of Upper Pimeria several years before the US government
acquired the Arizona Territory with the Gadsen Purchase in 1853. Daughter of
Jose Maria, who was appointed village governor when the Papagos came under
American supervision, Chona spent her girlhood in a traditional Papago setting
little changed since the coming of the Kino expedition in the late seventeenth
century. Her father's status in the village made her privy to important events and
led to her later characterization of herself as "a woman who knows things." Raised
in a family of medicine men, she too exhibited signs of medicine power in
childhood but was not permitted to develop her gift. She participated in a
traditional puberty ceremony and was married into another medicine family but
returned to her family when her husband accepted a second wife, a common
practice for medicine men at the time but one that she found impossible to
accept. She was later married to a man considerably older than she was who
encouraged her to develop her healing powers; she was able to fulfill her medicine
gift in her later years and became well known as a curer of infant maladies.

In the early 1930s Chona became the guide and primary informant for
anthropologist Ruth M. Underhill, who was compiling the first comprehensive
study of Papago culture. In the course of their work and travels together, Chona
narrated her life story, which was first published under the title *The Autobiography
of a Papago Woman* in 1936, then reissued with a comprehensive introduction by
Underhill under the title *Papago Woman* in 1979. Focusing on traditional Papago
village life, the autobiography is a striking and lyrical narrative of a woman
Underhill characterizes as "executive" for her capacity to satisfy her personal
goals and desires within the limits of her culture. The published text was hailed
as a breakthrough in ethnographic life history for its literary style and depiction
of a complex narrative persona.

Chona's autobiography provides an intimate portrait of traditional Papago
culture from a distinctly female viewpoint, with emphasis on family life, seasonal
cycles, ceremonial events, and movement on the desert landscape. The collaboration of Chona, a woman exceptionally knowledgeable about her culture, and
Underhill, an ethnographer with a literary bent, produced a text that has been
consistently praised for its historical, anthropological, and literary quality.

Chona spent the last years of her life alternating between living in Tucson and
with her daughter in Santa Rosa village on the Papago Reservation. She was well
known for her basketry, and though she was acquainted with modern American
ways, she chose to pursue a traditional way of life.

—Kathleen M. Sands

References

Bataille, Gretchen M., and Kathleen M. Sands. "Maria Chona." In *Native American Women Telling Their Lives*, 447-82. Lincoln: University of Nebraska Press, 1984.

Lurie, Nancy Oestreich. "A Papago Woman and a Woman Anthropologist." *Reviews on Anthropology* 7 (Winter 1980): 120.

Sands, Kathleen M. "Ethnography, Autobiography and Fiction: Narrative Strategies in Cultural Analysis." In *Native American Literature: Forum I*, edited by Laura Coltelli, 39-52. Pisa: Serrizo Editorale Universitario, 1989.

Underhill, Ruth M. "The Papago Family." In *Comparative Family Systems*, edited by M.F. Nimkoff, 147-62. Boston: Houghton Mifflin, 1965.

———. *Papago Woman*. New York: Holt, Rinehart, and Winston, 1979.

———. *Social Organization of the Papago Indians*. Columbia University Contributions to Anthropology 30. New York: Columbia University Press, 1936.

CHOUTEAU, YVONNE (b. 1929), a Cherokee, is one of the celebrated Indian ballerinas. Chouteau was born to parents of Cherokee/Shawnee ancestry in Ft. Worth, Texas. She began her illustrious career by receiving her general education at the Professional Children's School of New York. This allowed her to attend school while still focusing on her dancing, for she had already won a scholarship to the School of American Ballet. Beginning in 1941 at the age of twelve, she studied over a two-year period with such ballet luminaries as Anatole Vilzak and Ludmilla Sholler. Other noted tutors included Fronie Asher and Veronine Vestoff.

At the age of fourteen (1943), Chouteau joined the Ballet Russe de Monte Carlo as a member of the *corps de ballet*. In 1945 she first soloed in the role of "Prayer" in *Coppelia*, followed by other noted titles, such as the title character in *Paquila*, "Fanny Cerito" in *Pas de Quatre*, and "Jota" in *Capriccio Espagnol*. Her 1950 elevation to the position of ballerina was made official when she danced as "Juliette" in *Romeo et Juliette*.

In the mid-1950s, Yvonne Chouteau married fellow dancer Miguel Terekhov. In 1957 they moved to Montevideo, Uruguay, where they worked with ballet troupes for two years. In 1959 they moved to Norman, Oklahoma, to become artists-in-residence at the University of Oklahoma. In 1962 the college instituted a full degree in dance. Chouteau and Terekhov designed its first curriculum. They continued to teach in their school in Oklahoma City and organized their own ballet troupe. They have served as guest artists with other troupes, as well as working tirelessly to foster interest in Oklahoma's performing arts.

In 1976 Chouteau was again in the national spotlight, dancing in her work entitled *Indian Trail of Tears*, performed at the Kennedy Center. She continued to dance in performance until 1978. On September 16, 1983, she received Oklahoma's Governor's Arts Award for lifetime achievement in the arts.

Oklahoma Governor Walters has declared 1992 as the Year of the Indian, and in honor of Chouteau and the other Indian ballerinas, artist Mike Larsen has painted a mural depicting their lives. It was unveiled in the capital rotunda on November 17, 1991.

Today, Yvonne Chouteau, mother of two and grandmother of two, still teaches ballet with her husband at their school. In 1974 Phillips University in Oklahoma awarded her an honorary Doctor of Humanities degree. She lives in suburban Oklahoma City.

—Cynthia Kasee

References

Chujoy, Anatole, and P. W. Manchester, comps. *The Dance Encyclopedia.* New York: Simon and Schuster, 1967.
Gridley, Marion. *American Indian Women.* New York: Hawthorne Books, 1974.
Koegler, Horst. *Concise Dictionary of Ballet.* New York: Oxford University Press, 1977.
"Moon-Maidens: Five Part Indian Ballerinas." *Newsweek* 70 (November 1967): 101-2.

CHRYSTOS (b. 1946), poet, artist, and activist, was born and raised in San Francisco by her Menominee father and Lithuanian/Alsace-Lorraine mother. Active with Women for Big Mountain in Seattle, she lives on Bainbridge Island, in the Pacific Northwest.

Influenced and encouraged by Kate Millett and Audre Lorde, Chrystos has published her work in such publications and collections as *This Bridge Called My Back, A Gathering of Spirit, Sinister Wisdom, Conditions, Sapphic Touch, WomanSpirit, Sunbury, Plexus, Living the Spirit, Diversity: the Lesbian Rag, Lesbian Ethics, Fireweed, Taos Review, So's Your Old Lady, Naming the Waves, Intricate Passions, Naming the Violence: Speaking Out on Lesbian Battering, Gay and Lesbian Poetry of Our Time,* and *Making Face, Making Soul/Haciendo Caras.* Her *Not Vanishing* collects seventy-two of her highly imagistic poems, marked by her experiences as a former addict, prostitute, and mental patient. *Dream On* delivers a more forceful and feminist voice, one more confidently engaged in Indian and lesbian matters from a more pointedly political perspective.

Always aware of the duality of being both Native American and urban, Chrystos's passionate verse explores the issues of colonialism, genocide, class, and gender and how they affect women and Indian peoples, specifically from a feminist and lesbian perspective. Her work ranges from the anger of "Today Was a Bad Day Like TB," to the humor of "Poem for Lettuce," to the eroticism of "O Honeysuckle Woman," to the social and political outrage of "For Eli." Her subjects are inevitably the disenfranchised—Indians, women, lesbians, prostitutes, alcoholics, abused children, mixed-bloods, gays, the homeless, African

Americans—whom she champions with an insider's awareness and sensitivity. Simultaneously, she rages with vigor against the victimizers in contemporary society, never flinching from the gritty realities that have shaped many current social and political conditions. Both harsh and lyrical, her free verse is frequently prosaic in form, and her contributions are primarily in the force of her message and social vision, as well as her romantic and lyric eroticism.

—Rodney Simard

References

Chrystos. *Dream On*. Vancouver: Press Gang, 1991.

———. *Not Vanishing*. Vancouver: Press Gang, 1988.

Lerner, Andrea, ed. *Dancing on the Rim of the World: An Anthology of Contemporary Northwest Native American Writing*. Tucson: University of Arizona Press, 1990.

Roscoe, Will, ed. *Living the Spirit: A Gay American Indian Anthology*. New York: St. Martin's, 1988.

CLEGHORN, MILDRED IMOCH (b. 1910), Fort Sill Apache, was born to Richard Imoch and Amy Wratten, prisoners of war confined by the U.S. military at Fort Sill, on December 11, 1910. Cleghorn attended public school in Apache, Oklahoma, and the Haskell Business Institute in Lawrence, Kansas. The Kansas Bureau of Indian Affairs (BIA) is where Cleghorn worked until 1937. In 1941 she received her college degree in home economics and was a school teacher for one and one-half years at the Riverside School in Oklahoma. While working with Pawnees in Kansas, Cleghorn met her future husband, Bill, and after an extended courtship they were married during a double ceremony shared with Cleghorn's cousin, Kathleen Smith Kanseah, on the Mescalero Apache Reservation in New Mexico. Cleghorn, one of only approximately ten Apaches living today who was born in captivity, currently is the chairperson for the Fort Sill Apaches. She is an admired, outspoken leader who believes strongly in preserving Native traditions. She actively participates in such tribal activities as dancing, beadworking, game playing (slapstick), cooking, singing, storytelling, praying, reading and dollmaking. Mildred Cleghorn was elected Indian of the Year in 1989.

—Julie LaMay Abner

Reference

Stockel, Henrietta H. *Women of the Apache Nation: Voices of Truth*. Reno: University of Nevada Press, 1991.

COBB, ISABELLE (1858-1947), physician and educator, was born in Morgantown, Tennessee, the eldest child of Joseph B. Cobb, a white man, and Evaline Clingan Cobb, of mixed Cherokee-and-white lineage. She was educated in rural schools of Cleveland, Tennessee, until 1870, when her family moved to the Cherokee Nation in Indian Territory. Cobb then studied at the Cherokee Female Seminary, where she graduated in 1879. Afterwards, she enrolled in the Glendale Female College in Ohio for two years, but returned to her high school alma mater to teach from 1882 to 1887, along with her younger sister, Martha Cobb Clarke. Cobb graduated from the Women's Medical College of Pennsylvania with her medical degree in 1892, "specializing in women and children." She practiced medicine at the Nursery and Children's Hospital in West New Brighten, New York, and in Wagoner, Indian Territory (later Oklahoma), where she often performed surgery at her patients' homes since there were no hospitals in the vicinity. Cobb was an active Presbyterian and Republican, served as superintendent of the Oklahoma Rural Sunday Schools, and was a member of numerous literary societies in Wagoner County, Oklahoma.

—Devon A. Mihesuah

References

Cobb, Isabelle. In *Indian and Pioneer Histories*. Vol. 65. Edited by Grant Foreman, 184-218. Oklahoma City: Oklahoma Historical Society, n.d.
The Record-Democrat [Wagoner, OK] 14 August 1947: 1.
Starr, Emmett. *History of the Cherokee Indians and Their Legends and Folklore*. Oklahoma City: The Warden, 1979.
Who's Who Among Oklahoma Indians. Oklahoma City: Travis, 1928.

COCHRAN, JO WHITEHORSE (b. 1958), author, editor, educator who sees herself as an Indian/lesbian/feminist, was born in Seattle, Washington, to parents of Lakota and Norwegian descent. Cochran is a Reiki practitioner, a Seichim master, and among her environmental interests cites a wish to heal the planet. While attending the University of Washington, she co-instructed an introductory course in Women's Studies before attaining her MA in creative writing.

Cochran has served as editor for a variety of publications, including *Changing Our Power*, an introductory text to women's studies; *Gathering Ground*, an anthology of writing by Northwest women of color; and the journal *Calyx*, an anthology of Native American literature. In her editorial statement in *Calyx*, Cochran outlines her desire to create a community voice, bringing together the differing experiences and voices of Indian women. She adds that individuals must demonstrate the strength to write the truths found in their worldly experiences.

Cochran's own poetry not only presents a commitment to nature and the earth, but also vividly reflects human experience associated with being a Native American, a woman, and a contemplative individual. For example, "Halfbreed Girl in City School" speaks of the alienation one feels while living in diverse cultures, cultures still learning to coexist. "First of February, New Snow," and "Nearing Winter" express Cochran's understanding of the relationship that exists between nature and the experiences of life. Finally, "From My Grandmother" illustrates Cochran's ability to listen to the voices around her. Throughout her work, Cochran's commitment to an authentic representation of life clearly presents itself.

—Steven R. Price

References

Cochran, Jo, et al., eds. "Bearing Witness/Sobreviviendo: An Anthology of Native American/Latina Art and Literature." *Calyx: A Journal of Art and Literature by Women* 8 (1984).

Cochran, Jo, J. T. Stewart, and Mayumi Tsutakawa. *Gathering Ground: New Writing and Art by Northwest Women of Color*. Seattle: The Seal Press, 1984.

Cochran, Jo, ed. *Changing Our Power: An Introduction to Women's Studies*. Dubuque, IA: Kendall/Hunt, 1987.

Cochran, Jo Whitehorse. "Half-Breed Girl in City School." *Backbone: A Journal of Women's Literature* (Fall 1984).

Lerner, Andrea, ed. *Dancing on the Rim of the World: An Anthology of Contemporary Northwest Native American Writing*. Tucson: University of Arizona Press, 1990.

COOCOOCHEE (c. early 1740s–19th century), a Mohawk medicine woman and visionary, was born into the Bear Clan at an Indian village southeast of Montreal but lived most of her life amongst Chief Blue Jacket's Shawnees in the Ohio country region. Much of our knowledge of Coocoochee is the result of Oliver Spencer's writings, who at eleven years of age was captured by Coocoochee's son, White Loon, near Cincinnati. Spencer lived with Coocoochee and her family from July 1792 until February 1793 and maintained contact with the family throughout his life.

Subsequent to her marriage to the Mohawk warrior Cokundiawsaw, and the birth of a daughter and three sons, Coocoochee and her family emigrated to Ohio country in 1769. There they settled amongst the Shawnee on the west bank of the Scioto River. While Coocoochee and her family hoped this move would distance themselves from the persistent encroachments of white colonists, by 1774 there was nothing left of this dream. In that year the Governor of Virginia, Lord Dunmore, destroyed the Shawnee villages in the Muskingum Valley, halting a mere one hundred miles from the Shawnee enclave where Coocoochee resided.

With the outbreak of the American Revolution in 1777, Chief Blue Jacket and his people removed to the Mad River along the Ohio-Kentucky frontier. Coocoochee and her family followed. Pro-British, Coocoochee's husband and eldest son Wapanoo participated in anti-American expeditions during the American Revolution. Hostilities in the region continued unabated even after the American Revolution, due to ever-increasing pressure by Kentuckians for the Native population's land. As a result more and more Indians of diverse tribal affiliations settled in the Mad River Valley region and joined in the battle against the encroachers. Despite this alliance the Indians gave way before Benjamin Logan's expedition of 1786, which forced many of the inhabitants, including Coocoochee and her family, to flee. Again Coocoochee and her family followed Blue Jacket's Shawnees, and in 1787 settled near the Miami Towns along the Maumee River near Fort Wayne, Indiana. There they lived in relative peace until 1790 when the Miami Towns were torched by a military expedition led by General Josiah Harmar. Coocoochee's spouse, Cokundiawsaw, was killed during this raid. This resulted in Coocoochee's fourth removal, and along with Blue Jacket and others of the allied Indian forces, they sought refuge at the "Glaize" on the banks of the Maumee River at present-day Defiance, Ohio.

During her years among the Shawnee, Coocoochee had developed special skills as a healer, knowledgeable in the preparation and use of herbal medicines. She was also esteemed as a person of vision and wisdom and was often consulted before the start of a military expedition. Specific examples of this were recorded by Spencer. In the fall of 1792, the Glaize's inter-tribal council consulted Coocoochee on the prospects for success on a contemplated raid on a supply shipment being sent to three American outposts north of Cincinnati. After communing with the spiritual world on behalf of the inter-tribal council, she declared that the raid would be successful. It was.

The final dispersion of the Glaize's mixed-tribal community came in the summer of 1794 when a raid (the battle of Fallen Timbers), led by General Wayne, forced the community to scatter. After this event it is unclear what happened to Coocoochee. It is known that Coocoochee's daughter eventually took up residence near Malden, Ontario, where her husband George Ironside became a British Indian Superintendent. Coocoochee's sons, White Loon and Black Loon, resided in various Shawnee towns in Ohio. Although the exact date is not known, it is surmised she passed on early in the nineteenth century before the commencement of the War of 1812.

Coocoochee's position as medicine woman and seer gave her a special status within her mixed tribal community. This, along with her ability to successfully maintain her family and traditional way of life despite periodic removals and the ever-present threat of frontier warfare, give Coocoochee's life a special significance within the annals of colonial and frontier Euro-Indian relations.

—Faren R. Siminoff

References

Spencer, Oliver M. *The Indian Captivity of O.M. Spencer.* Edited by Milo Milton
Quaife. Chicago: R. R. Donnelley, 1917. Reprint. New York: Citadel Press,
1968.
Tanner, Helen Hornbeck. "Coocoochee: Mohawk Medicine Woman." *American
Indian Culture and Research Journal* 3 (1979): 23-41.
————, ed. *Atlas of Great Lakes Indian History.* Norman: University of Oklahoma
Press, 1986.

COOK-LYNN, ELIZABETH (b. 1930), a Crow Creek Sioux, was born in

Fort Thompson, South Dakota, and holds a BA degree in English and journalism
and an MA in educational psychology and counseling. For almost twenty years
she taught English and Indian Studies at Eastern Washington University, where
she was a founding editor of the nationally recognized Indian studies journal,
Wicazo Sa Review. To students of contemporary Native American literature, she
was initially known for her poetry and for mixed-genre experiments in prose and
poetry, especially *Then Badger Said This.* By the beginning of the 1990s, her fiction
began to attract attention. A collection of stories, *The Power of Horses,* appeared
in 1990 and a novel, *From the River's Edge,* in 1991.

Cook-Lynn identifies three dominant influences on her creative writing: a
rich family-tribal heritage, a powerful Northern Plains landscape, and N. Scott
Momaday's writings. Her father's and grandfather's experiences on the Crow
Creek Tribal Council helped to shape her social and political attitudes. Just as
important was the example of her grandmother and namesake, Eliza Renville, a
bilingual writer for Christian newspapers. Besides these specific family influences,
Cook-Lynn often notes the impact of family and reservation stories of the Crow
Creek Sioux. She's thankful she listened and remembered. She also remembers
the land. Strong visual images of skies and rivers, primarily the Missouri, and
powerful animals, particularly horses, as well as recollections of sounds as delicate
as a meadowlark's call define her sense of place. So do histories as old as Wounded
Knee and as recent as wounded rivers (a Missouri River dam project) and stories
as ancient as Dakotah creation narratives of Inyan, the rock, and as recent as
destruction narratives of brutal reservation murders. Momaday's *The Way to Rainy
Mountain* (1969) inspired Cook-Lynn to mix poetry, history, tribal narratives,
and personal memories and to perceive of herself as a consecrator of past and
current events that testify to the tragedies and successes of tribal and individual
survival.

Family, tribe, place, and Momaday helped shape Cook-Lynn's literary imagination; so did gender. Repeatedly in poems and fiction the narrative voice or
focus is feminine. But this is no monotone performance. The viewpoint can be
the insider's voice of a little girl riding on a reservation wagon (Section XI of
Badger); the insider/outsider voice of a young mother trying to get her children

back from the mother of her ex-husband ("A Family Matter") and a sister watching the sins of the father repeated in the drunken acts of her siblings ("Last Days of a Squaw Man"); the mature voice of the outsider Indian scholar desperately trying to locate a scholarship recipient and finding instead the stares of cold hatred, handfuls of gravel thrown at her car, and the corpse of the young man she sought ("A Good Chance"); or the sympathetic voice of the poem "At Dawn, Sitting in My Father's House" that recalls Cook-Lynn's father with the vitality of a young daughter and with the wisdom of a woman who has accepted the natural processes of life and death. The range and the intensity of these women's voices make many of Cook-Lynn's Crow Creek portraits accessible and moving for readers who have little knowledge of Dakotah tribal history, reservation life, or the banks of the Missouri.

In *From the River's Edge*, we again see powerful female perspectives, especially in Cook-Lynn's portrayal of the strong, beautiful, and independent Aurelia. The narrative focus of the novel, however, is the trial of John Tatekeya. Cook-Lynn uses the trial as a unifying touchstone to satirize the legal system. John is the victim of cattle rustling, but during the trial, he (not the white rustler) is presented as the guilty one (a careless ranch manager, drinker, and adulterer) and "winning" the case brings him no recompense. Cook-Lynn also uses the trial to examine the decay of Dakotah community and family relationships, the effects of damming the Missouri, and the impact of traditional Dakotah values. For John, some ceremonials and some family values still work (sometimes) despite the severe tensions exposed by the trial. For Aurelia, John's long-time lover, Dakotah values have lost their ability to sustain her against the separation from John, weak family support, the oppression of Dakotah people and land, and the harsh South Dakota winds. *From the River's Edge* is a tough book. It implies that sometimes and for some Indian people, tribal traditions can still sustain and enrich life. Nonetheless, in a pragmatic, honest, and tragic way, Aurelia realizes that tribal values and landscapes cannot heal her, despite her strengths and strong desire for healing.

—Kenneth M. Roemer

References

Cook-Lynn, Elizabeth. "As a Dakotah Woman." Interview by Joseph Bruchac. In *Survival This Way: Interviews with American Indian Poets*, edited by Joseph Bruchac, 57-71. Tucson: University of Arizona Press, 1987.

———. *From the River's Edge*. New York: Arcade-Little, Brown, 1991.

———. *The Power of Horses and Other Stories*. New York: Arcade-Little, Brown, 1990.

———. *Seek the House of Relatives*. Marvin, SD: Blue Cloud Quarterly, 1983.

———. *Then Badger Said This*. 1977. Reprint. Fairfield, WA: Ye Galleon Press, 1983.

———. "'You May Consider Speaking about Your Art. . . .'" In *I Tell You Now: Autobiographical Essays by Native American Writers*, edited by Brian Swann and Arnold Krupat, 55-63. Lincoln: University of Nebraska Press, 1987.

Roemer, Kenneth M. Review of *Then Badger Said This*, by Elizabeth Cook-Lynn. *ASAIL Newsletter* n.s. 2 (Winter 1978): 55-58.

Ruppert, James. "The Uses of Oral Tradition in Six Contemporary Native American Poets." *American Indian Culture and Research Journal* 4 (1980): 87-110.

CORDERO, HELEN QUINTANA [DAIYROWITSA] (b. 1915), famous Native American potter and inventor of the Storyteller Doll, is the second daughter of Pablo and Caroline Trujillo Quintana from the Keres Pueblo of Cochiti, New Mexico. Unlike most Pueblo women, she did not learn pottery making as a child, preferring farming and men's work to housework and schoolwork. She did, reluctantly, attend St. Catherine's Indian School in Santa Fe from third grade to eighth. The most important teacher in her youth, however, was her grandfather Santiago Quintana, a respected storyteller and religious leader in the Pueblo. In addition to telling stories to his many children, grandchildren, and great grandchildren, Santiago Quintana shared his wisdom with several generations of anthropologists, notably Bandelier, Curtis, and Ruth Benedict, who published many of his stories in *Tales of the Cochiti Indians*. It was the image of him telling stories to the children that Cordero remembered in 1964 when folk art collector Alexander Girard asked her to make a larger "singing mother" with more children, and she shaped the first storyteller figure.

In 1932 she married Fernando (Fred) Cordero, who has been a leading drummer and drum maker in the Pueblo and who has held many tribal offices, including governor. In addition to four children of their own, Dolly, Jimmy, George, and Tony, they raised two foster sons, Gabriel and Leonard Trujillo. Cordero did not begin working with clay until the late 1950s, as an alternative to bead and leatherwork. She spent six months "under" Juanita Arquero, her husband's cousin, but could not master bowls and jars. Arquero suggested she try figures instead. Helen's creativity blossomed, and her "little people" revived a longstanding but moribund Cochiti figurative tradition and began what has become a revolution in Pueblo ceramics. She shaped the first Storyteller in 1964 and took first, second, and third prizes that year at the New Mexico State Fair. In 1965 she won the first of many first prizes at Santa Fe Indian Market, and in 1968, the first of many at the Annual Indian Arts and Crafts Exhibit at the Heard Museum, where she had her first one-person show in 1976. Since then she has demonstrated her pottery making from Bandelier National Monument to Kent State University and has had countless shows at galleries and museums throughout the country, notably the *Tales for All Seasons* exhibit at the Wheelwright Museum in Santa Fe in 1981–82.

In addition to countless prizes for her figures, Cordero has been much honored. In 1982 she received the New Mexico Governor's Award, and in 1986 a Heritage Fellowship from the National Endowment for the Arts. The popularity and success of Cordero's figures have changed the shape of Pueblo pottery, resulted in a new valuation of figurative ceramics, and brought economic benefits to her own and other Pueblos. By 1973 at least six other Cochiti potters were making storytellers and related figurines; ten years later there were ten times that number at Cochiti, including her own children, grandchildren, and hundreds of other potters from Taos to Hopi. She has indeed "really started something."

—Barbara A. Babcock

References

Babcock, Barbara A. "'At Home, No Women Are Storytellers': Potteries, Stories, and Politics in Cochiti Pueblo." *Journal of the Southwest* 30 (1988): 356-89.
———. "Clay Changes: Helen Cordero and the Pueblo Storyteller." *American Indian Art* 8 (1983): 30–39.
———. "Helen Cordero, The Storyteller Lady." *New Mexico Magazine* 56 (1978): 6-8.
———. "Modeled Selves: Helen Cordero's 'Little People.'" In *The Anthropology of Experience*, edited by E. Bruner and V. Turner, 316-43. Urbana: University of Illinois Press, 1986.
———. "Taking Liberties, Writing from the Margins, and Doing It with a Difference." *Journal of American Folklore* 100 (October/December 1987): 390–411.
———, and Guy and Doris Monthan. *The Pueblo Storyteller: Development of a Figurative Ceramic Tradition.* Tucson: University of Arizona Press, 1986.
Benedict, Ruth Fulton. *Tales of the Cochiti Indians.* 1931. Reprint. Albuquerque: University of New Mexico Press, 1981.
Monthan, Guy, and Doris Monthan. "Helen Cordero." *American Indian Art Magazine* 2 (1977): 72-76.

CROW DOG, MARY [MARY BRAVE BIRD, OHITIKA WIN, BRAVE WOMAN] (b. 1953), a political activist, is a Sioux born on the Rosebud Reservation in South Dakota. She is a member of the "Burned Thigh" or the Brule Sioux. Crow Dog tells a compelling story of what it is like to be a Native American woman in her autobiography, *Lakota Woman.* The narrative that Crow Dog delivers in this work is not chronological; rather, it is a cyclical pattern of development told in colloquial language.

Crow Dog describes herself as an *iveska*, or half-blood, and relates a childhood and adolescence of dismal realities: alcoholism, rebelliousness, and poverty. She was primarily raised by her grandparents while her mother trained as a nurse. She also had close contact with extended members of her family, such as her grand-uncle Dick Fool Bull, who took her to her first peyote meeting when she was still a young girl, and her Aunt Elsie Flood, a medicine woman. From them, she learned the oral tradition of her people. She also attended the mission school at St. Francis during the early 1960s, an unhappy experience of beatings and racism that caused her to drop out before she graduated.

The turning point in Crow Dog's life came with her first encounter with the American Indian Movement (AIM, which began in 1968) at a powwow held in 1971 at Leonard Crow Dog's home after a Sun Dance. According to her, the AIM movement boosted the morale of Native Americans at a time when it was critically needed, and the Indian rights movement was first a spiritual movement with ancient religion at its heart. Crow Dog joined the Trail of Broken Treaties, a caravan that followed the Cherokees' Trail of Tears, and was in the group that took over the BIA building in Washington, DC, in 1972. Crow Dog was also present at the siege of Wounded Knee in 1973, where she gave birth to her first child. It is this siege, with its echoes of the past injustices forced upon Native Americans, that forms the focal point of her narration.

Crow Dog married Leonard, a medicine man, in 1973. As a medicine man's wife, she has learned more of the traditions and rituals of the Sioux, looking to Native American religion as the cornerstone of her life. She and Leonard have three children and live in both Phoenix and Rosebud.

While Crow Dog tells the story of Leonard and the AIM movement, the story is also one about Native American women who have been in a double bind of victimization, caught between eroding traditions and a neglectful and misinformed white dominant culture. Hers is ultimately the story of one Lakota woman who, in spite of oppression, has emerged strong and whole.

—Laurie Lisa

Reference

Crow Dog, Mary, and Richard Erdoes. *Lakota Woman*. New York: Grove Weidenfeld, 1990.

CRYING WIND [LINDA STAFFORD, GWENDLELYNN LOVEQUIST]
(b. 1943) was abandoned by her mother and raised by her Kickapoo grandmother, Shima Sani, on an Indian reservation. She attended the University of Colorado, 1961; University of Texas, 1966; University of New Mexico, 1967; and the University of Alaska, 1969.

Under the name Crying Wind she has published a self-illustrated historical novel, *I Remember Divide* (Stafford Publishers, 1978), and two autobiographical novels, *Crying Wind* and *My Searching Heart*. The autobiographies are based on her experiences with poverty, prejudice, conversion to Christianity, and her search to find herself. These books have been translated into over a dozen foreign languages.

Using the pseudonym Gwendlelynn Lovequist, she has published numerous love stories and romances and contributed over two hundred stories to various magazines such as *Writer's Digest*. As Linda Stafford, she has authored articles on child rearing, home life, and humor. She is the proprietor of art galleries in Santa Fe, New Mexico; Anchorage, Alaska; and Oklahoma City, Oklahoma.

She married Don B. Stafford, a steel worker, in 1965, and they reside in Anderson, Missouri, with their four children. All of her books have a message of hope and the optimistic theme of not giving up because things will get better. She likes to leave the reader with a smile and a happy ending.

—Joyce Ann Kievit

References

Crying Wind. *Crying Wind*. Chicago: Moody Press, 1977.
———. *My Searching Heart*. Eugene, OR: Harvest House, 1980.
Fraser, Gordon. *Rain on the Desert*. Chicago: Moody Press, 1975.

CUERO, DELFINA (1900?-1972) was one of the few survivors of forced displacement of Kumeyaaye (Diegueño) people by non-Indian (Anglo-American and immigrant Asian) settlers in the San Diego area at the beginning of the twentieth century. In the 1960s Delfina Cuero narrated her life history to Florence Shipek. In doing so, she contributed not only an account of personal courage and endurance, but invaluable knowledge of the ecology of coastal southern California and traditional Kumeyaaye arts and sciences.

Delfina Cuero was born near Mission San Diego, but she and her family were considered squatters on the land they had occupied for centuries. Their band had to move frequently as more and more land was claimed as property for non-Indian agriculture, ranching, and settlement. She was married in her early teens to Sebastian Osun, a hard-working man chosen by her parents, and they had five surviving children: Aurelio, Lupe, Eugenia, Lola, and Santos. Shortly before her marriage, Cuero's parents had moved with her to Baja California (Mexico), where the displaced Kumeyaaye were relatively unharassed and could maintain crops and domestic animals on the land they occupied. Sebastian Osun died when their oldest child was eleven years old; Cuero remained in Mexico where she raised her children under harsh circumstances. Wage labor brought little income, generally in food or second-hand clothing rather than money, while previous sources of sustenance were no longer accessible. Some of Cuero's children were indentured in abusive homes, and she herself suffered from more than one abusive companion. One of Delfina Cuero's purposes in telling her life story, according to Florence Shipek, was to validate her claim to US citizenship by birth, and thus to secure the right to return to live with relatives in southern California. In 1967 she was able to move permanently back to the San Diego area, where she lived until her death in 1972.

—Helen Jaskoski

Reference

Cuero, Delfina. *The Autobiography of Delfina Cuero.* Edited by Florence Shipek.
    Translated by Rosalie Pinto Robertson. Pasadena: Dawson's Book Shop, 1968.
    Reprint. Morongo Indian Reservation, Banning, CA: Malki Museum Press,
    1970.

CULLETON, BEATRICE [BEATRICE MOSIONIER] (b. 1949), a Métis
author, was born in St. Boniface, near Winnipeg, the youngest child of Louis and
Mary Clara Mosionier. At the age of three, she and her two sisters and one
brother became wards of the Children's Aid Society, who put them into different
foster homes. Culleton grew up around Winnipeg in a non-Native foster family.
She attended grades one to ten in the Catholic schools in St. Norbert, Manitoba,
and transferred in grade eleven to St. Charles Academy, near Winnipeg. She
began grade twelve at Gordon Bell High School but dropped out before
graduation. Later, she attended George Brown College in Toronto.

While Culleton's personal experiences in a foster home were positive, her
sisters fared much worse. They suffered racism, cruelty, and abuse, forcing them
into the "Native girl syndrome." Both sisters committed suicide, traumatic
experiences affecting Culleton profoundly. After the death of her second sister in
October 1980, she decided to write fiction as a therapeutic inward quest for
identity. The result of this inward journey was her first novel, *In Search of April
Raintree*, which was published by Pemmican Publications, Winnipeg, in 1983. A
slightly edited school edition, *April Raintree*, followed a year later. The novel is
the fictional account of the lives of two Métis sisters, who grow up in foster
families, and who try to find a meaningful way of life in a society that is marked
by prejudice, racism, and sexual violence. While the first person narrator, April,
"passes" as white for years and marries into a rich Torontonian family, Cheryl
develops pride in her Métis roots but is unable to achieve her goal of improving
the lot of her people. Instead, she finally ends up on skid row and commits suicide,
whereas April separates from her husband, returns to Winnipeg, and decides to
raise Cheryl's son, conscious and proud of their Native heritage. The straightfor-
wardly told, realistic novel gives a graphic depiction of the plight of Native
children who become wards of the government due to their parents' addictions.
Their immense struggle to retain their humanity, within a surrounding environment bent on making them fail, provides a plot that is both moving and full of
suspense.

After the publication of the novel, Beatrice Culleton served as an editor for
Pemmican Publications, a publishing house affiliated with the Manitoba Métis
Federation. Her historical novella, *Spirit of the White Bison*, came out in 1985. It
depicts the wanton slaughter of the North American bison by the white intruders
as a parable of the genocide against Native Americans, to which it was so closely
and consciously linked. This book for young readers addresses issues of ecology

and international solidarity vis-à-vis Western linear concepts of growth and progress threatening the survival of all people.

For the last years Culleton has lived in Toronto with her husband, George Moehring. She has just finished the second draft of a play, entitled *Night of the Trickster*, and will be working on a script for a National Film Board screenplay about racial prejudice, directed by Canadian Native film director Alanis Obomsawin. Presently, she is Playwright-in-Residence at Native Earth Performing Arts in Toronto.

—Hartmut Lutz

References

"Beatrice Culleton [Interview]." In *Contemporary Challenges: Conversations with Canadian Native Authors*, edited by Hartmut Lutz, 97-105. Saskatoon, SK: Fifth House, 1991.

Culleton, Beatrice. *In Search of April Raintree*. Winnipeg: Pemmican Publications, 1983.

————. *Night of the Trickster*. Play, unpublished.

————. *Spirit of the White Bison*. Winnipeg: Pemmican Publications, 1985.

Fee, Margery. "Upsetting Fake Ideas: Jeannette Armstrong's 'Slash' and Beatrice Culleton's 'April Raintree.'" *Canadian Literature* 124-25 (Spring/Summer 1990): 168-80.

Garrod, Andrew. "Beatrice Culleton." In *Speaking for Myself: Canadian Writers in Interview*, edited by Andrew Garrod, 79-96. St. John, NF: Breakwater Books, 1986.

Grant, Agnes. "Contemporary Native Women's Voices in Literature." *Canadian Literature* 124-25 (Spring/Summer 1990): 124-32.

Klooss, Wolfgang. "Fictional and Non-Fictional Autobiographies by Métis Women." In *Minority Literatures in North America: Contemporary Perspectives*, edited by Wolfgang Karrer and Hartmut Lutz, 205-25. Frankfurt: Peter Lang, 1990.

CUNY, SR. GENEVIEVE (b. 1930) is a Franciscan educator and administrator who herself was a product of Franciscan education. Cuny was one of fifteen children born into an Oglala Lakota family homesteading the Badlands of Pine Ridge Reservation, South Dakota. She attended Catholic boarding schools staffed by Franciscan Sisters, first in Pine Ridge for twelve years, then in Sioux City, Iowa, for college. In 1954 she professed her vows. For several years thereafter she taught and also later administered at Franciscan staffed schools in the Rosebud and Pine Ridge Reservation vicinities and furthered her studies with a BS degree in history from Regis College, Denver, Colorado, and an MS degree in business education from the University of Detroit.

During the 1970s, the Catholic church created new opportunities for Indian church leadership and participation in response to demands for self-determination and the declining availability of non-Indian church personnel on reservations. Cuny reacted to these needs by redirecting her work towards religious education, where she became an advocate for including Native spirituality and values in the teaching of the Catholic faith. She first served as a local church educator and pastoral minister in the Rosebud Reservation area. Then, after completing an advanced religious education degree at Loyola University, Chicago, she became a Native religious education consultant for the Rapid City Diocese, a support position to local educators within five rural reservations and one urban Indian church.

Since 1976 Cuny has been a national advocate for more Indian self-determination within the Church. As a member of the Tekakwitha Conference Board of Directors, she has been a principal architect in transforming it from a regional missionary support group into a Native North American Catholic association for revitalizing local urban and rural Indian Catholic parishes. Moreover, she has served on several teams to further religious education among Native American Catholics, including a traveling national training team for catechists, a US Catholic Conference Multi-Cultural Catechesis Task Force, and a writing team for Seasons of Faith, a preschool to adult textbook series for family-centered multicultural catechesis. In 1990 she became Director of Catechetics at the Tekakwitha Conference National Center, Great Falls, Montana.

—Mark G. Thiel

References

Cross and Feather News. Great Falls, MT: Tekakwitha Conference National Center, 1-10, 1982-1991.

Cuny, Genevieve. "Leadership and Professional Development in the Light of the Native American Experience." In Faith and Culture: A Multicultural Catechetical Resource, edited by United States Catholic Conference, Department of Education, 53-61. Washington, DC: United States Catholic Conference, 1987.

Freye, Mariella, ed. The Story and Faith Journey of Seventeen Native Catechists. Great Falls, MT: Tekakwitha Conference National Center, 1982.

West River Catholic. "Cuny Authors Article about Native Catechesis." Rapid City, SD: Diocese of Rapid City, 15 (1987): 17.

D

DAHTESTE [TAH-DES-TE] (b. 1865?), Apache, was a woman warrior who actively participated in battles and raiding parties with her husbands, Anandia and Coonie, and Geronimo. According to one source she was as "courageous, daring, and skillful as the men." Apaches are traditionally matrilocal societies, and women are taught warfare skills without ridicule and are praised for mastering the difficult talents these skills require. Women are also responsible during these raiding parties for moral and spiritual support, as well as cooking, cleaning, and nursing when necessary. Dahteste was also a skillful horse rider and hunter and became a trusted scout, messenger, and mediator between the US cavalry and Geronimo and his band. She was instrumental, along with Lozen, in bringing about the final surrender of Geronimo in 1886; she was incarcerated along with Geronimo and his followers and was transferred to Fort Sill in 1894. She lived on that Oklahoma military facility until 1913, when she and her family moved to the Mescalero Apache Reservation and lived in a tent until their home was built.

Dahteste was able to survive personal as well as military battles. She survived both pneumonia and tuberculosis. After her divorce from Anandia in the "Indian way," when he left her to return to his previous wife, Dahteste married a widower with three children. He was an Apache scout for Fort Apache; Kuni (Coonie) became Dahteste's second husband. Besides Kuni's children, they also had his nephew and two orphans (or three nephews) living with them. A beautiful woman, Dahteste has been described as wearing her long dark hair straight, always traditionally well dressed, with beads, turquoise, belts, and bags. The elderly Dahteste lived at Whitetail with her niece, Elizabeth Coonie, and at the Mescalero Indian Reservation until she died of old age.

—Julie LaMay Abner

References

Ball, Eve, and Lynad Sanchez. "Legendary Apache Women." *Frontier Times* (October/November 1980): 8–12.
Buchanan, Kimberly Moore. *Apache Women Warriors*. El Paso: Texas Western Press, 1986.
Stockel, Henrietta H. *Women of the Apache Nation: Voices of Truth*. Reno: University of Nevada Press, 1991.

DAT-SO-LA-LEE [LOUISA KIZER or KEYSER] (c. 1835–1925), the famous basketmaker, was a full-blooded Washo woman born near Woodfords, California. Her parents named her "Dabuda," and she eventually came to be known as Dat-So-La-Lee or "Big Hips" (some sources state that her name was derived from S.L.

Lee, a prominent Carson City physician). She is mentioned in Captain Fremont's journals, which record his journey through the Carson Valley in January, 1844. She first married a Washo man named Assu, but he and their two children died early. She then married Charley Kizer, a Washo-Miwok craftsman, in 1888, becoming Louisa Kizer. Eventually, she and her husband came to live with Abram and Amy Cohn in Carson City, Nevada, where she worked first as a laundress but where her basket weaving attracted the fascination of Amy Cohn. The Cohns came to monopolize ownership of all Washo basketry for a time, especially the baskets of Louisa Kizer. The Cohns supported the Kizers in return for ownership of every basket Dat-So-La-Lee wove, so she never received any money herself for her work. It is generally agreed that Louisa Kizer single-handedly transformed Washo basketmaking, introducing curio functions and the incurving *degikup* shape, the hallmark of the coiled basket style.

She did adopt some ideas and materials from the neighboring Maidu and Pomo, and then dramatically transformed her own already innovative style, especially impressive when we remember she used a piece of glass to scrape the willows, or her teeth and fingernails, or later, a tin can lid to evenly size narrower splints, ultimately achieving thirty stitches per inch. Dat-So-La-Lee was continually experimenting but made her most significant contribution in the finely stitched, two-color *degikup*, often with flame motifs in a scatter design or decorative bands in symmetrical or alternating formats. She created in her baskets "art for art's sake," nevertheless maintaining the reserved, ordered, and integrated look of "tradition."

She journeyed to the St. Louis Exposition in 1919 with Abram and Amy Cohn to exhibit her baskets and demonstrate her abilities, but such large and public demonstrations were uncomfortable to her as she felt basket art should be passed to family members only. She died in Carson City, Nevada, in the house the Cohns had provided.

—Gretchen Ronnow

References

Cohodas, Marvin. "Dat-So-La-Lee and the 'Degikup.'" *Halycon: A Journal of the Humanities* 4 (1982): 119–40.

"Dat-So-La-Lee's Basketry Designs." *American Indian Art Magazine* (Autumn 1976): 22–31.

Dat-So-La-Lee. *Life Stories of Our Native People: Shoshone, Paiute, Washo.* Published by the Inter-Tribal Council of Nevada. Salt Lake City: University of Utah Printing Service, 1974.

Gigli, Jane Green. *Dat-so-la-lee, Queen of the Washo Basket Makers.* Nevada State Museum Anthropological Papers. Carson City, Nevada, 1974.

James, George Wharton. *Indian Basketry.* New York: Dover Publications, 1972.

Porter, Frank W., ed. *The Art of Native American Basketry: A Living Legacy.* Contributions to the Study of Anthropology, no. 5. New York: Greenwood Press, 1990.

Price, John A. *The Washo Indians: History, Life Cycle, Religion, Technology, Economics, and Modern Life.* Nevada State Museum Occasional Papers, no. 4. Carson City, Nevada, 1980.
Waltrip, Lela, and Rufus Waltrip. *Indian Women.* New York: David McKay, 1964.

DAUENHAUER, NORA MARKS (b. 1927) was born in Juneau, Alaska;

she grew up in Juneau and Hoonah, as well as on the family fishing boat and in seasonal subsistence sites around Icy Straits, Glacier Bay, and Cape Spencer. She was raised speaking the Tlingit language, and it was not until she entered school at the age of eight that she began to learn English. Almost all of her work as a writer, an anthropologist, and a cultural conservationist has grown from and is flavored by her sense of living in two languages.

Dauenhauer received her BA in anthropology from Alaska Methodist University in 1976. She is married to writer and former poet laureate of Alaska, Richard Dauenhauer. She has four children and thirteen grandchildren. Although her family maintains a central prominence in her life, she has also earned an international reputation for her transcription, translation, and explication of Tlingit oral literature.

Her extensive research in Tlingit oral literatures culminated in 1987 with the publication (with Richard Dauenhauer) of *Haa Shuka, Our Ancestors: Tlingit Oral Narratives.* Carefully transcribed and produced in both English and Tlingit, the work is not only an invaluable text for anthropologists and those interested in Northwest languages and cultures, but it is also distinguished by its artistic appeal. Its imaginative freshness, its imagery and vision make the collection an outstanding work of literature. The Dauenhauers' sensitivity and expertise in the native Tlingit produce an authentic version of the narratives. Finally, their decision to produce the collection in a bilingual format reveals their sense of the two audiences for the text. Their work challenges the classic anthropological tradition of appropriating Native materials to present to mainly white audiences. This text is perhaps most strongly geared for a Tlingit audience, and thus it has served as a model for other indigenous communities who are seeking to take control of collecting and preserving their own cultural legacies. Dauenhauer, in collaboration with her husband, continues to work on Tlingit language projects in her capacity as principal researcher for the Sealaska Heritage Foundation. Their years of commitment and interest in Alaska's indigenous peoples and their languages have resulted in three additional publications. The first, *Because We Cherish You: Sealaska Elders Speak to the Future,* offers elders' stories and perceptions of the delicate balance between traditional life and the contemporary world we live in. The Dauenhauers have also produced two language texts: *Beginning Tlingit* and *Tlingit Spelling Book.*

Nora Marks Dauenhauer has also received much acclaim for her prose and poetry publications. In 1988 Black Currant Press published her first volume of poetry, *The Droning Shaman*. This volume is thoroughly infused with her interest in place, particularly the Alaskan landscape, as well as her interest in language and translation. While many of the poems written in English use phrases and words from Tlingit, she also demonstrates her facility and interest in translation by presenting a number of her own translations into Tlingit of poems by Basho, E. E. Cummings, and Gary Snyder's reworkings of Han Shan. Her poetry and prose have also appeared in a number of widely known anthologies, including *New Worlds of Literature*, *Harper's Anthology of 20th Century Native American Poetry*, *Earth Power Coming: Short Fiction in Native American Literature*, and *Alaska Native Writers, Storytellers, and Orators*, the latter edited by Dauenhauer with her husband and Gary Holthaus.

Dauenhauer's work has garnered her many prizes; in 1989 she was presented with the Governor's Award for the Arts, while in 1980 the Alaska Humanities Forum voted her Humanist of the Year. In her poetry, her prose, and her texts in Tlingit oral history and language, Dauenhauer's work resonates with her commitment to her traditions, her ancestry, and her language.

—Andrea Lerner

References

Dauenhauer, Nora Marks. *The Droning Shaman*. Haines, AK: The Black Currant Press, 1988.

Dauenhauer, Nora Marks, and Richard Dauenhauer, eds. *"Because We Cherish You . . ." Sealaska Elders Speak to the Future*. Juneau, AK: Sealaska Heritage Foundation, 1981.

———. *Beginning Tlingit*. A joint publication of Alaska Native Language Center, Alaska Native Education Board, and Tlingit Readers, Inc., 1976.

———. *Haa Shuka, Our Ancestors: Tlingit Oral Narratives*. Seattle: University of Washington Press, 1987.

———. *Tlingit Spelling Book*. Juneau, AK: Sealaska Heritage Foundation, 1974.

Dauenhauer, Nora Marks, Richard Dauenhauer, and Gary Holthaus, eds. *Alaska Native Writers, Storytellers, and Orators*. Special issue of *Alaska Quarterly Review*. Anchorage: University of Alaska, 1986.

Green, Rayna, ed. *That's What She Said: Contemporary Poetry and Fiction by Native American Women*. Bloomington: Indiana University Press, 1984.

Niatum, Duane, ed. *Harper's Anthology of 20th Century Native American Poetry*. San Francisco: Harper and Row, 1988.

Ortiz, Simon, ed. *Earth Power Coming: Short Fiction in Native American Literature*. Tsaile, AZ: Navajo Community College Press, 1983.

DAVIDSON, FLORENCE EDENSHAW [STORY MAID] (b. 1896),

a Haida, was born on September 15, 1896, in the village of Masset, one of the two Queen Charlotte Islands, off the coast of British Columbia. She was born in her father's home while being assisted into this world by her grandmother, Amy Edenshaw. Because her parents, Chief Charles (the carver) and Isabella Edenshaw, believed in both traditional ceremonies and Christianity simultaneously, Davidson had her ears pierced at four days of age and was also christened and baptized into the Anglican church. Chief Charles always favored Davidson because he believed her to be the reincarnation of his mother, Qawkuna, since the first words that Florence spoke were, "Dad, I'm your mother." Davidson sporadically attended the mission school at Masset until the fourth level because she was often needed to assist her Aunt Martha or at home. Haida culture has defined gender roles and is a matrilineal society, thus Davidson's childhood ended suddenly with her puberty seclusion and arranged marriage to Robert Davidson, a man twice her age, on February 23, 1911, when she was fourteen years old. She defiantly announced to her mother that she would not marry "that old man," and later stated, "I wish I were dead." The years melted her bitterness, and Davidson began to speak fondly of her husband; together they bore nineteen children.

In her adult life, Davidson was an active member of the Anglican church, choir, and women's auxiliary, and she also worked in a cannery and yet found time to fish and bake much of her family's sustenance. In 1929 her entire family moved from their small cottage into the large two-story house that Robert built for them. Two elders entitled the new home, "it's summertime inside," and "the main road runs by the house." In 1952 tragedy struck, and their home was destroyed by fire; the family began a two-year project of rebuilding their home. Davidson, throughout her life, strived to preserve her heritage that was so important to her. Most of her life was filled with caring for her children; her home was often filled with visitors, and her warmth and kindness were well known among her people.

—Julie LaMay Abner

Reference

Blackman, Margaret B. *During My Time: Florence Edenshaw Davidson, a Haida Woman*. Seattle: University of Washington Press, 1982.

DE CLUE, CHARLOTTE (b. 1948) is an Osage poet originally from Enid, Oklahoma. She attended Oklahoma State University at Stillwater and the University of Missouri at Kansas City. Her poetry reflects her strong interest in Osage history and culture. Her works have appeared in many collections, such as *Songs from this Earth on Turtle's Back*, *A Gathering of Spirit*, and *That's What She Said*. De Clue and her husband have a grown son and make their home in Lawrence, Kansas.

—Cynthia Kasee

76   *De Clue, Charlotte*

References

Brant, Beth, ed. *A Gathering of Spirit.* Rockland, ME: Sinister Wisdom, 1984.
Bruchac, Joseph, ed. *Songs from this Earth on Turtle's Back.* Greenfield Center, NY: Greenfield Review Press, 1983.
———. Special Issue on Native American Writers. *Greenfield Review* 9 (Fall 1981).
Cochran, Jo, et al., eds. "Bearing Witness/Sobreviviendo: An Anthology of Native American/Latina Art and Literature." *Calyx: A Journal of Art and Literature by Women* 8 (1984).
Green, Rayna, ed. *That's What She Said.* Bloomington: Indiana University Press, 1984.

DEER, ADA (b. 1935) was born and raised on the Menominee Indian Reservation in northern Wisconsin. The eldest of five children, her father is Menominee and her mother Euro-American. For the first eighteen years of her life, Deer lived with her family near the Wolf River in a small log cabin without electricity or running water. In 1957 she earned a BA degree in social work, the first Menominee to graduate from the University of Wisconsin, Madison. In addition, she was the first Native American to earn an MA in social work from Columbia University (1961). She also studied law briefly at the University of Wisconsin, Madison, and the University of New Mexico, Albuquerque, and was a Fellow at the Harvard Institute of Politics, J.F.K. School of Government, in 1977. Since 1977 she has held the position of senior lecturer in the School of Social Work and the Native American Studies Program at the University of Wisconsin, Madison. In 1991 she added a third academic affiliation, this one with the Women's Studies Program. A member of the board of directors of the Native American Rights Fund from 1984–90, she served as its chair from 1989–90.

A social worker, educator, and activist, Deer is best known for her political activism in the 1960s and early 1970s when she led the struggle to regain federal recognition for her tribe. As part of the federal government's policy of forced Indian assimilation, the US Congress passed an act terminating the Menominee Reservation (1954). Known as the Menominee Termination Act, this legislation (which was fully implemented by 1961) meant the end of federal control over tribal affairs. In short, the Menominee were no longer recognized by the federal government as Indians. The consequences for the Menominee were drastic: the loss of the health and education services and the potential loss of their tribal land. In an effort to reorganize during the implementation period following the Termination Act, the Menominees voted to become a separate county and were soon in serious financial difficulty. In 1970 Ada Deer, Jim White, and others created a new Menominee political organization known as Determination of the Rights and Unity for Menominee Shareholders (DRUMS). The long-term goal of DRUMS was to repeal the Termination Act, but first DRUMS leaders replaced the generally discredited Menominee government officials. With legal assistance from the Native American Rights Fund, Deer and other DRUMS leaders led the long fight to regain federal recognition for the Menominee. From 1972–73, Deer served as vice-president and chief lobbyist for the DRUMS-originated National Committee to Save the Menominee People and Forest, Inc. Their efforts were rewarded when, in 1973, President Nixon signed into law the Menominee Restoration Act which restored federal recognition and thus health and education benefits to the tribe.

After the Restoration Act, Ada Deer was elected chair of the Menominee Restoration Committee, a position she held from 1974 to 1976. Her new job was to complete the transition back to reservation life. Throughout the process she had to negotiate the criticism of some Menominee detractors, the bias of some of the media, as well as the alternative strategies of more radical activists who became known as the Menominee Warriors. By 1976 the new structure for the Menominee tribal government was set up and adopted. Her work completed, Ada Deer resigned.

In addition to her well-known efforts to restore federal recognition for her people (an historic reversal of American Indian policy in the US), Deer has labored diligently on behalf of numerous causes. Since 1958 she has worked to provide community services, particularly education, health, and legal services for youth, women, and Native Americans. Deer has a contagious belief in the possibility of pursuing social and political change from the bottom up. She does not wait for political powers at the top to initiate action. Over the years, Ada Deer has been honored with numerous awards for her activism. In 1982 she was one of eighteen women presented the Wonder Woman Award by the Wonder Woman Foundation in New York City. That same year, the Girl Scouts USA awarded Deer their Woman of the Year Award. The prestigious Indian Achievement Award was presented to her in 1984, while in 1985 she was named "Poster Woman" by the National Women's History Project, chosen as one of twelve honored women to be depicted in the *Heroine* Calendar, and along with other valiant women like Ida B. Wells and Amelia Earhart, selected for the Gallery of Women by the Adolph Coors Company. In addition, she has received the Politzer Award presented by the Ethical Culture Society (1975) and the White Buffalo Council Achievement Award (1974). Most recently she received the 1991 Distinguished Service Award from the American Indian Resources Institute.

She has served as a board member on such national committees as Girl Scouts of the USA, American Indian Policy Review Commission, National Association of Social Workers, Americans for Indian Opportunity, and the Housing Assistance Council. She has also contributed her energies to the National Women's Education Fund, the National Indian Advisory Committee of Honor, and the Quincentenary Committee for the Smithsonian Institution. Deer has remained active in such local and state political organizations as the Wisconsin Women's

Council and the Democratic Party of Wisconsin. In 1978 and 1982, Deer was a candidate for Wisconsin Secretary of State. She is past president of the Wisconsin chapter of the National Association of Social Workers.

Ada Deer has devoted her life to working for social justice, particularly with and for Native people and women. With her indomitable spirit and contagious optimism, Deer continues to serve as a role model, exhorting and inspiring individuals to become politically active.

—Hertha D. Wong

References

Anderson, Owanah, ed. *Ohoyo One Thousand: A Resource Guide of American Indian/Alaska Native Women, 1982*. Wichita Falls, TX: Ohoyo Resource Center, 1982.

Bletzinger, Andrea, and Anne Short, eds. *Wisconsin Women: A Gifted Heritage*. Milwaukee, WI: American Association of University Women, Wisconsin State Division, 1982.

Deer, Ada, with R.E. Simon, Jr. *Speaking Out*. Chicago: Children's Press Open Door Books, 1970.

Directory of Significant 20th Century American Minority Women. Nashville, TN: Fisk University, 1978.

Fanlund, Lari. "Indians in Wisconsin: A Conversation with Ada Deer." *Wisconsin Trails: The Magazine of Life in Wisconsin* 24 (March/April 1983): 8–21.

Graf, Karen. "Ada Deer: Creating Opportunities for Minority Students." *On Wisconsin* 9 (April 1987): 8.

McClanahan, A.J. "Indian Leader Says Keep Tribal Ties." *The Anchorage Times* 9 March 1984: B6.

Peroff, Nicholas C. *Menominee Drums: Tribal Termination and Restoration, 1954–1974*. Norman: University of Oklahoma Press, 1982.

Who's Who in American Politics. New York: R.R. Bowker, 1979.

Wong, Hertha. Written personal communication with Ada Deer, 25 February 1991.

Zweifel, Dave. "Ada Deer Is Finally Given 'Heroine' Status." *The Capital Times* [Madison, WI] 18 March 1985: 2.

DELORIA, ELLA CARA

DELORIA, ELLA CARA (1889–1971), a linguistic anthropologist, was a Yankton Sioux born at White Swan, South Dakota, on the Yankton Sioux Reservation. In 1890 her father was assigned to St. Elizabeth's Mission as a deacon of the Episcopal church, and the family moved to the Standing Rock Reservation; he was ordained to the priesthood in 1892. Deloria and her siblings were taught according to the doctrines of Episcopalian Christianity and also were greatly influenced by the Sioux culture and language with which they lived.

Deloria attended St. Elizabeth's Mission in Wakpala, South Dakota, and All Saint's School in Sioux Falls, South Dakota, taking the college preparatory course from 1906 to 1910. She attended the University of Chicago from 1910–11 and finished her course work at Oberlin College in Ohio. She then enrolled at Columbia University and began her lengthy association with Dr. Franz Boas. She graduated from Columbia with a BS degree in June of 1915.

Deloria returned to South Dakota and taught at All Saints from 1915 to 1919. She then accepted a job with the Young Women's Christian Association (YWCA) in an experimental program that would demonstrate to the Indian Bureau the value of physical education for Native American girls. The Haskell Indian School in Lawrence, Kansas, employed her to teach physical education in 1923.

In 1927 Deloria reestablished her connection with Franz Boas, the preeminent American anthropologist of the time, and assisted him as a research specialist in American Indian ethnology and linguistics until his death in 1942. The first project began when Boas asked her to translate and edit some written Sioux texts. She gathered and translated additional stories, legends, and works as well. As a result of these efforts, "Sun Dance of the Oglala Sioux" was published in the *Journal of American Folklore* in 1929. This was followed by *Dakota Texts* (1932), a bilingual collection of Sioux tales, and *Dakota Grammar* (1941), a collaboration with Boas. *Speaking of Indians*, a description of Indian, particularly Sioux, culture was published in 1944. *Waterlily*, a novel of a Teton Sioux woman's life, was written during the early 1940s and published posthumously in 1988.

Deloria received the 1943 Indian Achievement Medal and during the 1940s was recognized as the leading authority on the Sioux. She continued her scholarly research, writing, and lecturing throughout her life, collecting voluminous folkloristic and linguistic materials and translations. She also held the position of director of St. Elizabeth's Mission from 1955–58. At the time of her death on February 12, 1971, she was working on a Lakota dictionary.

Deloria is buried beside her sister, Susan Marble, and her mother, Mary Sully Deloria, in the St. Phillip's Cemetery at Lake Andes, South Dakota. Deloria's upbringing among the Sioux, devotion to Christianity, and training as an ethnologist give her work an unique and invaluable place in the study of her culture.

—Laurie Lisa

References

Deloria, Ella Cara. *Dakota Texts*. Edited by Agnes Picotte and Paul N. Pavich. Vermillion: Dakota Press, 1978.

———. *Speaking of Indians*. Introductory notes by Agnes Picotte and Paul N. Pavich. Vermillion: Dakota Press, 1979.

———. *Waterlily*. Lincoln: University of Nebraska Press, 1988.

Medicine, Bea. "Ella C. Deloria: The Emic Voice." MELUS 7 (Winter 1980): 23–30.

Murray, Janette K. "Ella Deloria: A Biographical Sketch and Literary Analysis." PhD diss., University of North Dakota, 1974.

Rice, Julian. "Why the Lakota Still Have Their Own: Ella Deloria's Dakota Texts." Western American Literature 19 (November 1984): 205–17.

DICK, LENA FRANK (1889?-1965)

DICK, LENA FRANK (1889?-1965) was born in Coleville, in Antelope Valley, California, the daughter of Charley and Lucy Frank, and belonged to the Washoe tribe. Dick was a teenager when she married George Emm, and had her only child, Juanita. She married Levi Dick around 1906, when George Emm left her soon after the birth of Juanita.

Dick learned basket weaving from her mother, who was a skilled basket maker also. Due to this early influence, Dick's sister, Lillie Frank James, and Jessie Frank Wade became known as accomplished basket weavers also. Although Dick was a very traditional Washoe woman, she became an innovator in the techniques, designs and use of color in basket weaving. During the time when she was actively weaving, from around 1920 to 1935, she acquired the patronage of Roscoe A. Day, a San Francisco area orthodontist, through an agent, Fred Settelmeyer, a Carson Valley rancher. Neither Day nor Settelmeyer promoted Dick's work to other collectors or took the time to meet her. Due to Day and Settelmeyer's interest in the art and not the artist, much of Dick's work was mistakenly identified as the work of other weavers, after baskets had passed out of possession of Day, and she was not fully given credit for all of her work until the late 1970s.

Dick's excellence as a weaver was centered in an extreme fineness of technique, usually finer than twenty-five stitches per inch, conservation and expansion of serrated diamond and V-designs, triangle or nested V's, and characteristic non-standardized arrangements of lines and triangles, in addition to juxtaposing red and black in the same motif in the creation of a traditional degikup basket.

After about 1935, due to failing eyesight from years of fine and detailed basket weaving, Lena gave up weaving the extremely fine baskets in favor of utilitarian baskets.

—Julie A. Russ

References

Cohodas, Marvin. "Lena Frank Dick: An Outstanding Washoe Basket Weaver." American Indian Art 4 (Autumn 1979): 32–41, 90.

———. "Washoe Innovators and Their Patrons." In The Arts of the North American Indian: Native Traditions in Evolution, edited by Edwin L. Wade, 203–20. New York: Hudson Hills, 1986.

DIETZ, ANGEL DeCORA [HINOOKMAHIWI-KILINAKA, HENOOK-MAKHEWE-KELENAKA]

(1871–1919) was a prominent personality of the Allotment Era, at the turn of the present century. She was an institutionally trained, professional artist, a teacher, a popular lecturer on Indian affairs, occasional writer, and an active member of the Society of American Indians.

Angel DeCora was born on May 3, 1871, on the Winnebago Reservation in Nebraska. Her father, David DeCora, a descendant of the Dakaury family, was of French-Winnebago ancestry; her mother was a member of the La Mere family. According to Dockstader, her parents died when she was still a young girl, and she was consequently brought up by her maternal relatives.

She first attended the local reservation school and afterward, at the age of twelve, was sent to Hampton Institute, where she graduated in 1891. According to her own autobiographical sketch, written in 1911, her transfer to Hampton was not voluntary, but arranged by some "strange white man" without consent of her relatives. She continued her education at the Burnham Classical School for Girls in Massachusetts and then enrolled for a four-year course in the Smith College Art Department, studying there under Dwight T. Tryon. Later she transferred to Drexel Institute in Philadelphia to study illustration with Howard Pyle for approximately two years. Following a brief sojourn at the Cowles Art School, she perfected her artistic skills for another two years at the Boston Museum of Fine Arts School.

Following completion of her academic training, Angel DeCora set up a private studio in Boston and did some illustrative work for a number of major publishing firms there, before moving on to New York City. Here she managed to establish herself somewhat as a book illustrator, working on such books as Francis La Flesche's *The Middle Five*, Gertrude Bonnin's *Old Indian Legends*, Natalie Curtis's *The Indian's Book*, and Elaine Goodale Eastman's *Yellow Star*. While preparing the illustrations for *Old Indian Legends*, she struck up what would become a long-lasting friendship with Gertrude Bonnin, with whom she would later cooperate in matters of Indian politics.

Angel DeCora's most important role during the Allotment Era was as director of the Leupp Art Department at Carlisle Indian School from 1906 to 1915. Here she developed an intensive art program for Indian students, encouraging them to apply Indian designs to modern art media, and this at a time when practically all things Indian were viewed as mere hindrance to the progress of Indian "civilization." She believed firmly that young Indians had a special "talent for pictorial art" and that her students at Carlisle would possibly develop it to the point of someday making a marked contribution to American art. Her work at Carlisle must not always have been easy, as it was vehemently opposed by Richard Pratt, who referred to it as plain "humbug." Nevertheless, DeCora's views were already becoming manifest with the emergence of the so-called "San Ildefonso School" of Indian artists in the Southwest at about that time (1910), a period which is viewed by art historians as the "renaissance" of Indian art, and they became a part of official Indian policy during the Indian New Deal Era with the creation of an Indian Arts and Crafts Department in 1935.

At Carlisle she also met Sioux artist William Dietz, whom she married in 1908 and with whom she returned to live in New York State at the outbreak of World War I, taking a position at the New York State Museum in Albany as draftswoman. She divorced William Dietz in 1918 and then moved back to New York City to continue her illustrating work.

Angel DeCora lectured widely on the subject of Indian affairs in general, as well as Indian art in particular, and was an active supporter of the Society of American Indians. It was to this first supra-tribal Indian political organization that she bequeathed her modest life savings. She was also the author of a number of articles (most of which are still unrecorded), including two on Indian art, as well as two autobiographical sketches and a short story titled "The Sick Child" that was published in Harper's Monthly in 1899.

Angel DeCora died in New York City on February 6, 1919.

—Bernd Peyer

References

Bonnin, Gertrude. *Old Indian Legends*. Small, Maynard, 1901.
Curtis, Natalie. "An American Indian Artist." *Outlook* 124 (January 1920): 64–66.
———. *The Indian's Book*. New York: Harper and Brothers, 1907.
DeCora, Angel. "An Autobiography." *Red Man* 3 (March 1911): 279–85.
Dockstader, Frederick J. "Angel DeCora Dietz." In *Great North American Indians*, edited by Frederick J. Dockstader, 71. New York: Van Nostrand Reinhold, 1977.
Eastman, Elaine G. "In Memoriam: Angel DeCora Dietz." *American Indian Magazine* 7 (Spring 1919): 51–52.
———. *Yellow Star*. Boston: Little, Brown, 1911.
La Flesche, Francis. *The Middle Five*. Boston: Ginn, 1900.
Littlefield, Daniel F., and James W. Parins. *A Biobibliography of Native American Writers, 1772–1924*. Metuchen, NJ: Scarecrow Press, 1981. Expanded edition, 1985.
McAnulty, Sarah. "Angel DeCora: American Indian Artist and Educator." *Nebraska History* 57 (1976): 143–99.

DORION WOMAN [MARIE IOWA, MARIE LaGUIVOISE, MADAM MARIE IOWA DORION VENIER TOUPIN] (1786–1853), an Iowa Indian, was born in the area around the Arkansas or Red River. Referred to as the Dorion Woman, she appears in the narratives of various explorers of the Wilson Price Hunt expedition from St. Louis, Missouri, to the Pacific Northwest, which began in 1811. Her husband, Pierre Dorion, a mixed-blood Métis and Yankton-Sioux, was employed by Hunt because of Dorion's command of several American Indian languages.

When the group set out for the West, the Dorion Woman accompanied them with her two children, Baptiste and Paul—a circumstance that would not have been allowed had Hunt not needed Pierre Dorion's services so badly. Along the journey Dorion Woman gave birth to a third child, which died a week after it was born due to the harsh winter storm conditions and starvation the group experienced passing over the mountains. Once the group had successfully traversed the Rockies, they split into two groups to set up posts for trading and trapping; Pierre Dorion and his family went with John Reed. They then split into three groups. While Pierre was out hunting, Dog Rib Indians attacked and killed all in his party and at the two other posts. When the Dorion Woman was warned of the attacks, she fled with her children. She found one badly wounded man from her husband's party still alive and heard of her husband's death. She attempted to save both him and her children by hiding, but he died in the night. She headed out alone, eventually set up camp for the winter and kept her children alive by killing her two horses and smoking and drying the meat. After a long, arduous journey east in the spring, she found a new home among the Walla Wallas.

On April 17, 1814, when the rest of the original party stopped at the Walla Walla camp, Dorion Woman told her story to Gabriel Franchere, who carried the news with him to Montreal and who published his narrative version five years later. Alexander Ross heard the Dorion Woman's story and published it in London in 1849; others took the story back with them to St. Louis. None of the men knew her Indian name, but later, after her third marriage, she took on the name Marie LaGuivoise when she was baptized and christened for her marriage to John Toupin, a mixed-blood Canadian. Venier was her second husband's name. She died in the Williamette Valley near Salem, Oregon, in 1853.

The Dorion Woman, as her name suggests, became legendary more for the role she played in relation to Anglo-American efforts to "win the West" than she did as a person in her own right. Nevertheless, she was by all accounts a woman of courage, dignity, and fortitude.

—Kathryn W. Shanley

References

Allen, A. J. *Ten Years in Oregon, Travels and Adventures of Dr. E. White and Lady.* Ithaca, NY: Mack-Andrus, 1848.

Barry, J. Neilson. *Redskin & Pioneer: Brave Tales of the Great Northwest.* New York: Rand McNally, 1932.

Defenbach, Byron. *Red Heroines of the Northwest.* Caldwell, ID: Caxton, 1929.

Franchere, Gabriel. *Narrative of a Voyage to the Northwest Coast of America in the Years 1811, 1812, 1813, and 1814.* Translated and edited by J.V. Huntington. New York: Redfield, 1854.

Irving, Washington. *Astoria or Anecdotes of an Enterprise Beyond the Rocky Mountains*. Chicago: Belford-Clark, 1836.

Ross, Alexander. *Adventures of the First Settlers on the Oregon or Columbia River, Being the Narrative of the Expedition Fitted by John Jacob Astor to Establish the "Pacific Fur Company. . . ."* London: Smith-Elder, 1849.

E

EATON, RACHEL CAROLINE (1869–1938), historian, was the eldest child of George W. Eaton, a white man, and Nancy Elizabeth Williams Eaton, of mixed Cherokee-and-white lineage. Eaton was born in Indian Territory and was educated in the Cherokee public schools, including the Cherokee Female Seminary where she graduated in 1887. She received her BA degree in 1895 from Drury College, graduating cum laude. Eaton then returned to the Cherokee Nation to teach in the public schools and at the Female Seminary, along with her sister, Pauline. She later earned her MA (1911) and PhD (1919) degrees in history from Chicago University.

During her long and productive career, Eaton served as the head of the History Department at the State College for Women in Columbus, Missouri, professor of history at Lake Erie College in Paineville, Ohio, Dean of Women and the History Department head at Trinity University in Waxahachie, Texas, and as superintendent of schools in Rogers County, Oklahoma. Eaton is the author of *Domestic Science Among the Primitive Cherokees, Historic Fort Gibson, John Ross and the Cherokee Indians, Oklahoma Pioneer Life, The Battle of Claremore Mound,* and *History of Pioneer Churches in Oklahoma*. She was an active member of the Presbyterian church, and she was also a member of the Order of the Eastern Star, the Rebecca Lodge, the Oklahoma Author's League, the Tulsa Women's Indian Club, and the La-kee-kon Club. In 1932, the Tulsa Historical Society formed the "Rachel Caroline Eaton Chapter," and in 1936 Eaton was inducted into the Oklahoma Hall of Fame.

—Devon A. Mihesuah

References

"Editorial." *Chronicles of Oklahoma* 10 (March 1932): 8.
Starr, Emmett. *History of the Cherokee Indians and Their Legends and Folklore.* Oklahoma City, OK: Warden, 1979.
Who's Who Among Oklahoma Indians. Oklahoma City, OK: Travis, 1928.
Wright, Muriel. "Rachel Caroline Eaton." *Chronicles of Oklahoma* 16 (March/December 1938): 509–10.

ENDREZZE, ANITA [ENDREZZE-DANIELSON, ENDREZZE-PROBST] (b. 1952), of European and Yaqui heritage, is a widely acclaimed visual artist, poet, and short story writer. Endrezze was born in Long Beach, California, and was raised in California, Hawaii, Oregon, and Washington; she now makes her home in Spokane, Washington.

The author of two collections of poetry, *Burning the Fields* and *The North People*, Endrezze's work has been widely recognized for its imagistic and deeply spiritual artistry. Her poetry draws heavily upon her Native American heritage and infused throughout it is a distinctly feminist vision. At times rooted in the daily domestic realm, the poems make startling jumps to a universal realm. At the center of much of her work is the artist's deeply felt relationship to the earth and the natural world. The poems successfully meld Endrezze's ecofeminist view to her own brand of American Indian spirituality and offer, in poignant and artistic frames, a new lens through which to posit the relationship between humans and the landscape, as well as the relations between men and women, the body and the spirit. Her words offer soaring insights and leaps of imaginative fancy which are truly transformative. Yet the writer remains a craftswoman, never forsaking her scrutiny to form, to language, and to sound. Endrezze's writing has appeared in virtually all of the leading anthologies of Native American writing, including *Voices of the Rainbow*, *A Gathering of Spirit*, *Songs from this Earth on Turtle's Back*, and most recently, *Dancing on the Rim of the World* and *Harper's Anthology of 20th Century Native American Poetry*. Her work has been translated into a number of languages, including French, German, Danish, and Italian. Fluent in the Danish language, she published a children's novel, *The Mountain and the Guardian Spirit*, in that language.

Her writing has garnered several awards and international praise. In 1990 she was invited to participate in a forum at the University of Milan; the year before she was a featured speaker in Grenoble, France. More locally, she has received awards from the Northwest Writer's Conference, as well as Seattle's acclaimed Bumbershoot Writers-in-Performance Award.

Endrezze is equally well known as a painter and visual artist. Like her writing, much of the imagery in her art stems from dream and vision and works to capture something of the eternal feminine energy which, for Endrezze, is the basis of all healing. Her artwork has been used to illustrate a number of collections of American Indian writing, including the cover of *Harper's Anthology of 20th Century Native American Poetry*, as well as the cover of a special American Indian issue of *The Wooster Review*.

Endrezze has served as Poet-in-Residence with the Washington State Arts Commission and has edited newsletters for the Audubon Society and the Indian Artists Guild. She is also a member of ATLATL, a Phoenix, Arizona, based Native American arts organization. She has also offered numerous workshops on poetry, painting, storytelling, and poetry and art as therapy.

—Andrea Lerner

References

Brant, Beth. *A Gathering of Spirit*. Rockland, ME: Sinister Wisdom, 1984.
Bruchac, Joseph, ed. *Songs from this Earth on Turtle's Back: Contemporary American Indian Poetry*. Greenfield Center, NY: Greenfield Review Press, 1983.

Endrezze, Anita. *Burning the Fields*. Lewiston, ID: Confluence Press, 1983.

————. *The Mountain and the Guardian Spirit*. Denmark: CDR Forlag, 1986.

————. *The North Country*. Marvin, SD: Blue Cloud, 1983.

Lerner, Andrea, ed. *Dancing on the Rim of the World*. Tucson: University of Arizona Press, 1990.

Niatum, Duane, ed. *Carriers of the Dream Wheel*. New York: Harper and Row, 1975.

————. *Harper's Anthology of 20th Century Native American Poetry*. San Francisco: Harper and Row, 1988.

Rosen, Kenneth, ed. *Voices of the Rainbow*. New York: Viking Press, 1975.

ERDRICH, LOUISE (b. 1954), known for her poetry, novels, and short stories, was born in Little Falls, Minnesota, and raised in Wahpeton, North Dakota. Her mother, a Chippewa, and her father, of German descent, both taught at the Wahpeton Indian School, and her grandfather was tribal chair of the Turtle Mountain Chippewa Reservation in North Dakota for a number of years. Erdrich is a member of the Turtle Mountain Band of Chippewas.

Erdrich received her BA from Dartmouth in 1976 where she was awarded prizes for fiction and poetry, and she taught in the Poetry in the Schools Program and was visiting poet and teacher for the North Dakota State Arts in 1977–78. In 1978 she received a fellowship to teach composition and creative writing at Johns Hopkins University. After completing her MA from Johns Hopkins in 1979, Erdrich moved to Boston to become editor of the Boston Indian Council newspaper, *The Circle*. Erdrich was a MacDowell Colony Fellow in 1980, a Yaddo Colony Fellow in 1981, and was awarded a National Endowment for the Arts Fellowship in 1982.

Besides the recognition she received while in college, Erdrich has won several awards for her 1984 novel, *Love Medicine*, including the National Book Critics Circle Award in 1985, the Sue Kaufman Prize for Best First Novel from the American Academy and Institute of Arts and Letters, the Virginia McCormack Scully Prize for Best Book of 1984 dealing with Indians or Chicanos, the Best First Fiction Award from the Great Lakes College Association, and the American Book Award from the Before Columbus Foundation. In addition, many of her short stories have been published in various periodicals, and in 1982, Erdrich won the Nelson Algren Short Fiction Award for her short story, "The World's Greatest Fisherman." Erdrich also won The Society of Magazine Editors' Award in 1983 and the National Award for Fiction.

Erdrich, now a full-time writer, lives in Cornish, New Hampshire, with her husband, Michael Dorris (Modoc), and their children. She and Dorris, a professor in the Native American Studies Program at Dartmouth College, often collaborate while writing, but *Crown of Columbus*, published in 1991, is the only novel on which both of their names appear.

—Janet L. Peterson

References

Bruchac, Joseph, ed. "Whatever Is Really Yours: An Interview with Louise Erdrich." In *Survival This Way: Interviews with Native American Poets*, 73–86. Tucson: University of Arizona Press, 1987.

Coltelli, Laura. *Winged Words: Native American Writers Speak*. Lincoln: University of Nebraska Press, 1990.

Dorris, Michael, and Louise Erdich. *The Crown of Columbus*. New York: HarperCollins, 1991.

Erdrich, Louise. *Baptism of Desire*. New York: Harper and Row, 1989.

———. *The Beet Queen*. New York: Henry Holt, 1986.

———. *Jacklight*. New York: Henry Holt, 1984.

———. *Love Medicine*. New York: Holt, Rinehart, and Winston, 1984.

———. *Tracks*. New York: Henry Holt, 1988.

George, Jan. "Interview with Louise Erdrich." *North Dakota Quarterly* 53 (Spring 1985): 240–46.

Kroeber, Karl, ed. "Louise Erdrich: *Love Medicine*." *Studies in American Indian Literatures* 9 (Winter 1985): 1–41.

Nowik, Nan. "Interview with Louise Erdrich." *Belles Lettres* (November/December 1986): 9.

EVANS, MARY AUGUSTA TAPPAGE (b. 1888), elder and poet of the Soda Creek Indians of Cariboo country, British Columbia, is the maternal granddaughter of William Longshem, hereditary Shuswap Chief. Daughter of Mary Ann Longsheim and Christopher (Alex) Tappage, she was educated at the St. Joseph's Mission, in Onward Valley, near Williams Lake, and married George Evans, half Indian and half Welsh (died 1931) in 1903, after which she became non-status because she married a non-Indian. They established a ranch on the banks of Deep Creek, near her birthplace and where she has always lived, and had two daughters (both stillborn) and two sons.

Evans's status as a "poet" is marginal in the conventional sense, for while she has been anthologized and her work is collected in a volume along with photographs, tales, and children's stories, hers are "spoken poems," traditional narratives shaped into poetic form by her editor, Jean E. Speare. Nevertheless, her experiential stories, and those traditional tales she relates, often have mythic dimensions. Such works as "Smallpox," an account of the impact of various diseases on her family, and "Changes," a meditation about marriage and changing custom, are genuinely affecting as modern poetry.

—Rodney Simard

References

Day, David, and Marilyn Bowering, eds. *Many Voices: An Anthology of Contemporary Canadian Indian Poetry*. Vancouver: J. J. Douglas, 1977.

Speare, Jean E., ed. *The Days of Augusta*. Vancouver: J. J. Douglas, 1973.

F

FOLWELL, JODY (b. 1942) is a member of the distinguished Naranjo family of artists and potters from Santa Clara Pueblo, New Mexico. Fluent in Tewa and English, Folwell was educated at Santa Clara Day School and in Taos, New Mexico. She also studied at the College of Santa Fe and the University of New Mexico, receiving her BA in history and political science.

After twelve years as a teacher and educator, she turned to pottery making full-time in 1974. In a family noted for its artistic accomplishments (her sister is Nora Naranjo-Morse), Folwell has emerged as an unparalleled innovator in design. While her methods of pottery making are time honored—she gathers her own clay and tempers it with volcanic ash; she builds her pots by the coil method and hand polishes them to a high sheen; and she fires outside—her designs are distinctly individual, characterized by asymmetry, unusual color combinations of sienna, charcoal, amber and ocher, and bold political and personal statements incised onto the surface through the *sgraffito* method of etching.

Controversial for several years because of her departure from the classic polished red and black ware of Santa Clara Pueblo, Folwell began attracting major collectors and galleries in the late 1970s and has been the recipient of numerous awards, including the prestigious Best of Show Award at the 1985 Indian Market in Santa Fe, sponsored by the Southwestern Association on Indian Affairs, for a jar on which she and the sculptor Robert Haozous collaborated.

Upon the slightly irregular surface of her dome shaped vessels, Folwell carves stories that reflect her concerns of the moment, whether it is airplanes that symbolize the overly rapid technological explosion of this country, or dogs, the abandoned strays of many Indian reservations, whom she supports with the sale of her dog pots until she finds proper homes for them.

The subject of articles and a PBS-TV special on prominent American Indian artists, Folwell has opened the door for American Indian potters to explore the limits of their own creativity and to build today the traditions of tomorrow. Her work is in numerous private and corporate collections, as well as museums, including the Heard Museum. In "Literary Pottery" by Ron McCoy, Folwell says: "Traditional and contemporary are the same. What's contemporary today is traditional tomorrow. What's traditional today becomes contemporary down the road. That's a perpetual cycle artists must go and grow through in order to succeed creatively. . . . Ancient Southwestern pottery represents abstract design. The thought behind a design is traditional. Yet as abstraction, it falls on the borderline of 'then' and 'now.'"

—Dexter Fisher Cirillo

References

American Indian Artists 11. 30 min. 1983. Distributed by the Native American Public Broadcasting Consortium, Lincoln, NE. A video documentary.

Arnold, David. "Pueblo Pottery—2000 Years of Artistry." National Geographic 162 (November 1982): 593–605.

Cortright, Barbara. "Jody Folwell, Potter." Artspace (Summer 1982): 33–35.

Jacka, Jerry, and Lois Essary Jacka. Beyond Tradition: Contemporary Indian Art and Its Evolution. Flagstaff, AZ: Northland Publishing, 1988.

Lichtenstein, Grace. "The Evolution of a Craft Tradition." Ms. 11 (April 1983): 58–60, 92.

McCoy, Ron. "Literary Pottery." Southwest Profile (January 1987): 14–17.

———. "Made in America." America West 1 (February 1987): 51–67.

Perlman, Barbara. "Courage: Her Greatest Asset." Arizona Arts and Lifestyle (Summer 1980): 20–21.

Trimble, Stephen. Talking with the Clay—The Art of Pueblo Pottery. Santa Fe, NM: School of American Research Press, 1987.

"Women of Sweetgrass, Cedar, and Sage." Catalogue for show curated by Harmony Hammond and Jaune Quick-to-See Smith, June 1–29, 1985. Gallery of the American Indian Community House, New York City.

FRANCISCO, NIA (b. 1952), a Navajo poet and educator, was born in Fort Defiance, Arizona, of the Red Bottom People and of the Salt People. Her reverence for Navajo language and culture illuminates Blue Horses for Navajo Women, her first full-length collection of poems. Birth, death, motherhood, love, dreams, the deep connectedness of families, the sexual abuse of children, and the semi-permeable membrane that separates Navajo from Anglo culture are recurring subjects. Blue Horses for Navajo Women is divided into four sections, each representing one of the four sacred directions and four sacred mountains of the Navajo. Holy beings (blue horses, white shell, turquoise, black thunder clouds) reflect Francisco's spirituality and reveal the complexities of life lived at the eastern edge of the Navajo Reservation.

Nia Francisco's work has been recognized by grants from the National Endowment for the Arts, the Arizona Commission on the Arts, and the New York Commission on the Arts. Francisco holds an AA in Indian education and Navajo Studies from Navajo Community College and a certificate in graphic and performing arts from the Institute of American Indian Arts in Santa Fe, where her exposure to the beauty of other Native cultures increased her appreciation for the beauty of her own. Currently, Francisco is pursuing a BA in elementary education and a BS in communicative disorders at Northern Arizona University in Flagstaff.

Presently employed as a social service representative in the Parent Aide Program of the Navajo Division of Social Services (Fort Defiance Agency), Francisco has worked as an educator in the Navajo Tribe Division of Education, the Fort Defiance Division of Child Development, the Chinle School District, the Navajo Academy, and the Navajo Community College.

Francisco's spiritual beliefs include the assumption that there are holy beings in every religion. Raised by her grandparents, she credits them for instilling in her a reverence for the traditional ways of knowledge of the Navajo. She attends the Baptist church and the Native American church, and she practices Navajo beliefs and healing ceremonies. Francisco lives in Navajo, New Mexico, with her five children: four boys and one girl.

"To me," Francisco said in a recent letter, "writing is my art form. I've refined it. I enjoy doing it. I also write Navajo language, speak it fluently. In the Navajo, when a person is bilingual—knows another tongue—it is said that person can 'hear.'"

—Rhoda Carroll

References

Bruchac, Joseph, ed. *Songs from this Earth on Turtle's Back: Contemporary American Indian Poetry.* Greenfield Center, NY: Greenfield Review Press, 1983.
Dunsmore, Roger. "Review of *Blue Horses for Navajo Women,* by Nia Francisco." *Studies in American Indian Literatures* n.s. 2 (Fall 1990): 41–43.
Francisco, Nia. *Blue Horses for Navajo Women.* Greenfield Center, NY: Greenfield Review Press, 1988.
———. "Navajo Traditional Knowledge." In *The Sacred: Ways of Knowledge, Sources of Life,* edited by Peggy V. Beck and Anna Lee Walters, 277–97. Tsaile, AZ: Navajo Community College Press, 1977.
———. Unpublished interview with Dexter Fisher. Navajo Community College, Tsaile, AZ, 26 January 1977.
Kopp, Karl, and Jane Kopp, eds. *South West: A Contemporary Anthology.* Albuquerque, NM: Red Earth, 1977.

FRY, MAGGIE ANN CULVER (b. 1900), a widely known writer, was born at Vian, Cherokee Nation, and was educated in the elementary schools of the Indian Territory and later Oklahoma. After four years as a sales clerk and telephone operator, she returned to high school but was forced to drop out. She married Merrit Fry, who like her was an enrolled Cherokee. They made their home near Claremore, Oklahoma, where she was a farm wife, mother, and active worker in Agricultural Economic Clubs and 4–H Clubs. During the New Deal era, she worked for the Oklahoma Emergency Relief Administration in Rogers County (1933–35).

Though interested in writing since childhood, she did not pursue a writing career until after World War II. In 1954 she published her first volume of poetry, *The Witch Deer,* which was followed by five books: *The Umbilical Cord,* which was nominated for the Pulitzer Prize, and *Buckskin Hollow Reflections,* collections of poetry; A Boy Named Will, a life of Will Rogers for juvenile readers; Sunrise Over Red Man's Land (1981), an autobiography; and Cherokee Female Seminary Years, a collection of historical pieces and reminiscences. In addition, she has published more than 750 free-lance articles, stories, and poems in publications as wide ranging as religious and devotional magazines, the Chicago Tribune and other newspapers, literary magazines, agricultural publications, American Mercury, and Organic Gardening. Her writing has won a number of awards, including the office of Poet Laureate of Oklahoma since 1977 and writer-in-residence at Claremore Junior College.

In addition to writing, Maggie Fry served as a Sunday school teacher for six decades after 1917, a church musician, a radio Sunday school teacher each week for station KWPR in Claremore (1962–73), legislative assistant to the president pro tem of the Oklahoma state senate (1964–65), editor of the Rogers County Observer (1968–69), columnist for the same newspaper (1968–71), and a teacher and civic leader in many other capacities.

Maggie Fry's writings and public careers reflect two strong influences: pride in her Cherokee heritage and an unfaltering Christian faith. She remains interested in writing and is contemplating a work about famous Cherokee men.

—Daniel F. Littlefield, Jr.

References

Authors in the News. Vol. 1. Detroit: Gale Research, 1976.
Claremore Progress [Claremore, OK] 8 August 1975: 1; 21 July 1977: 1; 23 December 1990: Spotlight Section, 1.
Fry Files. Legislative Reference Division, Oklahoma Department of Libraries, Oklahoma City; Muskogee Public Library, Muskogee, Oklahoma; Will Rogers Public Library, Claremore, Oklahoma.
Fry, Maggie Culver. A Boy Named Will: The Story of Young Will Rogers. N.p.: Oklahoma Publishing, 1971.
———. Buckskin Hollow Reflections. Muskogee, OK: Five Civilized Tribes Museum, 1978.
———. Cherokee Female Seminary Years: A Cherokee National Anthology. Claremore, OK: Rogers State Press, 1988.
———. The Umbilical Cord. Chicago: Windfall Press, 1971.
———. The Witch Deer: Poems of the Oklahoma Indians. New York: Exposition Press, 1955.
Kay, Ernest, ed. International Who's Who in Poetry. 2nd ed. London: International Who's Who in Poetry, 1970.

G

GLANCY, DIANE (b. 1941), of German/English/Cherokee descent, was born in Kansas City, Missouri, and attended the University of Missouri. She holds an MA from Central State University in Oklahoma and an MFA from the University of Iowa (1988). Currently, she teaches at Macalester College in St. Paul, Minnesota, and has been artist-in-residence in Tulsa for the State Arts Council. She has published widely in leading literary journals. Her work has received the Pegasus Award from The Oklahoma Federation of Writers (for *Brown Wolf Leaves the Res*) and the Lakes and Prairies Prize from *Milkweed Chronicle* (for *One Age in a Dream*). She was laureate for the Five Civilized Tribes from 1984 to 1986. In addition to her literary and professional accomplishments, she is the mother of two children, David and Jennifer.

In her autobiographical essay, "Two Dresses" in Swann and Krupat's *I Tell You Now*, Glancy writes movingly of her mixed-blood heritage, her sense of history, and her relationship to the landscape of the Plains, all elements which infuse and inform her writing. Poetry reveals "underlying meanings and relationships" that permit her to "face the wilderness within." Part of that wilderness is the result of being a part of two cultures, yet belonging wholly in neither. Another aspect of wilderness is the sense of being split between two dimensions, "between the visible and the invisible worlds, between earth and heaven," a split that characterizes both the Indian and poetry. "Poetry is a ghost dance in which one world seeks the other. Though the two worlds are opposed, they long to be united," and this longing for fusion can be seen in the tension she evokes between the smallness of the individual and the vastness of the landscape, between the intersections of a people's sense of historical place and the mobility of the present, and in her use of contemporary English words and poetic forms interspersed with ancient Indian chants.

—Kathleen Donovan

References

Bruchac, Joseph, ed. *Songs from this Earth on Turtle's Back: Contemporary American Indian Poetry.* Greenfield Center, NY: Greenfield Review Press, 1983.

Foss, Phillip. *The Clouds Threw this Light.* Santa Fe, NM: Institute of American Indian Arts Press, 1983.

Glancy, Diane. *Brown Wolf Leaves the Res and Other Poems.* Marvin, SD: Blue Cloud Quarterly Press, 1984.

———. *Iron Woman.* Minneapolis, MN: New Rivers Press, 1990.

———. *Offering: Aliscolidodi.* Duluth, MN: Holy Cow!, 1988.

———. *One Age in a Dream.* Minneapolis, MN: Milkweed Editions, 1986.

———. *Trigger Dance.* Boulder, CO: Fiction Collective Two, 1990.

————. *Traveling On.* Tulsa, OK: Myrtlewood Press, 1982.

————. "Two Dresses." In *I Tell You Now: Autobiographical Essays By Native American Writers*, edited by Brian Swann and Arnold Krupat, 167–83. Lincoln: University of Nebraska Press, 1987.

Salisbury, Ralph, ed. *A Nation Within.* Hamilton, New Zealand: Outrigger, 1983.

GONZALES, ROSE [ROSE CATA]

GONZALES, ROSE [ROSE CATA] was born and raised in the Tewa-speaking San Juan Pueblo of New Mexico's Northern Rio Grande. In 1920 she married Robert Gonzales and moved to his home, San Ildefonso Pueblo, where she learned the art of pottery making from her mother-in-law, Ramona Sanchez Gonzales. This personal training expanded with study at the Institute of American Indian Arts in Santa Fe, New Mexico, the school of many San Ildefonso artists.

Gonzales continues to play a part in the San Ildefonso Artistic Renaissance that began in the 1930s with the movement from pottery with polychrome decorations to pottery with matte black designs on a polished black surface. This development sparked tremendous commercial success and revitalized the ceramic industry at San Ildefonso Pueblo. Since that time, Gonzales has further enhanced the development of pottery making by being the first potter to use a carving technique as decoration, a style that has become quite popular among Pueblo potters.

Her work is characterized by the rounded edges of its carved areas and by the fine polishing throughout. Gonzales works in varied shapes ranging from closed bowls to canteens; however, she consistently incorporates designs like "Awanyu" the serpent, "Kiva Steps," clouds, lightening, and "Thunderbird" into her black on black works.

Gonzales has shown widely throughout the United States as a contributor to specialized showings of Native American art. However, her works can be found in the collections of the Museum of New Mexico, the Maxwell Museum of Anthropology in Albuquerque, Texas Tech University Museum at Lubbock, and The School of American Research in Santa Fe. Additionally, Gonzales exhibits throughout the Southwest at the Heard Museum Arts and Crafts Show, the Southwestern Association of Indian Affairs Indian Market, the Gallup Ceremonial, and the Eight Northern Indian Pueblo Artists and Craftsmen Show.

Like her own mother-in-law, Gonzales taught and continues to inspire two generations of potters who carry on the specialized art of pottery making at San Ildefonso Pueblo. As an artist and as an active member of the Pueblo, Gonzales has contributed to the artistic and cultural growth of the San Ildefonso Pueblo, as well as to the society at large.

—Michelle Savoy

References

Fox, Nancy. "Rose Gonzales." *American Indian Art Magazine* 2 (Autumn 1977): 52–57.

Maxwell Museum of Anthropology. *Seven Families in Pueblo Pottery*. Albuquerque: University of New Mexico Press, 1975.

GOOSE, MARY (b. 1955) was born in Des Moines, Iowa, but grew up around the Mesquakie Settlement near Tama. Her mother is a member of the Mesquakie tribe, and Mary Goose is Mesquakie and Chippewa with most of her tribal influence coming from the Mesquakie. After attending public schools in Des Moines and Tama, she graduated from Tama High School in 1974. Goose then enrolled at Iowa State University where she planned to study veterinary medicine but found that her interests lay elsewhere and graduated in 1980 with a BA in anthropology and minors in art and American Indian Studies. In 1985 she added a BS in speech communications with an emphasis in the tele-communication arts. She now lives in Des Moines, Iowa, with her son Lucas.

Mary Goose's love for works of creative fiction started with her mother translating comic books into Mesquakie for her before she was old enough to read and has continued into her adult life. Although interested in a broad range of literature, she found that science fiction most stimulated her imagination. She received little encouragement from the public school system but was persuaded to try her hand at writing through exposure to college classes in creative writing and Native American literature. She found that poetry came very easily to her and provided an outlet for her creative talent. She lists the works of Ray Bradbury and the TV series "Star Trek" as two of her main sources of inspiration.

Mary Goose's poetry has appeared in anthologies such as *The Remembered Earth*, *Songs from this Earth on Turtle's Back*, and *The Clouds Threw This Light* as well as the spring 1985 issue of *North Dakota Quarterly*. An up-coming anthology, edited by Joy Harjo, will also include some of her poems. Goose has been asked to participate in the Oklahoma Writers Conference in July of 1992. In the future she would like to write and produce her own film.

—Arlon Benson

References

Benson, Arlon. Personal communication with Mary Goose, 17 March 1992.

Hobson, Geary, ed. *The Remembered Earth: An Anthology of Contemporary Native American Literature*. Albuquerque, NM: Red Earth Press, 1979.

GOULD, JANICE MAY (b. 1949) was born in San Diego, California, on April 1, the second of three daughters of a British immigrant father (Gould) and an Irish, French, and Maidu mother (Beatty). When Gould was nine years old, she moved from San Diego 700 miles north to Berkeley, California, where she lived until her graduation from Berkeley High School in 1967. During that tumultuous time of war protests and race riots, Gould was deeply affected by the Civil Rights Movement and the Free Speech Movement which originated in Berkeley. Although her mother had told her that the family was Konkow, they were tribally enrolled as Maidu in the 1960s.

After high school, Gould traveled regularly, moving back and forth between Portland, Oregon, and Boulder, Colorado. In 1979 she returned to Berkeley to attend the University of California, Berkeley, where she earned her BA degree in linguistics, with high honors and distinction, in 1983 and her MA degree in English in 1987. Currently, she is completing the PhD program in the Department of English at the University of New Mexico in Albuquerque. Her focus is Native American literature with an emphasis on poetry.

Gould has published numerous poems in journals, such as *Sinister Wisdom; Calyx: A Journal of Art and Literature by Women; Ikon; Berkeley Poetry Review; Conceptions Southwest; Evergreen Chronicles;* and *Fireweed: A Feminist Quarterly,* as well as in anthologies like *A Gathering of Spirit; Naming the Waves; Living the Spirit: A Gay American Indian Anthology; Spider Woman's Granddaughters; Haciendo Caras, Making Face, Making Soul;* and *Recollections of Judy Greenwood.* In 1989 Gould was presented a National Endowment for the Arts Award for her poetry. Her first book of poems, *Beneath My Heart,* was published in 1990.

Although she is primarily a poet, Gould has published one somewhat autobiographical short story, entitled "Stories Don't Have Endings," under the pseudonym, Misha Gallagher (her grandmother's first husband's last name). The story appears in *Spider Woman's Granddaughters: Traditional Tales and Contemporary Writings by Native American Women* (Beacon Press, 1989), an anthology edited by Paula Gunn Allen. Also, scholarly and creative essays by Gould are forthcoming in *Reinventing the Enemy's Language* edited by Joy Harjo, *Decolonizing the Subject: Politics and Gender in Women's Autobiography* edited by Sidonie Smith and Julia Watson, *Growing Up Different* edited by Christian McEwen, and *An Intimate Wilderness* edited by Ruth Gundle.

In addition to writing, Janice Gould is a gifted musician. Like her mother, who studied voice, piano, and flute at The Juilliard School of Music and who taught private music lessons, Gould has studied and worked as a musician. Unlike her mother's classical training, Gould prepared to be a folk musician. She studied oboe, guitar, mandolin, and accordion and has performed an eclectic selection of music, from folk to country to Irish to Tex-Mex. Her best known contribution, though, is her graceful and sensitive writing about the search for a personal and Native identity, a central theme for many Native American women writers.

—Hertha D. Wong

References

Cochran, Jo, et al., eds. "Bearing Witness/Sobreviviendo: An Anthology of Native American/Latina Art and Literature." *Calyx: A Journal of Art and Literature by Women* 8 (1984).

Gould, Janice. *Beneath My Heart*. Ithaca, NY: Firebrand Books, 1990.

Wong, Hertha. Personal communication with Janice Gould, November 1990.

———. Written personal communication with Janice Gould, January 1991.

GREEN, RAYNA DIANE (b. 1942), a Cherokee, was born in Dallas, Texas, and raised in Oklahoma. She received her BA (1963) and MA (1966) from Southern Methodist University and a PhD (1973) in Folklore and American Studies from Indiana University. She has taught at several universities, including the University of Arkansas, the University of Massachusetts, the University of Maryland, Yale University, George Washington University, and Dartmouth College. Green has served as a planner for the Department of History of Science and Technology for the development of a Native American Program for the Museum of American History at the Smithsonian Institution and directed the Native American Science Resource Center at Dartmouth College. She has also served as Director of the Project on Native Americans in Science at the American Association for the Advancement of Science.

As a folklorist and cultural historian, Green has published material on Native American women, folk and material culture, Native American stereotypes, and contemporary Native American literature and art. Her interests range from scholarly publications to poetry and scripting. She was the author of the script for the film *More Than Bows and Arrows* and has contributed to several television productions. Green has served on several boards, including the board of the Indian Law Resource Center, the Ms. Foundation on Women, and the Phelps-Stoke Fund.

Green has also contributed numerous articles and reviews to such publications as *Ms.*, *Southern Exposure*, *Folklore Forum*, and *Southern Folklore Quarterly*. In the area of Native American women's studies, she was the editor and contributor to *That's What She Said: A Collection of Poetry and Fiction by Contemporary Native American Women* and author of *Native American Women: A Contextual Bibliography*. Currently, Green is the Director of American Indian Programs for the National Museum of American History at the Smithsonion Institution. She continues to write, research, and lecture in many fields, including program and policy development for Indian tribes and institutions, folklife, Native American studies, women's studies, museum studies, and ethnoscience.

—Laurie Lisa

References

Green, Rayna. "The Beaded Adidas." In *Time and Temperature: A Centennial Retrospective*, edited by Charles Camp, 66–67. Washington, DC: American Folklore Society, 1989. Reprinted in *The Messenger* (Wheelwright Museum Newsletter), 1989; *The Runner* (Smithsonion American Indian Newsletter), 1990; Bruchac, ed., *Contemporary Cherokee Prose Writing*. Greenfield, NY: Greenfield Review Press, 1991.

———. "Diary of a Native American Feminist." *Ms.* 11 (July/August 1982): 170–72, 211–13.

———. "The Image of the Indian in American Popular Culture." In *The Handbook of North American Indians*, vol. 4, edited by Wilcomb Washburn, 587–606. Washington, DC: Smithsonian Institution Press, 1988.

———. *Native American Women: A Contextual Bibliography*. Bloomington: Indiana University Press, 1983.

———. "Native American Women: The Leadership Paradox." *Women's Educational Equity Communications Network News and Notes* 1 (1980): 1, 4.

———. "The Pocahontas Perplex: The Image of Indian Women in Popular Culture." *Massachusetts Review* 16 (1975): 698–714.

———. Resource Guides to: *Museums as Educational Tools for Indian Education; Resources in American Indian Performing Arts* and *Resources in American Indian Literature*. Washington, DC: ORBIS Associates, 1986.

———, ed. *That's What She Said: Contemporary Poetry and Fiction by Native American Women*. Bloomington: Indiana University Press, 1984.

H

HAIL, RAVEN [AWO, GO-LA-NV, LYNN DAVIS] (b. 1921) was born in Washington County, Oklahoma, on land leased for oil drilling, north of Dewey, and is an active member of the Cherokee Nation. She attended West Anthracite and Prairie Center elementary schools while living with her mother on their Cherokee land allotment near Welch (Craig County), Oklahoma, and she spent two years at Oklahoma State University and one at Southern Methodist University. A member of the Cherokee River Culture Church, she married and divorced Henry Frank Davis; their only child, Henry Frank Davis, Jr., married Paulette Blessing and they have two children, Megan and Adam. After her divorce, Hail legally changed her surname to her mother's maiden name.

Her poetry and essays on Cherokee culture have appeared in various publications, including *The Cherokee Advocate*, *The Cherokee Nation News*, *Arizona Women's Voice*, *The Clouds Threw This Light*, *The Remembered Earth*, *Poetry Dallas*, *The Texas Anthology*, *The Blue Cloud Quarterly*, *Fiction International*, *Nimrod*, *Cimarron Review*, *Translation*, *The Little Balkans Review*, *The State*, *The Archer*, *Quetzaal*, *Gray Day*, *Tosan*, *Indian Voice*, *Daybreak*, *Lacuna*, *The Wayside Quarterly*, *The Herbalist*, *The Herb Quarterly*, *Bestways Magazine*, and *Circle of Motion*.

Among the diverse accomplishments of Raven Hail are a recording, *The Raven Sings*, consisting of Native American songs; *The Raven and the Redbird*, a three-act play about the life of Sam Houston and his Cherokee wife, Talihina (Diana) Rogers; and *The Raven Speaks*, originally published as monthly newsletters written from April 1968–March 1972. She has also written three novels and a cookbook: *Windsong*, the story of Rebecca Bowles (the daughter of a Texas Cherokee named Warlord and wife of Sequoyah's son) and her experiences on the Texas frontier; *The Raven's Tales*, consisting of bilingual Cherokee legends; *The Pleiades Stones*, about a mysterious circle of stones and a journey into the unknown through the use of a magic crystal; and *Native American Foods (Foods the Indians Gave Us) Coloring Book*, a book of traditional recipes and a coloring book. Hail also lectures on many aspects of Cherokee culture and is an instructor of such traditional skills as beadwork, basketry, singing, dancing, and folklore.

Raven Hail's unique style of prose is living "literature," at once both domestic and aesthetic, which embraces a multi-faceted, participatory interaction between teller and audience as she mixes prose, poetry, and visual elements, while using both the English and Cherokee languages. Her primary literary accomplishment is seguing the Native oral tradition with the Euro-American literary-based novelistic form, thus preserving her Native American heritage.

—Julie LaMay Abner

References

Hail, Raven. *Native American Foods (Foods the Indians Gave Us) Coloring Book.*
     Mesa, AZ: Raven Hail Books, 1979.
————. *The Pleiades Stones.* Mesa, AZ: Raven Hail Books, 1988.
————. "The Raven and the Redbird: Sam Houston and His Cherokee Wife."
     N.P., 1965.
————. *The Raven Sings.* Wayfarer 1001–1. (33–1/3 RPM).
————. *The Raven Speaks.* Mesa, AZ: Raven Hail Books, 1987.
————. *Windsong: Texas Cherokee Princess.* Mesa, AZ: Raven Hail Books, 1986.

HAILSTONE, VIVIEN (b. 1915), Indian businesswoman, cultural consultant, educator, artisan, and political activist, was born to Geneva Orcutt (Yurok/
Karok) and David Risling (Karok and a member of the Hupa tribe) in Morek,
California. During her youth, there were no roads or stores in this area, and it
wasn't until Hailstone started school that she first saw a non-Indian, the
schoolmaster.
     Hailstone's elders, great-grandmother Jane Young (Yurok) and parents,
educated Hailstone in her people's traditions. For a time she worked in a Hoopa
sawmill her father owned, doing whatever was needed, from manual labor to
keeping books. During World War II, she moved to Eureka with husband Albert
Hailstone and son Albert, Jr., where she learned welding and worked in shipyards.
Later, she and her brother Anthony established a logging operation and built a
new sawmill at Hoopa. Still later she owned and operated an Indian gift shop.
     Seeking to raise Indians' cultural pride in an era when they were made to feel
ashamed of who they were, and traditional basketry materials were difficult to
obtain, Hailstone became a founding member of a 1940s pottery guild which
incorporated Indian basketry designs into its pottery. She served on a Human
Rights Commission which met in Eureka and, as a member and later chair of the
College of the Redwood Extension Board of Directors (1950s), was key to
opening the way for an elder to teach Northwest California Indian basketry and
jewelry classes to interested Indians at the college, classes which have now
expanded in scope and location. Hailstone teaches basketry classes which
incorporate Indian stories, history, songs, and language at DQ-University in
Winters, and her own jewelry pieces have won many awards.
     In the 1960s, while raising an adopted son, Damon, Hailstone became
concerned about teaching methods which promoted Indian stereotypes and
assailed Indian children's pride. She became a founding member of Northern
Indian California Education (NICE), and with the encouragement of her
brother, David, Jr., helped initiate a grassroots organizing and lobbying effort in
support of establishing a California Indian Education Association (CIEA). Once
established, CIEA was the foundation for California Indian Legal Services,

National Indian Legal Service, and the Indian Teachers Educators Program at Humboldt State University.

Hailstone assisted in the 1971 establishment of CIEA's Shasta County Chapter, Local Indians for Education (LIFE), which became an independent, non-profit corporation in 1978. In an effort to expand educational and economic opportunities for Indians, Hailstone helped organize leather working, knitting, jewelry, airbrush painting, basketry, and sewing classes through the LIFE Center. This was the basis for the establishment of an Indian Art & Design Gift Shop concession (1980s) at Old Shasta State Park as an outlet for locally produced Indian arts.

As the first Indian ever to serve on the State of California Department of Parks and Recreation Commission (1970s), Hailstone helped promote Indian names for two parks and several park locales, a reburial policy for Indian remains and associated grave goods, a traditional materials gathering policy for Indians, and the elimination of Indian stereotypes from park displays. Presently, as a Friends of the Museum member, Hailstone is promoting a California State Indian Museum and collaborations between Indians and the state parks.

Hailstone's efforts helped further Indian pride, education, and political opportunities. She helped revitalize Indian skills in northwest California by blending these skills with non-traditional media and forms to create opportunities for their continuance while acknowledging Indians as people of today.

—Bev Ortiz

References

Ortiz, Bev. "Baskets of Dreams." *News from Native California* 2 (September/ October 1988): 28–29.
———. "Beyond the Stereotypes." *News from Native California* 5 (November 1990/January 1991): 32–33.
———. Oral and taped interviews with Vivien Hailstone, 1988–90.
———. Personal Communication with Darlene Marshall, February 1991.

HALE, JANET CAMPBELL (b. 1946), poet, novelist, and teacher, was

born in Riverside, California, and is a member of the Coeur d'Alene tribe of northern Idaho. As a child, Hale lived on the Coeur d'Alene, Colville, and Yakima Reservations and continues to have a strong connection with reservation life and tribal cultures.

Hale attended Wapato High School in Washington and transferred as a junior to the Institute of American Indian Arts in Santa Fe, New Mexico, where she pursued her interest in writing and the arts. In 1974, she received her BA from the University of California at Berkeley, then studied law at both the University of California at Berkeley and Gonzaga Law School in Spokane, Washington.

Since that time, Hale has earned her MA in English from the University of California at Davis (1984) and has taught literature courses at UC Berkeley, UC Davis, DQ University in Davis, Western Washington University in Bellingham, University of Oregon, and Lummi Community College in Bellingham, Washington.

Throughout her career, Hale has contributed to numerous anthologies of both Native American and minority literature; her poems, as well as her novels, address the complexities of the modern Native American living in a multi-cultural world. Hale received positive reviews for *The Owl's Song*, praising it for its potential influence on young Americans' perceptions of tribal cultures. Additionally, *The Jailing of Cecilia Capture* was nominated for the Pulitzer Prize, as well as five other literary awards. Currently, Hale lives in New York City, where she is working on a new novel.

—Michelle Savoy

References

Allen, Terry D., ed. *The Whispering Wind*. Garden City, NY: Doubleday, 1972.

Bruchac, Joseph, ed. *The Next World: Poems by 32 Third World Americans*. Trumansburg, NY: Crossing Press, 1987.

————, ed. *Songs from this Earth on Turtle's Back: Contemporary American Indian Poetry*. Greenfield Center, NY: Greenfield Review Press, 1983.

Colonese, Tom, and Louis Owens. *American Indian Novelists: An Annotated Critical Bibliography*. New York: Garland, 1985.

Dodge, Robert K., and Jospeh B. McCullough, eds. *Voices from Wah'Kon-tah*. New York: International Publishers, 1974.

Fisher, Dexter, ed. *The Third Woman: Minority Women Writers of the United States*. Boston: Houghton Mifflin, 1980.

Hale, Janet Campbell. *Custer Lives in Humboldt County and Other Poems*. Greenfield Center, NY: Greenfield Review Press, 1978.

————. *The Jailing of Cecilia Capture*. New York: Random House, 1985.

————. *The Owl's Song*. New York: Doubleday, 1974.

Hobson, Geary, ed. *The Remembered Earth: An Anthology of Native American Literature*. Albuquerque, NM: Red Earth Press, 1979.

Lerner, Andrea, ed. *Dancing on the Rim of the World: An Anthology of Contemporary Northwest Native American Writing*. Tucson: University of Arizona Press, 1990.

Rosen, Kenneth. "American Indian Literature: Current Condition and Suggested Research." *American Indian Culture and Research Journal* 3 (1979): 57–66.

————. *Voices of the Rainbow: Contemporary Poetry by American Indians*. New York: Viking, 1978.

HAMPTON, CAROL CUSSEN McDONALD (b. 1935) was born in Oklahoma City, Oklahoma. A Caddo Indian, Carol Hampton received a BA degree in philosophy, and MA and PhD (1984) degrees in history at the University of Oklahoma. Her scholarly work has been on the Native American Church. She has taught courses on Native American religions and philosophy at the University of Oklahoma, and she served as director of the American Indian Studies Program at the University of Science and Arts of Oklahoma in Chickasha from 1981 to 1984. She also served the Caddo tribe as a member of the Tribal Council from 1976 through 1983 and as tribal historian from 1979 to 1984. She was appointed a member of the Advisory Committee on Social Justice of the Oklahoma State Regents for Higher Education in 1983. From 1985 to 1987 she was associate director of the Consortium for Graduate Opportunities for American Indians in Berkeley, California, and she co-directed a National Endowment for the Humanities Summer Institute for College Teachers, "Great Traditions in American Indian Thought," held in Berkeley in the summer of 1987. She was appointed national field officer for American Indian/Alaska Native Ministry by the Episcopal church in 1987, and she is a member of the Joint Strategy Action Committee, Inc., of the Indian Ministries Task Force and a commissioner of the Programme to Combat Racism, a program of the World Council of Churches.

In addition to her work with Indian programs, Hampton has been active in a number of civic organizations in Oklahoma City, including the Junior League, the Oklahoma Symphony Board, the Oklahoma Art Center, the Oklahoma Heritage Association, and the Oklahoma Foundation for the Humanities. She is also a member of a number of professional societies in the field of history, including the Western History Association, the Organization of American Historians, and the American Historical Association. She is also a founding member of the Association of American Indian Historians.

Hampton and her husband live in Oklahoma City. They have four children and four grandchildren.

—Clara Sue Kidwell

Reference

Anderson, Owanah, ed. *Ohoyo One Thousand: A Resource Guide of American Indian/Alaska Native Women, 1982*. Wichita Falls, TX: Ohoyo Resource Center, 1982.

HARDIN, HELEN BAGSHAW [LITTLE CORN TASSLES, TSA-SAH-WEE-AH, LITTLE STANDING SPRUCE] (1943–1984) was born in Albuquerque to a Santa Clara Pueblo mother, Pablita Velarde, and Anglo father, Herbert Hardin. Helen Hardin had, by the age of thirty-five, become one of the leading contemporary Indian women artists. Much of her childhood during and following World War II was spent at Santa Clara Pueblo among her mother's people. This daughter of an internationally renowned painter won her first prize for a drawing when she was six and, as a child, sold pictures at Gallup Ceremonial with her mother. For most of her life, Hardin lived and was educated in the Anglo world, and frequently described herself as "Anglo socially and Indian in [her] art." She graduated in 1961 from St. Pius X High School in Albuquerque, where she concentrated on art. Subsequently, she studied art history and anthropology at the University of New Mexico and attended a Special School for Indian Arts at the University of Arizona, funded by the Rockefeller Foundation. In 1962, at the age of nineteen, Hardin had her first one-woman show at Coronado Monument. Two years later she gave birth to a daughter Margarete and had her first "formal" gallery show at the Enchanted Mesa in Albuquerque. In 1968, she separated herself from difficult relationships both with her mother and with Pat Terrazas, the father of her child, by visiting her father in Bogota, Colombia. While there, she had a very successful show at the American Embassy, which resulted in another three years later in Guatemala City. This was followed by numerous exhibitions at home and abroad and many Grand Awards, Best of Show, and First Prizes at the National Indian Arts Exhibition in Scottsdale, Santa Fe Indian Market, Philbrook Art Center, and the Inter-Tribal Ceremonial at Gallup among others. Hardin has been featured in several national magazines, including *Seventeen* when she was in high school and a cover story in *New Mexico Magazine* in 1970. She was also featured in the 1976 PBS series on American Indian Artists. Her art has been reproduced in many contexts and during her lifetime she also received several commissions, notably from the Franklin Mint to design coins for the series, "History of the American Indian," and from Clarke Industries to illustrate two of their children's books.

Eschewing the "tourist-pleasing cliches" of many Indian painters, Hardin developed a contemporary and highly individual art, influenced by Joe H. Herrera—an art that seems both old and new, combining modern techniques with tribal images and mythic figures: "I use tradition as a springboard and go diving into my paints." Her "point of departure" is the "ancient art history of my own people, as evidenced on the walls of caves and pottery of the Pueblo." Using acrylics, acrylic varnish, inks, washes, and architects' templates with precision, discipline, and control, this "high priestess of the protractor" created spiritual surfaces that have frequently been likened to Klee and Kandinsky. In more indigenous terms, her paintings revitalized an "art," like kiva murals and sandpainting, that was/is a ritual to restore the harmony of natural forces through the intuitive placement of life and color. Her artistic recognition in the last decade of her life was combined with a happy marriage to Anglo photographer, Cradoc Bagshaw, a highly successful venture into the media of etching beginning in 1980, and civic work related to the arts. She served as a member of the board of directors of the Southwest Association of Indian Affairs and of the Wheelwright Museum in Santa Fe. They lived in Tesuque and then in Albuquerque where she died of cancer in 1984.

—Barbara A. Babcock

References

Culley, LouAnn Faris. "Helen Hardin: A Retrospective." *American Indian Art* 4 (1979): 68–75.

DeLaurer, Marjel. "Helen Hardin." *Arizona Highways* 52 (August 1976): 28–29, 44–45.

Hardin, Helen. "Helen Hardin, Tewa Painter." In *This Song Remembers: Self-Portraits of Native Americans in the Arts,* edited by Jane B. Katz, 116–23. Boston: Houghton Mifflin, 1980.

Scott, Jay. *Changing Woman: The Life and Art of Helen Hardin.* Flagstaff, AZ: Northland Publishers, 1989.

Wilks, Flo. "A Spiritual Escape from the World of Reality." *Southwest Art* (August 1978): 66 69.

HARJO, JOY (b. 1951) was born in Tulsa, Oklahoma, to Allen W. (Creek) and Wynema (Baker) Foster. She is the mother of two children, Phil Dayn and Rainy Dawn.

Harjo attended high school at the Institute of American Indian Arts in Santa Fe, New Mexico. In 1976 she received her BA at the University of New Mexico, Albuquerque, and in 1978 her MFA at the University of Iowa. In 1978–79 she was an instructor at the Institute of American Indian Arts, Santa Fe, and in 1980–81 a part-time instructor in creative writing and poetry at Arizona State University, Tempe. She has also taught at the University of Colorado, Boulder, and at the University of Arizona, Tucson. Currently, she teaches creative writing at the University of New Mexico, Albuquerque.

She is on the board of directors for the National Association for Third World Writers, on the policy panel of the National Endowment for the Arts, and a member of the board of directors for the Native American Public Broadcasting Consortium. She is also contributing editor of *Contact II* and *Tyuony,* and the poetry editor of *High Plains Literary Review.*

Her third book of poetry, *She Had Some Horses,* was highly praised, and her recent *In Mad Love and War* won the Poetry Society of America's William Carlos Williams Award, the Delmore Schwartz Memorial Poetry Prize, sponsored by New York University, and the Pen Oakland Josephine Miles Award.

Her Creek heritage, history, and mythology are very important elements in her creative process and her poetry. Her ethnic background deeply affects her relationship with the land, a geography of the remembered earth that in Harjo's work has three physical directions, spectacular and complementary to each other: the Oklahoma red earth, the land of her people and her childhood; the Southwest and the desert landscape which in many instances conveys the sense of a mythic womanhood; and the third direction that has its center in Alabama—the tribal land of the Creeks before the Removal Act—a land which is the original place, lost forever and forever recreated in the original memory.

Her powerful poetic language creates images of beauty and images of grief, looking for perfection of love in all its manifestations. The rhythm is very often the incantatory, ceremonial sound of the old Indian chants, that Indian oral tradition in which, in Harjo's words "the knowledge was kept by remembering," and for that very reason, memory "swims deep in blood/a delta in the skin. . . ."

—Laura Coltelli

References

Allen, Paula Gunn. "Answering the Deer: Genocide and Continuance in the Poetry of American Indian Women." In *The Sacred Hoop*, 155–64. Boston: Beacon Press, 1986.

"Bibliography of Fourteen Native American Poets: Joy Harjo." *SAIL* 9 (Supplement 1985): 18–23.

Bruchac, Joseph. "Interview with Joy Harjo." *North Dakota Quarterly* 53 (Spring 1985): 220–34.

———. "The Arms of Another Sky: Joy Harjo." In *The Sacred Hoop*, 165–83. Boston: Beacon Press, 1986.

Coltelli, Laura. "Joy Harjo." In *Winged Words: American Indian Writers Speak*, 55–68. Lincoln: University of Nebraska Press, 1990.

Harjo, Joy. *In Mad Love and War*. Middletown, CT: Wesleyan University Press, 1990.

———. *The Last Song*. Las Cruces, NM: Puerto del Sol Press, 1975.

———. *Secrets from the Center of the World*. Sun Tracks Series, vol. 17. Tucson: University of Arizona Press, 1989.

———. *She Had Some Horses*. New York: Thunder's Mouth Press, 1983.

———. *What Moon Drove Me to This*. New York: I. Reed, 1979.

Ruppert, James. "Paula Gunn Allen and Joy Harjo: Closing the Distance Between Personal and Mythic Space." *American Indian Quarterly* 7 (Winter 1983): 27–40.

Wiget, Andrew. "Nightriding with Noni Daylight: The Many Horse Songs of Joy Harjo." In *Native American Literatures*, edited by Laura Coltelli, 185–96. Pisa: Seu, 1989.

HARNAR, NELLIE SHAW (1905–1985), a Neh-muh or Northern Paiute Indian, was born in Wadsworth, Nevada, on the Pyramid Lake Reservation. Her parents were James and Margie Shaw who had nine children. Harnar attended day school in Wadsworth but also learned the songs and legends of the tribe from the elders. She attended Carson Indian School at Stewart, Nevada, and graduated from Carson City High School and the Normal Training Course at Haskell Institute in Lawrence, Kansas. She received a BA degree from Northern Arizona University in Flagstaff, Arizona, in elementary education in 1936 and an MA degree from the University of Nevada at Reno in 1965. Her master's thesis, which she dedicated to her people, the Neh-muh, was *The History of the Pyramid*

Lake Indians—1842–1959. Along with all of her formal education, she still maintained her fluency in Paiute and her interests in the stories, histories, and traditions of her tribe. She dedicated her life to teaching and counseling in the Bureau of Indian Affairs schools in Arizona, Kansas, New Mexico, Wyoming, and Nevada.

She continued throughout her life to be active in many state and national service, social, and honorary societies, actively sponsoring the movement in Nevada to get monuments erected to the memory of Sarah Winnemucca (Hopkins) and Louisa Keyser (Dat-So-La-Lee); in 1975 she was named Nevada's Outstanding Woman of the Year.

She was baptized and confirmed in the Episcopal church. She married Curtis Sequoyah Harnar, and together they had one son, Curtis, Jr. She and her husband spent their retirement on the Pyramid Lake Reservation, and she died in Reno. She is respectfully remembered by educators and historians, Anglo and Indian alike, and she left a significant impression upon all who met her.

—Gretchen Ronnow

References

"Harnar, Nellie Shaw." Computer biography on file. Alumni Association, University of Nevada, Reno.

Harnar, Nellie Shaw. *The History of the Pyramid Lake Indians, 1843–1959, and Early Tribal History, 1825–1834*. Sparks, NV: Dave's Printing and Publishing, 1974.

———. *The Indians of Coo-Yu-Ee Pah (Pyramid Lake): The History of the Pyramid Lake Indians in Nevada*. Sparks, NV: Western Printing and Publishing, 1974.

"Nellie Shaw Harner." *Indian Historian* 2 (October 1965): 17.

HARRIS, LaDONNA (b. 1931), president and executive director of Americans for Indian Opportunity, was born in Temple, Oklahoma, to a Comanche mother and an Irish-American father. She spent her early years with her maternal grandparents, speaking only Comanche until she started school. As a result of her involvement in civil rights issues and her knowledge of political contacts, information gained firsthand during her husband's tenure as Senator (first state-level, and later in the US Congress), Harris organized the first intertribal organization in Oklahoma. This was the early 1960s, and Oklahomans for Indian Opportunity (OIO) allied sixty tribes for purposes of economic development. During this era, Harris's current hometown, Lawton, was not yet integrated, so OIO was a vanguard organization.

With her husband's move to Washington, DC, Harris became involved with feminist issues and became one of the first members of the National Women's Political Caucus. In honor of this, and many other groundbreaking projects, Harris was named to President Ford's US Commission on the Observance of

International Women's Year. By this time, she had nurtured her national version of OIO, Americans for Indian Opportunity (AIO), for several years. With the recognition of Presidents Ford, and later, Carter, Harris's organization grew and became a very influential force in the economic development of Indian Country. Always busy with numerous intersecting plans, Harris simultaneously served as special advisor to Sergeant Shriver in the Office of Economic Opportunity and on the National Committee for Full Employment and the National Commission on the Mental Health of Children. An outgrowth of her investigations into the various methods of reaching full employment and seeking economic development of depressed areas was the founding of the Council of Energy Resources Tribes, a controversial but still very influential group.

An untiring advocate of Indian self-determination, LaDonna Harris has continuously revamped AIO to meet the changing needs of Native communities. Lately, the organization has been involved in Indian youth programs, conflict resolution, and the formation of venues for Natives to identify, discuss, and determine problem-solving plans for local concerns. AIO is also now involved in international indigenous concerns, with plans to study indigenous populations in Africa, the Pacific, Central America, and the USSR.

A frequent lecturer across the country, Harris has also taught at the Washington School of the Institute for Policy Studies. She has several honorary degrees, including a Doctor of Laws from Dartmouth. She is the mother of three, including Katherine Harris Tijerina, president of the newly reorganized Institute of American Indian Arts in Santa Fe, New Mexico. LaDonna Harris is a board member of many organizations, among them the National Organization for Women, Save the Children, and the National Urban League. In 1979 *Ladies Home Journal* named LaDonna Harris "Woman of the Year and of the Decade."
—Cynthia Kasee

References

Harris, LaDonna. "American Indian Education and Pluralism." In *Contemporary Native American Addresses*, edited by John R. Maestas. Provo, UT: Brigham Young University, 1976.
Josephy, Alvin M. *Now That the Buffalo's Gone*. New York: Alfred A. Knopf, 1982.
"LaDonna Harris." *Americans for Indian Opportunity Information Packet* (1987): 23–25.
Morris, Terry. "LaDonna Harris: A Woman Who Gives a Damn." *Redbook* 134 (February 1970): 74, 115, 117–18.
Philip, Kenneth, ed. *Indian Self Rule*. Chicago: Howe Brothers, 1986.
Who's Who of the American Indian. New York: Todd, 1986.

HENRY, JEANNETTE (b. 1908) was born to the Turtle Clan of the Carolina Cherokee. She married Rupert Costo in 1950. Together they co-founded the American Indian Historical Society in 1962 and the Indian Historian Press in 1969, and have been responsible for publishing *Wassaja*, a national newspaper, *The Indian Historian*, a quarterly journal, and *The Weewish Tree*, a children's magazine. The efforts of all the above organizations have been to educate and inform Indians on national Indian issues, controversies, and opportunities for cooperation between Indian media and people. She is currently working on a long-researched comprehensive text on the Indians of California.

—Julie A. Russ

References

Bahr, Donald, and Susan Fenger. "Indians and Missions: Homage to and Debate with Rupert Costo and Jeannette Henry." *Journal of the Southwest* 31 (Fall 1989): 300–21.

Costo, Rupert, and Jeannette Henry, eds. *The Missions of California: A Legacy of Genocide*. San Francisco: Indian Historian Press, 1987.

———, and Jeannette Henry. *Indian Treaties: Two Centuries of Dishonor*. San Francisco: Indian Historian Press, 1977.

———. *A Thousand Years of American Indian Storytelling*. San Francisco: Indian Historian Press, 1981.

Henry, Jeannette. *Textbooks and the American Indian*. San Francisco: Indian Historian Press, 1970.

———, ed. *American Indian Reader*. 4 vols. San Francisco: Indian Historian Press, 1972–74.

HETH, CHARLOTTE ANNE WILSON (b. 1937) was born in Muskogee, Oklahoma, and is currently chair of the Department of Ethnomusicology and Systematic Musicology at the University of California at Los Angeles. She is a member of the Cherokee Nation of Oklahoma. She received her BA and MA degrees in music at the University of Tulsa, and she received a Ford Foundation Fellowship to complete her PhD in ethnomusicology at UCLA in 1975. Her doctoral dissertation was an analysis of Cherokee Stomp Dance music in Oklahoma. She has taught music at the high school and college level and served a two-year stint in the Peace Corps in Ethiopia, where she taught English to high school students. She joined the faculty of the Music Department at UCLA in 1974, and she also served as director of the American Indian Studies Center there from 1976 to 1987. During that time, she coordinated the development and implementation of the first American Indian Studies Master's Degree Program. From 1987 to 1989 she served as director of the American Indian Studies Program at Cornell University. She returned to UCLA in 1989 to assume the position she now holds.

In addition to teaching and administration, she has maintained an active research record. She has published six record albums and eight videotapes of Indian music and co-authored a needs assessment on American Indian higher education. She has received grants from federal and state agencies to do research on Cherokee hymns and the Iroquois condolence ceremony. She has received postdoctoral fellowships from the D'Arcy McNickle Center for the History of the American Indian at the Newberry Library in Chicago and from the Ford Foundation.

Heth has served as a consultant to numerous arts organizations and media projects and was the primary consultant on music for the highly acclaimed television series "Roanoak," which appeared on PBS in 1987. She has been a member of the Advisory Committee of the American Folklife Program at the Smithsonian Institution, the California Council for the Humanities, the Advisory Council of the D'Arcy McNickle Center for the History of the American Indian at the Newberry Library in Chicago, and numerous other advisory boards and committees. She is also active in the Society for Ethnomusicology. As a musician and educator, she has played a significant role in disseminating information about American Indian music to Indian and non-Indian audiences nationally. Through her work with the American Indian Studies Center at UCLA, Heth has been instrumental in offering opportunities for graduate study to many American Indian students.

—Clara Sue Kidwell

References

Heth, Charlotte, ed. *Selected Reports in Ethnomusicology* 2 (1980).
Who's Who in American Music. New York: R. R. Bowker, 1983.
Who's Who in the West. Chicago: Marquis Who's Who, 1949—.
Who's Who of American Women. Chicago: Marquis Who's Who, 1958—.

HIGHWALKING, BELLE (1892–1971) was born on the Northern Cheyenne Reservation in Montana. Because her mother died in childbirth, Highwalking was raised by her grandmother while her father, Teeth, served in a special corps of Cheyenne scouts for the US Army at Fort Keogh until they were disbanded in 1895. At that time he became a policeman on the reservation, and Highwalking and her grandmother came to live with him and her stepmother in Lame Deer. Her father married six times, and of the children, only Highwalking and her brother, John Teeth, survived. One other brother, John Stands In Timber, from her mother's first marriage, was the author of *Cheyenne Memories*. Highwalking's maternal grandmother, Blackbird Woman, was a Crow, and Highwalking often visited the nearby Crow Reservation.

Highwalking attended Busby School, at which her uncle Red Hat taught. She and Floyd Highwalking were married by the Mennonite minister on January 23,

1912. They attended the Catholic church briefly, but the death of her daughter and the priest's objections to her Cheyenne peyote meetings convinced Highwalking to quit. She was pleased that the Mennonite church taught her to read the Bible in Cheyenne and included her on their committees even when she was old.

Belle and Floyd Highwalking had many children, all delivered at home; the last daughter, Theresa, was born when her youngest brother was fifteen years old. Floyd and Belle often travelled to other reservations in North Dakota, Wyoming, Oklahoma, and New Mexico; after Floyd died in July of 1964, Highwalking complained that, "I never go anywhere." In later life she lived with her oldest son, George Hiwalker, until her death on October 30, 1971.

Highwalking told her life history to Katherine M. Weist, partly in English and partly in Cheyenne, beginning the interviews at Weist's home in Missoula, Montana, in 1970 and finishing the recordings a month before she died. Her daughter-in-law, Helen Hiwalker, translated the Cheyenne tapes in preparation for Weist's subsequent editing of Highwalking's narrative, which was published in 1979.

—Thelma J. Shinn

References

Stands In Timber, John, and Margot Liberty. *Cheyenne Memories*. New Haven, CT: Yale University Press, 1967.

Weist, Katherine M., ed. *Belle Highwalking: The Narrative of a Northern Cheyenne Woman*. Billings: Montana Council for Indian Education, 1979.

———. "Giving Away: The Ceremonial Distribution of Goods Among the Northern Cheyenne of Southeastern Montana." *Plains Anthropologist* 18 (1973): 97–103.

———. "The Northern Cheyennes: Diversity in a Loosely Structured Society." PhD diss., Ann Arbor, Michigan, University Microfilms, 1970.

HILBERT, VI [taqʷseblu] (b. 1918) is an Upper Skagit elder born in Lyman, Washington. A linguist, educator, and storyteller, she has devoted much of her life to the study, promotion, and preservation of her childhood language, Lushootseed Salish, and the oral literature and culture of her people. A quarter century of unflagging research has resulted in a remarkable collection of audiotapes and videotapes of Lushootseed language, oral history, and cultural information shared by elders from the Skagit and neighboring communities. Hilbert has carefully transcribed and translated the materials into English, making available information which otherwise would have been lost to future generations of Lushootseed people. Working with low quality, early recordings, she has also transcribed and translated a large body of material in Lushootseed taped by anthropologists twenty years before she began her research, at a time when many elders still spoke only Lushootseed. Many of these elders were the best storytellers of their time, and Hilbert sought to preserve this art form by memorizing their works, and analyzing and emulating their traditional type in classes on Lushootseed language and literature at the University of Washington. She translated several such stories into English and edited them in *Haboo: Native American Stories from Puget Sound.* When she retired from teaching in 1988, her former students begged her to tell the stories publicly, and Hilbert became a storyteller herself. Her unique blend of the traditional language with line-by-line English translation, uncommon in oral performance, has delighted audiences from all over the world; she is frequently invited to speak and tell stories by Native groups, the National Association of Professional Storytellers, various local storytelling groups, and educators at all levels. Throughout her public storytelling career, she has continued her research. Her collaboration with linguists and anthropologists has produced two pedagogical grammars and several research papers, a forthcoming volume of texts in Lushootseed with English translations, and a revised and expanded version of the only dictionary of the language is in preparation. She is currently involved in a project to archive her collection.

—Dawn Bates

References

Bierwert, Crisca, ed. *Lushootseed Texts.* Lincoln: University of Nebraska Press, in press.

Hess, Thom, and Vi Hilbert. *Lushootseed I and II.* Seattle: Daybreak Star Press, United Indians of All Tribes Foundation, 1976.

Hilbert, Vi. *Haboo: Native American Stories from Puget Sound.* Seattle: University of Washington Press, 1985.

———. "To a Different Canoe: The Lasting Legacy of Lushootseed Heritage." In *A Time of Gathering: Native American Heritage in Washington State*, edited by Robin K. Wright. Thomas Burke Memorial Washington State Museum Monograph 7. Seattle: University of Washington Press, 1991.

HILL, JOAN,

originally from Muskogee, Oklahoma, is a painter and advocate of the arts. Her family lineage includes chiefs of the Cherokee and Creek Nations. Her Indian name is Chea-se-quah, which means redbird. She studied art with Dick West, famous Cheyenne artist, at Bacone College in Muskogee and taught for four years in the Tulsa public schools before resigning to devote herself full-time to her art. Her paintings are in the permanent collections of the United States Department of the Interior, the Philbrook Art Center in Tulsa, the Heard Museum in Phoenix, the Museum of the American Indian in New York City, and the Smithsonian Institution in Washington, DC. She has won two hundred fifty-five awards, including the Grand Master Award from the Five Civilized Tribes Museum in Muskogee, the Waite Phillips Special Artists Trophy from the

Philbrook Museum, a special commission award from the Daybreak Star Indian Center in Seattle, and a commemorative medal from Great Britain. She has traveled and studied in thirty-six foreign countries with the T. H. Hewitt Painting Workshops. Her most memorable participation was in the first Painters Cultural Interchange with the People's Republic of China. Photographs of a one-woman show of her work are still being circulated in China.

Her most well-known work is characterized by a traditional style and content, which is sometimes inspired by dreams of incidents told to her by her parents and grandparents. It is also characterized by extensive research in historical documents to assure complete authenticity of detail. She works primarily in acrylics, although she is also skilled with watercolors, which are generally abstract.

Hill has also served the state of Oklahoma as a member of the Oklahoma Curriculum Improvement Commission and recently as a member of the Governor's Commission on the Status of Women.

The power of Joan Hill's paintings comes from her natural talent, the support and encouragement of her parents during her youth, and her pride in her Indian heritage. She has honed her skill in painting and her scrupulous attention to historical detail to become one of the outstanding Indian painters of the twentieth century.

—Clara Sue Kidwell

References

Strickland, Rennard. *Native American Art at Philbrook*. Tulsa, OK: Philbrook Art Center, 1980.

Who's Who in American Art. New York: American Federation of the Arts, R.R. Bowker, 1978.

Who's Who of American Women. Chicago: Marquis Who's Who, 1958–.

HOGAN, LINDA (b. 1947) was born in Denver to Charles Henderson (Chicksaw) and Cleona Bower. She is divorced and a mother of two adopted children, Sandra Dawn Protector and Tanya Thunder Horse.

She received her MA in English and creative writing in 1978 from the University of Colorado at Boulder. In 1979 she was one of the organizers of the Colorado Cultural Program. In 1979 she was Poet-in-the-Schools for the states of Colorado and Oklahoma; in 1981–84, assistant professor in the Tribes Program at Colorado College, Colorado Springs; and in 1982–84, associate professor of American and American Indian Studies at the University of Minnesota. A member of the board of directors of the Denver Indian Center since 1984, she is currently an associate professor of Native American and American Studies at the University of Colorado at Boulder. She is also a volunteer worker at Colorado Wildlife Rehabilitation Clinic.

She has been the recipient of a Newberry Library Fellowship and in 1982 of a Yaddo Colony Fellowship. Other awards include the Five Civilized Tribes Playwriting Award, 1980; the short fiction award from *Stand Magazine*, 1983; Western States Book Award honorable mention, 1984; and a fellow of Colorado Independent Writers, 1984 and 1985.

One of the most accomplished American Indian writers, she began her literary career in 1979 as a poet. Recently, she has published two collections of short stories and a novel, *Mean Spirit*, which gained a Pulitzer Prize nomination in 1991.

Very active in antinuclear and pacifist movements, her work reflects her deep involvement in her tribal history, the relationship between humans and other species, intense spirituality, and a profound understanding and concern for the human community.

Her views on the status of minority women are thus expressed: "To be a woman and a minority woman in this country is like a double-whammy, or maybe even a triple-whammy. It's hard enough to be one or the other. I think also here minority women and the white women's movement have completely different sets of priorities . . . it's like trying to break in and survive, versus trying to have a position equal to a white man in a corporation."

—Laura Coltelli

References

Allen, Paula Gunn. "Answering the Deer: Genocide and Continuance in the Poetry of American Indian Women." In *The Sacred Hoop*, 155–64. Boston: Beacon Press, 1986.

———. "Let Us Hold Fierce: Linda Hogan." In *The Sacred Hoop*, 163–83. Boston: Beacon Press, 1986.

Balassi, William, John F. Crawford, and Annie O. Eysturoy, eds. *This Is about Vision: Interviews with Southwestern Writers*. Albuquerque: University of New Mexico Press, 1990.

Bruchac, Joseph, ed. "To Take Care of Life: An Interview with Linda Hogan." In *Survival This Way: Interviews with Native American Poets*, 119–34. Tucson: University of Arizona Press, 1987.

Coltelli, Laura. "Linda Hogan." In *Winged Words. American Indian Writers Speak*, 71–86. Lincoln: University of Nebraska Press, 1990.

Hogan, Linda. *Calling Myself Home*. Greenfield Center, NY: Greenfield Review Press, 1979.

———. *Daughters, I Love You*. Denver, CO: Loretto Heights College, 1981.

———. *Eclipse*. Los Angeles: UCLA American Indian Studies Center Press, 1983.

———. *Mean Spirit*. New York: Atheneum, 1990.

———. *Red Clay: Poems and Stories*. Greenfield Center, NY: Greenfield Review Press, 1991.

———. *Savings*. Minneapolis: Coffee House Press, 1988.

———. *Seeing Through the Sun*. Amherst: University of Massachussets Press, 1985.

————, Judith McDaniel, and Carol Bruchac, eds. *The Stories We Hold Secret*. Greenfield Center, NY: Greenfield Review Press, 1986.

————, and Charles Colbert Henderson. *That Horse*. Acoma, NM: Acoma Press, 1985.

"*SAIL* Bibliography, no. 6: Linda Hogan." *SAIL* 8 (Spring 1984): 1–2.

Scholer, Bo. "A Heart Made Out of Crickets: An Interview with Linda Hogan." *Journal of Ethnic Studies* 16 (Spring 1988): 107–17.

HOPKINS, SARAH WINNEMUCCA [THOCMETONY, TOS-ME-TO-NE, SHELL FLOWER, SONOMETA, SOMITONE, SA-MIT-TAU-NEE, WHITE SHELL] (1844?-1891) was a major figure in the history of the Paiute tribe and a spokeswoman for the plight of her tribe and Indian peoples in the later part of the nineteenth century. Granddaughter of Chief Truckee, who had guided early whites across the great basin, and daughter of Chief Winnemucca, an antelope shaman and leader, she became a legendary and controversial figure during her own lifetime.

Her first encounter with whites terrified her, and she did not want to travel from Humboldt Sink, in Nevada, to California with her family in 1847, but encounters with generous settlers along the way dissolved her fear. In California she attended a convent school where she learned to write and speak English. She also learned Spanish and knew three Indian dialects. By adolescence her skill as a translator and her position in a prominent family brought her the role of interpreter at Camp McDermitt in northern Nevada and later at the Malheur Agency in Oregon. She also became the personal interpreter and guide for General Oliver O. Howard during the Bannock Wars in 1878. She distinguished herself as a warrior in that conflict, taking her fallen uncle's place in the battle.

Her skills rapidly gained her recognition as spokeswoman for her people and led to lectures in major western cities on behalf of justice for Indians. In 1883 she went east to lecture and plead the cause of Indian rights. In Boston she became the protégée of Elizabeth Palmer Peabody and her sister Mary (Mrs. Horace) Mann, who volunteered to edit the manuscript of Winnemucca's autobiography, a record not only of her own life, but also a history of her tribe and a strong plea for redress as the title indicates: *Life Among the Paiutes: Their Wrongs and Claims*. The intent of her autobiography was to bring her crusade for justice to a wider audience and to convince white society that the Paiutes were decent people willing to co-exist with whites. Her narrative ends with a plea to Congress to restore land and rights to her people.

Winnemucca's crusade for justice and an end to corruption in administration of reservations met with limited success—she was unable to regain land lost to the tribe when it was moved to the Yakima Reservation in Washington state. She was controversial because some of her white patrons were actually not advocates of Indian sovereignty and rights, and she was an unconventional representative of

Indian women in white society and an unconventional woman within her tribe. Yet Winnemucca was an important lobbyist for reform in Indian policy, a woman who dared to make great personal sacrifices and take great risks for her causes. Before her death, she returned to her people to open a school for Paiute children.

—Kathleen M. Sands

References

Brimlow, George. "The Life of Sarah Winnemucca: The Formative Years." *Oregon Historical Quarterly* 53 (June 1952): 103–34.
Canfield, Gae Whitney. *Sarah Winnemucca of the Northern Paiutes.* Norman: University of Oklahoma Press, 1931.
Gehm, Katherine. *Sarah Winnemucca.* Phoenix: O'Sullivan, Woodside, 1975.
Hopkins, Sara Winnemucca. *Life Among the Paiutes: Their Wrongs and Claims.* Edited by Mrs. Horace Mann. Boston: Putnam's, 1883.
———. "The Pah-Utes." *California, A Western Monthly Magazine* 6 (1882): 252.
Morrison, Dorothy Nafus. *Chief Sarah: Sarah Winnemucca's Fight for Indian Rights.* New York: Antheneum, 1980.
Richey, Elinor. "Sagebrush Princess with a Cause: Sarah Winnemucca." *American West* 12 (November 1975): 30–33, 57–63.
Stewart, Patricia. "Sarah Winnemucca." *Nevada Historical Society Quarterly* 14 (Winter 1971): 23–38.

HORN, KAHN-TINETA (b. 1940), Mohawk activist, daughter of Mohawk

high-steel worker, Assennaienton Horn of the Kahnawake Mohawk Nation Territory (Caugnawaga Reservation in Quebec, Canada), was born in Brooklyn, New York. Horn was primarily raised on Kahnawake and attended school both at Kahnawake and at Akwesasne (St. Regis Indian Reservation near Cornwall, Ontario). As the daughter of a longhouse chief and member of the Bear Clan, she was raised in accordance with the traditional Mohawk way of life. She has attributed her activism to childhood memories of both her father's activism and her grandfathers' struggle against the joint American-Canadian St. Lawrence Seaway Project, which ultimately expropriated 1260 acres of Kahnawake land.

During the 1960s Horn was best known as a fashion model, actress, and seller of cosmetics who advocated Indian control of their lands, resources, government, and a return to the traditional ways of the Hodinasaunnee (People of the Longhouse). On December 18, 1968, Horn formed part of a group of Mohawk Indians protesting Canada's failure to live up to the terms of the 1795 Jay Treaty granting the Mohawks duty-free passage across the United States-Canadian border. During that protest Horn, along with sixty others, was arrested on Cornwall Island, Ontario, for blockading the entranceway to the Canada-US International Bridge.

From 1973 to 1990 Horn worked for the Canadian Department of Indian Affairs as a programme officer. In the spring of 1990, the town of Oka, Quebec, decided to extend a golf course onto 55 acres claimed by the Mohawks. This included an Indian burial site and an area known as "The Pines" considered sacred by the Mohawks. This decision resulted in the blockade of a dirt road traversing the Pines. Horn, who was on an educational leave from her job, states that she became involved in this incident as part of a negotiating team which was seeking a peaceful resolution to this crisis. Its resolution on September 26, 1990, resulted in Horn's arrest. Among the casualties was Horn's fourteen-year-old daughter, Waneek, who Horn says was stabbed in the chest by soldiers while protecting her four-year-old sister, Ganyetahawi. Subsequent to her arrest she was fired from her position with Indian Affairs and lost custody of Ganyetahawi. The Ministry of Indian Affairs cites her unauthorized absence from work during the time of the uprising as justification for her termination. Horn has countered that the firing was politically and racially motivated and done in reprisal for her association with the Oka uprising.

She is currently challenging her dismissal and has since regained custody of her daughter. Kahn-tineta Horn is representative of the social and political leadership role which Mohawk women have fulfilled within traditional Mohawk society.

—Faren R. Siminoff

References

Allan, Chris. "Baby By-the-Falling-Waters Joins the Fight." *Akwesasne Notes* 3 (March 1971): 27.

Broussand, C. "Mohawk Beauty with a Mission." *Look* 28 January 1964, 91–94.

Platiel, Rudy. "Kahn-Tineta Wants Her Sister Evicted." *Akwesasne Notes* 3 (1971): 38.

HUNGRY WOLF, BEVERLY [SIKSKI-AKI, BLACK-FACED WOMAN]

(b. 1950) was born in the Blood Indian Hospital on the Blood Indian Reserve in Canada in 1950, a member of the Little Bear family, the Blood tribe, the Blackfoot Nation. She was educated at the boarding school on the reserve, and after finishing her college education, returned there as a teacher. Although her Catholic education discouraged any adherence to her cultural traditions, her marriage to a German, born Adolph Gutöhrlein, led her to a new appreciation of and desire to preserve these traditions. Gutöhrlein had come to America in 1954, and as he grew he pursued his interest in American Indians, finally adopting the name Adolph Hungry Wolf, which was given to him by an elderly Blackfoot Indian named Makes Summer. His appreciation of traditional Indian culture led him finally to Canada, where he met Beverly. He and his wife, Carol, first considered Beverly an "adopted sister," but when their marriage ended, Beverly and Adolph were wed.

Beverly and Adolph encountered some enmity among the Indians who could not understand why a white man should choose to live as an Indian, and their co-authored book, *Shadows of the Buffalo*, tells of their experiences. Earlier, Hungry Wolf had assisted her husband in gathering information for his book, *The Blood People*, and he in turn encouraged her to collect the wisdom of the women of the Blackfoot Nation in her own book, *The Ways of My Grandmothers*. Adolf has also published independent works.

The women who served as sources for *The Ways of My Grandmothers* included Beverly Hungry Wolf's actual grandmother, AnadaAki, whose name means Pretty Woman and who later was known as Hilda Heavy Head, Hilda Beebe, and Hilda Strangling Wolf because of later marriages. Although the daughter of a German father named Joe Trollinger and educated in a girls' school run by a British matron, AnadaAki still grew up amidst the songs and ceremonies of the Blackfoot Nation and shared their stories. AnadaAki was in her nineties and living with Ruth Little Bear, Hungry Wolf's mother, when her stories were collected for this book.

It is tribal custom, however, to consider all of the older women as grandmothers, and Beverly Hungry Wolf collected information and stories from these other "grandmothers" as well. A particularly important source was Paula Weasel Head, who was noted for her wisdom and her knowledge of the Medicine Pipe Bundles important to the tribe, and who honored Hungry Wolf by taking her as an "adopted child." Additional stories came from Hungry Wolf's aunt, Mary One Spot, and other elders within the Blood Clan. Other information is also preserved in the book, such as recipes, craftwork, dances, and childhood memories of the traditions and lifestyle of the Blackfoot Nation.

Beverly Hungry Wolf now lives with her husband and their five children in a cabin in the wilderness of the British Columbia Rockies.

—Thelma J. Shinn

References

Hungry Wolf, Adolph. *The Blood People: A Division of the Blackfoot Confederacy.* New York: Harper and Row, 1977.

———. *Shadows of the Buffalo: A Family Odyssey Among the Indians.* New York: William Morrow, 1983.

Hungry Wolf, Beverly. *The Ways of My Grandmothers.* New York: William Morrow, 1980.

I

IGNACIO, CARMELLA (b. 1942) is the first registered nurse at Grossmont Hospital in San Diego, California, to reach Level IV for clinical nurses. Ignacio has worked at Grossmont Hospital since 1968, where she has been in charge of the ophthalmology and orthopedic service in the operating room. She belongs to the National Association of Operating Room Nurses and the United Nurse Association of California. Ignacio has served as president of the Heartland Youth Symphony Orchestra, but she is known nationally for her work in American Indian health. In 1984 she was elected to the board of directors of the San Diego American Indian Health Center, a very successful health care facility in the San Diego metropolitan area.

Ignacio is Tohono O'odham (Papago) and was born at Sells, Arizona. Her mother was of the Chico family, while her father was a Pablo family member. As a child she attended Topawa Elementary School and St. John's Indian School. Upon graduation she attended the University of Arizona and St. Mary's School of Nursing, where she became a registered nurse. She has contributed significantly to the health of Native Americans by assuring quality medical service to thousands of Indians at the Indian Health Center. She is well known to the Indian Health Service and has worked with state and federal agencies to improve health care to urban Indians throughout California.

—Clifford E. Trafzer

Reference

Trafzer, Clifford. Personal communication with Carmella Ignacio, 1990.

INDIAN EMILY (1856?-1873) was an Apache girl who was found lying badly wounded by Lieutenant Tom Easton in 1868, after an Apache raid on Fort David (in what is now Texas). After being nursed back to health by his mother, Emily (the Eastons' name for her) spent the next several years with the lieutenant and his mother. As the story goes, she learned to speak, read and write in English and otherwise adapted to white ways, to the point of falling in love with the young lieutenant, Tom Easton. When his affections turned toward Mary Nelson, the daughter of a post family—about two years later—Emily ran away. In 1873 the soldiers went on alert, for Apaches had been attacking stagecoaches and wagon trains. One night a sentry, hearing approaching footsteps and calling out without getting a response, fired on what he thought was an intruder; he shot and mortally wounded Emily, who had returned to warn Tom and his mother that Emily's Apache band was going to attack the fort. Emily is reputed to have given her life for her friends, the whites, and with having saved the garrison from massacre.

—Kathryn W. Shanley

References

Raht, Carlysle Graham. *The Romance of the Davis Mountains and the Big Bend Country.* El Paso, TX: Rahtbooks, 1919.

Twitchell, Ralph Emerson. *The Leading Facts of New Mexico History.* Cedar Rapids, IA: Torch Press, 1911.

Waltrip, Lela, and Rufus Waltrip. *Indian Women: Thirteen Who Played a Part in the History of America from the Earliest Days to Now.* New York: David McKay, 1964.

ISOM, JOAN SHADDOX (b. 1940) was raised in eastern Oklahoma's hills, learning all she could about her Cherokee people's myths, legends, and culture. As she grew, she developed equal interests in poetry and drawing. Isom saw both as ways to preserve Cherokee traditions and express her interpretations of them. She received a BA in education from Central State University (now Central Oklahoma State University) in Edmond in 1965 and an MFA from the University of Arkansas in 1970.

Joan Shaddox Isom's one-act plays, *The Living Forest, A Pound of Miracles, Paint Me a Memory, The Halloween Visitor,* and *Boy Medicine,* were all published in 1975 by Oklahoma City's Melody House. *Free Spirits,* published by Plays, Inc., of Boston in 1975, won a special recognition award in the Best Plays of the Year Contest. Isom was commissioned to write the bicentennial play for Fort Gibson, Oklahoma; it was first performed in 1976 and continues as an annual summer drama.

Isom is also an artist and her work was exhibited in the 1968 Prix de Paris Competition, winning an award for its role in representing current trends in American art. Likewise, in 1968 her work placed fourth in the Olympic Art Competition, held in Rimini, Italy.

A versatile artist and educator, she has taught all levels of school from elementary to college, was a producer for a children's theatre group, and directed the Fine Arts Program for her region in 1971. Bringing art to schoolchildren has always been a priority, and she has designed fine arts curricula, as well as serving as director of Oklahoma's Arts and Humanities Council.

Joan Shaddox Isom is most widely known for her collections of poems *Foxgrapes* and *The Moon in Five Disguises.* She illustrated both volumes and is a founding member of the Foxmoor Publishing Co-op, which published *The Moon in Five Disguises.* Individual works have appeared in many periodicals, such as *The Indian Historian.* Her poem "The Visit" creates a haunting picture of an adult Isom going through the broken-down ruins of her childhood home, a home lost during the Oklahoma Dustbowl. It won first place in the 1971 Beta Sigma Phi International Poetry Contest.

Joan Shaddox Isom makes her home in Tahlequah, Oklahoma.

—Cynthia Kasee

References

Brant, Beth, ed. *A Gathering of Spirit*. Rockland, ME: Sinister Wisdom, 1984.
Campbell, Gilbert, ed. *Authors Files*. Palmer Lake, CO: Filter Press, 1991.
Isom, Joan Shaddox. *Foxgrapes*. Palmer Lake, CO: Filter Press, 1975.
————. *The Moon in Five Disguises*. Tahlequah, OK: Foxmoor Publishing Co-op, 1981.

J

JARVIS, ROSIE

JARVIS, ROSIE (c. 1851–1955) was born on the Haupt Ranch in Sonoma County, California, where many of the Kashaya Pomo settled after the Russians abandoned Fort Ross in 1842. Jarvis's mother, Mollie, subsequently married Charlie Haupt, a squatter with a large tract of land, forsaking her marriage to Chico Jarvis, Rosie's Indian father, to secure a home for her Kashaya people. Rosie Jarvis became a type of hand curer; she massaged muscles and rubbed out pains. But her greatest contribution to the Kashaya Pomo and to other Indians was the vast knowledge she passed on as tribal historian. She raised her granddaughter, Essie Parrish, who would become the last great Kashaya religious and political leader, and schooled her in the history of the land and people. Because of Rosie Jarvis this oral history is alive and well today; every Kashaya person, if interested, can trace his or her heritage to ancestors living in specific locales at the time of European contact nearly two hundred years ago.

Jarvis married more than once. Her husband, Tom Smith, a Kashaya Pomo/Coast Miwok, was a well-known powerful Indian doctor and dreamer. Their son, Robert, became chief of the Kashaya tribe. In 1919 she was among the first to settle on a plot of land, purchased by the US Government, to establish the Kashaya Reservation. Jarvis only knew a few words of English when she died in 1955. According to her great-granddaughter, Violet Chappell, daughter of Essie Parrish and current tribal historian, Jarvis "never stopped talking about the old days because it was important for us."

—Greg Sarris

Reference

Sarris, Greg. Personal communication with Violet Chappell. Kashaya Reservation, Stewart's Point, California, May 1990.

JEMISON, ALICE LEE

JEMISON, ALICE LEE (1901–1964) was born in the town of Silver Creek, just off the Cattaraugus Indian Reservation in the state of New York. The daughter of a Seneca mother and a Cherokee father, Jemison identified most strongly with her Seneca heritage and with a long-standing tradition of politically significant Iroquois women. Jemison graduated from Silver Creek High School in 1919, but her ambition to continue her education and become a lawyer went unfulfilled for lack of money. When her marriage to LeVerne L. Jemison, a Seneca steelworker, ended in separation in 1928, Jemison found herself accepting a wide variety of jobs, her choice determined almost solely by her responsibility to support her mother and two children. Thus began a struggle against poverty that would remain a constant throughout her life.

Alice Lee Jemison is best remembered as an outspoken critic of the Bureau of Indian Affairs (BIA), its New Deal program of the 1930s, and as a leader in the ultra-conservative American Indian Federation. Her use of inflammatory rhetoric and demagoguery, especially in opposition to New Deal legislation, led some of the government officials she criticized to cast her as an extremist. But a closer examination of Jemison's brand of conservatism reveals that it was complex and often misunderstood, especially when taken out of its cultural context. Jemison's anti-government positions were not rooted in an extreme ideology. Instead, they had two main sources: the general and widespread mistrust of non-Indian institutions typical of conservative Senecas, and the politically conservative climate prevalent in western New York.

To more fully understand Jemison's point of view, it is important to recognize her commitment to preserving Iroquois treaty rights, which she and others believed safeguarded an independent Iroquois sovereignty, not a sovereign status protected merely at the pleasure of the Congress of the United States. Much affected by the problems all Iroquois faced during her lifetime, Jemison got involved in tribal politics in the 1920s and remained active well into the 1940s. She served the Seneca people as a legal researcher and lobbyist, and she also worked together with members of the Iroquois Confederacy to organize Indian leaders into an Intertribal Committee for the advancement of the American Indian.

—Gretchen G. Harvey

References

Hauptman, Laurence M. "Alice Lee Jemison: Seneca Political Activist." *The Indian Historian* 12 (1974): 15–40.
———. "The Only Good Indian Bureau Is a Dead Indian Bureau: Alice Lee Jemison, Seneca Political Activist." In *The Iroquois and the New Deal*. Syracuse, NY: Syracuse University Press, 1981.
Jemison, Alice Lee. *Buffalo Evening News*, April 1933: 18–21.
———. File in the Office Files of Commissioner John Collier. Bureau of Indian Affairs, Record Group 75, National Archives, Washington, DC.

JIMULLA, VIOLA PELHAME [SICATUVA, "BORN QUICKLY"] (1878–1966), Chieftess of the Yavapai tribe (mistakenly called the Mojave-Apache), was the third of three daughters of Who-wah and Ka-hava-soo-ah who lived near Prescott, Arizona. Her father died when she was young, and Who-wah married Pelhame, under whose name Jimulla attended the Rice Arizona Indian School and the Phoenix Indian School. In 1901 she married Sam Jimulla ("Red Ants," who died in 1940 after being thrown from his horse), and together they had five daughters, three of whom died young.

In 1935, approximately 75 acres were established as the Prescott Yavapai Indian Reservation (expanded to 1,327 acres in the early 1950s), the smallest Indian reservation in the United States. Sam Jimulla was appointed Chief by the commissioner of Indian Affairs and elected simultaneously to the position by his people. After his death, his wife succeeded him as Chieftess and primarily managed tribal affairs for several years single-handedly, despite the formation of a five-person Tribal Council in 1940. At her death, her second daughter, Grace (Mrs. Don Mitchell), succeeded her, her appointment confirmed by the Tribal Council in 1967.

A progressive and compassionate leader, Jimulla was also involved in various aspects of her tribe's spiritual life. She was named an elder of the Yavapai Indian Mission (Presbyterian) in 1922 and was instrumental in the foundation of the Trinity Presbyterian Church of Prescott, Arizona, in 1957. She was also an accomplished basket weaver and teacher of basketry under WPA programs.

—Rodney Simard

Reference

Barnett, Franklin. *Viola Jimulla: The Indian Chieftess*. Prescott, AZ: Prescott Yavapai Indians, 1968.

JOE, RITA (b. 1932), the Micmac poet, was born the daughter of Joseph Bernard and Annie Googoo in Wycocomagh, Cape Breton Island, Nova Scotia. Her mother died in childbirth when Joe was five, and the loss of her mother, and the feeling of desertion matched by a longing to return to her mother's love, runs through Rita Joe's poetry to this day. After her mother's death, Joe's aging father saw to it that she and her brothers and sisters had foster families to grow up in, but without the attention of parents, Joe had a hard time learning the Micmac language and absorbing all the knowledge it transmits through the oral tradition. So she had to make a conscious and very successful effort to reclaim that part of her heritage. When she was twelve years old, she applied to go to Shubbenacadie Residential School, which she attended until eighth grade. In the early fifties she moved to Boston, Massachusetts, a city where many Micmac people found work then, and there she met her late husband, Frank Joe (Micmac). Together, they raised a large family, including adopted, biological, and foster children, and they made their way back to Micmac territory from Boston via Halifax to Eskasoni Reserve on Cape Breton Island, where Joe now lives.

In the late sixties, partly influenced by her children's experiences in public schools, partly out of her own intellectual curiosity and creative exuberance, Rita Joe began to write poetry. For years, she also wrote a column, "Here and There in Eskasoni," for the *Micmac News*, a tribal newspaper which found its readers all over the world. When in 1971 her eldest daughter, Evelyn, was subjected to racist slurs and ridicule by her teacher in an almost totally white public school, Rita Joe decided to use her pen to counteract the devastating effects of mental colonization, such as the distortion and displacement of Native history and the stereotyping of Native persons. Her first volume of poetry, *Poems of Rita Joe*, came out in 1974. Without ever being aggressive or launching attacks on the political level, the poems gently present the Native experience within dominant society, and they advocate love and understanding between peoples to overcome the barriers that impede communication and peace.

After the publication of her first book, Rita Joe received many invitations to speak to Native and non-Native audiences in community centers, libraries, schools and universities, including the University of British Columbia; the University of Maine; Acadia, Dalhousie, and McGill Universities; and Chico State College, Chico, California. Her poem about making axe handles together with her father, "untitled" in *Poems*, is now on display on tanned hide in the Canadian Museum of Civilization in Ottawa. Her second book of poetry, *Song of Eskasoni*, came out in 1988, and her poems have appeared in anthologies and periodicals, including *Canadian Women Studies/Les cahiers de la femme* (1989).

Rita Joe has received wide recognition for her literary and humanitarian efforts. In 1974 she won the poetry competition prize of the Nova Scotia Writers' Federation, which she accepted in Native dress, and in 1989 she was nominated for the Order of Canada, the highest honor Canada can bestow on her citizens. In April 1990, still suffering from the loss of her husband, Rita Joe accepted the award from the hands of the Governor General at Rideau Hall in Ottawa "on behalf of all the Native people," as she said in her acceptance speech.

Also in 1990, using her winnings from a successful game of bingo, Rita Joe established a small Micmac arts and crafts shop right by her house on the Eskasoni Reserve, where she sells products crafted by her community. The shop attracts customers from all over the world.

In 1991, the Year of the Aborigine, Rita Joe attempted to set up a Micmac cultural center and museum on the reserve to present to the world the richness of a heritage that has survived four hundred years of contact, and that has incorporated into Roman Catholicism, of which Rita Joe is a strong supporter, many of the traditions and customs of the original Micmac Nation.

Rita Joe is a gentle but strong voice, a shining example of courage and dedication, an untiring community worker and supporter of her own people, and a lovable partner in conversation. As such she is an encouraging role model for young Native people.

—Hartmut Lutz

References

Joe, Rita. "The Gentle War." *Canadian Women Studies/Les cahiers de la femme* 10 (Summer/Fall 1989): 27–29.

————. *Poems of Rita Joe*. Halifax, NS: Abanaki Press, 1978. Reprint. By the author, 1990.

————. *Song of Eskasoni*. Charlottetown, P.E.I.: Ragweed Press, 1988.

"Rita Joe [Interview]." In *Contemporary Challenges: Conversations With Canadian Native Authors*, edited by Hartmut Lutz, 241–64. Saskatoon: Fifth House, 1991.

Steele, Charlott Musical. "Rita Joe Wages Gentle War of Words." *Atlantic Advocate* 81 (January 1991): 11–13.

JOHN, MARY (b. 1913) is a member of the Carrier Indian Band on the Stoney Creek Reserve in northern British Columbia. She was born at Six-Mile-Lake, the home of her grandmother, to Anzell and Charlie Pinker, a white man. In 1920 she attended the mission school at Fort St. James, transferring to the mission school at Lejac in 1922. Her memories of the seven years she attended school focus on the hunger and desolation she experienced there. She married Lazare John in 1929, and from 1930 to 1949, she bore twelve children.

John's life is recounted in Bridget Moran's *Stoney Creek Woman*, an autobiography that chronicles the hardships endured by her people because of the Indian Act and a lack of government attention and funds, as well as John's personal struggles and victories over poverty, racism, and illness. In 1957 John went to work at the hospital in Vanderhoof, sometimes walking the nine miles when she lacked transportation. She worked at the hospital for thirteen years. In 1972 John was asked to teach the Native Carrier language and culture at St. Joseph's. The Stoney Creek Reserve began an Elders Society in 1978, and John was an active participant. The Rotary Club in Vanderhoof named her Citizen of the Year in 1979, acknowledging her contributions to Stoney Creek, other Native communities, and the entire community in Vanderhoof.

John says that if she had three wishes for her people she would wish for improved living conditions on the reservations, more education for the children, and the opportunity to find employment on the reservations. Her life has been a life of dedication to her family, loyalty to Stoney Creek, and service to the community at large.

—Laurie Lisa

Reference

Moran, Bridget. *Stoney Creek Woman: The Story of Mary John*. Vancouver: Tillacum Library, 1988.

JOHNSON, EMILY PAULINE [TEKAHIONWAKE] (1861–1913) was born near Brantford, Ontario, on the Six Nations Reserve. The daughter of the Mohawk chief George Henry Martin Johnson and the English-born Emily Susanna Howells, who was a cousin of the American novelist William Dean

Howells, Johnson absorbed Mohawk traditions from family members and Anglo-American traditions through reading such authors as Shakespeare, Byron, Emerson, and Longfellow. Johnson's interest in theatrical performance and dramatic literary readings, stemming from family entertainments, increased during her attendance at the Central Collegiate School in Brantford.

Johnson began writing her own poetry around 1879 and began to achieve recognition through publication and public readings of her work in the early 1890s. Building on good family connections with England, she traveled to London in 1894 to find a publisher for her poems. The trip was a success, and the prestigious Bodley Head Press published her important collection, *The White Wampum*, in 1895. Following the publication of her first book, Johnson toured extensively. Though especially popular in western Canada, the "Mohawk Princess," as she was billed, found audiences for theatrical performances of her writings throughout Canada, as well as Great Britain and the United States. A second collection of poems, *Canadian Born*, was published in Toronto in 1903.

In 1904 Johnson turned more to prose writing and was able to place her stories and essays in *The Mother's Magazine* and other respected periodicals. Important collections of her prose works include *The Legends of Vancouver*, *The Shagganappi*, and *The Moccasin Maker*. A final verse collection, *Flint and Feather*, contained poems from *The White Wampum* and *Canadian Born* as well as later material.

Johnson is particularly noted for her memorable portrayal of American Indians and of women. Her stories often feature Indian heroines, and she often describes the victimization of Indian women in love relationships with white men. Her writings frequently serve to counteract negative stereotypes of Native Americans. In addition to her significance as a writer within the traditions of Native American and women's poetry and fiction, Johnson is regarded as an important figure in the development of the national literature of Canada. She never married. Johnson died in Vancouver, British Columbia, in 1913.

—James Robert Payne

References

Foster, Mrs. W. Garland (Anne). *The Mohawk Princess, Being Some Account of the Life of Teka-hion-wake (E. Pauline Johnson)*. Vancouver: Lion's Gate, 1931.
Johnson, Emily Pauline. *Canadian Born*. Toronto: Morang, 1903.
———. *Flint and Feather*. Toronto: Musson, 1912. Reprint. Markham, ON: PaperJacks, 1973.
———. *Legends of Vancouver*. 1911. Reprint. Vancouver: McClelland, 1912, 1961.
———. *The Moccasin Maker*. 1913. Reprint. Edited with introduction and notes by A. LaVonne Brown Ruoff. Tucson: University of Arizona Press, 1987.
———. *The Shagganappi*. Introduced by Ernest Thompson Seton. Vancouver: Briggs, 1913.

————. *The White Wampum*. London: Bodley Head, 1895.

Keller, Betty. *Pauline: A Biography of Pauline Johnson*. Vancouver: Douglas, 1981.

McRaye, Walter. *Pauline Johnson and Her Friends*. Toronto: Ryerson, 1947.

————. *Town Hall To-night*. Toronto: Ryerson, 1929.

Van Steen, Marcus, ed. *Pauline Johnson: Her Life and Work*. Toronto: Hodder and Stroughton, 1965.

JOHNSTON, VERNA PATRONELLA [PATRONELLA JOHNSTON, PATRONELLA VERNA NADJIWON JOHNSTON] (b. 1909), a Chippewa, is

called "Verna" by her family though christened Patronella Verna Nadjiwon when she was born at the Cape Croker Reserve in Ontario, Canada. In 1926 she married Henry Johnston and spent the next nineteen years raising her five children. From 1945 until 1959, she worked at odd jobs in Toronto and then returned to Cape Croker where she worked for Children's Aid as a foster mother to Indian children. In 1965 Johnston returned to Toronto to "make a place in the city" for her two granddaughters who were attending business courses, and in 1966 this initial endeavor led her to open the first boarding house for Indian students in Toronto. Over the next ten years, Johnston developed her continuing interest in Indian adaption to urban life as she taught her boarders how to value their Indianness, how to handle themselves off the reserve, and how to deal with the various governmental organizations concerned with Indian people.

While running her boarding house, Johnston ran a craft training program for Indian Affairs, which took her to one hundred twenty-four different Canadian reserves and brought her into contact with Native peoples from all over Canada. As she puts it, she was "caught up in the upswing of Indian consciousness" and soon was in demand as a speaker who was knowledgeable about the reserve system and its flaws and about Native urban life. This led to Johnston's being asked to teach Indian culture classes at Sheridan College, York University, and Seneca College. She also taught orientation classes for the Northern Corps teachers, and as a member of the board of the Indian Friendship Centre, she helped Indians from the reserves to find places to live in the city.

In 1970 Johnston published *Tales of Nokomis*, the Ojibwa stories she had been told as a child by her grandmother. In 1973 ill health forced her to close her boarding house and return for a year to Cape Croker; but she was back in Toronto in 1974, working as a voluntary consultant and housekeeper for Anduhyaun House, a hostel for young Indian girls. In 1976 she was named Indian Woman of the Year by the Native Women's Association of Canada. Since then, she has continued to be a resource person for the Native community. According to her niece-by-marriage, Carol Nadjiwon, in the fall of 1990, Johnston at the age of eighty-one, was still very active at Cape Croker and "helping out wherever she could." Johnston, Nadjiwon noted, "had just finished organizing a public assembly for peace and natural law."

—Joni Adamson Clarke

References

Clark, Joni Adamson. Interview with Carol Nadjiwon. Indian Resource Center,
    University of Arizona, 25 January 1991.
Johnston, Patronella. *Tales of Nokomis*. Toronto: Musson Books, 1970.
Vanderburgh, Rosamund M. *I Am Nokomis Too: The Biography of Verna Patronella
    Johnston*. Don Mills, ON: General Publishing, 1977.

JUANA MARIA [LOST WOMAN OF SAN NICHOLAS ISLAND, LONE
WOMAN OF SAN NICHOLAS ISLAND] (1815?-1853) was found in 1853
living alone on San Nicholas Island in the Santa Barbara Island group. Under the
auspices of Junipero Serra, the inhabitants of these tiny islands were transported
presumably to protect them from raids by the Russian hunters from Alaska, and
to eliminate priests crossing rough seas to perform their offices; after transportation, these people were employed as agricultural and domestic workers.

According to several accounts, in 1835 or 1836, upon boarding the transport
ship, a young Nicoleño woman discovered that her nursing infant had been left
on the island, so she jumped overboard into a stormy sea to retrieve it (some
accounts say she discovered her child missing before boarding and walked back
to the village; others do not mention that she was nursing). The rising storm
required the ship's immediate departure, and so it could not wait or return for the
pair. After arrival on the mainland, all trace of her people quickly disappeared.
When she herself arrived at the Santa Barbara Mission eighteen years later, no
one could understand her language, though a few words were recorded. The
priests had offered a $200 reward for her safe removal from the island. Future
attempts at rescue were considered but never carried through, due to the
treachery of tides and winds. Otter and seal hunters who worked on the island
sometimes looked, but were never able to find her.

Finally, in 1853, Captain George Nidever and his men were hunting otter and
seal and found her whale rib house on the island; the next day they encountered
the woman, sewing with a bone needle and seal skin thread in front of her house.
After they had hunted for a month, they persuaded her to board their ship,
supposedly to follow her people. Her inability to communicate prevented anyone
from finding out exactly how she had survived, or what had happened to her
child. Baptized Juana Maria, or Juana Marie, at the mission, she soon contracted
a fatal dysentery. The Lone Woman of San Nicholas Island died seven weeks after
her "rescue." One of her water baskets, her beads, and a stone mortar were
presented to the California Academy of Sciences after her death and were
subsequently destroyed in the San Francisco earthquake and fire of 1906. A
luxurious cape of seal skin and cormorant feathers was reported to have been sent
to the Vatican but was lost.

These artifacts and the mere fact of her survival continued to fascinate the mainlanders, who thought of her as a real-life Robinson Crusoe and published several romantic and historical accounts about her. A children's novel, *Island of the Blue Dolphins* by Scott O'Dell, based on her story and published in 1960, won the Newberry Medal for children's literature and was made into a film for children. Like Ishi, Juana Maria was the last member of her tribe. She was buried in the Santa Barbara Mission Cemetery on October 19, 1853.

—Jay Ann Cox

References

Hardacre, Emma Chamberlain. "Eighteen Years Alone." *Scribner's Monthly* (September 1880): 657-64. Reprint. Santa Barbara, CA: Schauer Printing, 1950. Monograph.

Heitzer, Robert F., and Albert B. Elsasser, eds. "Original Accounts of the Lone Woman of San Nicholas Island." *Reports of the University of California Archaeological Survey*, no. 55 (June 1961). Reprint. Ramona, CA: Ballena Press, 1973. Monograph.

O'Dell, Scott. *Island of the Blue Dolphins*. Boston: Houghton Mifflin, 1960.

JUMPER, BETTY MAE (b. 1923) was born at Indiantown near Lake Okeechobee in southern Florida. Her mother was Ada Tiger, a full-blood Seminole Indian. When she was five years of age, the family moved to the Dania Indian Reservation near Fort Lauderdale. The Tiger family became devout Christians and members of the Baptist church. Over the protest of her grandmother, she learned English and attended the reservation day school. The school was closed in 1936, but Jumper and a few other Seminole youngsters were ultimately sent to a federal residential school for Indians at Cherokee, North Carolina. There she made the adjustment to white man's clothing and schooling, as well as to living among the mountains and seasonal changes. In 1945 Jumper and her cousin became the first Seminoles to receive high school diplomas.

After graduation she went to the Kiowa Indian Hospital in Oklahoma and completed a year of nurse's training in the public health field. She then returned to Florida and worked with the public health nurse serving the Seminole Reservations. During this time she married Moses Jumper, a young Seminole who had also attended school at Cherokee. He was one of only three Seminoles who volunteered and served in the military during World War II. They raised a family of two sons and a daughter.

When the Seminole tribe was formally organized in 1957, Jumper was elected to the Tribal Council for a two-year term. This was followed by four years of service on the board of directors, which supervised tribal business enterprises. In 1967 the Seminole people elected Betty Mae Jumper as the first—and to this date only—woman to serve as chairman of the Seminole Tribal Council. During the four-year term she worked to improve health, employment, education, welfare, law and order, and housing conditions for her people. The tribe also entered into a number of land leases and other financial arrangements to move toward economic self-sufficiency. At the national level Jumper was active in the National Tribal Chairman's Association, a founder of United Southeastern Tribes, and served on the National Council on Indian Opportunities. In 1970 she was named one of the "Top Indian Women" of the year and attended the National Seminar for American Indian Women held in Colorado. Since leaving office Jumper has held a variety of positions with the Seminole tribe and is currently associated with its communications department, which published her brief memoir entitled . . . *and with the Wagon came God's Word.*

—Harry A. Kersey, Jr.

References

Jumper, Betty Mae. . . . *and with the Wagon came God's Word.* Hollywood, FL: Seminole Tribe, 1980.

———. Interview by Harry A. Kersey, Jr. 17 June 1969. Tape recording SEM 8A, University of Florida Oral History Archives, Gainesville, FL.

———. Interview by Harry A. Kersey, Jr. 2 January 1985. Tape recording SEM 196A, University of Florida Oral History Archives, Gainesville, FL.

Kersey, Harry A., Jr. "Federal Schools and Acculturation among the Florida Seminoles, 1927–1954." *Florida Historical Quarterly* 59 (1980): 165–81.

———. *The Florida Seminoles and the New Deal, 1933–1942.* Gainesville: University Presses of Florida, 1989.

Seminole Tribe of Florida and Seminole Tribe of Florida, Inc. 1977. *20th Anniversary of Tribal Organization, 1957–1977, Saturday, 20 August 1977.* Hollywood, FL: Seminole Tribe. Mimeo.

JUNEAU, JOSETTE (1803–1855) was a humanitarian known for promoting peace and hospitality in frontier Milwaukee, Wisconsin. Her public life spanned thirty-two years while the region was in transition from Indian to non-Indian control. Her charity and good works were acknowledged by a gift from Pope Leo XII, and she was eulogized by the local press upon her death.

Juneau was born into a family of twelve children at Sheboygan, Wisconsin. She was the daughter of Jacques Vieau, an itinerant French Canadian fur trader, and a Menominee mother. Her maternal relatives included influential Menominee leaders Ahkanepoway and Onaugesa. She was reared a Catholic, and during her youth, she served at the St. Francis Xavier Mission near Green Bay, Wisconsin. She was fluent and literate in French, and she was also fluent in Menominee, Chippewa, Potawatomi, and Winnebago.

At age seventeen, she married Solomon L. Juneau, a French Canadian who worked under her father's supervision at Milwaukee. At that trade outpost, she proved to be an energetic woman who managed the home life and also the trading post when her husband was absent. She bore at least seventeen children, of whom fourteen survived childhood. (Her son Joseph later became a co-founder and the namesake of Juneau, Alaska.) In addition, she regularly accommodated guests within her home and extended nursing care, charity, and education in domestics and Christian doctrine.

In 1835 her influence within the Native community was tested severely. A few Yankees squatting on local Potawatomi lands caused the Potawatomi to plan a revenge attack on the Yankee settlement during her husband's absence. Because none of the warriors wished to confront Juneau, she succeeded in foiling the plan by keeping an all-night vigil within the settlement.

Juneau mingled little with the incoming Yankees and rarely spoke English, despite her husband's civic prominence throughout the region (he had a variety of business interests and served as Milwaukee's first mayor). She longed for the rural life and more contact with her Menominee kin. Later she persuaded her husband to build a second home at Theresa, Wisconsin, a village north of Milwaukee in proximity to the Menominee Reservation. This home served initially as their summer residence, and after 1852, as their retirement home. In 1855 she returned to Milwaukee for treatment of a lingering illness. The treatment failed and she died soon after.

—Mark G. Thiel

References

Bruce, William G., ed. *History of Milwaukee: City and County.* Chicago: S.J. Clarke Publishing, 1922.

Fox, Isabella. *Solomon Juneau: A Biography, With Sketches of the Juneau Family.* Milwaukee: Evening Wisconsin Printing, 1916.

Gregory, John G. *History of Milwaukee, Wisconsin.* Chicago: S.J. Clarke Publishing, 1931.

Thwaites, Reuben G., ed. *Collections of the State Historical Society of Wisconsin.* Vol. 11. Madison, WI: Democrat Printing, 1888.

Waldman, Carl. *Who Was Who in Native American History: Indians and Non-Indians from Early Contacts through 1900.* New York: Facts on File, 1990.

K

KEAMS, GERALDINE (b. 1951) was born on the Navajo Reservation in Castle Butte, Arizona, and attended twelve different boarding and public schools before graduating from high school. The oldest of nine children in a family of sheepherders, she was most influenced by the storytelling of her grandmother and by her own love for reading, which lay the foundation for her future interest in preserving traditional Navajo tales and rituals in her poetry.

Keams studied English and American Indian literature at the University of Arizona, where she was recruited in 1971 by La Mama Theater in New York. Working there with Lee Breuer, later co-chair of the Yale Drama School, and Robert Shorty, a Navajo visual artist, she translated her grandmother's version of the Navajo creation story into English as the basis of a theater piece which began in New York and toured the country in 1971–72. She credits Breuer with her growing interest in "weaving words and visuals together," which would lead to her work in film, theater, and performance poetry with the Lee Strasberg School and Cafe La Mama in New York in the 1970s and in Los Angeles in the 1980s.

A member of Writers Guild of America West and co-founder of the Big Mountain Support Group of Los Angeles, Keams has served as consultant on such films as *Broken Rainbow*, has produced *Trail of Pollen*, her own full-length film, and is probably best known for her performance in the Clint Eastwood film, *The Outlaw Josey Wales*, although she has also acted in such other films as *Born to the Wind* and *The Legend of Walks-far-woman*. Her ambition in film is to, "do the classic cowboy and Indian movie in reverse and do it all from the Indians' side." Meanwhile, she writes and performs her poetry in Los Angeles and involves herself in current theater projects, such as *Asian Eyes*, which was performed at Olio on three levels, including both a video projection of Keams and her simultaneous appearance on stage performing poetry and a Navajo ritual. Through such multi-media approaches, she succeeds in combining the oral traditions of her heritage with her desire to preserve those traditions in ongoing artistic formats, such as film and poetry.

—Thelma J. Shinn

References

Bataille, Gretchen M. "An Interview with Geraldine Keams." *Explorations in Ethnic Studies* 10 (January 1987): 1–7.

Stein, Julia. "The New Ellis Island: L.A.'s Poet Innovators." *High Performance* 38 (1987): 40–45.

KEESHIG-TOBIAS, LENORE (b. 1950) is an Ojibway/Pottawatomi writer, storyteller, and cultural activist residing in Toronto. The daughter of Keitha and Donald Keeshig grew up on the Nawash Reserve on the Bruce Peninsula where she received her schooling at St. Mary's Indian Day School. She attended York University, Toronto, between 1977 and 1984, graduated with a BFA, general honors, with an emphasis on creative writing and presentation.

Throughout her adult life, Keeshig-Tobias has been actively promoting the production and dissemination of Native literature in Canada, working in close connection with other Native authors (Daniel David Moses, Tomson Highway, Beatrice Culleton) and initiating and co-founding the Committee To Re-establish the Trickster (CRET).

She has published articles, poetry, children's literature and drama and has helped develop curricular material for use in Native schools. She has also lectured and conducted workshops on Native literature and history and Native contributions to world cultures at universities and cultural centers in Canada and the USA. She has given public readings throughout Canada and has been successful in educational and literary audio and audiovisual recording. Keeshig-Tobias has been an editor of *Ontario Indian* (1981–82) and a co-founder and editor of *Sweetgrass—The Magazine of Canada's Native Peoples* (1982–85). She is now editing *The Magazine to Re-Establish the Trickster*.

Her incessant and selfless literary campaigning has won her several grants and awards, some of which are from the Department of Indian Affairs and Northern Development (1979, 1980), the Ontario Arts Council (1986–89), and a 1987 Author's Award for a Feature Article co-authored with David McLaren and published by *This Magazine*.

Keeshig-Tobias has come out strongly on several occasions against the appropriation of Native culture and philosophy by non-Native writers like Anne Cameron or Lynn Andrews. The wide attention this issue is receiving from Native and non-Native writers alike is mainly due to Keeshig-Tobias's panel discussion at The Writer's Union of Canada AGM in the Spring of 1989. Keeshig-Tobias has five children and shares her life with partner David McLaren.

—Hartmut Lutz

References

Keeshig-Tobias, Lenore. "He Was A Boxer When I Was Small" (and other poems). In *Seventh Generation*, edited by Heather Hodgson, 64–71. Penticton, BC: Theytus Books, 1989.
———. "Stop Stealing Native Stories." *Globe and Mail* [Toronto] 26 January 1990: A7.
———, ed. *The Magazine to Re-Establish the Trickster*, 1988ff.
"Lenore Keeshig-Tobias [Interview]." In *Contemporary Challenges: Conversations with Canadian Native Authors*, edited by Hartmut Lutz, 79–88. Saskatoon, SK: Fifth House, 1991.

KEGG, MAUDE MITCHELL [NAAWAKAMIGOOKWE, "MIDDLE OF THE EARTH LADY"] (b. 1904), Chippewa (Ojibwe) tradition-bearer, was

born in a birch bark wigwam at a wild rice harvesting camp in Crow Wing County, Minnesota, near the Chippewa villages of Mille Lacs Lake. She learned tribal lore and skills from Aakogwan, her maternal grandmother, who raised her in ricing, maple sugar, and berry picking camps and in the family's winter house. She attended the local country school with white settlers and completed the eighth grade. She married Martin Kegg in 1922, and they eventually made their home on the Mille Lacs Reservation and raised ten children.

For many years a guide at the Mille Lacs Indian Museum of the Minnesota Historical Society, she is an interpreter of her people's traditional way of life to both Indian and non-Indian. In 1969 she began teaching the Ojibwe language to scholars and dictating her memoirs and historical legends in Ojibwe. From this work have appeared so far two bilingual books (both in several editions), as well as a technical grammar and a student dictionary, widely used in Ojibwe language and culture classes in the United States and Canada.

Skilled in traditional crafts with birch bark, basswood bark fiber, and deer hide and beads, she was featured in the 1986 exhibition *Lost and Found Traditions: Native American Art 1965–1985*. In 1990 she received a National Heritage Fellowship from the National Endowment for the Arts in recognition of her achievements as a folk artist and a cultural interpreter.

—John D. Nichols

References

Coe, Ralph. *Lost and Found Traditions: Native American Art 1965–1985*. Seattle: University of Washington Press, 1986.

Kegg, Maude. *Gabekanaamsing/At the End of the Trail: Memories of Chippewa Childhood in Minnesota*. Edited by John Nichols. Occasional publications in Anthropology Linguistic Series, no. 4 (1978). University of Northern Colorado Museum of Anthropology.

———. *Gii-Ikwezensiwiyaan/When I Was a Little Girl*. Edited by John Nichols. Onamia, MN: Private printing, 1976.

———. *Nookomis Gaa-inaajimotawid/What My Grandmother Told Me*. Edited by John D. Nichols. 2d ed. Bemidji, MN: American Indian Studies, Bemidji State University, 1990.

———. *Portage Lake*. Edited by John D. Nichols. Edmonton: University of Alberta Press, 1991.

Nichols, John D. "Ojibwe Morphology." PhD diss., Harvard University, 1980.

———, and Earl Nyholm, eds. *Ojibwewi-ikidowinan: An Ojibwe Word Resource Book*. Occasional Publications in Minnesota Anthropology, no. 11. St. Paul: Minnesota Archaeological Society, 1979.

KELLOGG, LAURA CORNELIUS [LAURA MIRIAM CORNELIUS, MINNIE KELLOGG]

(1880–1947) was born into the Oneida Indian community of Wisconsin and became a baptized member of the Episcopal church. She descended from two influential Oneida leaders, Chief Daniel Bread and Chief Skenandore. Kellogg, like her forebears, built her reputation as an Oneida leader using her gifts for oratory. Unlike many of her contemporaries who went to Indian boarding schools, Laura Cornelius attended Grafton Hall, a private finishing school for girls in Fond du Lac, Wisconsin. After graduating in 1898, she spent two years traveling in Europe, and she later studied at a number of institutions of higher learning including Stanford, Barnard College, Columbia, Cornell, and the University of Wisconsin.

As one of the founders of the Society of American Indians, Kellogg contributed to the emergence of a national Indian voice at the Society's first meeting in 1911. In her address she asked the Society's leadership for a commitment to Indian self-sufficiency and independence, goals she believed were attainable by instituting plans for self-sustaining economic development on Indian reservations. While her message did not prove overwhelmingly popular among national Indian leaders, Kellogg did find a supportive constituency among the Iroquois. Thereafter she began more and more to devote her considerable talents, which included fluency in Oneida, to the recovery of New York and Wisconsin lands previously taken from the Oneida people.

Minnie Kellogg's special genius as a leader of the Oneida land claims struggle included her use of traditional Iroquois images and institutions to solve modern problems. The strategies she developed have influenced all subsequent twentieth-century campaigns to reclaim Iroquois lands. Unfortunately, Minnie Kellogg's legacy as an Iroquois leader is marred by accusations of fraud and mismanagement of donations. Minnie Kellogg, never able to recover her reputation, died in obscurity in New York City in 1947.

—Gretchen G. Harvey

References

Campisi, Jack. "Ethnic Identity and Boundary Maintenance in Three Oneida Communities." PhD diss., State University of New York, Albany, 1974.

Cornelius, Laura M. "Industrial Organization for the Indian." In *Report of the Executive Council on the Proceedings of the First Annual Conference, 12–17 October 1911*, Society of American Indians, 46–49. Washington, DC: Society of American Indians, 1912.

———. "Overalls and the Tenderfoot: A Story." *The Barnard Bear* 2 (March 1907): 5–18.

Hauptman, Laurence M. "Designing Woman: Minnie Kellogg, Iroquois Leader." In *Indian Lives: Essays on Nineteenth- and Twentieth-Century Native American Leaders*, edited by L.G. Moses and Raymond Wilson, 158–86. Albuquerque: University of New Mexico Press, 1985.

Kellogg, Laura Cornelius. *Our Democracy and the American Indian.* Kansas City, MO: Burton Publishing, 1920.

———. "Some Facts and Figures on Indian Education." *The Quarterly Journal* 1 (April 15, 1913): 37.

McLester, Thelma Cornelius. "Oneida Women Leaders." In *The Oneida Indian Experience: Two Perspectives,* edited by Jack Campisi and Laurence Hauptman, 108–25. Syracuse, NY: Syracuse University Press, 1988.

KIDWELL, CLARA S. (b. 1941) has been an associate professor of Native American Studies at the University of California, Berkeley, since 1974. She began her professional career in 1966, serving first as a collegiate instructor in history and then as a publications coordinator for a university research unit. In 1970 Kidwell became an instructor and chair of the Social Science Division at Haskell Indian Junior College, Lawrence, Kansas. She then was appointed as assistant professor in the University of Minnesota American Indian Studies Department, Minneapolis.

Kidwell's research and publications have flourished since her arrival at Berkeley. Her writings and lectures span a variety of topics reflecting her historical interest in interaction between Europeans and Native Americans in North America, including civil rights, education, ecology, medicine, women, world view, and the Choctaw tribe. She received fellowships from the Newberry Library, Chicago, and the Smithsonian Institution, among others. She served in 1980 as a visiting scholar and associate professor at Dartmouth College, Hanover, New Hampshire, and in 1989 became a trustee of the National Museum of the American Indian in Washington, DC. At Berkeley she has served as chair of the Department of Ethnic Studies, associate dean in the Graduate Division, and director of the Consortium for Graduate Opportunities for American Indians.

Kidwell was born in Tahlequah, Oklahoma, and raised in Muskogee, Oklahoma. She is of Choctaw and Chippewa parentage. She attended a Catholic grade school and a public high school in Muskogee. She earned her BA in Letters, and her MA and PhD degrees in History of Science at the University of Oklahoma, Norman, the latter in 1970.

—Mark G. Thiel

References

Kidwell, Clara S. "American Indian Attitudes Toward Nature: A Bicentennial Perspective." In *Contemporary Native American Address,* edited by John R. Maestas. Provo, UT: Brigham Young University Publications, 1975.

———. "Aztec and European Medicine in the New World, 1521–1600." In *Anthropology of Medicine,* edited by Lola Romanucci-Ross, Daniel Moerman, and Lawrence Tancredi. South Hadley, MA: J. F. Bergin, 1982.

————. "The Choctaw Struggle for Land and Identity in Mississippi, 1830–1918." In *After Removal: The Choctaw in Mississippi*, edited by Samuel J. Wells and Roseanna Tubby. Jackson: University Press of Mississippi, 1986.

————. "The Power of Women in Three American Indian Societies." *The Journal of Ethnic Studies* 6 (Winter 1979): 113–21.

————. "Science and Ethnoscience: Native American World Views as a Factor In the Development of Native Technologies." In *Environmental History: Critical Issues in Comparative Perspectives*, edited by Kendall E. Bailes. Lanham, MD: University Press of America, 1985.

Thiel, Mark G. Personal communication with Clara Sue Kidwell, 12 December 1990.

————. "Science and Ethnoscience." *The Indian Historian* 6 (Fall 1973), 43–54.

KILPATRICK, ANNA GRITTS (b. 1917) was born in Echota, Oklahoma, and earned a BS from Southern Methodist University in 1958. She spent her professional life as a teacher in the Dallas, Texas, public school system, and she pursued an active second career as a writer and collaborator with her husband, Jack Frederick Kilpatrick, a professor of music at SMU.

As a result of their shared interest in ethnomusicology, Kilpatrick and her husband investigated the relation of traditional Cherokee music patterns and tropes to symphonic music. This interest in blending the tribal with the European musical tradition led him to compose a symphony for the Oklahoma semi-centennial in 1957; at the time of his death, he was composing a symphony based on the rhythms and euphony of Native music. The Kilpatricks also brought to print many translations of Cherokee history, charm and love songs, folktales, and oral traditions. Theirs was apparently very much an intellectual and emotional partnership, one committed to both preserving and adapting the cultural heritage of the Oklahoma Cherokee. Their edited translation of *New Chota Letters* made available material from the first Native language periodical in America, which was a Cherokee publication. After her husband's death in 1967, Kilpatrick continued to prepare for publication their collaborative works on the Oklahoma Cherokee culture.

—Jennifer L. Jenkins

References

Kilpatrick, Anna Gritts, and Jack F. Kilpatrick. *Friends of Thunder: Folktales of the Oklahoma Cherokees*. Dallas, TX: Southern Methodist University Press, 1964.

————. *Muskogean Charm Songs Among the Oklahoma Cherokees*. Smithsonian Contributions to Anthropology, vol. 3, no. 3. Washington, DC: Smithsonian Press, 1967.

————. *Notebook of a Cherokee Shaman.* Smithsonian Contributions to Anthropology, vol. 2, no. 6. Washington, DC: Smithsonian Press, 1970.

————. *Run Toward the Nightland: Magic of the Oklahoma Cherokees.* Dallas, TX: Southern Methodist University Press, 1967.

————. *Walk in Your Soul: Love Incantations of the Oklahoma Cherokees.* Dallas, TX: Southern Methodist University Press, 1965.

————, eds. *New Chota Letters.* Dallas, TX: Southern Methodist University Press, 1968.

————, eds. *The Shadow of Sequoyah: Social Documents of the Cherokees, 1862–1964.* Translated by Anna Gritts Kilpatrick and Jack F. Kilpatrick. Civilization of the American Indian Series, vol. 81. Norman: University of Oklahoma Press, 1965.

KIRKNESS, VERNA J. (b. 1935) holds a BA, MEd, and DEd and is the founder and director of the First Nations House of Learning, University of British Columbia. Kirkness is widely known for her contributions to the development of Indian controlled education. Her career spans thirty-seven years and includes having been an elementary school teacher and principal, education supervisor, curriculum development researcher and consultant, and education director for the Manitoba Indian Brotherhood. Kirkness joined the Education Department faculty, University of British Columbia, in 1981 as the director of the Native Indian Teacher Education Program (NITEP). In 1983 she became the director of Native Indian Education (NIEducation) and developed the Ts'kel Education Administration Graduate Program, which began in 1984. In 1987 she assumed her present position and continues as director of NITEP.

Kirkness's publication record spans eighteen years and includes three books and more than twenty articles and papers on various aspects of Indian education in Canada. Since 1986 she edited one issue each year of the *Canadian Journal of Native Education.* She is also widely credited for her research, writing, and campaigning for the development of a national Indian Post-Secondary Education Assistance Program (1977). Since then, the program has sponsored thousands of Indian students pursuing technical and professional training at the postsecondary levels.

Much of her spare time is spent in private consultation work evaluating and advising local controlled Indian band schools, doing workshops, and lecturing. Kirkness has lectured and presented papers at a wide range of forums. She is a world traveller and attended the "World Conference: Indigenous People's Education" held in New Zealand (1990).

Kirkness has been widely recognized and applauded for her contributions to, and promotion of, Indian education issues. She has received the Golden Eagle Feather Award (1988) from the Professional Native Women's Association, the title of Fellow (1988) at the Ontario Institute for Studies in Education, the honor of President Emeritus (1988) of the Mokakit Indian Education Research

Association, which she founded in 1983, Canadian Educator of the Year Award (1990), an Honorary Doctorate of Human Letters from Mount St. Vincent University (1990), University of British Columbia Alumni Award (1990), the University of British Columbia's 75th Anniversary Medal (1990), and the British Columbia Educator of the Year Award (1990). One of the most outstanding honors she received from her own community was the opening of the Kirkness Adult Learning Centre (1984) in Winnipeg, Manitoba. The Centre was named to honor Kirkness as "a distinguished teacher and author on education of Native Indians."

Verna Kirkness is of Swampy Cree origins from the Fisher River First Nation at Koostatak, Manitoba. She teaches and speaks her language fluently. Her example as a role model and activist has been important in opening the doors for indigenous women in the professions and in making Indian education a national priority.

—Winona Stevenson

References

Kirkness, Verna J. "Indian Control of Indian Education: Over a Decade Later." In
    Mokakit Indian Education Research Association—Selected Papers, 74–79.
    Vancouver: University of British Columbia, 1986.
McGlaughlin, Peter. "MSVU Convocation without Incident, Threats." *The Daily
    News* [Halifax] 12 May 1990: 4.
"A Tribute to Verna Kirkness, President Emeritus, Mokakit." *Mokakit Newsletter* 1
    (1989): 1.
West, Doug. "Educator Wins National Award." *Kahtou* 1 May 1990: 3.

KREPPS, ETHEL C. was born in Mountain View, Oklahoma, and is secretary of the Kiowa tribe. She has been an active voice for the importance of education for Indian peoples, receiving both nursing and law degrees. She graduated with her JD from the University of Tulsa College of Law in 1979. In addition to her duties within her own tribe, Krepps has been active as a national officer of American Indian/Alaskan Native Nurses Association, staff attorney for Native American Coalition of Tulsa for Indian Child Welfare Act, state chairperson for the Indian Child Welfare Association, and secretary of the Native American Chamber of Commerce.

Krepps provides legal services to Indian tribes and individuals, contributing free legal counsel to obtain custody of Indian children for Indian parents, and has served as a family crisis counselor. She has presented testimony before the Committee on Equality of Education for Women, has been an advisor to the Ohoyo Resource Center, served on the Region VI Adoption Task Force, was the national essay winner for the Trial Lawyer's Association of the American Bar Association in 1979, and was an Oklahoma Conference presenter in 1981.

—Julie A. Russ

References

Krepps, Ethel C. *A Strong Medicine Wind.* Austin, TX: Western, 1979.
———. "A Strong Medicine Wind." *Oklahoma Memories,* edited by Anne Morgan and Rennard Strickland, 145–61. Norman: University of Oklahoma Press, 1981.
———. "A Strong Medicine Wind." *True West* 26 (March/April 1979): 7–10, 40–42.
———. "Equality in Education for Indian Women." *Wassaja/The Indian Historian* 13 (June 1980): 9–10.

L

LaDUKE, WINONA (b. 1959), an Ojibwa (Chippewa) Anishinabe, is an enrolled member of the Mississippi band from the White Earth Reservation, Minnesota. LaDuke lives in Canada with her husband Randy Kapashesit, a chief of the Moose Factory, Ontario, Cree band, and their daughter Waseyabin and son Ajawak. LaDuke also spends a few weeks several times a year on the northern Minnesota White Earth Reservation, her father's tribal homeland.

After her parents' divorce when LaDuke was five years old, she was raised by her mother. Today, her Chippewa father, Vincent LaDuke (Sun Bear), is a well-known New Age author. Her mother, Betty LaDuke, who is Jewish, is an artist and activist who has supported her daughter Winona's exploration of and identification with her Native background.

In 1982 LaDuke received a BA from Harvard in Native economic development. She also studied at the Massachusetts Institute of Technology, in 1983, in the Department of Urban Studies Community Fellows Program. LaDuke received her MA in rural development from Antioch University in 1989.

Winona LaDuke is a tireless author, economist, legal researcher, lecturer, and activist. She has published extensively on issues of Native economic development and on environmental and legal issues related to Native affairs. She speaks out for the social, political, economic, and environmental rights of other tribes besides her own. She has been involved in the resistance movement by the Big Mountain Diné (Navajo) who are fighting forced relocation from their ancestral homeland. Currently, LaDuke is expanding her scope to address concerns of indigenous peoples worldwide.

In 1989 LaDuke received one of the first international Reebok Human Rights Awards recognizing human rights activists under the age of thirty. With her award she initiated the White Earth Land Recovery Project, an effort which will return to tribal members some of the 830,000 acres of the White Earth Reservation that were promised to the original Chippewa settlers.

She is a member of the Women of All Red Nations (WARN) and president of the continental Indigenous Women's Network, support/activist groups which address specific needs of Native women. She is also steering committee representative of the International Council of Indigenous Women, a global organization seeking "Non-governmental Organization" status at the United Nations. Besides these groups, LaDuke is coordinator or board member of various other local and national organizations working for social change.

—Elizabeth A. McNeil

145

References

Fireweed: A Feminist Quarterly 22 (Winter 1986). Special Issue.

Florio, Maria, and Victoria Mudd. *Broken Rainbow*. 1985. Distributed by Earthworks Films.

LaDuke, Betty. "Winona: In Celebration of a Rite of Passage." *Woman of Power* 13 (Spring 1989): 32–33.

LaDuke, Winona. "Indian Treaty Rights Are a Critical Environmental Issue." *Utne Reader* 37 (January/February 1990): 57.

———. "In Honor of the Women Warriors." *off our backs* 11 (February 1981): 3–4.

———. "Interview with Roberta Blackgoat, a Diné Elder." *Woman of Power* 4 (Fall 1986): 29–31.

———. "The Political Economy of Radioactive Colonialism." *Union of Radical Political Economics* (Spring 1979): n.p.

———. "They Always Come Back." In *A Gathering of Spirit: A Collection by North American Indian Women*, 2d ed., edited by Beth Brant, 62–67. Ithaca, NY: Firebrand Books, 1988.

———. "The White Earth Land Struggle." International Working Group on Indigenous Affairs, Document No. 62 (January 1989).

———. "Words from the Indigenous Women's Network Meeting." *Akwesasne Notes* 17 (Winter 1985): 8–10.

———, and Ward Churchill. "Native America: The Political Economy of Radioactive Colonialism." *Insurgent Sociologist* 13 (Spring 1986): 51–78.

Levy, Paul. "The Land and the Blood." *Star Tribune Sunday Magazine*, 14 May 1989, 8–15.

LaFLESCHE FARLEY, ROSALIE (1861–1900) was born on the Omaha

Reservation in Nebraska in 1861, the second daughter of Joseph LaFlesche (Insta Maza, or Iron Eye), and Mary Gale (Hinnuagsnun, the One Woman). Joseph was half white and half Ponca, while Mary was white and Omaha. Iron Eye had become a chief of the Omahas in 1853, remaining in that position until 1866. He was an influential member of the tribe at a time of great transition and upheaval in its history. Joseph LaFlesche preached the doctrine of assimilation to his people and to his children, insisting that they must provide a white education for young members of the tribe and adopt white ways of living.

LaFlesche was one of four sisters who made an impact on the history of their people, the others being Susette, Marguerite, and Susan. Her half-brother, Francis, became a noted ethnologist. Like Iron Eye's other children, LaFlesche attended school on the reservation. While her three sisters went on to attend school in the East, LaFlesche remained behind; nonetheless, she played an important role in the drama that was unfolding on the reservation at the time. Two issues were debated hotly on the Omaha Reservation after the allotment of land in severalty was completed in 1884: leasing of unallotted tribal land and self-government for the tribe.

On one side of the issue stood LaFlesche and her husband, Ed Farley, along with Joseph and most of the rest of the LaFlesche family. Opposing them were Susette LaFlesche, or Bright Eyes, and her husband, Thomas H. Tibbles, a newspaperman and reformer. The Tibbles were outspoken in their belief that the Indians' best interests lay in citizenship and immediate assimilation into white society. LaFlesche and other family members believed in self-government for the Omaha, a system that would make them independent of both the federal government and the State of Nebraska. They contended further that leasing pasture land not used by the Indians would result in badly needed income for the tribe. Ed and Rosalie became the managers of a large tract of unallotted lands that they leased to white cattlemen in the area. They also managed the allotted lands of some Indians who wished to rent their property rather than work it. LaFlesche handled most of the business, including negotiating with the government and the tribe, handling accounts for individuals, and making contracts. The leased pasture led to several disagreements with white squatters and land speculators, but LaFlesche defended the tribe's interests vigorously. The self-government question was settled in 1887 when the Omahas were made citizens and came under the jurisdiction of the State of Nebraska.

Although she did not attain national prominence, Rosalie LaFlesche Farley was recognized as a leader of her people who was unafraid to speak out eloquently on their behalf.

—James W. Parins

References

Green, Norma Kidd. *Iron Eye's Family: The Children of Joseph LaFlesche*. Lincoln, NE: Johnsen Publishing, 1969.
LaFlesche Family Papers. Nebraska State Historical Society, Lincoln.

LaFLESCHE PICOTTE, SUSAN (1865–1915) was born on the Omaha Reservation in Nebraska on June 17, 1865, the daughter of Joseph LaFlesche (Insta Maza, or Iron Eye) and Mary Gale (Hinnuagsnun, or the One Woman). Iron Eye, a chief of the Omaha, was half white and half Ponca, while his wife was white and Omaha. The influential LaFlesche family supported bringing white education to the reservation and made certain that each of the children received a good education.

Susan LaFlesche attended school on the reservation, after which she followed her elder sister Susette to the Elizabeth Institute for Young Ladies in New Jersey. In 1882, three years after leaving for the East, she returned home to teach at the mission school. In 1884 LaFlesche began her studies at the Hampton Normal and

Agricultural Institute in Virginia, a school for blacks and American Indians, graduating with honors in spring, 1886. In October of that year, she entered the Woman's Medical College in Philadelphia. Susan LaFlesche excelled as a medical student, graduating at the head of her class in 1889. She thus became the first American Indian woman doctor of medicine.

LaFlesche returned to the Omaha Reservation upon completing a four-month internship in Philadelphia and worked as a physician at the local school. A few months later, she was appointed physician for the Omaha Agency, a post she served in from 1889 until 1893. The work was difficult, and her duties extended beyond the purely medical; she also served as advisor, teacher, interpreter, and nurse to the Omahas. In 1893 the young physician temporarily took leave from her position to care for her mother, who by this time was infirm. LaFlesche was in ill health herself by then, her condition no doubt worsened by her regimen of hard work, travel of long distances, often in inclement weather, and exposure to diseases of every kind.

Despite her ill health and against the advice of family and friends, LaFlesche announced her intention to marry Henry Picotte in 1894. Picotte was a Yankton Sioux, the brother of Charles Picotte, who had married Susan LaFlesche's sister Marguerite six years earlier. Susan LaFlesche Picotte and her husband settled in Bancroft, Nebraska, where she practiced medicine and he farmed. The couple had two sons, Caryl and Pierre. Even though her practice placed demands on her, Susan Picotte continued to serve her people during this period. She acted as interpreter and helped many families and individuals in the transition Omaha society was experiencing at the time.

After Henry's death in 1905, Picotte was appointed missionary to the Omahas by the Presbyterian Board of Home Missions. She had been active in the church in Bancroft and, after her appointment, continued to minister to the needs of the area's people. She was politically active as well and in 1910 headed a tribal delegation to the nation's capitol, where she addressed the Secretary of the Interior on the issues of citizenship and competency for the Omahas. But it was in the area of health care that Picotte made her biggest contribution. She insisted that the Omaha adopt modern hygienic practices and other preventive measures to halt the spread of disease. Further, soon after she moved to the new town of Walthill, she began a campaign to build a hospital for the people there. The facility was opened in 1913.

Susan LaFlesche Picotte served her people well in a variety of ways, administering to their physical, spiritual, and personal needs. She also repre-sented the Omahas well in white society, serving, from time to time, as their representative to the government. But more often, Picotte was the one who spoke for the Omahas in an unofficial but nonetheless clearly recognized capacity. She represented her people to disparate groups from the East and from Nebraska, ranging from women's clubs to missionary, educational, and medical organiza-

Paula Gunn Allen

Rountry/Williams

Tsianina Redfeather Blackstone

Eugene Hutchinson

Gertrude Simmons Bonnin

Sr. Genevieve Cuny

Diana Luppi

Joy Harjo

Amy Suber

Charlotte Anne Wilson Heth

Vi Hilbert

Joan Hill

Linda Hogan

Josette Juneau

Violet Chappell/Greg Sarris

Essie Parrish

Ken Olson

Agnes Picotte

Arthur Murata

Wendy Rose

Marquette University

Sacred White Buffalo,
Mother Mary Catherine

Virginia Driving Hawk Sneve

Leslie Marmon Silko

tions. Until her death in 1915, she was an effective role model for hundreds of young Omahas.

—James W. Parins

References

Clark, Jerry E., and Martha Ellen Webb. "Susette and Susan LaFlesche: Missionary." In *Being and Becoming Indian: Biographical Studies of North American Frontiers*, edited by James A. Clifton, 137–59. Chicago: The Dorsey Press, 1989.
Green, Norma Kidd. *Iron Eye's Family: The Children of Joseph LaFlesche*. Lincoln, NE: Johnsen Publishing, 1969.
LaFlesche Family Papers. Nebraska State Historical Society, Lincoln.
Mathes, Valerie Sherer. "Dr. Susan LaFlesche Picotte: The Reformed and the Reformer." In *Indian Lives: Essays on Nineteenth- and Twentieth-Century Native Americans*, edited by L. G. Moses and Raymond Wilson, 61–90. Albuquerque: University of New Mexico Press, 1985.
———. "Susan LaFlesche Picotte: Nebraska's Indian Physician, 1865–1915." *Nebraska History* 63 (1982): 502–30.

LaFLESCHE PICOTTE DIDDOCK, MARGUERITE (1862–1945)

was born on the Omaha Reservation, the daughter of Joseph LaFlesche (Insta Maza, or Iron Eye) and Mary Gale (Hinnuagsnun, or the One Woman). Her father was Ponca and white, and her mother was Omaha and white. LaFlesche attended school on the reservation as a youngster and later attended the Elizabeth Institute for Young Ladies in New Jersey, following in the footsteps of her older sister Susette. She was accompanied to the East by her sister Susan, and the pair remained at the Institute for three years. In 1882, after completing their course of study there, they returned to the reservation. LaFlesche took a job teaching at the Presbyterian mission school there.

In 1884 Marguerite and Susan again departed for the East, this time to Hampton, Virginia. It was there that they enrolled in the Hampton Normal and Agricultural Institute, a school for blacks and American Indians. LaFlesche studied in the Normal course at Hampton for a year before returning home. In 1886 she reentered Hampton and graduated in 1887. As part of the commencement ceremonies, LaFlesche read her senior composition, "Customs of the Omahas," a piece for which she had received special honors.

After graduation LaFlesche began her career as a teacher on the Omaha Reservation. While at Hampton, she had met Charles Felix Picotte, Jr., a Sioux, who had also become a teacher and was now back at the Yankton Agency. In late 1888 the two decided to marry. Picotte left Yankton to join his new wife in Nebraska, where she continued to teach, and he took up management of much of the family farm after the death of Joseph LaFlesche. During the winter of 1889–

90, Picotte accompanied Susette LaFlesche and her husband, Thomas H. Tibbles, to Pine Ridge, where they reported on the Ghost Dance Movement and the later violence at Wounded Knee. Picotte acted as interpreter for the two journalists until January, 1891, when he returned to the Omaha Reservation. By this time his health was failing rapidly; he died the next year.

LaFlesche continued to teach at the Omaha Agency government school. At the time, the agency's "Industrial Farmer" was Walter Diddock. In this position, he was in charge of the farm and of teaching agriculture to boys from the school. In time, the two became engaged and were married in June, 1895. Eventually, they built a house on the reservation at Walthill, near the home of Susan Picotte LaFlesche. It was here that they reared five children. During the first decades of the century, LaFlesche was active in the social, political, and educational affairs of the Omahas. She participated in negotiations with the federal government at the end of the trust period in 1910 and worked hard to bring library facilities to the area. She also served on the election board once the Nineteenth Amendment came into effect.

Marguerite LaFlesche Diddock lived until 1945; she died in the Susan Picotte Memorial Hospital.

—James W. Parins

References

Green, Norma Kidd. Iron Eye's Family: The Children of Joseph LaFlesche. Lincoln, NE: Johnsen Publishing, 1969.
LaFlesche Family Papers. Nebraska State Historical Society, Lincoln.

LaFLESCHE TIBBLES, SUSETTE [INSHTA THEAMBA, BRIGHT EYES] (1854–1903)

was born on the Omaha Reservation in Nebraska. Her father, Joseph LaFlesche (Insta Maza, or Iron Eye) was Ponca and French, and while he spent some of his early life working with his father as a trader, he eventually made his home with his Ponca mother, who lived with the Omahas. LaFlesche's mother was Mary Gale (Hinnuagsnun, or the One Woman), who was white and Omaha. The LaFlesche family was an influential one on the reservation, since Joseph had become chief in 1853, a post he held until 1866. The elder LaFlesche was an early advocate of white education for Omaha children and supported efforts by missionaries and others to establish schools among his people. He also saw to it that his children, Louis, Susette, Rosalie, Marguerite, and Susan, received an education; the children of his second wife, an Omaha woman named Ta-in-ne (Elizabeth Esau), were educated by white teachers as well.

LaFlesche attended the mission school on the reservation until 1869 when it closed. In 1872 she entered the Elizabeth Institute for Young Ladies in New Jersey, which was conducted by one of her former teachers. She was a good student, excelling in literature and writing; some of her school essays were published in a New York newspaper before her graduation in 1875. She returned to the reservation, intending to teach, but it was two years before she was able to secure a position at the government school, in spite of an Indian Service policy to give preference to properly qualified Indian applicants. She taught at the reservation school from 1877 to 1879.

During this time, events were unfolding among the Poncas, a neighboring tribe. In 1878, the Poncas were forcibly removed to the Indian Territory by the US Army. This action was of particular concern for the Omahas, who feared that if a peaceful group like the Poncas could be forced off their land despite their treaties, so could they. In addition, many of the Omahas had relatives among the Poncas; Bright Eyes's uncle, Joseph's brother White Swan, was a Ponca leader. During the winter of 1878–79, the Ponca chief, Standing Bear, led a party of his people back to the banks of the Niobrara River, their traditional home in Nebraska. When he was arrested and brought to trial in April 1879, the event caused a great stir among the Omahas. LaFlesche took up the Ponca cause and offered expert testimony at the trial. Her appearance there and her subsequent report on conditions among the Ponca people were to launch her career as a writer, orator, and defender of Indian rights.

During 1878 and 1879, LaFlesche and her half-brother Francis, who later became a noted ethnologist, visited the East with Standing Bear to bring the Poncas' plight to the attention of the public. The tour, organized by Thomas Henry Tibbles, assistant editor of the *Omaha Herald*, featured appearances by Standing Bear in traditional garb and the eloquent oratory of Bright Eyes, as she was billed. Tibbles, a former Army scout and preacher, organized the six-month tour, during which LaFlesche spoke to civic groups, Indian reform organizations, and literary clubs in Chicago, Pittsburgh, Boston, New York, and Washington, DC. Bright Eyes's fame spread as the group proceeded on their mission. At one point, Henry Wadsworth Longfellow attended her lecture, declaring that he had found Minnehaha. On the journey, she became friends with Helen Hunt Jackson, who later published *A Century of Dishonor*, and Alice C. Fletcher, who subsequently worked with Francis LaFlesche on several important ethnological projects. In March and December 1880, LaFlesche testified before the Senate concerning Ponca removal. Her clear and forceful remarks reflected her firsthand knowledge of the situation, acquired by her friendship with Standing Bear, her work as an interpreter among the Poncas, and her correspondence with Ponca leaders, such as White Swan.

After the death of Tibbles's wife, he and LaFlesche married. She continued her efforts on behalf of American Indians, working for citizenship and the allotment of land in severalty. LaFlesche and her husband visited England and Scotland in 1887 where she lectured extensively. In 1890 and 1891, the pair were at Pine Ridge where they reported on the events surrounding the Ghost Dance movement there and on the subsequent tragedy at Wounded Knee. LaFlesche published works in *St. Nicholas* and *Wide Awake* and contributed the introduction to William Justin Harsha's 1881 Indian reform novel, *Ploughed Under*. LaFlesche was a correspondent for the *Omaha World Herald* and later contributed to Tibbles's Populist newspaper, *The Independent*. Except for her year in Britain and a brief sojourn in Washington, DC, LaFlesche lived on or near the Omaha Reservation. Until her death in 1903, she used her considerable writing and speaking skills to fight for what she considered right for her people, in spite of differences of opinion with other family members.

—James W. Parins

References

Clark, Jerry E., and Martha Ellen Webb. "Susette and Susan LaFlesche: Reformer and Missionary." In *Being and Becoming Indian: Biographical Studies of North American Frontiers*, edited by James A. Clifton, 137–59. Chicago: The Dorsey Press, 1989.

Green, Norma Kidd. *Iron Eye's Family: The Children of Joseph LaFlesche*. Lincoln, NE: Johnsen Publishing, 1969.

LaFlesche Family Papers. Nebraska State Historical Society, Lincoln.

Wilson, Dorothy Clarke. *Bright Eyes: The Story of Susette LaFlesche, An Omaha Indian*. New York: McGraw-Hill, 1974.

LaROQUE, EMMA (b. 1949), of Cree/Métis descent, was born in Big Bay, Alberta. She received her BA from Goshen College (Indiana) in 1973, her MA in religion and Peace Studies in 1976, and an MA in Canadian history in 1980 from the University of Manitoba, where she is currently a professor of Native Studies.

LaRoque's 1975 handbook for educators of Native students, *Defeathering the Indian*, argues that since European contact Native peoples have been defined by outsiders of the dominant culture, a situation which has resulted in "psychological violence" against Native peoples in general and against Native schoolchildren in particular. Among the issues she explores with candor are the nature and result of stereotyping, the exclusion of Native and Métis people from Canadian history texts and the misinformation disseminated when they are included, the confusion between culture and heritage, and the possible negative results of intercultural education. She advocates the inclusion of Peace Studies in school curricula to end the cultural and individual stereotyping that is so damaging to the self-image of Indian children.

LaRoque is also a poet. Her work appears in *Canadian Literature* (Spring/Summer 1990). Her brief, imagist poems are inspired by her Cree heritage and the landscape of the Canadian plains. In "The Red in Winter," she evokes the beauty of the river in winter: "The blushing river the Cree called her/She wears no rouge today/She speaks no Cree/I ask about her other lifetimes/beneath her white mask." In "Nostalgia," she asks: "Where does it go/the log-cabins,/woodstoves and rabbit soups/we know/in our eight year old hearts?" And, in the ironically titled "Progress," she describes "Earth poet/So busy/weaving/magic/into words" whose artistry is obscured by "mad modern man" and his creations, the "cold steel spires/ stealing earth and sun/dance."

—Kathleen Donovan

References

LaRoque, Emma. *Defeathering the Indian*. Agincourt, AB: Book Society of Canada, 1975.

———. "Racism/Sexism and Its Effects on Native Women." In *The Canadian Human Rights Commission Report on Women and Racial Discrimination* (1990).

———. "Tides, Towns, and Trains." In *Living the Changes*. Manitoba: University of Manitoba Press, 1990.

LAVELL, JEANNETTE [CORBIERE-LAVELL, JEANETTE VIVIAN], an Ojibwa, was raised on the Wikwemikong Reserve in Ontario, Canada, on Manitoulin Island and has worked in Toronto as an executive secretary and a social worker at the Canadian Indian Centre of Toronto. In 1965 she was selected as Indian Princess Canada and later, with the Young Canadians, travelled extensively across Canada working with Native communities. She was one of the founding members and a president of the Ontario Native Women's Association and was elected as one of the vice-presidents of the Native Women's Association of Canada. She also served as president of both Nishnawbe Institute, an organization which promotes Native culture and its relevance to contemporary life, and Anduhyaun Inc., a residence for Native women in the city of Toronto. She studied for and received her teaching certificate and is still teaching today.

In 1970 Lavell lost her legal status as an Indian person through marriage. Subsequently, she decided to contest section 12(1)(b) of the 1951 Indian Act, which set forth that an Indian woman who marries a non-Indian is automatically deprived of her Indian status and her band rights from the date of her marriage. Under this act, male Indians who married non-Indians were still considered Indians, and their wives were also considered Indians, so the basis of Lavell's case was that the gender discriminatory provisions of section 12(1)(b) were contrary to the Canadian Bill of Rights, which guarantees protection of the law to all citizens regardless of race, sex, creed, etc. The case, which lost in the County Court and won in the Federal Court of Appeals, became a political vehicle for both the government and Native peoples and came before the Supreme Court of Canada in 1973 where it lost by one vote.

Though Lavell lost her case, she felt it a "victory and worth all the worry and anxiety it produced because now Native people as well as our political native organizations are looking at the whole question of Indian status and [band] membership." Indeed, the issue of Indian women's status acquired, for many people, the dimensions of a moral dilemma—the rights of all Indians against the rights of a minority of Indians—namely, Indian women. The case led, in 1975, to a joint Canadian National Indian Brotherhood Cabinet consultative committee to revise the Indian Act, and eventually, in 1985, to a revision of the Indian Act.

—Joni Adamson Clarke

References

Cheda, Sherill. "Indian Women." In *Women in Canada*, edited by Marylee Stephensen, 203–4. Toronto: General Publishing, 1977.
Jamieson, Kathleen. *Indian Women and the Law in Canada: Citizen Minus.* Ottawa: Canadian Government Publishing Centre, 1978.
Secretary of State. "Jeanette Corbiere-Lavell." *Speaking Together: Canada's Native Women.* Toronto: Hunter Rose, 1975.
Whyte, John D. "The Lavell Case and Equality in Canada." *Queen's Quarterly* 81 (1974): 28–41.

LAWSON, ROBERTA CAMPBELL (1878–1940), a noted leader in

women's clubs, was born at Alluwe, Cherokee Nation, a member of the well-known Journeycake family of Delawares. She was educated privately at home, in Independence, Missouri, and finally, at Hardin College in Mexico, Missouri, where she studied music.

From the time of her marriage to Edward B. Lawson in 1901, she was active in numerous local women's clubs and civic projects, first at Nowata and then Tulsa, where her husband's law practice and oil and banking interests took them. In 1917 she was elected president of the Oklahoma Federation of Women's Clubs, and thereafter, rose steadily through the ranks of the General Federation of Women's Clubs of America, holding a number of offices before she became president in 1935.

Lawson chose "Education for Living" as the theme of her administration, during which the General Federation favored the leveling of capital and labor, birth control, civil service and the merit system, and the control of venereal diseases. It also became the parent organization of the Women's Field Army for the American Society for the Control of Cancer, favored federal assistance to women who needed vocational training, and debated such issues as uniform marriage, divorce, and narcotics laws and revision of tax codes. Upon retirement from the presidency in 1938, Lawson returned to Tulsa, where she remained active in local club and civic affairs until her death.

Lawson's career included other significant achievements. She published *Indian Music Programs for Clubs and Special Music Days* and served as executive chair of the administrative committee for the Will Rogers charity fund for drought relief (1931) and on Eleanor Roosevelt's committee on Mobilization for Human Needs (1933–34). In 1933 she was also a member of the first World Federation Tour to Europe, where she gave performances of Indian music. In 1934 she was one of the General Federation's first delegates to the Pan-Pacific Conference. She was active throughout her career in the Presbyterian church and the Democratic party, and she was for many years a member of the board of regents of Oklahoma College for Women and of the board of trustees for the University of Tulsa.

—Daniel F. Littlefield, Jr.

References

Debo, Angie. "Roberta Campbell Lawson." In *Notable American Women 1607–1950: A Biographical Dictionary*, edited by Edward T. James, 376–77. Cambridge, MA: The Belknap Press of Harvard University Press, 1971.

Lawson, Roberta Campbell. *Indian Music Programs for Clubs and Special Music Days.* Nowata, OK: N.p., 1926.

Rainey, Luretta. *History of Oklahoma State Federation of Women's Clubs.* Guthrie, OK: Cooperative Publishing, 1939.

Tulsa Tribune, 31 December 1940: 1, 12.

LEWIS, LUCY (c. 1895–1992), an Acoma, was born around 1895 to Lola Santiago and Martin Ortiz and has lived most of her life on the high mesa at Sky City, Acoma Pueblo, in New Mexico. Lewis does not know her exact age or birthdate, but she celebrates her entrance into the world on November 2. In the 1960s Lewis was struck by lightning and survived, although at the time her fate was not sure. She attended McCarty Day School through the third grade and speaks Keresan. Lewis married Toribio Lewis (Hashkaya) and together they reared nine children. She is a nationally renown potter who learned her craft in the traditional manner at a very early age by watching her great aunt, Helice Vallo. Lewis received the Award of Merit at the first exhibition she entered at the 1950 Intertribal Indian Ceremonial in Gallup, New Mexico, and also first place at the Santa Fe Indian Market Competition in the same year. She has since received national acclaim and has permanent displays in museum collections and exhibitions. Her work toured the American embassies in Europe and the Near East, and she has been invited to the White House.

—Julie LaMay Abner

References

Collins, John. *A Tribute to Lucy M. Lewis, Acoma Potter.* Fullerton, CA: Museum of North Orange County, 1975.

Oleman, Minnie. "Lucy Lewis: Acoma's Versatile Potter." *El Palacio* 75 (1968): 10–12.
Peterson, Susan. *Lucy M. Lewis: American Indian Potter.* Tokyo: Kodansha International, 1984.
———. *Master Pueblo Potters.* New York: ACA Gallery Catalog, 1980.

LOLOMA, OTELLIE (b. 1922), like many Hopi children, made little unfired clay toys, but she received no formal or informal instruction until 1945 when she received a three-year scholarship to Alfred University in New York to study ceramics. Ironically, Loloma almost refused the scholarship in order to stay at Shipaulovi, her home on Second Mesa, where she worked as a substitute teacher at Shungopovi, Keams Canyon, Polacca, and Oraibi Day Schools. After returning from Alfred, Otellie Loloma also attended Northern Arizona University, Flagstaff, and the College of Santa Fe.

In the late 1950s, Otellie Loloma and her husband at the time, Charles, moved to Scottsdale, Arizona, where they perfected their crafts and opened the Kiva Craft Center. During the summers Loloma taught at Arizona State University, and in 1961 she was an instructor for the Southwest Indian Art Project at the University of Arizona, Tucson. In 1962 Otellie Loloma joined the faculty of the newly created Institute of American Indian Arts (IAIA), where she continues to teach.

During the 1960s Otellie Loloma's ceramics won wide critical acclaim, and she won prizes for her work at the Arizona State Fair, the Scottsdale Indian Art Exhibition, and the Philbrook Art Center, Tulsa, Oklahoma. Her work was also included in several exhibitions that traveled throughout the US, Latin America, and Europe. Consequently, her work is held in a number of permanent collections, such as the Museum of the American Indian, Heye Foundation, New York; the Heard Museum; Philbrook Indian Art Center; IAIA; and by many private collectors.

Otellie Loloma has executed work on canvas and in bronze and has designed jewelry, but it is in ceramics that she excels. The subject matter is subtly Hopi. There are human female forms with characteristic maiden whorls or buns above the ears, or bowls with masks or faces, but Loloma's manipulation of the clay is anything but Hopi. Some pieces are wheel thrown, others, especially the sculptures, are constructed; surfaces are textured and turquoise beads and leather dress the sculpture. However modern the treatment of the clay, Otellie Loloma's heritage transfuses it, as recorded by Monthan and Monthan: "When I start making a piece of pottery or a ceramic sculpture, I begin with an idea drawn from Hopi life and legends. As the piece progresses, the idea becomes part of the clay, subordinated to the overall design. In the finished piece the symbols may not be obvious, but they are there. They are like the seed: they have given their strength to make the plant grow."

Otellie Loloma's creative energies and time, however, are supplanted by the demands of her students at IAIA: "I stick with my students pretty close because of the fact that they are just now starting out. . . . If I'm going to make a creative artist out of them, I've got to be working close with them. . . . I'd rather have them come out of my class knowing something than me going out and doing my own exhibits, because I'm hired as an instructor, as a teacher."

—Laura Graves

References

Hammond, Harmony, and Juane Quick-to-See Smith. *Women of Sweetgrass, Cedar and Sage*. New York: Gallery of the American Indian Community House, 1985.
Loloma, Otellie. Interview. 8 January 1988. Manuscript Collection, Wheelwright Museum of Indian Art, Santa Fe.
Monthan, Guy, and Doris Monthan. *Art and Indian Individualism: The Art of Seventeen Contemporary Southwestern Artists and Craftsmen*. Flagstaff, AZ: Northland Press, 1975.
Nordness, Lee. *Objects: USA*. New York: Viking Press, 1970.

LONE DOG, LOUISE, resident of New York City and local spiritualist, is the author of *Strange Journey: The Vision Life of a Psychic Indian Woman*, a peculiar meld of 1960s metaphysics, traditional Indian spirituality, and Christianity. Self-professed to be of Mohawk and Delaware heritage, Lone Dog evinces much stereotypical but little legitimate tribal thinking in her work, a chronicle of her experiences with her spiritual guide, Chief White Feather, among others (including Joan of Arc and John Kennedy), along with various childhood reminiscences and psychic predictions. While the book exhibits vestigial, and possibly confused if not fraudulent, Native American traces, such as herbalism, homogenized Christian beliefs predominate, among such other disciplines as communion with "haunts" and astral projection. All are juxtaposed against ridicule of witchcraft and voodoo and skepticism of reincarnation and metaphysical organizations. Her volume, which concludes with testimonial letters from several New York women about primarily domestic predictions of Lone Dog, is perhaps best viewed as an artifact of the subjective and individual spiritual movements of the 1960s, in part influenced by the renewed popularity of such works as *Black Elk Speaks*.

—Rodney Simard

Reference

Lone Dog, Louise. *Strange Journey: The Vision Life of a Psychic Indian Woman*. Edited by Vinson Brown. Healdsburg, CA: Naturegraph, 1964.

LOWRY, ANNIE (1866–1943), a Northern Paiute, was born to Sau-tau-nee, who was called Susie, and Jerome Lowry, a white man, in Lovelock, Nevada. She said that the whites considered her just "plain old Paiute," and her Indian neighbors thought she acted as though she were better than they since she had adopted certain white customs, but in spite of that, she associated herself with her Paiute bloodline, feeling a great affinity for her tribe. To the white teachings, as she said, her mind was closed.

Under the auspices of the Writer's Project of the Works Progress Administration, Lalla Scott, a white woman, met Annie Lowry to record her version of local history and culture. Scott ultimately published this work as *Karnee: A Paiute Narrative*. In *Karnee* are recorded Lowry's memories of Sau-tau-nee's stories of Cap John's encounter with the first white men to enter the area of Pyramid Lake and the Humboldt River—men such as Peter Skene Ogden, Joseph Walker, and John C. Fremont. Lowry speaks of the last great Paiute Council in Nevada, traditional Paiute life and legends, and the battles at Pyramid Lake. She speaks of her own personal observations of her people's encounters with ranchers, miners, gamblers, and Chinese immigrants in Nevada. She speaks of boarding with whites to attend school in Lovelock and of the harshness of existence after she and her mother were abandoned by Jerome Lowry, and they were left to struggle to survive.

Lowry married a Paiute man named Sanny, and they had nine children, four of whom died young. Even though the words of this story are Lalla Scott's, there is an eloquence in the procession of experiences in the life of Annie Lowry, including the deaths of these children and Sanny, her first husband. She later married John Pascal, an English-speaking Paiute and mediator among the bands, and they lived out their lives in the Lovelock, Nevada, area.

In spite of, or perhaps because of, the "embeddedness" of the text—Lowry's story retold in Lalla Scott's words, "authenticated" by Eva Wasson Pancho and Mabel Summerfield (Lowry's daughters), introduced by Robert Heizer, obtrusively annotated and commented upon, even patronizingly contradicted, by Charles Craig—Lowry was a Paiute woman well worth knowing. Her story makes a fascinating analogue to that of Sarah Winnemucca (Hopkins).

—Gretchen Ronnow

References

Numa: A Northern Paiute History. Reno: Inter-Tribal Council of Nevada, 1976.
Scott, Lalla. *Karnee: A Paiute Narrative*. Reno: University of Nevada Press, 1966.

LOZEN (c. 1840–1890), Chiricahua Apache warrior woman, was born in Apacheria (New Mexico, Arizona, Northern Mexico) in approximately the 1840s. The sister of Victorio, famous Warm Springs Apache war leader, Lozen was remarkable among traditional Apache women in that she remained single and achieved honor and respect as a warrior and person of power.

According to Apache informants recorded by Eve Ball, Lozen's uniqueness was visible early in her life and revered by her tribespeople, who protected her from criticism for her breaking of gender behavior rules. As a child, she could outrun boys in foot races, but her ability was respected, not resented. At the time of her puberty ceremony, she was given Power to find the enemy, sensing their direction and distance by the intensity of a tingling sensation in her palms as she prayed with hands outstretched. She decided not to marry, but to devote her life to the aid of her people, who needed her greatly in the difficult years of the late nineteenth century, when they were constantly fighting Mexico and/or the United States. In addition to her talent for reconnaissance, Lozen also was reportedly an excellent shot, cunning strategist, knowledgeable healer, and effective messenger. Often acting as a shaman, she sang war songs and directed dances of war parties prior to their going into action.

At the time of the Tres Castillos massacre in Mexico in 1880, which decimated her brother Victorio's band and led to his death, Lozen was assisting a Mescalero Apache woman in childbirth and escorting her back to her people in New Mexico. Many Chiricahuas believed that the tragic ambush would not have happened if Lozen had been with them. Lozen was with Geronimo at the time of his final surrender; in fact, she was one of two women he sent as messengers to arrange a meeting with the American troops when he had decided to surrender. Lozen was among the Apaches sent as prisoners of war first to Fort Marion, Florida, in 1886, and then to Mount Vernon Barracks in Alabama in 1887. She died while the group was in Alabama, probably of tuberculosis.

—Helen M. Bannan

References

Ball, Eve, and Lynda Sanchez. "Legendary Apache Women." *Frontier Times* (October/November 1980): 8–12.

———, with Nora Henn and Lynda Sanchez. *Indeh: An Apache Odyssey*. Provo, UT: Brigham Young University Press, 1980.

———, with James Kaywaykla. *In the Days of Victorio: Recollections of a Warm Springs Apache*. Tucson: The University of Arizona Press, 1970.

Buchanan, Kimberly Moore. *Apache Women Warriors*. Southwestern Studies Series, no. 79. El Paso: Texas Western Press, 1986.

Cole, D.C. *The Chiricahua Apache 1846–1876, From War to Reservation*. Albuquerque: University of New Mexico Press, 1988.

Stockel, H. Henrietta. *Women of the Apache Nation*. Reno: University of Nevada Press, 1991.

M

MANKILLER, WILMA (b. 1946) is the first woman to become principal chief of the Cherokee Nation of Oklahoma. One of eleven children, Mankiller was born on "allotted" Oklahoma land to a full-blood Cherokee father and a Dutch-Irish mother. Her father was directly related to tribal members who were tragically removed from the southeastern Appalachian states in the 1838–1839 Trail of Tears forced emigration. In 1957, when Mankiller was twelve, her family was relocated to a low-income housing project in San Francisco because of a federal program that attempted to "urbanize" rural Indians. During the 1960s Mankiller married, had two children, and studied sociology at San Francisco State University. She attributes the 1969 takeover of the former prison at Alcatraz by the American Indian Movement, which was in protest to the US government's treatment of Native Americans, as changing the direction of her life.

Mankiller began doing volunteer work among Native Americans in the Bay Area during the 1970s, becoming angry at the historical and contemporary treatment of the Cherokee. The US government granted the Cherokees self-determination in 1975, and shortly afterwards, in 1977, Mankiller divorced and returned to Oklahoma with her children. She worked in community development, helping to obtain grants and introduce services in such areas as housing, employment, education, and health care. In 1979 another event changed the course of her life. A car accident left her face crushed, ribs broken, and legs shattered. After a series of operations and plastic surgery, she developed myasthenia gravis, which was followed by thymus surgery and steroid therapy.

Mankiller returned to work in December of 1980, a more introspective and dedicated advocate of the Cherokee Nation. Drawing upon humanistic and progressive precepts handed down by the Cherokee elders, she helped to obtain a grant to build a twenty-six mile waterline for the rural Cherokees. In 1983 she was asked to run for deputy chief and became the principal chief in 1985. In 1987 Mankiller was elected the first women Cherokee chief for a four-year term and was re-elected for four years, with eighty-three percent of the vote, in 1991.

Chief Mankiller's accomplishments in economic development, health care, and tribal self-governance are well known in the Native American community. While acknowledging the crises still faced by the Cherokee community, Mankiller's tireless advocacy of self-reliance and self-sufficiency continues to help her people achieve the goals so long denied them. Mankiller currently lives with her husband, Charlie Soap, and his son, Winterhawk, in Oklahoma.

—Laurie Lisa

References

Griffin, Connie. "Relearning to Trust Ourselves: An Interview with Chief Wilma Mankiller, Tahlequa, Oklahoma." *Women of Power* 7 (Summer 1987): 38–40, 72–74.
Wallis, Michael. "Hail to the Chief: Wilma Mankiller Is the First Woman to be Elected Cherokee Nation Chief." *Phillip Morris Magazine* (October 1989): 37–39.
Whittemore, Hank. "She Leads a Nation." *Parade Magazine*, 18 August 1991: 4–5.

MANN, HENRI [HENRIETTA WHITEMAN, THE WOMAN WHO COMES TO OFFER PRAYER] (b. 1934), educator, was born in Clinton, Oklahoma, the elder of two children of Leonora and Henry Mann, Sr., a Cheyenne farming family enrolled in the Cheyenne-Arapaho tribes of Oklahoma. Her early schooling in Oklahoma culminated in her BA in English education from Southwestern Oklahoma State University and MA in English from Oklahoma State University. The recipient of a Danforth Foundation Fellowship, she earned her PhD in American Studies from the University of New Mexico in 1982.

Mann has played a leading role in the development of Native American studies at the university level, emphasizing the importance of its connectedness to Indian communities and its role in fostering cultural continuity and student self-awareness. She began teaching at the University of California, Berkeley, in 1970, and later became coordinator of Native American Studies there. In 1972 Mann became director of Native American Studies at the University of Montana, a post she has held for eighteen years. During that time, she took leaves of absence to complete her doctorate, to teach at Harvard, and to serve for eighteen months in the Indian Education Office of the Bureau of Indian Affairs before she resigned in protest of Reagan administration policies in 1987. In 1991, she became a professor of Native American Studies at the University of Montana, freed from administrative responsibilities to devote more of her time to writing. She is now coordinator for American Indian Religious Freedom Coalition with the Association on American Indian Affairs.

In addition to her academic work, Mann has been active in service to her people. She has been a member of the business committee for the Cheyenne-Arapaho Tribal Council and has assisted in developing educational programs for the northern Cheyenne tribe of Montana. She has served on Indian education committees for the city of Missoula and the state of Montana, as a trustee of Bacone College, as well as on the boards of directors of several national Indian-oriented organizations. She has been honored as National American Indian Woman of the Year by the American Indian Heritage Foundation in 1988, Outstanding Woman in the greater Missoula area by the local YWCA in 1987, and as Cheyenne Indian of the Year at the American Indian Exposition in 1982.

Henri Mann is the mother of four children, one of whom died in young adulthood. An eloquent and sought-after speaker, she is truly bicultural; her knowledge of her Native Cheyenne heritage is as extensive as her academic background. She synthesizes both traditions in her life and in her work, consistently demonstrating the contemporary viability of traditional Native American culture and values. Nationwide, she is deeply respected as a person of insight, integrity, loyalty, and wisdom.

—Helen M. Bannan

References

Morton, Henri Mann, and James Prier Morton. "'Doctor'—Doctor." *Winds of Change* 5 (Winter 1990): 54–58.

Whiteman, Henrietta. "Cheyenne-Arapaho Education, 1871–1982." PhD diss., University of New Mexico, 1982.

———. "Insignificance of Humanity, 'Man Is Tampering with the Moon and the Stars': The Employment Status of Native American Women." In *Conference on the Educational and Occupational Needs of American Indian Women*, 37–61. Arlington, VA: National Institute of Education, 1980.

———. "Native American Studies, the University and the Indian Student." In *The Schooling of Native America*, edited by Thomas Thompson, 104–16. Washington, DC: American Association of Colleges for Teacher Education, 1978.

———. "White Buffalo Woman." In *The American Indian and the Problem of History*, edited by Calvin Martin, 162–70. New York: Oxford University Press, 1987.

MARACLE, LEE [BOBBI LEE] (b. 1950) was raised with her brothers and sisters by her Métis working mother in a poor North Vancouver neighborhood. In her adolescence she rejected the racism imposed upon her by dominant society, rebelled, dropped out of school, drifted into the hippie subculture, worked side by side with Chicanos in the western states, experienced drugs and drinking on skid row in Canadian urban centers, and finally became politically active in the Red Power Movement and later the Liberation Support Movement in and around Vancouver. Her as-told-to autobiography, based on eighty hours of tape, *Bobbi Lee: Indian Rebel*, was published by the Liberation Support Movement Press in 1975. As the straight record of the life of one of Canada's oppressed but fighting and resisting people, the autobiography is a celebration of Native survival and ranks with the autobiographical and political writings by fellow Métis authors/activists Maria Campbell and Howard Adams. Maracle's book had only limited circulation, went out of print for many years, and was reissued in an expanded version by the Women's Press in 1990. It was also published in a German translation by Trikont, a small publishing cooperative that existed in Munich in the 1970s.

From the time of her first publication until today, Lee Maracle has remained untiring as a cultural worker, writer, speaker, and political activist for the humanity of those oppressed by sexism, racism and capitalist exploitation. An extended stay in China showed her the strength and dignity a people can win through united struggle, built on solidarity against imperialist oppression and internal exploitation. In later years, Lee Maracle focused more and more on her development as a writer, drawing strength from a conscious return to her Native roots, a connecting with other Native authors throughout North America. She is presently a full-time student at Simon Fraser University, Vancouver. Besides, she workshops, teaches, and studies at En'Owkin Center, the first fully Native operated School of International Writing, in Penticton, British Columbia.

Her second book, I Am Woman, is the literary reflection of her struggle for liberation. It draws on the tradition of Big House oratory from the West Coast, as well as on feminism and theories of decolonization, bringing them together in one powerful individual voice that moves easily across the mental boundaries defined as "genre" by western literary criticism. In 1990 Lee Maracle contributed substantially to, and co-edited, Telling It: Women and Language Across Cultures. She has edited other Native authors (Rita Joe) and contributed to anthologies, journals, and magazines. She is one of the few Native authors who has been "around" for an extended time, and who has acquired international standing through her continued contribution to Native literature in Canada. Her latest work, Sojourner's Truth, is a collection of short stories, both modern and traditional.

Lee Maracle lives in Sardis with her husband, Dennis. Her daughters, Tania and Columpa, are already on the way to following the strong cultural and political commitments of their mother.

—Hartmut Lutz

References

Godard, Barbara. "The Politics of Representation: Some Native Canadian Women Writers." Canadian Literature 124–25 (Spring/Summer 1990): 183–225.

Grant, Agnes. "Contemporary Native Women's Voices in Literature." Canadian Literature 124–25 (Spring/Summer 1990): 124–36.

"Lee Maracle [Interview]." In Contemporary Challenges: Conversations with Canadian Native Authors, edited by Hartmut Lutz, 169–79. Saskatoon, SK: Fifth House, 1991.

Lee, S., L. Maracle, D. Marlatt, and B. Warland, eds. Telling It: Women and Language Across Cultures. Vancouver: Press Gang, 1990.

———. Bobbi Lee: Indian Rebel. 2d rev. ed. Toronto: Women's Press, 1990.

———. I Am Woman. Vancouver: Write-on Press, 1988.

———. Sojourner's Truth. Vancouver: Press Gang, 1990.

Petrone, Penny. Native Literature in Canada: From the Oral Tradition to the Present. Toronto: Oxford University Press, 1990.

MARTINEZ, MARIA MONTOYA [POVEKA, YELLOW POND LILY]

(1886–1980) was born in the Tewa Pueblo of San Ildefonso, New Mexico, the second of five daughters of Tomas and Reyecita Pena Montoya. Martinez was baptized Catholic, and as a child, made a pilgrimage to the Sancturio at Chimayo after recovering from smallpox. She attended St. Catherine's Indian School in Santa Fe for two years. She learned to make pottery as a child from her maternal aunt, Nicolasa. In 1904 she married Julian Martinez, and they spent their honeymoon at the St. Louis World's Fair—the first of countless times they would demonstrate Pueblo art and culture for Anglo observers. In 1907 Julian began working at the Pajarito Plateau excavations under the direction of Dr. Edgar Hewett. Julian copied pottery and wall designs from the ruins, and Martinez was asked to reproduce ancient pottery. They were encouraged in their experimentation by the Museum of New Mexico, where they lived and worked from 1909–12. Martinez shaped pots, and when he had finished his janitorial duties, Julian painted them, making famous the *avanyu*, or water serpent design. By 1919 they had developed the black-on-black, matte-and-polish pottery that initiated a major revival of Pueblo ceramics and made them and their Pueblo world famous. Martinez is generally regarded as the greatest of modern Pueblo potters. She is unquestionably the most photographed and written about and was, beginning in the mid-1920s, the first to sign her pots.

The Martinez family had four children who survived infancy: Adam, Juan, Tony, and Philip. After her husband's death in 1943, Martinez collaborated with her daughter-in-law Santana (wife of son Adam) and then, beginning in 1956, with her son Tony, who used his Indian name, Popovi Da. There are now six generations of the Martinez family "making their way with the clay," two of the most famous being grandson Tony Da and great granddaughter Barbara Gonzales. Among them, they have set new standards and styles for contemporary Pueblo pottery. Beginning with the first Santa Fe Indian Market in 1922, the pottery that Martinez made with various members of her family consistently won prizes and commanded the highest prices. In 1934 Martinez was the first Native American woman to receive a bronze medal for Indian Achievement from the Indian Fire Council. This was the first of many national and international awards and honors, including several honorary degrees and four visits to the White House.

Called the "Mother of the Pueblo," Martinez has been credited not only with keeping her family together and improving the economic conditions of her Pueblo, but also with reversing the process of deculturation by engendering a revolution in Pueblo ceramics that transformed a "craft" into an "art." Martinez and her pottery have become important links not only between the traditional and the modern, but also between Pueblo and Anglo-American cultures. Because of her, the role and position of the Native American artists and the valuation of indigenous art have substantially changed.

—Barbara A. Babcock

References

Gridley, Marion E. "Maria Martinez: Master Artisan." In *American Indian Women*, 105–18. New York: Hawthorn Books, 1974.

Marriott, Alice. *Maria, the Potter of San Ildefonso*. Norman: University of Oklahoma Press, 1945.

McGreevy, Susan Brown. *Maria: The Legend, The Legacy*. Santa Fe: Sunstone Press, 1982.

Nelson, Mary Carroll. *Maria Martinez*. Minneapolis: Dillon Press, 1974.

Peterson, Susan. *The Living Tradition of Maria Martinez*. Tokyo: Kodansha International, 1977.

Spivey, Richard. *Maria*. Flagstaff: Northland, 1979.

MAYO, SARAH JIM (c. 1860–1945) was a Washoe basket maker who introduced representational designs during the period of the flourishing of Washoe basketry. Her father, Captain Jim, was the most influential spokesman in dealing with the whites in the Carson Valley during the late nineteenth century. After the death of her husband in 1918, Mayo took back the prestigious name of her father. Her proud claims to a prestigious status might have led to some resistance from other women in the tribe.

Mayo's life followed the traditional pattern within the cultural context of the Washoe. In late spring and early summer, the Washoe camped on the south shore of Lake Tahoe; in the winter, they returned to Carson Valley. Mayo, like other women, worked in ranch houses as a domestic and bartered and sold her baskets to tourists. Her relationship with Margaretta (Maggie) Dressler, whose husband owned a large ranch in the Carson Valley, led to Dressler's large collection of Washoe baskets (many attributed to be Mayo's work but later not substantiated) and her photography of Mayo. Dressler also photographed a special basket that Mayo made to present to Woodrow Wilson in 1914 when Captain Pete Mayo led a delegation to Washington, DC, to argue land claims before the federal government. The present location of this basket is unknown.

Mayo introduced representational, or pictorial, designs around 1905, and this continued until around 1925 when her eyesight began to fail. Her designs (which are in contrast to Louisa Keyser's) are characterized by large-scale motifs that usually alternate in an *a b a b* pattern. The results are powerful and dramatic, with the pictorial images reaching the full size of the design field; she also combined the representational images in illusionistic settings and with narrative action and figure groupings. In addition, Mayo experimented with color. She added the brown of undyed bracken-fern root and experimented with yellow, green, gray, and willow dyed pink. The most documented of Mayo's artistry is from the period of 1913–18. However, she influenced a significant amount of the Washoe fancy basketry by most major weavers between 1912 and 1925.

—Laurie Lisa

References

Cahodas, Marvin. "Sarah Mayo and her Contemporaries: Representational Designs in Washoe Basketry." *American Indian Art Magazine* 6 (Autumn 1981): 52–59, 80.

———. "Washoe Innovators and Their Patrons." In *The Arts of the North American Indian: Native Traditions in Evolution*, edited by Edwin L. Wade, 203–20. New York: Hudson Hills Press, 1986.

McCLOUD, JANET (b. 1934) is a Tulalip woman whose name is synonymous with Indian activism. Born on the Tulalip Reservation, which was created in 1934 for the Duwamish, Suquamish, and other smaller tribes, she has lived in Yelm, Washington, since her marriage to Don McCloud (Puyallup/Nisqually). This mother of eight first came to national prominence as a result of her unceasing work on behalf of Indian fishing rights.

Beginning in January 1961, state officials arrested several Nisqually fishermen, in direct violation of longstanding treaties. Two of those arrested were McCloud's brothers-in-law. To maintain a constant presence in the boats, McCloud and other Native women took up fishing as soon as the men were arrested. After their release, the men returned to their boats, while McCloud returned to her efforts with the Survival of American Indians Association (which she organized in 1964).

By 1968 national Native rights groups were becoming active in the "fish-ins." Many local people, McCloud included, watched as so-called "outside Indians" slowly took over the protests. Eventually, the presence of celebrities turned this very serious issue into a media circus. However, bigger headlines loomed elsewhere, and McCloud and her sisters persevered until they were again at the helm of their own movement.

Now widely known herself, Janet McCloud was drawn into the national arena to work for better Indian education, preservation of cultures, languages and religions, and the rights of Native prisoners. Soon after working on the Native American Rights Fund book, *Our Brother's Keeper* (1975), she helped organize the Brotherhood of Indian Prisoners. Concerned with the loss of traditions, and startled by the increase in the number of Native women being sterilized, she founded and is still a coordinator for the Northwest Indian Women's Circle. Her lifetime efforts have been rewarded with her placement in the Elders Circle, an intertribal elders council that strives to keep traditions alive. Her most recent project has been to expose "plastic medicine men," those who commercialize Native religions.

—Cynthia Kasee

References

Bomberry, Dan, ed. "Sage Advice from a Longtime Activist." *Native Self-Sufficiency* 6 (1981): 4–5, 20.

Churchill, Ward. "Spiritual Hucksterism." *Z Magazine* (December 1990): 94, 96–98.

Josephy, Alvin M., Jr. *Now That the Buffalo's Gone.* New York: Alfred A. Knopf, 1982.

Payne, Diane. "Each of My Generations Is Getting Stronger: An Interview with Janet McCloud." *Indian Truth: Special Issue on Native Women* 239 (May/June): 5–7.

Vogel, Virgil J. *This Country Was Ours.* New York: Harper and Row, 1972.

McDANIEL, WILMA ELIZABETH (b. 1918), a poet of Anglo-Cherokee descent, is a native of Stroud, Oklahoma. The daughter of sharecroppers, McDaniel grew up in the Creek Nation during the Great Depression. She migrated to California's San Joaquin Valley during the Dustbowl Exodus of the 1930s and since settling there has composed a short novel, several collections of stories, and more than a dozen volumes of poetry. She has also written a regular column for *The Valley Voice*, a central California newspaper. Her work, which James D. Houston has termed "absolutely unique and magical," not only reflects her Creek heritage, but chronicles a childhood lived on the cusp of poverty in rural Oklahoma and years of toil as a migrant worker in central California. It speaks to us through language richly colloquial ("Ain't this something, Papa," says Melvin in "Progress," "five years in California/and we have went/from fresh fruit on our/table/to wax apples in a bowl"), conveying not merely a verisimilitude of place and person but a universal vision of a world where suffering is mitigated by hope.

—Eric Severson

References

Cox, Carol. Review of *Toll Bridge,* by Wilma Elizabeth McDaniel. *American Book Review* (May/June 1981): 8.

Haslam, Gerald W., and James D. Houston, eds. *California Heartland; Writing from the Great Central Valley.* Santa Barbara, CA: Capra Press, 1978.

Kates, J. Review of *Sister Vayda's Song,* by Wilma Elizabeth McDaniel. *Village Voice,* 25 January 1983: 42.

McDaniel, Wilma Elizabeth. *Day Tonight/Night Today Presents Wilma Elizabeth McDaniel: A Special Issue of Selected Short Stories.* Hull, MA: Day Tonight/Night Today, 1982.

———. *The Fish Hook: Okie and Valley Prose and Poems.* Big Timber, MT: Seven Buffaloes Press, 1978.

———. *A Girl from Buttonwillow*. Stockton, CA: Wormwood Books and Magazines, 1990.

———. *Going Steady with R.C. Boley*. Portlandville, NT: MAF Press, 1984.

———. *I Killed a Bee for You*. Marvin, SD: Blue Cloud Quarterly, 1987.

———. *The Peddlers Loved Almira*. Tulare, CA: Stone Woman Press, 1977.

———. *A Primer for Buford*. Brooklyn: Hanging Loose Press, 1990.

———. *The Red Coffee Can: Poems and Stories of the Unique Spirit of a San Joaquin Valley People*. Fresno, CA: Valley Publishers, 1974.

———. *Sand in My Bed*. Tulare, CA: Stone Woman Press, 1980.

———. *This Is Leonard's Alley*. Tulare, CA: Stone Woman Press, 1979.

———. *Toll Bridge*. New York: Contact II, 1980.

———. *The Wash Tub: Stories of a People Who Knew the Wash Tub as an Integral Part of Life in America*. Fresno, CA: Pioneer, 1976.

———. *Who Is San Andreas: Poems to Survive Earthquakes*. Marvin, SD: Blue Cloud Quarterly, 1984.

Shafarzek, Susan. "Small Press Roundup: Best Titles of 1982." *Library Journal* 107 (1982): 2306.

McKAY, MABEL (b. 1907) was born on a ranch in Nice, Lake County, California, where her father, Yanta Boone, a Potter Valley Pomo, worked as a ranch hand. Shortly after McKay's birth her mother, Daisy Hansen, a Long Valley Cache Creek Pomo (often referred to by ethnographers as Patwin) moved with McKay to Rumsey. There McKay was raised by her maternal grandmother, Sarah Taylor, whose brother Richard Taylor initiated, in 1871, the revivalistic Bole Maru and Bole Hesi movements among the Pomo and Southwestern Wintun. Richard Taylor was the first Bole Maru (Dream Dance) doctor and prophet; Mabel McKay would be the last.

McKay began dreaming at the age of five and began her work as medicine woman at age eighteen. Among the Pomo, she is the last sucking doctor, that is, a doctor who combines song, hand power, and sucking to cast out disease. She began weaving basketry at age seven and today is regarded as the foremost Pomo basketweaver. Her basketry is associated with power and prophecy; she dreams the designs and patterns and follows strict rules with her art. She is especially well known for her miniatures and feather baskets, which are held in permanent collections in museums in this country and in Europe.

Today McKay is the last living representative of the Long Valley Cache Creek Pomo, and therefore, the last to speak the language and know the history and culture of her people. She has been hounded by countless linguists, art historians, folklorists, anthropologists, and others interested in her life and work. McKay has taught basketry for nearly fifty years and has lectured in numerous colleges and universities. California State Governor Jerry Brown appointed McKay to the first board of the Native California Heritage Commission, through which she served for many years. In her lectures and interactions with others, McKay is known for her witty remarks, through which she reminds people that she is not merely a relic from a lost past but a contemporary woman living her life in a world shared by others. "You are an Indian doctor," a student once said. "What do you do for poison oak?" McKay answered, "Calamine lotion."

McKay married Charles McKay, a Wintun Indian, and they adopted a son, Marshall. Charles McKay died when Marshall was quite young, so McKay worked many years in the local apple canneries to support herself and Marshall. However, she never stopped doctoring and weaving and she worked closely with the Kashaya Pomo dreamer, Essie Parrish. As another Pomo once said, "McKay is the old way. She is our history, our hope, our power."

—Greg Sarris

References

Sarris, Greg. "On the Road to Lolsel." *News From Native California* 2 (Sept/Oct 1988): 3–6.

———. Personal Communication with Mabel McKay. Santa Rosa, CA, and vicinity, 1957–present.

———. "Strawberry Festival." *National Women's Studies Association Journal* 2 (Summer 1990): 408–24.

———. "The Verbal Art of Mabel McKay." *MELUS* 16 (Spring 1991): 95–112.

MEDICINE, BEATRICE A. (b. 1924), a Lakota (Sioux) Sihasapa, born on the Standing Rock Reservation, Wakpala, South Dakota, has recently retired from her career as anthropologist, teacher, and author.

Medicine is a nationally known scholar who has worked to dispel anthropological myths which have tended to oversimplify and homogenize Native American cultures. Through her writings and teaching, Medicine has opened a way toward establishing a more realistic picture of the plurality and diversity of Native American life—past and present—from real, complex, Native American perspectives. Medicine has been especially interested in the changing American Indian family and in Native American women's roles, real and perceived, past and present.

Medicine received a BS at South Dakota State University and later went on to receive her MA and PhD degrees from Michigan State University. She has taught at many universities and has directed Native American studies programs, including the Native American Studies Program at San Francisco State College and the Native Centre at the University of Calgary, Alberta. She has been awarded numerous fellowships and other honors and has been a member of many US and Canadian organizations in her areas of interest. Besides her work as a teacher and scholar, Medicine has dedicated herself to helping to develop Indian leadership and to establish urban Indian centers.

Even though Medicine has lived in an academic atmosphere, she has always maintained strong ties to her reservation home. She has involved herself in political matters as well as in traditional religious and ceremonial events. Medicine was chosen Sacred Pipe Woman in the revival of the Lakota Sun Dance in 1977. Married and later divorced, Medicine has also brought up her son, Clarence, in traditional Lakota culture.

—Elizabeth A. McNeil

References

Albers, Patricia, and Beatrice Medicine, eds. *The Hidden Half: Studies of Plains Indian Women.* Washington, DC: University Press of America, 1983.

Gridley, Marion E., ed. and comp. *Indians of Today.* 4th ed. Chicago: ICFP, 1971.

Medicine, Beatrice. "American Indian Family: Cultural Change and Adaptive Strategies." *Journal of Ethnic Studies* 8 (Winter 1981): 13–23.

———. "The Anthropologist as the Indian's Image Maker." *Indian Historian* 4 (Fall 1971): 27–29.

———. "The Changing Dakota Family and the Stresses Therein." *Pine Ridge Research Bulletin* 9 (1969): 1–20.

———. "Child Socialization Among Native Americans: The Lakota (Sioux) in Cultural Context." *Wicazo Sa Review* 1 (Fall 1985): 23–28.

———. "An Ethnography of Drinking and Sobriety Among the Lakota Sioux." PhD diss., University of Wisconsin at Madison, 1983.

———. "Higher Education: A New Arena for Native Americans." *Thresholds in Education* 4 (1978): 22–25.

———. "Ina, 1979." In *A Gathering of Spirit: A Collection by North American Indian Women,* edited by Beth Brant, 109–11. 2d ed. Ithaca, NY: Firebrand Books, 1988.

———. "Indian Women: Tribal Identity as Status Quo." In *Women and Nature,* edited by R. Hubbard and M. Lowe, 63–73. New York: Pergamon Press, 1983.

———. "Native American (Indian) Women: A Call for Research." *Anthropology and Education Quarterly* 19 (1988): 86–92.

———. *The Native American Woman: A Perspective.* Austin, TX: National Educational Laboratory Publishers, 1978.

———. "Professionalization of Native American (Indian) Women: Towards a Research Agenda." *Wicazo Sa Review* 4 (Spring 1988): 31–42.

———. "Role and Function of Indian Women." *Indian Education* 7 (January 1977): 4–5.

———. "The Role of Women in Native American Societies: A Bibliography." *Indian Historian* 8 (Summer 1975): 50–53.

MEDICINE FLOWER, GRACE [WOPOVI POVIWAH, TAFOYA] (b.

1938) was born Grace Tafoya on December 13 at Santa Clara Pueblo, New Mexico, into a distinguished family of potters that includes Camilio Tafoya (her father), Agapita Silva (her mother), Joseph Lonewolf (her brother), and Margaret Tafoya (her aunt and father's sister). Fluent in Tewa, she learned English in elementary school at Santa Clara Day School and graduated from nearby Espanola High School in 1957, after which she took a secretarial course at Brownings Commercial School.

In 1962 Medicine Flower returned to Santa Clara to take up pottery full-time, studying with her father. Her first pieces included miniature bowls and turtles in a plain style with either a highly polished red or black glaze.

In the late 1960s, she began carving her ceramic pieces, and in the mid 1970s, she began to etch the surfaces of her pottery with a technique called *sgraffito*, for which she and her brother have become famous. *Sgraffito* is a delicate form of incising the surface of a pot so that the design is literally scraped away from the slip that has been applied to the pot and polished to a high sheen before it is fired. By refining this technique with consummate skill, Medicine Flower transformed pottery making into fine art, assuring herself a permanent place in Pueblo pottery history.

Her designs are integrated to the shape of the pot and may include such delicate and intricate figures as butterflies, hummingbirds, flowers and deer, or the more "traditional" designs of kiva steps, bear paws, water serpents, and feathers. In the style of her ancestors, she gathers the materials for clay, temper, and slips from the surrounding land of her reservation, handbuilds her pots, and fires them outside. In addition to the classic Santa Clara red, tan, and black colors, she has introduced a range of pastels to her pots, including subtle purples and greens that bring out the details of her floral motifs.

From an interview with Jane Katz in 1978, Medicine Flower describes how she makes a pot:

> We go to the hills near Santa Clara to get enough clay for a whole season. . . . We put the clay in the sun to dry, soak it in water for about three days, then put it through a fine screen to get all the impurities out. . . . When the clay has just the right consistency, I begin my pot, using the old coil method. I mold the coils by hand, then use gourds to smooth them. After the pot is formed and completely dry—that takes days—I sandpaper it and wet it down to remove the sandpaper lines. I cover the bowl with a red earth clay. . . . I hand-polish the bowl with stones. . . .
>
> Then it's time to incise designs onto the pot, freehand. . . . I use knives and special tools . . . . fashioned from nails.
>
> The firing is done in the open on the ground. It has to be a really calm day, with no wind. . . . We put wood chips on the ground. Tin cans hold a steel grate, and a wire basket containing the pots is placed on the grate.

. . . You have to watch the fire carefully. If the wind blows and soot gets on the pot, it is ruined.

The recipient of dozens of awards over the years, Medicine Flower was especially honored in February, 1974, when she was selected as one of twenty-eight Hopi and Pueblo artists to be invited to the White House. Again in 1974, she was included in the important "Seven Families in Pueblo Pottery" show at the Maxwell Museum of Anthropology at the University of New Mexico. And in 1976, she became one of seven artists chosen for the American Indian Artists Film Series produced by PBS.

—Dexter Fisher Cirillo

References

Arnold, David. "Pueblo Pottery—2000 Years of Artistry." *National Geographic* 162 (November 1982): 593–605.
DeLauer, Marjel. "Joseph Lonewolf and Grace Medicine Flower." *Arizona Highways* 52 (August 1976): 42–43.
Houlihan, Patrick T. "Southwestern Pottery Today." Special Edition of *Arizona Highways* 50 (May 1974): 2–6.
Jacka, Jerry, and Lois Essary Jacka. *Beyond Tradition: Contemporary Indian Art and Its Evolution.* Flagstaff, AZ: Northland, 1988.
Katz, Jane. *This Song Remembers—Self Portraits of Native Americans in the Arts.* Boston: Houghton Mifflin, 1980.
LeFree, Betty. *Santa Clara Pottery Today.* Albuquerque: University of New Mexico Press, 1975.
McCoy, Ron. "Homage to the Clay Lady." *Southwest Profile* (March 1990): 21–23.
Monthan, Guy, and Doris Monthan. *Art and Indian Individualists.* Flagstaff, AZ: Northland Press, 1975.
Seven Families in Pueblo Pottery. Albuquerque: University of New Mexico Press, 1974. Catalogue from show at the Maxwell Museum of Anthropology.
Trimble, Stephen. *Talking with the Clay—The Art of Pueblo Pottery.* Santa Fe, NM: School of American Research Press, 1987.

MEDICINE SNAKE WOMAN [NATAWISTA] (1825–1893), a Blood woman, daughter of Men-Es-To-Kos or Father of All Children, played an important role in maintaining peaceful relations between factions around Fort Union in the Upper Missouri (Montana) between 1840 and 1858. She was married to the "bourgeois . . . 'Major' Culbertson" sometime in 1840 at the age of fifteen. They had five children, Jack, Julia, Nancy, Fannie, and Joseph. Fannie drowned sometime after 1851 in the Missouri, resulting in the removal of the other children to convents and military schools for their education.

Her brother, Seen-From-Afar, rose to the position of head chief of the Blood tribe. Her cousin, Little Dog, was head chief of the Piegan tribe. She assisted

Lewis Henry Morgan, an early anthropologist, when he traveled up the Missouri in 1862 by furnishing him with information on Blackfoot and Gros Ventre kinship systems. Governor Isaac Stevens chose Culbertson to accompany and assist his Pacific Railway survey party because of Culbertson's relationship with Medicine Snake Woman. White fear of "those 'most bloodthirsty Indians of the Upper Missouri'" was allayed by Medicine Snake Woman, who "mixed with the Indians, kept them in good spirits . . . listened to their conversations, and reported their reactions to Governor Stevens through her husband."

She was described by white men who met her as beautiful and intelligent. She loved wearing "white women's gowns" and was fond of colorful jewelry. Her skills as hostess, horsewoman, swimmer, porcupine quillworker, and diplomat helped bridge the two worlds of Anglo-American men and the indigenous peoples with whom she remained close.

Medicine Snake Woman and Culbertson first retired to Peoria, Illinois, in 1858, after he had amassed a fortune in the Indian trade. However, their fortune was soon dissipated, and they returned to the Upper Missouri in 1868. She never learned to speak English, and after living in the white world in lavish style, she left Culbertson, disillusioned, to return to her own people. She lived in the log house of her nephew, Chief Old Moon, and ultimately drew a regular Indian ration from the Canadian government. She died on the Blood Reserve in 1893 and was buried in the Indian cemetery near Standoff, Alberta.

—Renae Moore Bredin

References

Ewers, John E. *Indian Life on the Upper Missouri*. Norman: University of Oklahoma Press, 1968.
————. "Mothers of the Mixed-Bloods." *El Palacio, A Quarterly Journal of the Museum of New Mexico* 69 (1964): 20–29.
McDonnell, Anne. "Mrs. Alexander Culbertson." *Contributions to the Montana State Historical Society* 10 (1941): 243–46.
Morgan, Lewis Henry. *Lewis Henry Morgan, The Indian Journals, 1859–62*, edited by Leslie A. White. Ann Arbor: University of Michigan Press, 1959.

MODESTO, RUBY (1913–1980) was born at Martinez Reservation in the Coachella Valley of southern California. Her father was one of the Desert Cahuilla people from this area, while her mother was a Serrano woman from Morongo Reservation. Their family was known as the Dog Clan. Modesto's mother took her to the Moravian church on the reservation, and Modesto considered herself a Christian until she later became a Cahuilla *pul* or medicine woman. She then felt a need to choose between Christianity and the ancient belief of her people that "the power of a *pul*, the Dream Helper, comes from *Umna'ah*," because it became clear to her that the Christians considered her shamanistic power as witchcraft rather than the blessing she felt it to be.

Modesto's father, grandfather, and great grandfather had all served as clan *nets*, or ceremonial leaders, and many of her uncles and grand-uncles were medicine men. Her grandfather Francisco was the last to maintain a *kiva* before the clan adopted "the whiteman's law." Although she lived with her husband David and their family, Modesto described him as her companion and asserted that as a shaman she was dependent only on *Umna'ah*.

Besides her shamanistic services to her clan, Modesto also taught Cahuilla language classes in the Martinez tribal hall. She often provided information to anthropologists, even co-authoring one article, and she guest-lectured at local colleges even before she met Guy Mount in 1976, with whom she collaborated to create *Not for Innocent Ears*, a book designed for educational purposes and in which Modesto hoped to preserve accurate information about her people and her own spiritual beliefs. Her Uncle Charlie, also a *pul*, provides many of the examples of shamanistic ceremonies in the book, but her own autobiographical information and the Cahuilla folktales she recounts offer the most comprehensive picture of her people. The book was published in 1980, shortly after Modesto died on April 7 of that year.

—Thelma J. Shinn

References

Lando, Richard, and Ruby E. Modesto. "Temal Wakish: A Desert Cahuilla Village." *The Journal of California Anthropology* 4 (1977): 95–112.

Mount, Guy, and Ruby Modesto. *Not for Innocent Ears*. Angelus Oaks, CA: Sweetlight Books, 1980.

Wilke, Phillip J. *Late Prehistoric Human Ecology at Lake Cahuilla: Coachella Valley, California*. Contributions of the University of California Archaeological Research Facility, no. 38. Berkeley: UC Department of Anthropology, 1978.

MOMADAY, NATACHEE SCOTT (b. 1913) is a retired teacher, poet, and painter. Born in Fairview, Kentucky, of Cherokee, French, and English descent, she was educated at Haskell Junior College, Crescent College, and the University of New Mexico. She became a teacher and aspired to be a newspaper reporter. A woman of incredible beauty, she married in 1933, had her only child in 1934, and taught at various remote schools in the Southwest. She began teaching at the Jemez Day School on the Jemez Springs, New Mexico, Reservation in 1936, where she taught for twenty-five years. For this service, she was awarded the Bureau of Indian Affairs Service Medal for outstanding achievement. In 1954 she received a BA from University of California, Los Angeles. In 1975 the University of New Mexico awarded her a Doctorate in Humane Letters.

Since retirement, she has divided her energy between writing, painting, and lecturing. Her children's books include *Woodlawn Princess*, *Velvet Ribbons*, and *Owl in the Cedar Tree*, about a Navajo boy who paints the stories of his grandfather. In 1972 Momaday edited a critically acclaimed reader for the classroom, *American Indian Authors*, which is thought to be the first such collection of traditional and contemporary stories by Native authors. She has lectured at New York University, City University of Toulouse, and Oxford University. Her paintings in oil and pastel have won prizes in various art shows across North America, and she also works in pen and ink and charcoal.

She is the widow of Al Momaday (illustrator of *The Way to Rainy Mountain*) and mother of Pulitzer Prize-winning novelist, poet, and painter N. Scott Momaday. (Due to the similarity of their names, Natachee Scott Momaday's work is sometimes erroneously identified as her son's.) In 1978 the American Association of University Women named Momaday as one of thirteen women in New Mexico with outstanding cultural contributions to New Mexico and the Southwest. She currently lives in seclusion in the Jemez Mountains with her Belgian police dogs and a very protective black cat.

—Jay Ann Cox

References

Momaday, Natachee Scott. *American Indian Authors*. Boston: Houghton Mifflin, 1972.
———. *Owl in the Cedar Tree*. Illustrated by Don Perceval. San Francisco: Northland Press, 1975.
Momaday, N[avarro] Scott. *The Names: A Memoir*. New York: Harper and Row, 1976.

MOREZ, MARY (b. 1943) is a Navajo painter, and her work reflects the way

in which she has integrated the disparate events of her life into a cohesive whole. Mary Morez was born near Tuba City, Arizona, on the Navajo Reservation where she lived with her parents and, following their deaths, with her grandparents. As a young child she moved to Phoenix, Arizona, to live with her adopted family. As a child Morez spent some time in a Chicago hospital undergoing polio-related surgery. Following her return to Phoenix, she graduated from Phoenix Indian School in 1960, entered the University of Arizona and attended the Ray Vogue School of Art in Chicago, where she majored in fashion illustration. After she graduated in 1963 she worked as a fashion illustrator and draftsman until turning to painting full-time in 1969.

Morez's paintings reflect her bicultural education and experiences. Unlike a number of Navajo artists, her subjects are not confined to reservation scenes or the problems of the culturally disenfranchised. Instead Morez explores the abstractions of what it means to her to be Navajo. Although her treatment of this complex topic clearly reflects the influences of Picasso and Kandinsky, the elements are distinctly Navajo. Mary Morez's work transcends cultural and tribal boundaries and successfully explores the universality of human experiences, and in this sense, her work reflects her Navajo beliefs and her Navajo sense of herself.

Another theme in Mary Morez's life centers around the Phoenix Indian Hospital where she is a volunteer. After suffering through her own traumatic hospital visit as a child, Morez attended her second husband, Bill, as he suffered and succumbed to cancer. She has been honored there as "Outstanding Volunteer," is a past inductee in the Phoenix Indian School's Hall of Fame, and has been recognized for her contributions to Indian education at Camelback High School in Phoenix. She is also the former curator of fine arts at the Heard Museum.

Since 1970 when she held her first one-woman show at the Heard Museum, her work has been shown at the Wheelwright Museum in Santa Fe, the Navajo Tribal Museum in Window Rock, and the Native American Art Gallery in New York, among many other museums and galleries. Of her life, Morez said, "When I grow old I want to know I've left something behind. Not as an artist, but as a human being who loves and cares and tends and helps other human beings. To do that is to walk in beauty."

—Laura Graves

References

Chase, Katherine. "Navajo Painting." *Plateau* 54 (1982): 24.
Katz, Jane B. *This Song Remembers: Self-Portraits of Native Americans in the Arts.* Boston: Houghton Mifflin, 1980.
"Navajo Artist will be Honored at Museum." *Navajo Times* 28 September 1983.
Niemi, K. Untitled Manuscript. Wheelwright Museum of Indian Art, 1978.
Warner, John Anson. "Continuity Amidst Change: The Navajo Artist Mary Morez." Manuscript collection. Wheelwright Museum, Santa Fe, NM.

MOUNTAIN WOLF WOMAN [LITTLE FIFTH DAUGHTER, XEHACIWINGA, HAKSIGAXUNUMINKA] (1884–1960), a Winnebago,

tells her life story—which demonstrates a remarkable ability to value her traditional culture and yet readily adapt to the changes presented to her by the twentieth century in *Mountain Wolf Woman, Sister of Crashing Thunder.* Born into the Thunder Clan at East Fork River, Wisconsin, she was cured as a child of a life-threatening illness by a woman named Wolf Woman and was thereafter given her name. Her family moved to Black River Falls, and later she attended school for two years in Tomah, Wisconsin. When her family moved to Wittenburg, Wisconsin, she changed schools, remaining there only a short time before she married. Her first marriage, arranged by her brother and against her wishes, ended after the birth of her second child; she remained in Black River Falls until her marriage to Bad Soldier. After her second marriage, Mountain Wolf Woman moved several times to find better employment or housing situations and took several shorter trips to trap muskrats, to dig yellow water-lily roots, to hunt deer, or to pick blueberries and cranberries. She had eleven children, three of whom died, several grandchildren and great-grandchildren. She was one of the first Winnebago women to own a car and once took a train to Oregon to visit her daughter. At seventy-four, she flew to Michigan to collaborate on her life story with anthropologist Nancy Lurie.

Mountain Wolf Woman was raised as a traditional Winnebago and participated faithfully in Winnebago ceremonies, including the Scalp Dance and the Medicine Dance. She was also a practicing Christian but counted as her most significant experience her conversion to the Native American Church and her participation in peyote meetings. She died quietly in her sleep on November 9, 1960, at Black River Falls and was given a funeral which epitomized her allegiance to all three religions.

—Joni Adamson Clarke

References

Bataille, Gretchen, and Kathleen Mullen Sands. "Culture Change and Continuity: A Winnebago Life." In *American Indian Women Telling Their Lives*, 69–82. Lincoln: University of Nebraska Press, 1984.

Mountain Wolf Woman. *Mountain Wolf Woman, Sister of Crashing Thunder: The Autobiography of a Winnebago Indian*. Edited by Nancy Ostreich Lurie. Ann Arbor: University of Michigan Press, 1966.

Radin, Paul. *The Autobiography of a Winnebago Indian*. New York: Dover, 1963.

Tsosie, Rebecca. "Changing Women: The Cross-Currents of American Indian Feminine Identity." *American Culture and Research Journal* 12 (1988): 1–37.

MOURNING DOVE [CHRISTAL, CHRISTINE QUINTASKET, HUMISHUMA] (1888–1936)

was born near Bonner's Ferry, Idaho, to Joseph Quintasket (Okanogan) and Lucy Stukin (Colville). Christal Quintasket took Morning Dove as a pen name in 1912 to symbolize the launching of her literary ambitions, changing the name to Mourning Dove in 1921 after she had seen the bird of that name in a Spokane museum. The phonetic spelling of the Okanogan word for Mourning Dove is *Humishuma*.

Her first marriage to Hector McLeod, a Flathead Indian, ended in divorce; in 1919, she married Fred Galler, a Wenatchee. She had no children by either marriage. Her education consisted of a smattering of government Indian schools, approximately three years at the Sacred Heart Convent in Ward, Washington, and some business school education when she was twenty-four.

In 1914, Mourning Dove met Lucullus V. McWhorter at a Frontier Days Celebration in Walla Walla, Washington—a meeting that initiated both a friendship and literary collaboration for the rest of her life. Founder of the

American Archaeologist and a scholar of encyclopedic interests, McWhorter encouraged Mourning Dove's literary aspirations. He was instrumental in inspiring her to collect the Okanogan "folklores" that would form the basis for *Coyote Stories* published in 1933. He also became her mentor and collaborator on her novel, *Co-Ge-We-A, The Half-Blood: A Depiction of the Great Montana Cattle Range*, published in 1927, thirteen years after she had completed the first draft. The title page acknowledges that the novel is "given through Sho-pow-tan," a pen name for McWhorter, and indeed, much of the formal and stilted language in the novel and the elaborate notes to the text clearly reflect McWhorter's influence.

However, the novel is Mourning Dove's from the story—a romance about a mixed-breed female, told from the Indian point of view—to the inclusion of unrecorded stories and beliefs of the Okanogan. Intent upon preserving her tribal heritage, but reluctant to divulge restricted material, Mourning Dove found her voice in the medium of fiction.

Her commitment to literature was profound, and she wrote under difficult circumstances. Often working as a migrant laborer in fields with her husband, she had only temporary shelter at night, but she always took her typewriter with her, so she could work through the night on her stories. Her correspondence with McWhorter is a revealing self-portrait of a woman dedicated to preserving her tribal history and to finding her own voice in the language of fiction.

—Dexter Fisher Cirillo

References

Brown, Alanna Kathleen. "Mourning Dove, an Indian Novelist." *Plainswoman* 11 (1988): 3–4.

———. "Mourning Dove's Canadian Recovery Years, 1917–1919." *Canadian Literature* 124–25 (Spring/Summer 1990): 113–23.

———. "Mourning Dove's Voice in *Co-Ge-We-A*." *Wicazo Sa Review* 4 (1988): 2–15.

———. "Profile: Mourning Dove (Humishuma) 1888–1936." *Legacy: A Journal of Nineteenth Century American Women Writers* 6 (Spring 1989): 51–58.

Fisher, Dexter. Introduction to *Co-Ge-We-A*, by Mourning Dove. Lincoln: University of Nebraska Press, 1981.

Mourning Dove. *Co-Ge-We-A, the Half-Blood: A Depiction of the Great Montana Cattle Range*. Boston: Four Seas, 1927.

———. *Coyote Stories*. Edited and illustrated by Heister Dean Guie with notes by Lucullus V. McWhorter and a Foreword by Chief Standing Bear. Caldwell, ID: Caxton Printers, 1933.

———. *Mourning Dove—A Salishan Autobiography*. Edited by Jay Miller. Lincoln: University of Nebraska Press, 1990.

———. *Tales of the Okanogans*. Edited by Donald M. Hines. Fairfield, WA: Ye Galleon Press, 1976.

MUSGROVE, MARY [MARY MATTHEWS, MARY BOSOMWORTH]

(c.1700–1763) was a major intermediary between the Creek Indians and the English colonists who settled Georgia in 1733. She was the niece of Brimms, a Creek leader. Her father was a white trader, but in the matrilineal system of Creek society, the fact that her Creek mother was sister to Brimms gave her high status. She was sent to a Christian mission school in Ponpon, South Carolina, at the age of ten. In 1715 she returned to the Creek territory where she met and married John Musgrove, part of an English delegation sent to make peace with the Creeks. By 1732 the couple had established an extensive trading post at Yamacraw Bluff, near Savannah.

When James Oglethorpe arrived in 1733, he met Mary Musgrove, and upon discovering that she could speak English, prevailed upon her to negotiate with the leaders of the Yamacraw community to allow him to settle near them and establish the colony he named Georgia. She continued to be an important advisor to Oglethorpe, establishing a new trading post on the Altamaha River where she could observe the Spanish colonies, which threatened war with the Georgia Colony, and rally the Indians in the area to Oglethorpe's side against the Spanish. In about 1740 John Musgrove died, and Musgrove promptly married Jacob Matthews, a former indentured servant who had risen to become commander of a group of white soldiers. After his marriage he became a braggart and drunkard, and his bad reputation in the Georgia colony tarnished Musgrove as well. He died in 1742, at about the same time that hostile Yamassee Indians destroyed her trading post on the Altamaha. Her establishment near Savannah was also ruined during the war between Georgia and the Spanish.

Oglethorpe left Georgia to return to England in 1743, and although he gave Musgrove his own diamond ring and £200 with the promise of £2000 more, he never followed through with the promise, and Musgrove's influence with the government of the Georgia colony declined.

She still had extensive land holdings, and she retained her influence with the Creeks. In about 1746 she married Thomas Bosomworth, an English ex-minister, and with him set up a new trading station at the confluence of the Ockmulguee and Oconee rivers. They made claims for even more land from both the Creeks and the trustees of Georgia, relying on Musgrove's reputation as being influential with the Indians and indeed ultimately asserting that Musgrove was "Queen of the Creeks." When the Georgia Council failed to honor her claims, despite her veiled threats of an Indian uprising, she took her case to the Board of Trade in England, which in 1759 also disallowed them but gave her £2100 from the sale of some of the land for her past service to the colony. Mary Musgrove Matthews Bosomworth died sometime around 1763, partly compensated but mainly thwarted in her attempts to convince the English that she was the "Queen of the Creeks" and rightful owner of large tracts of Creek land. Her reputation depended on her family connections and her influence with Oglethorpe, but her motivations in negotiating between whites and Indians seem largely those of self-interest, and her marriages to three white men, two of whom were of dubious reputation, diminished her standing with whites and ultimately undercut her status with the Creeks.

—Clara Sue Kidwell

References

Coulter, E. Merton. "Mary Musgrove, 'Queen of the Creeks': A Chapter of Early Georgia Troubles." *The Georgia Historical Quarterly* 11 (March 1927): 1–30.
Todd, Helen. *Mary Musgrove: Georgia Indian Princess.* Savannah, GA: Seven Oakes, 1981.

N

NAMPEYO [NAMPAYO, NAMPAYU, SNAKE GIRL] (b. 1859–1942) was a Hopi potter who reintroduced ancient forms and designs, later known as the *sikyatki* revival style, to revolutionize her tribe's ceramic art. Nampeyo was born in Hano on First Mesa, the daughter of Qotsvema, a member of the Snake Clan, and Qotcakao, a Tobacco Clan woman. Nampeyo married Kwivioya in 1879, but he left because he feared that her beauty would attract other men. In 1881 she married Lesso (sometimes spelled Lesou).

Nampeyo's first introduction to ceramic art was when she watched her grandmother making *ollas* and other vessels used in everyday activities. Nampeyo made variations on those designs then in use in the tribe, and her work brought good prices from the white traders. Sometime in the early 1890s, Nampeyo became interested in the ancient work of her people and searched for older pieces that she might study. In 1895 her husband was hired to help with the excavation of Kikyatki, an early Pueblo ruin. Nampeyo and Lesso traveled there, as well as to the ruins at Awatovi, Tsukuvi, and Payupki, to find shards to inspire her work. She also began to adapt her forms to some of the older shapes, such as the low wide-shouldered jars of the Sikyatki. Still, her ceramics were unique, and eventually the bold, fluid designs were characterized by the use of the background space as an essential element that became part of the whole creation.

Nampeyo became a symbol of Hopi culture used in promotional photographs and literature by the Santa Fe Railway and the Fred Harvey Company. According to the documented evidence, Nampeyo left the reservation three times: in 1905 and 1907 to the Hopi House at the Grand Canyon and in 1910 to the United States Land and Irrigation Exposition in Chicago. By the end of the first decade of this century, Nampeyo had been acknowledged in anthropological reports, had been photographed by well-known photographers, and her pots had been collected for the National Museum in Washington, DC.

Although the height of Nampeyo's career was from 1901–10, she continued to work into her old age. When her eyesight began to fail, she still formed the pottery, and Lesso helped to duplicate her artistry. Nampeyo's daughter, Fannie, carried on the tradition after his death in 1932. Nampeyo died on July 20, 1942. Her four daughters—Annie, Cecilia, Fannie, and Nellie—have carried on the art of ceramics to some degree.

—Laurie Lisa

References

Ashton, Robert, Jr. "Nampeyo and Lesou." *American Indian Art Magazine* 1 (Summer 1976): 24–33.

Collins, John. *Nampeyo, Hopi Potter: Her Artistry and Her Legacy*. Fullerton, CA: Muckenthaler Cultural Center, 1974.

Colton, Mary Russell F., and Harold S. Colton. "An Appreciation of the Art of Nampeyo and Her Influence on Hopi Pottery." *Plateau* 15 (January 1944): 43–45.

Kramer, Barbara. "Nampeyo, Hopi House and the Chicago Land Show." *American Indian Art Magazine* 14 (Winter 1988): 46–53.

McCoy, Ronald. "Nampeyo: Giving the Indian Artist a Name." In *Indian Lives: Essays on Nineteenth- and Twentieth-Century Leaders*, edited by L.G. Moses and Raymond Wilson. Albuquerque: University of New Mexico Press, 1985.

Monthan, Guy, and Doris Monthan. "Dextra Quotskuyva Nampeyo." *American Indian Art Magazine* 2 (Autumn 1977): 58–63.

Nequatewa, Edmund. "Nampeyo, Famous Hopi Potter." *Plateau* 15 (January 1943): 40–42.

NAMPEYO, DAISY HOOEE (b. 1910) is Tewa-Hopi and grew up in the Hopi village of Hano on First Mesa. She is the daughter of Anne and Willie Healing and the granddaughter of the famous Hopi potter Nampeyo, from whom she learned the art of pottery. At the age of ten, while attending Phoenix Indian School, she was threatened with blindness from cataracts. Anita Baldwin, a patron of the arts, took her to California for surgery and more formal education, and then to Europe to study art in Paris.

In 1935, married to Ray Naha and living in Arizona, she worked with archaeologists from the Peabody Museum of Harvard University in conjunction with the excavation of Awatovi. The style and designs of her pottery were greatly influenced by the pots that were rediscovered in this ancient city. In 1938, after divorcing her first husband, Nampeyo moved to Zuni and married Leo Poblano, a prominent local silversmith. She took up sculpting and, together with Poblano, helped to introduce relief settings to the Zuni silversmiths. As the people of Zuni sought to recapture some of their traditions, Nampeyo returned to the making of traditional pottery, giving up sculpting for good. Nampeyo's second husband was killed while fighting a forest fire in California, and she married Sidney Hooee, also a Zuni silversmith.

Daisy Hooee Nampeyo maintains a workshop at Zuni where the traditional methods and designs of Zuni and Hopi pottery are practiced. Daisy still signs her pottery with the last name of Nampeyo in deference to the talented craftswoman from whom she is descended.

—Arlon Benson

References

Fowler, Carol. *Daisy Hooee Nampeyo.* Minneapolis: Dillon Press, 1977.
Kramer, Barbara. "Nampeyo, Hopi House, and the Chicago Land Show." *American Indian Art Magazine* 14 (Winter 1988): 46–53.
Peterson, Susan. "Matriarchs of Pueblo Pottery." *Portfolio* (November/December 1980): 50–55.

NARANJO-MORSE, NORA (b. 1953) is a Tewa Pueblo poet and potter. The youngest daughter and last child of Michael and Rose Naranjo of Santa Clara Pueblo, Nora has six sisters and three brothers, many of whom are themselves artists. She spent much of her youth in Taos Pueblo where her father was a Baptist missionary and graduated from Taos High School in 1971. After sorting mail in Washington, DC, and selling firecrackers in South Dakota, Naranjo-Morse "came home" to Santa Clara and to "working on clay" in 1976. Her mother and three sisters are all potters, and it was her sister Jody Folwell who reintroduced Naranjo-Morse to clay. In 1980 she graduated from the College of Santa Fe with a major in social welfare. By the time she graduated, she had become recognized as a potter and had married Greg Morse with whom she has had twins, Zakary and Eliza, and built an adobe house. The combination of marriage, children, and building a house has "made [her] flourish" and let herself "follow [her] heart." In the process, her ceramic sculptures have become much larger, but since clay limits the size of what one can do, she is now working in metal as well.

As the youngest in a family of recognized potters, Naranjo-Morse wanted to be different, so she began making small animals and people rather than bowls, combining Taos micaceous clay with Santa Clara clay. She began winning prizes at Santa Fe Indian Market in 1979 and in 1980 had the first of many gallery shows at Gallery 10 in Scottsdale, Arizona. She has received fellowships for her art both from the Southwest Association on Indian Affairs and the School of American Research. Her clay people have appeared in two important museum exhibits, *A Separate Vision* at the Museum of Northern Arizona and *Earth, Hands, and Life: Southwestern Ceramic Figures* at the Heard Museum. Her poems have been published in *Sun Tracks*, in several anthologies of Native American writers, and in her own book, *Mud Woman: Poems from the Clay.* She has read poetry and demonstrated pottery making from Flagstaff, Arizona, to Denmark and Germany, and has been featured in videotapes produced by the Museum of Northern Arizona and the Museum of New Mexico.

Naranjo-Morse describes her art as that of "an American Indian woman trying to make sense of these two cultures" in the late twentieth-century, where one day she is reading poetry in New York City and the next gathering clay as Santa Clara women have done for generations. Both the conflict and the humor of this double life are embodied in her clay friend and alter ego "Pearlene" and in poems such as "Mud Woman Encounters the World of Money and Business." In her "menagerie of characters inspired by culture and personal experience," Naranjo-Morse has taken an important Santa Clara figurative ceramic tradition in a new direction. Her "joyful play" has produced figures and scenes which combine humor and an abstracted and refined sophistication. Like the mocking pastiche of Pueblo clown performances, Naranjo-Morse's mixtures of ideas and materials often make a wry, satirical cultural critique of her multiple post-colonial worlds in which "nothing was in place anymore." As both a poet and a potter, Naranjo-Morse subverts traditional and widely accepted conceptions of Pueblo culture, Pueblo women, and Pueblo potteries.

—Barbara A. Babcock

References

Coe, Kathryn, and Diana F. Pardue. "Earth Symbols." *Native Peoples* 2 (Winter 1989): 42–47.
Eaton, Linda B. "A Separate Vision." *Plateau* 60 (Winter 1989): 10–17.
Lichtenstein, Grace. "The Evolution of a Craft Tradition: Three Generations of Naranjo Women." *Ms.* 11 (April 1983): 59–60, 92.
Naranjo-Morse, Nora. *Mud Woman: Poems from the Clay.* Tucson: University of Arizona Press, 1992.
Peterson, Ashley. "Nora Naranjo-Morse: Working with Enchantment." *Santa Fe Reporter* 20 August 1981: 81–82.
Trimble, Stephen. "Brown Earth and Laughter: The Clay People of Nora Naranjo-Morse." *American Indian Art* 12 (Autumn 1987): 58–65.

NEAKOK, SADIE BROWER (b. 1916), educator, community activist, and magistrate, was born and raised in the Alaskan North Slope Borough community of Barrow. One of thirteen siblings, Neakok is the daughter of the American pioneer, whaler, and entrepreneur Charles Brower and his second wife, Assianggataq, an Inupiat Indian. In 1940 she married Nate Neakok, a mechanic and full-blooded Inupiat. In addition to their twelve children, the Neakoks took on, from time to time, the temporary care of foster children.

While most of Neakok's life has been spent in Barrow, she did venture "outside" in 1930 when her father sent her to San Francisco, California, to finish her education. After receiving a high school degree there in 1934, she returned to Barrow. Her American clothes and "outside" education earned her the epithet "white lady."

From the date of her return, Neakok has devoted her life to community service, fulfilling the roles of teacher, welfare worker, and state magistrate. Her call to public service came shortly after her return from California. In 1934 Neakok was the first radio announcer to broadcast the news in the Inupiat language. That same year she became involved in the Bureau of Indian Affairs' (BIA) attempts to recruit young Native peoples for a vocational school outside of Anchorage. In 1938 she was recruited during her sophomore year at the University of Alaska by the BIA to teach full-time. But her most important public role came in 1960 when she was appointed by the State of Alaska to be a magistrate. As a magistrate, Neakok was instrumental in not only introducing and implementing the American legal system amongst the Inupiat, but also in assisting the community in learning how to benefit from the system. She served as Alaska's northern most magistrate for seventeen years, retiring in 1977.

Neakok's unique background and personal experiences aided her in becoming an important public figure in the Barrow community. She has used this position to assist her community in adapting to the changes which were first imposed upon it from the "outside," starting in the late nineteenth century, culminating in 1959 with Alaska's entry into the Union.

—Faren R. Siminoff

Reference

Blackman, Margaret B. *Sadie Brower Neakok: An Inupiaq Woman*. Seattle: University of Washington Press, 1989.

NELSON, MARGARET F. (b. 1922), an enrolled member of the Cherokee Nation, was born in Claremore, Oklahoma. She attended Oklahoma State University from 1940–42, then married and raised four children. In 1968 she enrolled in Northwestern University where she completed a BA in English; in 1971 she received an MA in English at Oklahoma State University, and in 1979 completed a PhD in American folklore at the same institution. She served on the faculty of Oklahoma State University from 1970 until retirement as associate professor in 1990.

Professor Nelson's publications and organizational work have contributed significantly to furthering American Indian education. She was appointed by President Ronald Reagan to the National Advisory Council on Indian Education and has held several offices in the North American Indian Women's Association. Her publications include *Ohoyo Okhana: A Bibliography of American Indian–Alaska Native Curriculum Material*, a guide book published by the Cherokee National Historical Society, and articles and book reviews for *American Indian Quarterly* and *Studies in American Indian Literatures*. Her many lectures and interviews have addressed Indian education, American Indian literature, and American Indian women's issues.

—Helen Jaskoski

References

Directory of American Scholars. New York: R.R. Bowker, 1982.
Nelson, Margaret F. *Ohoyo Okhana: A Bibliography of American Indian–Alaska Native Curriculum Material*. Wichita Falls, TX: Ohoyo Resource Center, 1982.

————. *Rural Village Guidebook*. Tahlequah, OK: Cherokee National Historical Society, n.d.

NETNOKWA (c.1740–50–c.1815–20) was born in the central Great Lakes area and was a member of the Ottawa tribe. She was a respected fur trade "captain," or leader, in the late eighteenth-century Great Lakes fur trade. She traded at Mackinac and led a band of trappers who were her sons and sons-in-law, among whom was the white captive John Tanner.

As is typical of mature women in Algonquian societies, Netnokwa possessed great wisdom, skills, personal charisma, and strong spiritual power. These enabled her to wield considerable authority within her family. All family property belonged to her, she made all major decisions for the family, and in crises she was able to call on spirit powers to affect weather and find game. Expert in the skilled tasks for which women were responsible (making rush mats, tanning hides, making clothing, and harvesting, preparing, and storing foods), her duties also included the giving of feasts for the first animals of each species killed by her sons and finding suitable wives for her sons.

In the late 1790s Netnokwa decided to go to Red River (present-day Manitoba) to visit relatives of her husband, Tawgaweninne. She persuaded other Ottawa to accompany her, and they were part of a wave of Ottawa and Ojibwa who entered the West about this time. She was widowed during the journey and never remarried, but spent the rest of her life leading bands of relatives in the Red and Assiniboine River areas.

Netnokwa's life also illustrates Indian involvement in the western fur trade. While a plentiful supply of beaver gave her ready access to desired trade goods, the use of alcohol in the fur trade was damaging to Native societies. As a trading chief, Netnokwa drank and got others drunk in semi-annual drinking parties at trading posts. Her redistribution of alcohol was an adaptation of traditional means of gaining status among Native people, but the drinking parties resulted in accidents and fights which caused many deaths—among them those of her husband and son-in-law.

Netnokwa died in the Red River Valley sometime after 1815. Her forceful character and life history demonstrate that women could and did play vital roles in leadership and decision-making among Algonquian societies in the historic era.

—Laura Peers

Reference

Tanner, John. *A Narrative of the Captivity and Adventures of John Tanner During Thirty Years' Residence Among the Indians in the Interior of North America*. Edited by Edwin James. Minneapolis, MN: Ross and Haines, 1956.

NUNEZ, BONITA WA WA CALACHAW [WA WA CHAW]

(1888–1972) was probably a member of the Rincon Band of the Luiseno tribe of Mission Indians in southern California. A white woman, Mary Duggan of New York City, who was delayed by a winter storm in 1888 while traveling in the area, carried away the newborn baby from the poverty-stricken mother. Wa Wa Chaw was raised by Mary Duggan and her brother, Cornelius Duggan, a prominent New York physician. These two affluent people were humanitarians and "Indian lovers," and they raised Wa Wa Chaw as their own daughter, taking care, however, always to dress her as they thought an Indian child should dress. They encouraged a mystical bent of her mind that they recognized as something extraordinary and encouraged her strong artistic abilities.

About the only information available about Wa Wa Chaw and her life is in her diaries discussed in Stan Steiner's *Spirit Woman*. She married and the marriage failed, and she had a child die at age three. Wa Wa Chaw once danced with Isadora Duncan, performed on the vaudeville stage, visited the White House, became and was arrested as an Indian rights activist. She ultimately journeyed alone to California in search of her real mother and tribe. She lived with her tribe for a time and also with the urban Indians of Chicago, New York, Philadelphia, and other major cities.

One of the earliest and most significant uses to which her striking artistic ability was put was to draw illustrations of the medical specimens Duggan brought home to her. She was adept at drawing bones, tissues, organs, tumors, and various bacteria. Her method was to meditate upon the subject until she "saw" it with mystical dimensions. She was in demand as a successful medical illustrator for the best medical journals of the day. As a fine artist Wa Wa Chaw had Expressionistic tendencies comparable to her contemporary, the Norwegian Edvard Munch; but as an early twentieth-century urban Indian activist and spokesperson for ethnically mixed ghetto neighborhoods, she also qualifies as a folk artist who intended her art to be used by the masses rather than preserved in galleries. In her later paintings she uses the earthy colors of red, yellow, brown, and black and white, creating a feeling of harmony with the earth and organic unity. Her heavy strokes, thick, dark lines, and bold designs imply strength and energy. Her subjects are often family or group scenes where the members are embracing or holding each other. Ultimately, her paintings speak her personality and experience.

—Gretchen Ronnow

References

Steiner, Stan. *The New Indians*. New York: Harper and Row, 1968.
———. *Spirit Woman: The Diaries and Paintings of Bonita Wa Wa Calachaw Nunez, An American Indian*. San Francisco: Harper and Row, 1980.

O

OSCEOLA, LAURA MAE (b. 1932), a member of the Panther Clan, has lived most of her life at the Seminole Reservation in Hollywood, Florida. Because Seminole children were not permitted to attend public school in Florida when she was young, Osceola was sent to the government boarding school for Indians at Cherokee, North Carolina. After completing school she returned to the reservation, and at age seventeen, married Max Osceola. She gained distinction as the first Florida Indian girl to apply for a marriage license or to have a marriage ceremony performed in a church. She is the mother of four children, three boys and a girl, and has several grandchildren. Her adopted son, James Billie, is the current chairman of the Seminole tribe.

Osceola inherited a tradition of service from her uncles Sam Tommie and Tony Tommie (the latter had attended the Carlisle Indian School in Pennsylvania), who were respected Seminole leaders earlier in this century. She made her own lasting contribution at a time of extreme difficulty when the Seminoles of Florida faced federal termination proceedings. With her education and ability to speak English, as well as fluency in both Seminole languages, Osceola was selected as the major interpreter for older Seminole leaders during the termination hearings of the 1950s. The Seminoles had no funds for a trip to the nation's capital to defend their lands, so Osceola spoke before numerous church and civic groups to secure donations. She was the only woman member of the tribal delegation which went to Washington, DC, in 1954 to testify at the congressional hearings on a Seminole Termination Bill. This was a major breakthrough for a woman in a traditionally male-dominated tribal political system. Osceola spoke forcefully for the elders, effectively answering the pointed questions of the Joint Senate-House Subcommittee and eloquently presenting the Seminole position that they needed twenty-five more years for education and training before they would be ready to manage their own affairs. This convinced the Florida congressional delegation that the Seminoles were not ready for termination of federal services, so the bill was ultimately defeated.

The Florida Seminoles then set out to organize their own government with a federal constitution and corporate charter. Osceola visited all of the reservations, helping to explain what the new tribal government would mean for the people, and it was overwhelmingly adopted. When the Seminole Tribe of Florida was formed in 1957, she was named secretary and treasurer, an extremely influential position in setting up the office management and bookkeeping systems and supervising elections for the new government, and she served in that capacity until 1967. Despite the respect and popularity which she gained through her contributions during the early years of tribal organization, Osceola never held an elective office; however, she was generally consulted when important decisions were made by the Tribal Council. She later served for many years as an employment assistance counselor for the Seminole tribe. Today her son, Max Osceola, Jr., a tribal councilman from the Hollywood Reservation, continues a family tradition of service to the Seminole people.

—Harry A. Kersey, Jr.

References

Gallagher, Peter B. "Hog Farm Signed into Federal Trust." *The Seminole Tribune* [Hollywood, CA] 13 January 1991: 1, 6.

Kersey, Harry A., Jr. "'Give Us Twenty-Five More Years': Florida Seminoles from Near-Termination to Self-Determination, 1953–1957." *Florida Historical Quarterly* 68 (1989): 290–309.

Seminole Tribe of Florida and Seminole Tribe of Florida, Inc. 1977. *20th Anniversary of Tribal Organization 1957–1977, Saturday, 20 August 1977.* Hollywood, FL: Seminole Tribe. Mimeo.

The Seminole Tribe of Florida. *On The Path to Self-Reliance.* 26 min. 1989. Videotape.

US Congress. Joint hearing before the subcommittees of the committees on Interior and Insular Affairs. *Termination of Federal Supervision Over Certain Tribes of Indians.* 83rd Congress, 2nd sess., 1954. S. Doc. 2747. H.R. 7321, pt. 8.

OWEN, ANGIE REANO (b. 1946) was born Angelita Reano at Santo Domingo Pueblo, New Mexico, into a family that made jewelry. As a child, she and her sisters drilled white gypsum for her mother to use in her mosaic jewelry of the early 1950s. When she was in the sixth grade, Owen sold the family's jewelry on the porch under the portals of the Palace of the Governors on the Plaza in Santa Fe. Educated at Santo Domingo Day School and Bernalillo High School, she graduated from Albuquerque High School in 1965. She worked briefly at a lumber mill before embarking on a jewelry career of her own.

In 1969 she married Don Owen, an Anglo trader and more recently coordinator of the annual Indian Market sponsored by the Southwestern Association on Indian Affairs. Encouraged by her husband and other friends, Owen began researching the prehistoric styles of mosaic jewelry created by the Hohokam and Anasazi cultures of the Southwest. She traveled extensively throughout the region, studying early pieces in museum and private collections to learn the techniques of her ancestors.

The mosaic style of jewelry—a pattern of small pieces of turquoise, coral, and other stones cut from the rough stone and set onto shell with epoxy and then ground and buffed and polished to a glossy and smooth finish—had been done in the 1940s and 1950s by Owen's mother and a few others at Santo Domingo. It was called "depression" jewelry because the only surfaces available to the jewelers were the backs of 78 records and old batteries. Few artists explored the format, however, because rolled beads, or "heishi," necklaces were much more popular at the time.

Among the many examples of prehistoric shell jewelry that particularly inspired Owen were the Glycymeris bracelets, which when cut, became bangle bracelets in any number of shapes that could be etched or overlayed with mosaic. The *tour de force* of overlaying a total circumference presented a technical and aesthetic challenge to Owen as it had to her predecessors. In 1974 she made her first mosaic bangle bracelet on green snail, producing at least one a year following that. But it was not until 1978 that she finally found in a shell shop in Malibu, California, the same Glycymeris shell used by the Hohokam. And in 1982, she made her first mosaic cuff bracelet out of a tiger cowrie shell.

Recognized early on by museums, traders, and other Indian artists for her single-handed revival of an ancient tradition of mosaic overlay, Owen did not achieve commercial success with her work until the late 1970s. Since then her work has been widely collected both privately and by museums here and in Europe, including the Albuquerque Museum, the Heard Museum and the Millicent Rogers Museum, among others. In 1990 the Smithsonian invited her to participate in a special Native American artists series in Washington, DC. She has received every major award for her work at the various competitions held throughout the Southwest, including Best of Division in Mosaic at the Heard Museum and the annual Indian Market in Santa Fe.

The shells and stones she most frequently uses are black lip and gold lip shell (mother-of-pearl), green snail, spiny oyster, pink mussel, Glycymeris, tiger cowrie, Olivella, Pecten, conch, Conus, clam, turquoise, jet, coral, lapis lazuli, pipestone, serpentine and ivory.

Owen's talent lies in the fact that her designs are organically determined by the shape of the shells. While the forms are classic, the aesthetic is modern, and the jewelry she creates is truly timeless. Perhaps, even more important, she has launched a revival at Santo Domingo in jewelry making that is providing numerous jewelers with new opportunities for both artistic expression and economic success.

—Dexter Fisher Cirillo

References

Cirillo, Dexter. "Back to the Past—Tradition and Change in Contemporary Pueblo Jewelry." *American Indian Art Magazine* 13 (Spring 1988): 46–63.

Cortright, Barbara. "Angie Reano Owen." *American West* 1 (February 1987): 68–69.

Jacka, Jerry, and Lois Essary Jacka. *Beyond Tradition: Contemporary Indian Art and Its Evolution.* Flagstaff, AZ: Northland Publishing, 1988.

Jernigan, E. Wesley. *Jewelry of the Prehistoric Southwest.* Albuquerque: University of New Mexico Press, 1978.

"One Space: Three Visions." Catalogue for show curated by Dextra Frankel, Albuquerque Museum, August 5th-November 4th, 1979.

OWL WOMAN (b. 1822–1849) was the daughter of Grey Thunder, keeper of the medicine arrows for the Cheyenne band of Yellow Wolf in the early 1800s. She was "given" in marriage to Colonel William Bent, who had traveled with his brother Charles to establish a fort and/or trading post on the upper Arkansas River in Colorado sometime around 1823–33. The tribal community thought that it would be "a good stroke of diplomacy" to give Bent one of its girls. Bent himself, as well as the family trading company Bent, St. Vrain & Company, was to benefit both economically and professionally from this alliance. The Cheyenne also clearly benefitted from the close ties with Bent because of his willingness to act as their advocate in dealing with white interests, both while Owl Woman was alive as well as after her death, with Bent eventually acting as agent for the southern Cheyenne.

Owl Woman and William Bent were instrumental in keeping the peace between area whites, as well as amongst the then battling Kiowas, Comanches, and Cheyennes. Bent's brother Charles, Governor of the provisional US territorial government of New Mexico at the time of the Mexican and Taos Pueblo uprising, was killed in that conflict. The Cheyenne were apparently eager to assist in "taking revenge" on Taos Pueblo, but Bent managed to dissuade them.

In 1838 Owl Woman gave birth to her first child, Mary. Two other children came shortly thereafter, Robert and George. There was a fourth child, Julia. It may be that Owl Woman died in childbirth at this time. It is also possible that she died of the cholera outbreak on the Cimarron. Owl Woman had apparently willed her children to her mother and her sister. William Bent married the sister, Yellow Woman, which assured his "claim" on his children.

Her son George continued as a trader in the area after having been educated, along with his brother Robert, in St. Louis. George also wrote *40 Years with the Cheyenne*, and Julia wrote and published a brief autobiographical piece for the *School News* at Carlisle Indian School in 1881. There is some dispute as to the birth mother of sons Robert and George. They are also noted to have been Yellow Woman's children, but it seems more likely that they were born to Owl Woman, then raised as her own by Yellow Woman.

—Renae Moore Bredin

References

Ellis, Richard N. "Bent, Carlson, and the Indians, 1865." *The Colorado Magazine* 46 (1969): 55–68.

Grinnell, George Bird. *The Cheyenne Indians: Their History and Ways of Life.* Vol. 1. Lincoln: University of Nebraska Press, 1972.

———. *The Fighting Cheyennes.* Norman: University of Oklahoma Press, 1956.

Seymour, Flora Warren. *Women of Trail and Wigwam.* New York: The Woman's Press, 1930.

P

PARKER, CYNTHIA ANN [PRELOCH] (1827–1870) was born in Clark County, Illinois, as the eldest child of Silas and Lucy Parker. In 1832 her family moved south to Texas as part of a branch of the Primitive Baptist church headed by her uncle, Elder John Parker. By the spring of 1834, the congregation decided to settle at the headwaters of the Navasota River in what is today Groesbeck, Texas. In order to protect themselves from marauding Indians, they built substantial walls around their settlement, which they called Fort Parker, and created a company of Texas Rangers.

On May 19, 1836, Fort Parker was attacked by several hundred Caddo, Comanche, and Kiowa Indians. At least five settlers were killed and five were abducted; among the captives was nine-year-old Cynthia Ann Parker. Within six years all of the captives were located and returned to white society, except for Parker. She was given to Chatua and Tabbi-nocca, a Tenowish Comanche couple who raised her like a daughter. She assimilated completely to Comanche life, and when attempts were made to ransom her in the 1840s, the band council refused to accept any offer, stating that she stayed with them by her own choice.

In 1845 Parker married Peta Nocoma, a young Quahadi Comanche chief famous for leading the Fort Parker attack and many other victorious raids. The marriage was apparently successful, and although prominent warriors sometimes married two or three women, Parker was Nocoma's only wife. They had two sons, Quanah and Pecos, and a daughter, Topsannah.

Peta Nocoma led many raids into Young, Jack, Parker, and Palo Pinto Counties, looting farms and ranches and killing settlers. On December 18, 1860, Captain Lawrence Sullivan Ross attacked Nocoma's camp on the Pease River. Nocoma was wounded, Quanah and Pecos escaped, and Parker and Topsannah were captured and taken to Camp Cooper. She was identified by her Uncle Isaac Parker in January 1861 and was taken to his farm in Birdville, Texas.

Although Parker never related her experiences as a Comanche captive, she became a legend in her own day. Many settlers took advantage of her name to publish memoirs, letters, or articles designed to incite anti-Indian sentiment. Others wrote historical fiction that over the years became accepted as fact. She returned to white society as unwillingly as she left it twenty-five years earlier. After her capture by white society she lived with various members of the Parker family but was unable to re-assimilate to a life she had only known for nine years and had forgotten. She never stopped grieving for Peta Nocoma and her sons.

In the fall of 1863, Parker received news that Pecos had died of smallpox; a few months later Topsannah succumbed to an influenza. Their deaths devastated her, and she died in 1870, heartbroken and weakened by self-inflicted starvation. Her other son, Quanah, survived his mother and became a notable Comanche war chief who distinguished himself by serving as a member of the Indian police and as a delegate for his people in Washington, DC. In 1875 he led the Quahada Comanche to a reservation in Oklahoma Territory, and in 1888 he was appointed one of three judges on the Court of Indian Offenses.

Quanah Parker searched for his mother for many years. When he discovered she was dead, he had her remains and Topsannah's remains moved to Cache, Oklahoma, for reburial. On February 21, 1911, Quanah died and was laid to rest at his mother's side.

—Joyce Ann Kievit

References

Hacker, Margaret Schmidt. *Cynthia Ann Parker: The Life and the Legend.* El Paso: Texas Western Press, 1990.
Parker Family Documents. Eugene C. Barker History Center, University of Texas, Austin.
Quanah Parker Files. Fort Sill Archives, Lawton, Oklahoma.
Waldraven-Johnson, Margaret. *White Comanche: The Story of Cynthia Ann Parker and Her Son, Quanah.* New York: Comet Press, 1956.
Waltrip, Lela, and Rufus Waltrip. *Indian Women.* New York: David McKay, 1964.

PARKER, JULIA F. (b. 1929), tribal scholar, cultural consultant, historian, educator, and basket weaver, was born at Graton, California, and spent her early years moving from tent camp to tent camp with her parents as they followed the crops. When she was six her father died, followed soon after by her mother Lily Pete (Kashia Pomo). Together with two younger sisters and two younger brothers, Parker was raised by a foster mother. In the eighth grade she and her siblings were taken out of public schools and sent to the Bureau of Indian Affairs' Stewart, Nevada, boarding school. Parker was among a group of children who hid way out on campus during weekend afternoons to do "Indian things" which were forbidden at school. At Stewart, she met her future husband, Ralph Parker (Yosemite Miwok/Paiute).

Parker moved to Yosemite National Park in 1948, where she worked in the laundry and was instructed in Miwok/Paiute tradition by Ralph's grandmother, Lucy Tom Parker Telles, who sometimes demonstrated basketry for the public in the park. One of Telles's baskets, which took four years to complete, was exhibited at the 1939 World's Fair.

In Yosemite Parker raised four children and assisted with the education and upbringing of two granddaughters and seven grandsons. After Telles died in 1956, the park service asked Parker to replace her as a cultural demonstrator. To prepare for the task, Parker studied basketry with Carrie Bethel and Minnie Mike (both Mono Lake Paiute/Southern Sierra Miwok) and Ida Bishop (Mono Lake Paiute). She later studied Pomo basketry with Elsie Allen (Cloverdale Pomo), Molly Jackson (Yokayo Pomo), and Mabel McKay (Cache Creek Pomo).

As cultural demonstrator, and more recently supervisor, for Yosemite's Indian Cultural Program, Parker has been instrumental in preserving Yosemite Miwok/ Paiute traditions, including traditional acorn and soaproot brush making, basketry, games, and tools. Her baskets have travelled as far away as Oslo, Norway, and in 1983, she presented Great Britain's Queen Elizabeth II with one of her baskets. Parker has been featured in numerous books and articles, and she is collaborating on a book about traditional Yosemite Miwok/Paiute acorn making. She is also assisting in an effort to achieve federal acknowledgment of the Miwok/Paiute.

Parker has taught others how to carry on the "old ways" through classes and demonstrations at Yosemite, other parks, various museums, elementary schools, and colleges in such disparate places as Palm Springs, California; Colter Bay, Wyoming; and the Smithsonian Institution in Washington, DC.

Her legacy is the inspiration she has given others to carry on the traditional ways. In her own words, "We should keep the old way here because of our children and our children's children and generations to come after us."

—Bev Ortiz

References

Ortiz, Bev. "It Will Live Forever: Yosemite Indian Acorn Preparation." *News from Native California* 2 (November/December 1988): 24–28.
———. *It Will Live Forever.* Berkeley, CA: Heyday Books, 1991.
———. Oral and taped interviews with Julia Parker, 1983–90.

PARRISH, ESSIE (1902–1979) was born on the Haupt Ranch in Sonoma County, California, where many of the Kashaya Pomo resided before settling on the present Kashaya Pomo Reservation. Early on, the Kashaya recognized that Parrish, daughter of Emily Colder and John Pinola, would be the last of four prophets to lead the Kashaya Pomo in political and religious matters. Parrish was raised by her maternal grandmother, Rosie Jarvis, the great tribal historian, and consulted in her early years with her predecessor as tribal leader, Annie Jarvis. Parrish began dreaming in early childhood and treated her first patient at age nine. In 1943, after the death of Annie Jarvis, Parrish became the official religious leader, or dreamer, of the Kashaya people. She doctored the sick and directed all religious activity, including the making of costumes for the numerous religious events and the teaching of rules and traditions associated with those events. This was no small feat; at a time when other tribes of Pomo had stopped most traditional activity and the influences of dominant American culture dissipated tribal cohesion among many Pomo groups, Parrish used her religion and knowledge to keep the Kashaya together. Consequently, the Kashaya Pomo are viewed by most Indian and non-Indian authorities as the most knowledgeable among the Pomo groups regarding religious and historical issues. With well-known anthropologists, Parrish made more than two dozen films on various aspects of the Kashaya Pomo culture, including films on her dream dances, doctoring, and the use and preparation of acorns as a food substance. Her film on acorn preparation, entitled *Chishkle*, or *Beautiful Tree*, won the Western Heritage Award in 1965. With UC Berkeley linguist Robert Oswalt, she compiled a Kashaya dictionary and the well-known *Kashaya Texts*, wherein many of the Kashaya legends and Parrish's personal experiences are recorded.

Parrish was also a basketweaver of national repute. Her baskets have been collected and displayed in museums throughout the country. She consulted with scholars at the Lowie Museum, UC Berkeley, not only on basketry, but on the use of native California plants by the Kashaya Pomo. In 1967 she met Robert Kennedy when he came to the Kashaya Reservation during his campaign. As head of state, Parrish, dressed in ceremonial attire, led Kennedy into the Roundhouse, the Kashaya religious center, and gave him a sacred basket she had woven. Later, after Kennedy left, she told her people that the basket was to help him, since he would not have much time left on this earth.

Parrish was not only a religious and political leader and a scholar who worked regularly with many colleges and universities, she was also a devoted mother to fifteen children. As her daughter Violet Chappell notes, "Mom was one of a kind. She could do anything. Play the piano, the accordion, the harmonica. She could cook. People used to come from the cities just to get her pies. She didn't believe in the word *can't*. And, above all else, she taught us to be proud, how great it was to be Indian and know who we are." As one anthropologist once remarked, summing up the cultural and historical contributions of Essie Parrish, "she was the most important California Indian of the twentieth century."

—Greg Sarris

References

Oswalt, Robert. *Kashaya Texts*. Vol. 36. Berkeley: University of California Publications in Linguistics, 1964.

Parrish, Otis, and Paula Hammett. "Parrish: A Pomo Shaman." *Native Self-Sufficiency* 6 (1981): 8–9.

Sarris, Greg. Personal Communication with Violet Chappell. Kashaya Reservation, Stewart's Point, CA, May 1990.

———. Personal Communication with Essie Parrish. Kashaya Reservation, Stewart's Point, CA, and vicinity, 1957–79.

PAUL, ALICE S., a contemporary Tohono O'odham, is a well-known educator in Arizona. She received her BA in 1958 in elementary education, her MEd in 1968 in elementary education, and her EdD in 1978 at the University of Arizona in elementary education and educational psychology.

She is the director of the Tucson Early Education Model Follow-through Program at the University of Arizona College of Education and has been the coordinator of educational development for that Model. She has taught in the Tucson public schools and is currently an associate professor of teaching and teacher education at the University of Arizona.

Paul sees her primary focus as centering on young children and their families. She is and has been especially interested in holding workshops for tribal peoples and parents on how to become involved in their children's educations. She has worked in this capacity with the San Carlos Apache, the Tohono O'odham, and the Choctaw tribal schools, as well as with the Native American Head Start Programs in Arizona, Nevada, North Dakota, Utah, and New Mexico. She has been a consultant with the National Head Start Bureau in Washington, DC, and a reader for American Indian Fellowship applications for the US Department of Education. She has given and continues to give numerous conference presentations on Native American child language development, on facts and myths of the Native American perspective, and on strategies for teaching "at-risk" children and strategies for parenting. She has also published on early childhood intervention and bilingualism.

When interviewed at her University of Arizona office, she indicated that one of her greatest concerns was to foster an awareness in teachers, students, and parents of the resources Native Americans have in their traditions and in their own families. She would also like to raise awareness about the many networking opportunities for Native American educators, as well as for educators teaching Native Americans.

Paul and her husband, Richard, live in Tucson. Family gatherings include four children and six grandchildren.

—Gretchen Ronnow

References

Paul, Alice. "The Transitional Model—Bilingualism Examined." In *Educational Models for Young Children*, edited by Jaipul Roopnarine and James Johnson. Columbus, OH: Charles E. Merrill, 1987.

———. "Two Decades of Early Childhood Intervention." In *Intergenerational Transfer of Cognitive Skills*. Applied Behavioral and Cognitive Sciences, Inc. In press.

Rennow, Gretchen. Personal Communication with Alice Paul. University of Arizona, Tucson, Arizona, 12 October 1990.

PAVATEA, GARNET (1915–1981) was like many young Tewa and Hopi

girls of her generation, learning to make pottery from her mother. As a young girl she accompanied her mother to Winslow, Arizona, where they sold their pottery to the Anglo tourists at the train station. For some women pottery-making was nothing more than a way to make money; for Garnet Pavatea, however, it became a continuation of a timeless cultural aesthetic, a vehicle for self-expression, and a means of defining herself vis-à-vis her people and the non-Tewa world.

In 1953 Pavatea entered her pottery in a judged exhibition and began what was to become a lifetime association with the staff of the Museum of Northern Arizona, Flagstaff, and its annual celebration of Hopi art, the Hopi Craftsmen Exhibition. Pavatea's polychrome bowls and jars won awards, and her engaging personality won her the pottery demonstrator's job at the Hopi show for the next two decades. Her pottery blended her own sense of cultural aesthetic with forms and decorative motifs popular with American consumers. In addition to the traditional bowl and jar forms, Pavatea also made the popular wedding vase, as well as a number of special request forms like fruit bowls and bean pots. She favored two decorative styles: One was the popular nineteenth-century *sikyatki* revival style which featured a yellowish-white background with red and black painted geometric and stylized bird motifs. The other was a design Pavatea reintroduced and perfected. Sometime in the early 1960s, she began producing plain, highly polished redware pieces that were often decorated with a punctate band made by pressing the triangular tip of a bottle-opener in the damp clay. During the winter of 1981, having narrowly missed the Pottery Division Award at the 1980 Hopi Show, Garnet Pavatea began trying to recreate the "really big" pots like her mother made. She was motivated by reclaiming the prize that had been "hers" and by trying to recapture a talent she felt Hopi potters had lost— the ability to make and fire large vessels. This was her goal despite the fact that she had lost both legs to diabetes and gathering clay had become something of a chore. The disease claimed her life two weeks after she reclaimed "her" prize with the largest jar she had made in years.

Pavatea's artistic talent and her popularity as a demonstrator at the museum insured that her house at Tewa Village was often visited by Anglo neophytes, as well as connoisseurs who prized her pottery and friendship. Her humor and graciousness also made her house a popular spot for Hopi and Tewa women to stop and visit, their laughter ringing out across the mesa.

—Laura Graves

References

Allen, Laura Graves. *Contemporary Hopi Pottery*. Flagstaff: Museum of Northern Arizona Press, 1984.

"Garnet Pavatea 1915–1981." *Museum Notes (MNA)* 28 (Fall 1981).

"Garnet Pavatea Exhibit Set at Museum through October." *The Sun* [Flagstaff] 21 September 1981.

PEASE-WINDY BOY, JEANINE (b. 1949) is known as "One Who Likes Places of Prayer" in her native Crow language. She was one of four children born to teachers working on the Colville Reservation in Washington. Her father was a Crow; her mother was German-English. In 1970 she received two BAs, one in sociology and one in anthropology, from Central Washington University. She served as a counselor at Navajo Community College in Tsaile, Arizona, in 1971, before moving on to a three-year stint as director of the Upward Bound Program at Big Bend Community College (Washington). In 1975, Pease-Windy Boy, now married, moved to Havre, Montana. There, she became director of the Adult and Continuing Education Commission of the Crow tribe, a post she held for four years.

By then (1979) a divorced mother of two, she took two years off work to devote to her children. Unfortunately, her former husband's unemployment forced her to accept public assistance, but the experience made her sensitive to the struggles of the many single, low-income mothers who scrape together resources to further their educations.

In 1981 Jeanine Pease-Windy Boy moved to Billings, Montana, where she worked in Eastern Montana College's Indian Career Services Department. One year later, in 1982, she launched the institution with which she has become synonymous.

With a tribal mandate, an abandoned house, two trailers and only $50,000, Jeanine Pease-Windy Boy founded Little Big Horn College. Over its nine-year history, LBHC has grown into a fully accredited two-year college, serving about three hundred of the Crow Reservation's seven thousand residents every year. Fifteen full-time and several part-time faculty members teach there, with many classes conducted entirely in Crow. Pease-Windy Boy is president, teaches math, psychology and English composition, car pools students to the college in bad weather, and mops floors. She donates $3,000 of her $26,000 salary back to the college every year. Recently, the college entered into a partnership with Montana State University to train Crow scientists and to locate a biomedical research lab at LBHC.

Jeanine Pease-Windy Boy received her MEd from Montana State University in 1987 and is approaching completion of her doctorate from MSU, also in education. She has honorary doctorates from Hood College (Maryland) and Gonzaga University (Washington). She won 1987's Outstanding Graduate Achievement Award from Montana State University and 1988's Outstanding Alumni Achievement Award from Central Washington University. In 1990, the National Indian Education Association named her Educator of the Year. She has served on the boards of the American Indian Higher Education Consortium (she was its president from 1983 to 1985), the Minority Concerns Advisory Commission, the Phelps-Stokes Fund, and was recently named a trustee of the Smithsonian's new National Museum of the American Indian.

Also an activist, Pease-Windy Boy has not avoided controversy. From 1983–86, a Montana court heard the redistricting case, *Windy Boy v. Bighorn County*. She successfully sued for a review of a redistricting plan to decrease Crow voting strength in non-tribal elections and to exclude Crow children from public schools. In 1990 several noted Soviet authors were invited to visit Montana, with the state requesting that Pease-Windy Boy host a tour of the Crow Reservation for them. When she found out the authors' anti-Semitic views, she retracted the offer, citing the need for all minorities to act as advocates for each other. For this, she won an award from the Torah Academy of Suffolk County (New York).

An active member of the First Crow Baptist Church and the Bighorn County Democratic Central Committee, Jeanine Pease-Windy Boy lives in the reservation community of Lodge Grass with her daughter, Roses, and her son, Vernon.

—Cynthia Kasee

References

Ebin, Barbara Burkhard. "On Indian and Jews: Cross-cultural support." *The Jewish Week* 1 March 1991: 28.

Kleinhuizen, Jeff. "A Boost for American Indians: Tribal Colleges Combine Academics and Heritage." *USA Today* 7 May 1991: 4D.

Mooney, Carolyn J. "Head of Blossoming Tribal College: 'A Product of My Community.'" *Chronicle of Higher Education*, 29 November 1989: A3.

Newell, Kathie. "Youthful strivers given name, 'dream-maker.'" *Havre Daily News* 21 March 1989: 3.

"NIEA Educator of the Year Award." *NIEA Newsletter* 23 (1990): 1.

PEÑA, TONITA [MARIA ANTONIA PEÑA, LITTLE BEAD, PINK SHELL, QUAH AH, QUAH H. AH, TONITA PEÑA A., TONITA P. ARQUERO] (1893–1949) was born at San Ildefonso Pueblo, New Mexico. There she lived with her parents and attended day school from 1899–1905. During an influenza epidemic she moved to Cochiti Pueblo to live with her aunt, Martina Montoya. Montoya was admired by San Ildefonso potter Maria Martinez and is credited with introducing the Cochiti slip to San Ildefonso potters. While under her aunt's tutelage, Peña learned to paint on pottery; at this time she also attended St. Catherine's Indian School in Santa Fe, where she studied art. Peña married Juan Rosario Chavez in 1908 and had two children with him; after his death in 1912, she returned to St. Catherine's to pursue her art studies. From 1913–20 she was married to Felipe Herrera; their son, Joe H. Herrera, also became a noted Pueblo artist. After Felipe Herrera's death, Peña taught art, pottery making, and pottery painting at the Indian schools in Santa Fe and Albuquerque. She married again in 1922, and with Epitacio Arquero she raised another family and pursued her career as an artist.

Peña is believed to be the first modern woman watercolorist of the Rio Grande Pueblo peoples. As early as 1909 she was identified as the only female member of the San Ildefonso Group, a group of Pueblo artists which also included her cousin, Romando Vigil, Alfredo Montoya, and the Hopi, Fred Kabotie. In the 1920s Peña displayed her paintings and pots in the arcade of the Palace of the Governors in Santa Fe, and the nearby La Fonda Hotel bought her work to decorate rooms and suites. Peña painted a series of murals for the Santa Fe Indian School in the 1930s, under the auspices of the Works Progress Administration. These panels soon were moved to the Albuquerque Indian School and then to the Southwest Museum in Los Angeles in 1934. She also painted a commemorative panel for the Coronado Quatrocentennial in 1940.

Peña's paintings depict Pueblo dances and pottery designs, while her murals blend Pueblo iconography with images from Anglo and Hispanic colonial history. Her watercolor renditions of seasonal dances place the dancers on a field of white, rather than in the panoramic scene of the Pueblo plaza. This isolation of the figures makes them seem timeless and emphasizes the dancer's persona and religious significance. Her paintings of pottery, also on a field of white, have been used as illustrations of Cochiti and San Ildefonso styles. Her legacy of watercolors is extensive and serves as valuable documentation of the dances and pottery forms she observed during the thirty years of her career as an artist.

—Jennifer L. Jenkins

References

Brody, J.J. *Indian Painters, White Patrons*. Albuquerque: University of New Mexico Press, 1971.

Cassidy, Ina Sizer. "Art and Artists of New Mexico." *New Mexico Magazine* 16 (November 1938): 22, 32–33.

———. "Indian Murals." *New Mexico Magazine* 12 (1934).

———. "Tonita Peña (Quah Ah)—Julian Martinez." *New Mexico Magazine* 11 (November 1933).

Dorman, Margaret. "A Study of the Water Color Paintings of Modern Pueblo Indians." Master's thesis, University of New Mexico, n.d.

Gray, Samuel L. *Tonita Peña: Quah Ah*. Albuquerque: Avanyu Publishing, 1990.

"Indian Drawings." *School Arts Magazine* 30 (March 1931): 461–63.

"Two Paintings of Tonita Peña and an Article on her Work." *Christian Science Monitor*, 22 April 1936.

PETERSON, HELEN (b. 1915) was born on the Pine Ridge Reservation in South Dakota. An enrolled member of the Oglala Sioux tribe, Peterson attended a public high school, Nebraska State Teachers College, and graduated with a degree in education from Colorado State College. First employed as a secretary for Head of the Education Department at Colorado State College, Peterson went on to serve as Director of the Rocky Mountain Council on Inter-American Affairs, located in Denver. In this capacity she attended the Inter-American Indian Conference in Peru as an advisor for the United States' delegate.

From 1948 until 1950, Peterson directed the Mayor's Committee on Human Relations in Denver, and after becoming an active member of the all-Indian National Congress of American Indians (NCAI) in 1948, she took over its executive director position in 1953. Later Peterson returned to Denver as the Director of Denver's Commission on Community Relations.

—Gretchen G. Harvey

Reference

Philp, Kenneth R., ed. *Indian Self-Rule: First-Hand Accounts of Indian-White Relations from Roosevelt to Reagan.* Salt Lake City, UT: Howe Brothers, 1986.

PICOTTE, AGNES [GOES IN CENTER] (b. 1935), research specialist with the Dakota Indian Foundation, at Chamberlain, South Dakota, has been editing the papers of Ella Cara Deloria and collecting letters, stories, and documents by other Dakota writers since 1975. She and Paul Pavich co-edited Deloria's *Dakota Texts*, reissued in 1978; Picotte's biographical sketch of Deloria is published with Deloria's novel, *Waterlily*; and she wrote the foreword to Zitkala-Ŝa's *Old Indian Legends*, reissued in 1985. Picotte's book, *An Introduction to Basic Dakota, Lakota and Nakota*, was published by the Dakota Indian Foundation in 1987; she is now working on a dictionary that will include the Dakota, Nakota and Lakota dialects, using Deloria's orthography to indicate the true sounds of the language.

Born at Hisle, South Dakota, Picotte grew up in the Wanblee district on the Pine Ridge Reservation. Her father, Oliver Goes in Center, was of the Oglala tribe; her mother, Mabel Romero Goes in Center, is the daughter of Manual Romero, originally from Mexico but adopted into the Oglala tribe. Picotte grew up speaking Lakota, living near her grandmothers, Katie Lip Goes in Center and Florence Hawk Romero, in the traditional way. But there were a number of white ranchers also in the Wanblee area, and the Goes in Center family, who also raised cattle, had friendly relations with them during the 1930s.

The youngest of four girls, Picotte, like her sisters, was sent to the Holy Rosary Mission School because the family lived seventeen miles from the nearest public grade school. Her father found occasional construction work in Rapid City and on the Ellsworth Air Force Base nearby. She and her family sometimes moved with him. She graduated from high school at St. Paul's Indian School, Marty, South Dakota.

Encouraged by her father to pursue her education, she attended Mt. Marty College in Yankton, South Dakota, where she completed a BA in education. She then taught at Red Cloud School on the Pine Ridge Reservation, where she was Indian Studies director.

After receiving an ethnic studies scholarship, she enrolled in graduate school at the University of Oregon, where she assisted in the development of the Ethnic Studies Department. She completed both the MA and PhD in education there and was the first Oglala to earn the PhD.

From 1975 through 1986, Picotte was adjunct professor of history and director of the Ella C. Deloria Project in Indian culture and language at the University of South Dakota. Picotte, her husband, Norbert, and their daughter, Mabel Grace, now live in Chamberlain, South Dakota.

—Norma C. Wilson

References

Hoover, Herbert, and Susan Peterson. Interviews with Agnes Picotte. Audiotapes 1046, 1047 and 1048. Vermillion, SD: American Indian Research Project, University of South Dakota, 1979.

Picotte, Agnes. *An Introduction to Basic Dakota, Lakota and Nakota.* Chamberlain, SD: Dakota Indian Foundation, 1987.

———. "Introductory biographical sketch of the author." *Waterlily*, by Ella Cara Deloria. Lincoln: University of Nebraska, 1988.

———. Foreword to *Old Indian Legends*, by Zitkala-Ŝa. Lincoln: University of Nebraska, 1985.

———, and Paul N. Pavich. Introductory Notes to *Dakota Texts*, by Ella C. Deloria. Vermillion, SD: Dakota Press, 1978.

Who's Who Among the Sioux. Vermillion, SD: Institute of Indian Studies, University of South Dakota, 1988.

PINKERMAN-URI, CONNIE REDBIRD (b. 1930) is Choctaw/Cherokee and was born in the vicinity of Wheatland, California. She was raised in a traditional rural Native American community, attended the local public school, and graduated from high school in 1947. After taking classes at Uba Junior College, she attended the University of Arkansas where she received a degree in medicine (MD) in 1955. She practiced medicine in the Los Angeles area for two decades before returning to college, earning a degree in law (JD) from Whittier College in 1979. She was the first Native American woman to hold degrees in both law and medicine.

Uri has been active in the areas of Native American civil rights and cultural preservation. In the mid 1960s she organized the first Indian Free Clinic in the Los Angeles area, in the back of a church. During the same time period she participated in an attempt to acquire and convert an abandoned army hospital, Ft. McArthur, into an Indian hospital and worked to alleviate health care problems at Chino State Prison in California. In the 1970s, her investigative work concerning the forced sterilization of Indian women helped to bring about new HEW regulations on sterilization in 1979. During the re-occupation of

Wounded Knee in 1973, she organized a caravan of medical supplies and helped arrange bail money for those participants who were put in jail. Uri helped the Northern Cheyenne use the Clean Air Act of 1970 to protect their environment from air pollution generated by factories outside the reservation. Throughout her career she has provided medical and legal services to the Los Angeles Indian community, often without charge.

In her professional capacity, Uri has worked with various groups to aid the process of organization within the Native American community. As a committee member of the Association of American Indian Physicians, she advocated the establishment of an Indian medical school. She has been a council member of Indian Women United for Social Justice since 1968. She has also been outspoken on the subjects of racism and sexism in the professional community.

—Arlon Benson

References

Anderson, Owanah, ed. *Ohoyo One Thousand: A Resource Guide of American Indian/Alaskan Native Women*, 1982. Wichita Falls, TX: Ohoyo Resource Center, 1982.
Benson, Arlon. Personal communication with Connie Uri, 22 March 1992.
Jarvis, Gayle Mark. "The Theft of Life." *Akwesasne Notes* 9 (Autumn 1977): 30–33.

POCAHONTAS (c. 1595–1617), born in eastern Virginia, was the daughter of Powhatan, the most powerful Indian leader of that area. Soon after her tenth birthday, Pocahontas and her people, the Powhaten, began to encounter the English, who settled at Jamestown in 1607. Because she was the favored daughter of an influential political leader, she traveled freely from her father's village to other Indian towns and to the English settlements; at times she may have visited Jamestown on missions for her father or she may have gone out of curiosity. There is no clear evidence that she brought food or was enamored of John Smith. When she reached age thirteen, she was placed in an arranged marriage with one of her father's supporters named Kocoum.

Her life changed dramatically in 1613 when she was kidnapped by the English and held in Jamestown for more than a year. During that period she fell in love with an English settler named John Rolfe, who obtained permission both from English authorities and Powhatan to marry Pocahontas. Early in 1614 she was first baptized into the Church of England as "Rebecca" and then married to Rolfe. This significant union, one of three legal Powhatan-English marriages in the seventeenth century, ushered in a brief period of relative peace on England's Virginia frontier. English officials anxious to capitalize on this harmony invited Pocahontas and Powhatan's chief advisor, Uttamatomakkin, to visit England. Included in the traveling party were several other Indians, as well as John Rolfe and the Rolfes' infant son, Thomas. Under the financial sponsorship of the Virginia Company of London, Pocahontas was introduced to English society in 1616; she and Uttamatomakkin were honored at the King's Twelfth Night Masque on January 6, 1617. During her stay in London, Pocahontas became ill, probably from some form of pulmonary disease. Although she boarded ship for Virginia in March of 1617, she sailed no farther than Gravesend. She was taken ashore, where she died and was buried on March 21, 1617.

Within three years, unfortunately, her story became larger than life through the writings of John Smith, one of Virginia's early leaders. In his 1624 *General History*, Smith alleged that Pocahontas had rescued him from execution in December, 1607. The story is questioned because Smith's two earlier works about Virginia did not mention the rescue. Although the account has been accepted by some historians and rejected by others, modern anthropologists have found no confirmation for it. The basic problem is Smith's capacity for self-glorification, when he transforms an Indian girl into a princess intervening on Smith's behalf against the imperial Powhatan. John Smith's reporting also clouds the information about the visit to England because only Smith described his interview in England with Pocahontas. Since romance seems more attractive than actuality, the Pocahontas of reality has become the Princess Pocahontas of novels and plays, as well as a symbol in modern poems by Sandburg, Lindsay, Crane, and Benet. Fortunately, twentieth-century anthropological research has stripped away the legends and returned Pocahontas to her rightful, if less epic, place in history.

—James H. O'Donnell III

References

Barbour, Philip L. *Pocahontas and Her World: A Chronicle of America's First Settlement*. . . . Boston: Houghton Mifflin, 1970.

Feest, Christian. "Pride and Prejudice: The Pocahontas Myth and the Pamunkey." *European Review of American Studies* 1 (1987): 5–12.

Mossiker, Frances. *Pocahontas: The Life and the Legend*. New York: Alfred A. Knopf, 1976.

Rountree, Helen C. *Pocahontas's People: The Powhatan Indians of Virginia Through Four Centuries*. Norman: University of Oklahoma Press, 1990.

————. *The Powhatan Indians of Virginia: Their Traditional Culture*. Norman: University of Oklahoma Press, 1989.

Woodward, Grace Steele. *Pocohontas*. Norman: University of Oklahoma Press, 1969.

POTTS, MARIE [CHANKUTPAN] (1895–1978) was born at Big Meadows, California, now the site of Lake Almanor in Plumas County. She belonged to the Northern Maidu tribe. She attended and was the first California Indian to graduate from the Carlisle Indian School in Pennsylvania, but returned to northern California, where she married and raised five children.

Throughout her life, Potts worked to improve the lives of all Native Americans. She traveled throughout the country lecturing on her heritage, urging cultural preservation, and speaking out for the welfare of Indians. She participated in the Indian occupation of Alcatraz Island, and confronted former Governor Ronald Reagan in her quest to use the governor's mansion for a prayer meeting.

Potts played a key role in establishing the American Indian Press Association and was co-founder of the Federated Indians of California Inter-Tribal Council. She was also a member of an *ad hoc* committee that later became the California Education Association. Potts taught at California State University, Sacramento, where she was considered an expert on American and California Indian history. She also founded *Smoke Signal*, the oldest Indian newspaper in America, which focuses on the struggle for Indian rights.

In 1975, the State of California honored her in recognition of her efforts to help the Indian people. She has also been honored by the establishment of the Marie Potts Journalism Achievement Award, the highest honor in Indian journalism given by the American Indian Press Association (AIPA). In 1977, the California State Parks and Recreation Department gave her a commendation at Sutter's Fort. The second floor of the California Health, Education, and Welfare Department building is named for her and includes a permanent lobby display recounting her achievements.

—Julie A. Russ

Reference

Potts, Marie. *The Northern Maidu*. Happy Camp, CA: Naturegraph, 1977.

PRETTY-SHIELD (c. 1858–late 1930s?) was born in March near the Missouri

River in what is now southeastern Montana. A member of the Sore-lip Clan of the Crow Nation and the fourth of eleven children, Pretty-shield's mother was Kills-in-the-night, her father Crazy-sister-in-law. She was given her name by her paternal grandfather, Little-boy-strikes-with-a-lance, who named her in honor of his handsome war-shield when she was four days old.

In 1932, when she was seventy-four years old, Pretty-shield agreed to tell her life story to Euro-American trapper and hunter, Frank B. Linderman. Since so many male warriors had narrated their personal histories, Linderman particularly wanted to hear "a woman's story." Responding to the questions of her amanuensis and with the help of her interpreter Goes-together, Pretty-shield told stories about growing up in pre-reservation days when her "people's hearts were . . . as light as breath-feathers." She tells how, as a child, she played with kickballs and dolls and with other children, organized a play sun-dance; and she recollects how she traveled with her people, fearing and fighting the Lakota, Cheyenne, and Arapahoe, the long-time enemies of her people. She describes childbirth and childrearing practices and the first time she saw white men, whom the Crow at first called Beta-awk-a-wah-cha (Sits-on-the-water, because they were first seen in canoes) and then called Masta-cheeda (Yellow-eyes). She narrates humorous stories about being chased by an angry buffalo cow and adventurous stories about how her father rescued her from a buffalo stampede. In addition, Pretty-shield shares her vision, explaining the origin of her personal medicine.

Married to Goes-ahead, a Crow scout for General George A. Custer, Pretty-shield recounts her husband's stories of the Battle of the Little Bighorn. But in order to balance the men's accounts of battle, she tells about the little-known Crow women warriors. She describes how a battle between the Crows and the Lakota was won by a sixty-year-old Crow woman named Strikes-two and how two Crow women warriors fought with Three-stars (General George Crook) at the Rosebud. Pretty-shield is one of the few Native American women who lived during pre-reservation days to share her life story with an amanuensis.

Dominated by the contrast between then and now, Pretty-shield's life story testifies to the overwhelmingly traumatic transformation suffered by many indigenous people in the late nineteenth century when they were forced onto reservations. The "times have changed so fast," Pretty-shield tells Linderman, "that they have left me behind. I do not understand these times. I am walking in the dark. Ours was a different world before the buffalo went away, and I belong to that other world." Even so, Pretty-shield's narrative offers a corrective to the stereotypes of indigenous women by depicting a lively, intelligent woman with a playful sense of humor and a survivor's spirit.

—Hertha D. Wong

References

O'Brien, Lynne W. *Plains Indians Autobiographies.* Boise, ID: Boise State College, 1973.

Pretty-shield. *Pretty-shield: Medicine Woman of the Crows.* Edited by Frank B. Linderman. 1932. Reprint of *Red Mother.* Lincoln: University of Nebraska Press, 1972.

Q

QUEEN ANNE OF PAMUNKEY is known from legal documents as the leader of the Pamunkey Indians of Virginia during the period from 1706 to 1718. She was the third female ruler of the Pamunkeys during the years between 1656 and 1718. Her primary role was to protect her people against the possibility of their being completely overwhelmed by the surrounding English colonials in Virginia. Over the years tribal lands had been reduced to a relatively small tract. Faced with a declining population which could not support itself, both because of numbers and because of an insufficient land base, the Pamunkeys often had resorted to selling off more land for income. Queen Anne complained that surveyors from Virginia sought to cheat the tribe by either arriving without notice or by surveying more lands than actually had been purchased. She also complained that too much liquor had been sold to the people of the tribe.

Consequently, she sought to stop the sales both of liquor and of land. If she had had her way, only leases would have been permitted; no more lands would have been sold by the tribe. Another source of difficulty for the Pamunkeys was the annual tribute which they had to pay to the British government. In light of her tribe's poverty, Queen Anne repeatedly asked that the tribe be forgiven this annual debt. In 1711 the governor of Virginia agreed to forgive the tribute if the Queen of Pamunkey would send her son to be educated at the College of William and Mary. As a consequence, Queen Anne sent her son and another young Pamunkey to the college.

During her brief term as Pamunkey leader, Queen Anne sought every possible means to guarantee the survival of her people, whether that necessitated land sales or leases, protests to the Virginia governor, or permitting her son to study at the College of William and Mary. If politics may be described as the art of compromise, Queen Anne understood politics and effectively employed that art in protecting her people.

—James H. O'Donnell III

References

Mathes, Valerie Shirer. "A New Look at the Role of Women in Indian Society." *American Indian Quarterly* 2 (1975): 131–39.

McCartney, Martha W. "Cockacoeske, Queen of Pamunkey, Diplomat and Suzeraine." In *Powhatan's Mantle: Indians in the Colonial Southeast*, edited by Peter Wood, et al., 173–95. Lincoln: University of Nebraska Press, 1989.

Minor, Nono. "The American Indian: Famous Indian Women in Early America." *Real West* (March 1971): 35, 78.

Rountree, Helen C. *Pocahontas's People: the Powhatan Indians of Virginia Through Four Centuries.* Norman: University of Oklahoma Press, 1990.

R

ROE CLOUD, ELIZABETH BENDER (1887?–1964?) was born on the

White Earth Indian Reservation in Minnesota. Elizabeth Bender, the daughter of an Ojibwa mother and a German father, attended Pipestone Boarding School and later Hampton Institute where she graduated in 1907. With additional coursework in education in Hampton, Virginia, and with nurses training in Philidelphia, she found employment as a teacher in the Indian Service at Indian schools in Browning, Montana, in Fort Belknap, Montana, and in Carlisle, Pennsylvania.

After her marriage to the Winnebago leader Henry Roe Cloud, she worked with him to establish the American Indian Institute in Wichita, Kansas. In 1939 they both moved to the Umatilla Indian Reservation in Oregon, where her husband became the agency superintendent. Once there Elizabeth Roe Cloud founded the Oregon Trails Club of Pendleton, an Indian women's club affiliated with the General Federation of Women's Clubs (GFWC). She later became the GFWC's national chairperson for Indian Affairs.

In 1950, shortly after her husband died, Elizabeth Roe Cloud was honored as Oregon Mother of the Year and as the American Mother of the Year. As the National Congress of American Indian's (NCAI) field secretary during this period, Roe Cloud directed a workshop in Indian community organization at Brigham City, Utah, in 1951. She continued to take part in subsequent Indian community development programs initiated by the NCAI. She died in Oregon at seventy-seven years of age.

—Gretchen G. Harvey

Reference

Bender, Elizabeth. Student File. Hampton University Archives, Hampton, Virginia.

ROESSEL, RUTH W. (b. 1934) was born in Rough Rock, Arizona, on the

Navajo Reservation, the daughter of Medicine Man Ashishie and Hasbah, her Navajo mother. While growing up, Roessel learned the traditional values, practices, and crafts of the Navajo; in fact, she began weaving at the age of five, a craft that continues to earn her numerous awards.

Roessel has devoted her life to educating Navajo children and adults, in both an academic manner preparing them for careers and a traditional Navajo manner preparing them for family life. This bi-cultural approach comes from the difficulties she faced as a young woman pursuing her own education. Despite the fact that she had a diploma from the only institution available to Navajo girls, Roessel was refused admission to colleges on the basis that her education was considered inadequate. After many letters, phone calls, and favors from understanding individuals, Roessel began her study in education and received her MA from Arizona State University in 1975.

Roessel has served as a teacher at Navajo Community College, Tolani Lake School, Rough Rock School, Rough Rock Demonstration School, and Pinon School; a director at Rough Rock Demonstration School; and a principal at Round Rock Elementary School. Currently, she is a resource teacher at Jeddito Puppy School where she also serves as president of the American Federation of Teachers.

In addition to teaching, Roessel has written and edited several books dealing with Navajo topics, and she started a Medicine Person Training Program for the Navajo tribe. She is involved in a number of activities in women's advocacy, including the Navajo Women's Association (president, 1978–80), North American Indian Women's Association (charter member and state president, 1976–77), and Arizona Women in Higher Education. In 1980, Roessel was honored by her tribe when she received the Navajo Woman of the Year Award.

Roessel, along with her husband Dr. Robert Roessel, Jr., who works in the Division of Education, remains committed to helping Navajo people maintain elements of their traditional culture. Since 1988, the Roessels have conducted summer workshops centering on Navajo issues such as alcoholism, jealousy, and the Navajo medicine person.

—Michelle Savoy

References

Roessel, Ruth, comp. *Navajo Livestock Reduction: A National Disgrace*. Chinle, AZ: Navajo Community College Press, 1974.

———, comp. *Navajo Stories of the Long Walk Period*. Tsaile, AZ: Navajo Community College Press, 1973.

———, ed. *Navajo Studies at Navajo Community College*. Many Farms, AZ: Navajo Community College Press, 1971.

———, comp. *Papers on Navajo Culture and Life*. Rev. ed. Many Farms, AZ: Navajo Community College Press, 1970.

———. *Stories of Traditional Navajo Life and Culture*. Tsaile, AZ: Navajo Community College Press, 1976.

———. *Women in Navajo Society*. Rough Rock, AZ: Navajo Resource Center, 1981.

ROSE, WENDY [BRONWEN ELIZABETH EDWARDS] (b. 1948), poet, artist, teacher, and anthropologist, was born in Oakland, California, the daughter of a mixed-blood Miwok mother and a Hopi father. She was raised in an urban environment just outside San Francisco, and her poetry reflects the experience of a mixed-blood Indian living apart from the reservation and away from the influence of a tribal culture. After dropping out of high school in El Cerrito, California, she became involved in the American Indian Movement, participated in the occupation of Alcatraz, and began a writing career under the pen-name Chiron Khanshendel.

With the influence of a "surrogate father," Rose became interested in anthropology and has attended Cabrillo College, Contra Costa College, and finally the University of California, Berkeley, where she earned her BA (1976), MA (1978), and is currently a PhD candidate in the Department of Anthropology. At this time, she continues working on her dissertation, an annotated bibliography and analysis of books written by Native Americans.

Rose has served as manager of the Lowie Museum of Anthropology of the University of California at Berkeley, editor of the *American Indian Quarterly*, and lecturer in Native American Studies for both the University of California at Berkeley, 1979–83, and California State University at Fresno, 1983–84. Currently, she is the coordinator of Native American Studies at Fresno City College in California where she lives with Arthur Murata, her husband of sixteen years.

Throughout her writing career, Rose has published widely in journals, anthologies, and collections. Her book of poems, *Lost Cooper* (1980), was nominated for a Pulitzer Prize. In addition to writing and teaching, Rose is a successful visual artist, having illustrated numerous books and journals, exhibited works around the country, and designed posters, post cards, and sport shirts.

Rose is an active member of various Indian organizations and has given many poetry readings in connection with powwows and tribal functions for literary audiences. Her accomplishments in poetry and scholarship work toward establishing Native American writing as a legitimate part of the American literary canon, as well as re-classifying Native American writers as literary artists, rather than "literate fossils" or anthropological voices.

—Michelle D. Savoy

References

Allen, Paula Gunn. "This Wilderness in My Blood: Spirituality in the Works of Five American Indian Women Poets." In *Coyote Was Here: Essays on Contemporary Native American Literature and Political Mobilization*, edited by Bo Scholer, 95–114. Aarhus, Denmark: University of Aarhus, 1984.

Bruchac, Joseph. "An Interview with Wendy Rose." *Greenfield Review* 12 (Summer/Fall 1984): 43–75. Reprint. *Survival This Way.* Edited by Joseph Bruchac, 87–104. Tucson: University of Arizona Press, 1987.

Hunter, Carol. "A MELUS Interview: Wendy Rose." *MELUS* 10 (Fall 1983): 67–87.

Rose, Wendy. *Hopi Roadrunner Dancing.* Greenfield Center, NY: Greenfield Review Press, 1973.

———. "Just What's All This Fuss About White Shamanism Anyway?" In *Coyote Was Here: Essays on Contemporary Native American Literary and Political*

Mobilization, edited by Bo Scholer, 13–24. Aarhus, Denmark: University of Aarhus, 1984.

———. *Lost Copper*. Banning, CA: Malki Museum Press, Morongo Indian Reservation, 1980.

———. "Neon Scars." In *I Tell You Now: Autobiographical Essays by Native American Writers*, edited by Brian Swann and Arnold Krupat, 251–61. Lincoln: University of Nebraska Press, 1987.

SAIL Bibliography No. 2: "Wendy Rose." *Studies in American Literatures* 6 (Spring 1982): 19–23.

Saucerman, James R. "Wendy Rose: Searching Through Shards, Creating Life." *Wicazo Sa Review* 5 (Fall 1989): 26–29.

ROSS, AGNES ALLEN (b. 1910) was born on the homestead of her parents, John Allen and Ida Wakeman, granddaughter of Chief Little Crow. Located west of Flandreau, South Dakota, the homestead was sold on their father's death to provide money for his nine children.

Ross attended Flandreau Public School, the sole Indian in a class of forty-eight. As a speaker of only the Dakota language, she had to learn English quickly. After graduation in 1929, she went to Haskell Institute where she earned a teacher's certificate in 1931. For most of the rest of her adult life until retirement, she earned a living as a teacher in government Indian schools.

From 1931–33, she taught in the Hayward Indian School in northern Wisconsin. When it closed, she was transferred to the Rosebud Reservation and taught in the boarding school there for two years. Resigning from this position, she went to Northern Arizona State University in Flagstaff and earned a bachelor's degree in education in 1938. That year she returned to teaching and was placed in a two-year internship in Pine Ridge. When her supervising teacher recommended that the second year be waived, the government agreed, and she was transferred to Horse Creek Day School in White River in 1939. That summer she was selected by the national YMCA to represent American Indian youth at the World's Conference of Christian Youth in Amsterdam, Holland.

She taught in Horse Creek Day School from 1939–43. She had married Harvey Ross in 1939, and when he went into the army in 1943, she stayed home to take care of their three small sons from 1943–52.

In 1952 she returned to teaching in the Pine Ridge Oglala Community School, where she remained until retirement in 1972. In 1958 she received an MS in education from Chadron State College in Nebraska. In that year she was selected as Teacher of the Year for South Dakota. She was a teacher, then teacher supervisor, and finally, education specialist for the entire Pine Ridge Reservation.

After retirement, she and Harvey moved back to Flandreau. From 1972–75, she worked for Dakota State University as coordinator for Title Programs conducted for the Flandreau Indian School. During one of these summers she taught the Dakota language for the University of South Dakota. In 1980 she was granted a doctorate at Oglala Lakota College of Kyle, South Dakota, in recognition of her help in establishing that college.

From 1972–74, she was tribal chair of the Flandreau Indians. She was instrumental in getting the tribal motel built and initiated tribal housing and health programs.

In recent years she is more proud of her four sons' achievements than her own. Two of these sons have doctorates and work in education. A third, who has finished course work for the doctorate in mathematics, is budget analyst for the Bureau of Indian Affairs in Aberdeen, South Dakota. The fourth has a master's degree in elementary education. In 1986 Ross and Harvey were honored by Black Hills State University for having four sons who received degrees there.

—Jack Marken

References

"Allen-Ross." In *Moody County History Book*, 194. Sioux Falls, SD: Jack Kilgore and Associates, 1984.

Ross, Agnes. *Dakota Language*. Aberdeen, SD: N.p., 1980.

———. *Dakota Language*. Bushnell, SD: Featherstone, 1983. Cassette.

Who's Who Among the Sioux. Vermillion, SD: Institute of Indian Studies State Publishing, 1988.

RUNNING EAGLE [BROWN WEASEL WOMAN, PITAMAKAN] (?–1878?) was known for her skills as a warrior. Running Eagle was probably born during the Hudson's Bay trading era, and she was a member of the Piegan tribe of the Blackfeet Nation.

Brown Weasel Woman assumed the household duties when her mother became ill, although she disliked domestic routine. She was taught early by her father, a warrior, to shoot a bow and arrow, and accompanied him on buffalo hunts where she learned to shoot well enough to kill buffalo. On one of these hunts they encountered an enemy party. Her father's horse was shot when they retreated to camp, and she returned and picked him up, unloading the fresh meat on her horse and escaping back to the camp, where she was praised for her bravery.

Her mother died after learning of the father's death, and Brown Weasel Woman took over the care of her brothers and sisters. Having no interest in marriage, she brought a widow woman into her lodge to help with the household and to care for the children. From then on she carried a rifle inherited from her father and acted as the head of the family.

Her first war experience came soon after her parents' deaths. Crow warriors had stolen some horses and the Blackfeet warriors went in pursuit of them. Told by the warriors to return to camp, she nevertheless trailed behind them. Several days later, the party reached the enemy camp. During the raid, Brown Weasel

Woman and a male cousin captured eleven valuable horses. On the return to their camp, while the rest of the party rested under cover, she kept watch on the trail from a nearby butte. When she saw two enemy riders approach the horses, she ran down the butte with her rifle, caught hold of the rope of the herd's lead horse to keep the rest from running away, shot one of the enemy, and forced the other to turn back. Instead of reloading her rifle, she grabbed the fallen enemy's and shot at, but missed, the man getting away.

Still not accepted as a full warrior, she followed the advice of the wise elders and went out to fast and seek a vision. After four days and nights alone, she received a vision giving her the power necessary for leading a successful warrior's life. From then on the people considered her as a person with special powers guided by the Spirits and she was named Running Eagle by the chief, Lone Walker. She went on many raids and was allowed to tell of her exploits in the medicine lodge ceremony. She became a member of the Braves Society of young warriors and led many war parties.

She died during one of these raids some time after 1878. Near the Sun River in a battle with a large party of Flathead warriors, she was clubbed from behind and killed. Trick Falls in Glacier National Park bore the name Pitamakan in honor of this woman warrior until it was renamed by white settlers.

Her name appears as Running Eagle Pe tu on the agency census of 1877–78, but it is absent after that time.

—Audrey M. Godfrey

References

Ewers, John. "Deadlier Than the Male." *American Heritage* 16 (June 1965): 10–13.

Hungry Wolf, Beverly. *The Ways of My Grandmothers*. New York: William Morrow, 1980.

Pratt, Grace Roffey. "Female War Chief of the Blackfeet." Reprint from *Frontier Times* (1971).

Schilz, Thomas, and Jodye Lynn Dickson Schilz. "Amazons, Witches and Country Wives: Plains Indian Women in Historical Perspective." *Annals of Wyoming* 59 (Spring 1987): 48–56.

U.S. Department of the Interior. Bureau of Indian Affairs. Blackfoot Agency Census. 1877–78.

S

SACAGAWEA [SACAJAWEA, BIRD WOMAN] (c. 1788), one of the most elusive women in American history, remains obscured by controversial scholarship surrounding every mention of her in historical records, from the spelling and meaning of her name to the assessment of her contributions to the Lewis and Clark expedition. The controversy extends into her post-expedition fate, since verifiable information about her exists only in the journals of the explorers and in a few of Clark's letters after the journey ended. Finally, in some revisionist views, Sacagawea, like Pocahontas and La Malinche, is the embodiment of collusion with the Euro-American invaders.

Sacajawea (Shoshone for "Boat Launcher") or Sacagawea (Hidatsa/Minnetaree for "Bird Woman"), as her name is alternately spelled, was probably born in 1788 or 1789 to Shoshone parents in eastern Idaho, near the present-day town of Salmon. Following Shoshone custom, shortly after birth she was promised in marriage to a Shoshone man, the marriage to commence when she reached puberty. When she was about ten or eleven, the Shoshone camp near Three Forks in Montana was attacked by Minnetaree (Hidatsa), and Sacagawea and another girl were taken prisoner to the Minnetaree camp. Eventually, the two young women were purchased by Toussaint Charbonneau, a French-Canadian fur trader in the region. While camped for the winter of 1804–5 at Fort Mandan in present-day North Dakota, Lewis and Clark hired Charbonneau as an interpreter to accompany the expedition. On February 11, 1805, Sacagawea gave birth to a son, Jean Baptiste, and when the Corps of Discovery resumed its westward trek in April of that year, Charbonneau, Sacagawea and her baby were members of the party.

In their journals, Lewis and Clark appeared to have differing assessments of Sacagawea and her usefulness. Lewis seldom mentions her. Two of his more noteworthy observations illustrate his ambivalence towards her. In the first, he states that she required only sufficient food and a few "trinkets" to make her happy; in the second, he worries that she is dangerously ill, anxious not only for her sake but also because her services would be needed when the Corps reached the Shoshone. Clark, on the other hand, frequently expresses his fondness for her baby, the value of her services to the party, and his concern for her welfare in the face of illness, danger, and physical abuse by Charbonneau. Clark portrays her as self-effacing in most instances, but she argues forcefully and successfully that she should be allowed to travel the final few miles to view the Pacific Ocean and a beached whale after traveling so far and enduring so many hardships.

Her specific contributions to the expedition are recounted in Clark's journal. She was needed as a translator and negotiator for horses with her own people, the Shoshone, and as a guide through her home territory. The fact that her brother,

219

Cameahwait, was the Shoshone leader enabled the explorers to procure the animals they needed for the mountain portage. Her services as a translator also were utilized among other Indian tribes who had Shoshone prisoners living among them. She saved valuable scientific equipment from being swept away when one of the pirogues capsized, maintaining a cool head when Charbonneau panicked. On the return trip, she guided Clark through the Bozeman Pass, saving him many miles. When food supplies were scarce, she found edible roots and berries. Perhaps most significantly, the presence of a woman and child on the expedition was proof of the Corps's peaceful intentions. As Clark noted, "The Wife of Shabono our interpreter We find reconsiles all the Indians, as to our friendly intentions. A woman with a party of men is a token of peace." For her efforts, Lewis and Clark named a river for her, while Charbonneau received the sum of $500.33 at the conclusion of the expedition. Clark recognized the inequity in a later letter to Charbonneau: "Your woman who accompanied you that long dangerous and fatiguing rout to the Pacific Ocian and back diserved a greater reward for her attention and serves on that rout than we had in our power to give her at the Mandans."

If Sacagawea was perceived by the Indians whose country the Corps traversed as a "token of peace," there is little peace associated with other elements of her life. Stolen from her family and people at a young age, she was sold to a man who abused her. When she was reunited with her brother, Cameahwait, she learned that all of her family was dead, save for him and her sister's son, whom she adopted. Clark wished to adopt her son, Jean Baptiste, and raise him in civilization. Because the child was not yet weaned, Charbonneau and Sacagawea agreed that one year later they would take the child to Clark in St. Louis. Charbonneau tried farming on land purchased from Clark, eventually deciding to return to hunting and trapping. Sacagawea appears to have remained in St. Louis for some period of time, but information on the remainder of her life is contradictory.

One theory contends that Sacagawea died of "putrid fever" on December 10, 1812, at Fort Manuel in present-day South Dakota, at the age of about twenty-five, leaving behind an infant daughter. Evidence supporting this theory comes from a notation by trader John C. Luttig and an annotation from 1825–26 in Clark's handwriting on his cashbook as to the fate of members of the expedition. After Sacagawea's name, he had written, "Dead."

The second theory, promoted by Eva Emery Dye, in a popular 1902 novel, and Grace Hebard, a professor at the University of Wyoming in a 1933 scholarly work based on oral histories of Indians and whites on the Wind River Reservation in Wyoming, holds that Sacagawea lived a long and fulfilling life after leaving Charbonneau because he took a third wife who displeased her. Traveling to the Comanches, who were linguistically close to the Shoshone, Sacagawea married a Comanche man, Jerk Meat, and bore five more children, two of whom survived. After Jerk Meat's death, her whereabouts are unknown for several years, but she eventually returned to Wind River where her son Jean Baptiste and her adopted son, Bazil, were living. By the accounts of Indians, Indian agents, and missionaries on the reservation, the woman they knew as Porivo (Chief) knew many details of the Lewis and Clark expeditions, and also wore a Jefferson Medal around her neck. She became a highly respected member of the tribe and was a close associate of Chief Washakie, attending and speaking at the meeting that led to the Fort Bridger Treaty. The woman's grandson, Andrew Bazil, credits his grandmother with introducing the Sun Dance to the Shoshone. By several accounts, she related her version of the expedition to Grace Irwin, wife of the Indian agent. Sometimes speaking in French, her few mentions of Charbonneau were bitter, but she spoke highly of Captain Clark. Unfortunately, Irwin's document was lost in a fire at the agency office at Fort Washakie in 1884 or 1885. Porivo died in 1884 and was buried in the white cemetery at Fort Washakie because whites perceived her as a friend for her role in the expedition and for her advocacy of agriculture as a way of life for the Shoshone in the last half of the nineteenth century. In 1924 the Bureau of Indian Affairs asked Dr. Charles Eastman to determine the location of Sacagawea's grave so that a monument might be erected on it. Taking into account the strong oral tradition among the Shoshone, he concluded that Porivo was indeed Sacagawea.

Because of the passage of time and the scarcity of documentation, the events of Sacagawea's life after the expedition may never be known with certainty. However, it is interesting to note that the conflict between the theories rests in the tension between scanty, but "authoritative," written evidence of Sacagawea's early demise versus substantial, but "unauthoritative," oral accounts of the Shoshone Indians. In addition, the two women who were early proponents of the longer-lived Sacagawea theory, Dye and Hebard, were frequently referred to as leaders of the Women's Suffrage Movement by opposing scholars, suggesting that the women's scholarship was rendered suspect not simply by Dye's choice of genre or Hebard's methodology, but also by their political activism.

—Kathleen Donovan

References

Anderson, Irving. "A Charbonneau Family Portrait." *American West* 17 (1980): 4–13, 63–64.

——. "Probing the Riddle of the Bird Woman." *Montana: The Magazine of Western History* 23 (1973): 2–17.

Chuinard, E.G. "The Bird Woman: Purposeful Member of the Corps or Casual 'Tag-along.'" *Montana: The Magazine of Western History* 26 (1976): 18–29.

Clark, Ella, and Margot Edmonds. *Sacagawea of the Lewis and Clark Expedition.* Berkeley: University of California Press, 1979.

Coues, Elliot, ed. *History of the Expedition under the Command of Lewis and Clark.* 4 vols. 1893. Reprint. New York: Dover, 1964.

Dye, Eva Emery. *The Conquest: The True Story of Lewis and Clark.* Chicago: A.C. McClurg, 1902.

Hebard, Grace Raymond. *Sacajawea: A Guide and Interpreter of the Lewis and Clark Expedition, with an account of the Travels of Toussaint Charbonneau, and of Jean Baptiste, the expedition papoose.* Glendale: Arthur H. Clark, 1933.

Howard, Harold P. *Sacajawea.* Norman: University of Oklahoma Press, 1971.

Kingston, C.S. "Sacajawea as a Guide: The Evaluation of a Legend." *Pacific Northwest Quarterly* 35 (1944): 2–18.

Ronda, James P. *Lewis and Clark Among the Indians.* Lincoln: University of Nebraska Press, 1984.

Schroer, Blanche. "Boat-Pusher or Bird Woman?: Sacagawea or Sacajawea?" *Annals of Wyoming* 52 (1980): 46–54.

SACRED WHITE BUFFALO, MOTHER MARY CATHERINE

[JOSEPHINE CROWFEATHER, PTESANWANYAKAPI, PTESAN-WANYAGAPIWIN] (1867–1893), daughter of Joseph Crowfeather, a Hunkpapa Lakota chief, was born near Standing Rock Agency, Dakota Territory (now North Dakota). Since infancy, Crowfeather was regarded as a sacred virgin because, while a newborn, her father had carried her into battle for protection, and they both returned unharmed. Hence, her Indian name, Ptesanwanyakapi, or "They see a white buffalo woman," compared her to the sacred virgin in a Lakota story. As a youth, she expressed a desire to become a Catholic sister and for four years she attended the Benedictine Sisters' School at Fort Yates, North Dakota.

From 1888 to 1890, Crowfeather trained to become a sister under the guidance of Rev. Francis M. Craft, a priest with Iroquois ancestry. She shared his vision of fulfilling the dream of the sixteenth century Mohawk convert Kateri Tekakwitha who had wanted to establish an Indian Christian sisterhood. With five other Lakota women, she first attended a Benedictine academy in Avoca, Minnesota, and then the Benedictine novitiate in Zell, Minnesota, where Crowfeather professed her vows in 1890. She then served as assistant cook at a Stephen, South Dakota, mission school until internal strife at the novitiate prompted the premature transfer of the fledgling community to its new convent at Elbowoods, North Dakota, on the Fort Berthold Reservation.

The next year, Crowfeather was elected the founding prioress-general of the new Congregation of American Sisters, and she assumed the title of "Mother." Although independent, her community followed Benedictine discipline through convent devotions and missionary work among the Arickara, Gros Ventre, and Mandan. The congregation taught English, cared for the sick, and directed Christian sodalities.

In 1893 Mother Catherine succumbed to tuberculosis. Her young community survived for seven years more and was to reach a membership of twelve. Despite chronic poverty, illness, and racism during its brief history, the order served to inspire future Native religious workers.

—Mark G. Thiel

References

Duratschek, Mary C. *Crusading Along Sioux Trails: A History of the Catholic Indian Missions of South Dakota*. St. Meinrad, IN: The Grail Press, 1947.

Ewans, Mary. "The Native Order: A Brief and Strange History." In *Scattered Steeples, the Fargo Diocese: A Written History of its Centennial*, edited by Jerome D. Lamb, Jerry Ruff, and William C. Sherman, 10–23. Fargo, ND: Burch, Londergan, and Lynch, 1988.

Mathes, Valerie S. "American Indian Women and the Catholic Church." *North Dakota History* 47 (1980): 20–25.

SAILA, PITALOOSIE [PITALOUISA, PITALOOSEE] (b. 1942) was born

in Arctic Canada on August 11. One of the well-known women Inuit printmakers, she lives at Cape Dorset. Pitaloosie is married to the noted sculptor Pauta Saila and is the niece of Oshoochiak Pudiat and the famed Cape Dorset sculptor and printmaker, Pudlo.

In the late 1950s Canadian artist and author James A. Houston, working as a civil administrator for the Department of Northern Affairs and National Resources, introduced drawing and printmaking to the Inuit people of Cape Dorset. Since then the production of art has been a creative outlet and a means of earning a livelihood for many Inuit people. Pitaloosie is of the second generation of Cape Dorset artists. She began drawing in the late 1960s, and her first piece was published in the 1968 Cape Dorset collection. Since that time her prints have appeared regularly in the illustrated catalogues of the annual collections of Inuit art and her work has been exhibited internationally.

Pitaloosie often draws scenes of seasonal activities, such as hunting and fishing. "Fisherman's Dream," a 1971 print, was reproduced on a twelve-cent stamp, which was issued in November 1977 by the Canadian government. Pitaloosie is best known, though, for her depictions of mothers and children. In 1983 her print, "Arctic Madonna," was selected to be reproduced on a UNICEF card. Much of her work conveys the Inuit sense of transformation and possibility.

—Hertha D. Wong

References

Barz, Sandra B., comp. *Inuit Artists Print Workbook*. New York: Arts and Cultures of the North, 1981.

Dorset 79: The Twentieth Annual Cape Dorset Graphics Collection. Toronto: M.F. Feheley, 1979.

Furneaux, Patrick. "Evolution and Development of the Eskimo Print." In *Arts of the Eskimo: Prints*, edited by Ernst Roch, 9–16. Barre, MA: Barre, 1975.

Rosshandler, Leo. "The Eskimo Print, an Appreciation." In *Arts of the Eskimo: Prints*, edited by Ernst Roch, 17–19. Barre, MA: Barre, 1975.

Schuldberg, Jane. "Pitaloosie Saila." Snow Goose Associates, Seattle. Photocopy.

SAINTE-MARIE, BUFFY (b. early 1940s), a Cree orphaned as an infant, was adopted and raised by a couple in Massachusetts. Living in a virtually all-white community, her adoptive mother, part Micmac Indian, spent many hours telling Sainte-Marie her Indian history. Sainte-Marie's musical interests began very early in life. At the age of four she was making up poems and taught herself to play the piano. She began to play guitar and to write her own songs when her father gave her a guitar for her sixteenth birthday. As a university honors student, Sainte-Marie studied Oriental philosophy, while continuing to play guitar and compose songs and to research her heritage. After graduation Sainte-Marie went to New York to perform in Greenwich Village coffee shops and was soon offered nightclub dates and a recording contract.

During the 1960s Buffy Sainte-Marie became an internationally known folk singer and songwriter who produced a number of gold records. Besides her popular love songs, she wrote anti-war ballads, as well as many songs which celebrate Native identity and protest injustices waged on Native American peoples. During the height of the anti-war era, some of her more controversial material was banned from radio and television.

Despite her perceived controversial nature, Sainte-Marie appeared on major television shows during the 1960s and early 1970s. When she accepted a television contract, she insisted that all Indian roles be played by Indian people, thus opening the door for other Native American performers.

A social and political activist, Sainte-Marie founded the Native North American Women's Association—a group which has sponsored theater, arts, and education projects. She also instituted the Nihewan Foundation, a law school scholarship fund for Native Americans that is funded by money from her concerts. By 1975 Nihewan Foundation scholarships had sent more than twenty people through law school.

Although less visible during the 1980s, as were the other folk and protest musicians of the Vietnam/civil rights era, Sainte-Marie has been active in Native rights movements. For instance, Sainte-Marie read the English translations of elders' words in Maria Florio's and Victoria Mudd's 1985 film about the big business-inspired forced relocation of Navajo and Hopi from their ancestral homeland.

—Elizabeth A. McNeil

References

Braudy, Susan. "Buffy Sainte-Marie: 'Native North American Me.'" *Ms.* 4 (March 1975): 14–18.

Florio, Maria, and Victoria Mudd. *Broken Rainbow.* 1985. Distributed by Earthworks Films.

Gridley, Marion E., ed. and comp. *Indians of Today.* 4th ed. Chicago: ICFP, 1971.

Sainte-Marie, Buffy. "Buffy." *Talking Leaf* 41 (August 1976): 8–9.

———. *The Buffy Sainte-Marie Songbook.* New York: Grosset and Dunlap, 1971.

————. "Refuse to Be a Victim." In *The Ethnic American Woman: Problems, Protests, Life-Style*, edited by Edith Blicksilver, 339–40. Dubuque, IA: Kendall/ Hunt, 1978.

SAKIESTEWA, RAMONA (b. 1949) does weavings that are a metaphor for her life; her family included a Hopi father, German-Irish mother, and Anglo-American stepfather. She was raised in Albuquerque, New Mexico, a city which successfully melds past and present and Native American, Hispanic, and Anglo cultures. Her textiles incorporate these environmental influences, as well as the region's rich textile heritage. Her weavings reflect her multicultural environment. The influences are clear in her interpretations of historic Navajo weavings, abstractions of kachina textile motifs, or her treatments of the southwestern landscape and unique architecture. However, each textile bears Sakiestewa's imprint; each is well designed and executed in clean, clear colors from either vegetal or aniline dyes.

Sakiestewa grew up surrounded by the Native arts of the Southwest in her home and in her job in an Albuquerque trading post. After teaching herself to weave by reading books written by the anthropologists Ruth Underhill and Kate Peck Kent, she moved to New York to study design. In 1975 Sakiestewa began a project at Bandelier National Monument to replicate the ancient techniques used in the manufacture of a spun turkey feather blanket, and in 1983 she replicated a cotton manta. Before turning to weaving as a full-time profession, Sakiestewa worked as an arts administrator for the Museum of New Mexico, New Mexico Arts Division, and was instrumental in establishing ATLATL, a national Native American arts and cultural services organization. In 1981 she traveled to Peru to consult with weavers on the creation of a weavers' guild. The next year she founded Ramona Sakiestewa Ltd. to produce and market functional textiles. Her studio has recently transformed Frank Lloyd Wright sketches into fiber.

Currently, Sakiestewa has been studying contemporary Pueblo textiles and experimenting with historic dyes. She continues to serve on the New Mexico Arts Commission, Southwest Association on Indian Affairs, the Wheelwright Museum of Indian Art Board, as president of the Santa Fe Indian Market, and she has served as a panel member for the National Endowment for the Arts. Her work has won awards at the Santa Fe Indian Market, Heard Museum, and Museum of Northern Arizona and is held in many public and private collections. She lives in Santa Fe with her husband Arthur Sze, a poet, and their son, Micah.

—Laura Graves

References

Baizerman, Suzanne. *Ramona Sakiestewa Patterned Dreams: Textiles of the Southwest.* Santa Fe: Wheelwright Museum of Indian Art, 1989.

Bender, Roberta. "Ramona Sakiestewa: Beyond Limits." *Native Peoples* 2 (Summer 1989): 30–34.

Hammond, Harmony, and Juane Quick-to-See Smith. *Women of Sweetgrass, Cedar and Sage.* New York: Gallery of the American Indian Community House, 1985.

Jacka, Lois Essary, and Jerry Jacka. *Beyond Tradition: Contemporary Indian Art and Its Evolution.* Flagstaff, AZ: Northland Press, 1988.

Traugott, Joseph. "Indian Weaver's Creations Art More than Artifacts." *Albuquerque Journal*, 28 May 1989.

SALABIYE, VELMA S. (b. 1948), a Navajo born at Bellemont, Arizona, was educated at Bellemont Hogan School and at St. Michael's. After graduating from high school in 1966, she attended the University of Arizona, from which she graduated with a BA in education in 1971. In 1974 she earned her MLS from the university's Indian Graduate Library Institute, a federally funded program. As part of this program, she interned at the Window Rock Public Library on the Navajo Reservation.

On the reservation in 1975, she began planning a library, later known as the Navajo Research and Statistics Center. She became the coordinator for a Special Libraries Association meeting on the Navajo Reservation in 1977. In 1979 she served as evaluator of major American Indian collections in California, and in that year she was awarded a D'Arcy McNickle Fellowship at the Newberry Library Center for the History of the American Indian for the purpose of studying the roles and contributions of Navajo women to American Indian society.

Since 1980 Salabiye (Vee, as she is known to family and friends) has been the librarian of the American Indian Studies Center, UCLA. Since 1988 she has served as an associate editor of *American Indian Culture and Research Journal*. She has been the author or co-author of various publications on American Indian library collections, believing that her major roles are to promote American Indian librarianship and to build a strong American Indian library collection.

On October 7, 1987, she was presented a Certificate of Appreciation from the Office of Educational Research and Improvement, US Department of Education, "in recognition of the outstanding service provided to the Library Services for Indian Tribes and Hawaiian Natives Program."

—Jack Marken

References

"Humor and Joking of the American Indian: A Bibliography." *American Indian Libraries Newsletter* 10 (Fall 1986): 2–4.

Salabiye, Velma. *American Indian Library Resources at UCLA.* Los Angeles: Institute of American Cultures, 1980.

————. "Library and Information Resources." In *Community-Based Research: A Handbook for Native Americans.* Los Angeles: American Indian Studies Center, UCLA, 1983.

————, and James R. Young. "American Indian Leaders and Leadership of the Twentieth Century: A Bibliographic Essay." *Journal of the West* 23 (July 1984): 70–76.

SANAPIA [MARY POAFPYBITTY; STICKY MOTHER] (1895–1984), Yapai Comanche medicine woman, was born in a tepee encampment near Fort Sill, Oklahoma, the sixth in a family of eleven children. Her father was a "progressive" Christian Comanche proselytizer, and her mother a staunch Comanche-Arapaho traditionalist and medicine woman. The maternal influences proved stronger.

As a young child, Sanapia was raised by her maternal grandmother, who stressed the importance of learning and recording tribal traditions and urged the girl to follow her mother's career as an eagle doctor. Sanapia's uncle, who cured her of influenza in the early 1900s, extracted a promise that she become a doctor when she regained her health. Seven years of boarding school education at Cache Creek Mission School ended when Sanapia was fourteen. Her training as a medicine woman began the summer before her last year of school and continued for three years after she returned home. By age seventeen, Sanapia had learned all the skills and knowledge she would need as an eagle doctor from her mother, who then transferred her healing power to Sanapia in a formal ceremony. Sanapia could not begin to practice, however, until she had reached menopause.

Once her training was complete, Sanapia's mother and brother arranged a marriage for her that ended shortly after her first son was born. Sanapia remarried within a year and had a son and a daughter before her husband died in the 1930s. Sanapia mourned his death for several years by "roughing it out" in wild self-destructive behavior that stopped when she began to use her healing powers in the 1940s. She married a third time as she began her healing career and was again widowed in old age.

By the late 1960s, Sanapia was the last surviving eagle doctor and had acquired the maximum power and prestige attainable by a woman in traditional Comanche society. She specialized in the treatment of "ghost sickness," an illness increasingly common as Comanches acculturated, involving facial paralysis believed caused by fearful contact with a ghost. Her very effective healing ritual combined elements of psychiatry, herbal medicine, and peyote with songs and prayers to invoke the intercession of spirits and her medicine eagle, a process that reintegrated patients into the traditionalist community and thus restored their health.

As she approached old age, Sanapia began thinking about transferring her power, but no obvious successor appeared ready. She consented to work with anthropologist David E. Jones, whom she adopted as a son, to record her life and preserve her medicinal knowledge and practices in case she died before she could completely train her successor. This was a wise decision; she probably did not have a chance to formally transfer her power before her death in Oklahoma in 1984.

—Helen M. Bannan

References

Jones, David E. "Face the Ghost." *New Directions in the Study of Man* 4 (1980): 53–57.
———. *Sanapia, Comanche Medicine Woman.* New York: Holt, Rinehart, and Winston, 1972.

SANCHEZ, CAROL LEE (b. 1934), is a Laguna Pueblo/Sioux born in Albuquerque, New Mexico, and raised in the village of Paguate. She later moved to a small, Roman Catholic, land grant Chicano town nearby until she was eighteen. Her mother is a Laguna/Sioux and her father is a Lebanese-American who speaks Spanish and Arabic. Sister of Paula Gunn Allen, Sanchez is a poet, painter, and educator. The poetry and art of Sanchez is heavily influenced by her multicultural and multilinguistic background. Her writing was also influenced by her experiences in San Francisco since her arrival there in 1964.

Sanchez received her BA in Arts Administration from San Francisco State University in 1978. In 1975, her book of poems *Conversations from the Nightmare*, was nominated for the American Academy of Poets Edgar Allan Poe award. In 1981, she was a speaker for meetings of the American Indian Women Painters and Third World Women in Arts. Also in 1981, she was conference coordinator for the National Women's Studies Association at San Francisco State University. She is Affirmative Action Committee chair for the California Association of English. She also has a growing reputation as an arts administrator for her work as coordinator of the First Western States Biennial Exhibition.

She is presently teaching at San Francisco State University in the School of Ethnic Studies. She is primarily a teacher of American Indian Studies but has also been active and vocal in the feminist arena teaching women's and third world women's literature in addition to lecturing.

—Lucy Leriche

References

Allen, Paula Gunn. "This Wilderness in My Blood: Spiritual Foundations of the Poetry of Five American Indian Women." In *The Sacred Hoop: Recovering the Feminine in American Indian Traditions.* Boston: Beacon Press, 1986.
Anderson, Owanah, ed. *Ohoyo One Thousand: A Resource Guide of American Indian/Alaska Native Women, 1982.* Wichita Falls, TX: Ohoyo Resource Center, 1982.

Green Rayna, ed. *That's What She Said: Contemporary Poetry and Fiction by Native American Women.* Bloomington: Indiana University Press, 1984.

Sanchez, Carol Lee. *Conversations from the Nightmare.* Berkeley: Casa Editorial Publication, 1975.

———. *Coyote's Journal.* Berkeley: Wingbow Press, 1981.

———. *Excerpts from a Mountain Climber's Handbook.* San Francisco: Taurean Horn and Out West Limited, 1985.

———. *Message Bringer Woman.* San Francisco: Taurean Horn, 1977.

———. *Morning Prayer.* Brooklyn: Strawberry Press, 1977.

———. *Time Warps.* San Francisco: Taurean Horn Press, 1976.

SAUBEL, KATHERINE SIVA (b. 1920) is a Cahuilla Indian elder born on the Los Coyotes Reservation and raised in Palm Springs, California. She grew up speaking her Native language and learning tribal traditions from her mother, Melan Seivatily, and her father, Juan C. Siva. After marrying Mariano Saubel, together they helped begin the Malki Museum, the first non-profit tribal museum on an Indian reservation in California. For many years Saubel served on the Riverside County Historical Commission, which selected her County Historian of the Year in 1986. The next year she was recognized as the Elder of the Year by the California State Indian Museum. Governor George Deukmejian appointed her to serve on the California Native American Heritage Commission in 1986, and she has served with distinction, preserving sacred sites and protecting Indian remains. Saubel has testified as an expert on Indian culture and history before the California legislature, the United States Congress, and several boards, commissions, and agencies.

A respected scholar on Cahuilla Indian history, literature, and culture, Saubel was University of California's lecturer at the University of California, Riverside; she has taught at the University of California, Los Angeles; California State University, Hayward; and the University of Cologne. She has worked closely with linguist Hansjakob Seiler to preserve the Cahuilla language. Saubel's publications are a result of her interest in "saving remnants of my culture in these books," which are designed "to tell everyone how it was." With Professor Lowell Bean, she has published: *Temalpahk: Cahuilla Indian Knowledge and Usage of Plants, Cahuilla Ethnobotanical Notes,* and *Oak.* Her other books include *Kunvachmal: A Cahuilla Tale, I'sniyatam,* and *Cahuilla Ethnobotanical Notes: Mesquite and Screwbean* (also with Lowell Bean). Katherine Saubel is known internationally as a Native American scholar, and she is considered one of the foremost Indian leaders in California.

—Clifford E. Trafzer

References

Bean, Lowell John, and Katherine Siva Saubel. *Cahuilla Ethnobotanical Notes: The Aboriginal Uses of Oak.* Archaeology Survey Annual Report, University of California, Los Angeles, 1961.

————. *Cahuilla Ethnobotanical Notes: Aboriginal Uses of Mesquite and Screwbean.* Archaeology Survey Annual Report, University of California, Los Angeles, 1963.

————. *Temalpakh: Cahuilla Indian Knowledge and Uses of Plants.* Banning, CA: Malki Museum Press, 1972.

Jeffrey, Cheryl. "Katherine Saubel." *Local Daughters of the Desert* 2 (December 1989): N.p.

Saubel, Katherine Siva. *I'sniyatam Designs, a Cahuilla Word Book.* Banning, CA: Malki Museum Press, Morongo Indian Reservation, 1977.

Trafzer, Clifford E. Personal communication, 1990.

SEKAQUAPTEWA, HELEN [DOWAWISNIMA] (1898–1990) was born
into a turbulent time in Hopi history during a period of rapidly accelerating
Anglo influence on the remote mesas of her tribal land. She was the second
daughter in a family residing in the most traditional and conservative of the Hopi
villages of northern Arizona; her family was forced to move to Hotevilla when a
split at Oraibi village ended in eviction of nearly half the families. Hopis resisted
sending their children to school, and Sekaquaptewa was hidden from truant
officers but finally discovered and sent to boarding school at Keams Canyon; her
father was jailed for one year for his resistance to government interference in
tribal organization and traditional education.

Though, like other children at the time, Sekaquaptewa suffered from illness
and the family rupture caused by removal to school, she also became a good pupil,
and when the opportunity to attend the Phoenix Indian School was offered, she
chose to enter and complete secondary school. There she became adept at
domestic skills as well as academic subjects and aspired to open a laundry business
on the Hopi Reservation. However, when she returned to Hopi, her family and
other villagers were suspicious of her non-traditional ways, and she felt alienated.
She soon married Emory Sekaquaptewa, whom she had met at school, and
together they moved to a ranch on the perimeter of the reservation where they
raised a large family, several of whom were to become prominent in tribal politics
and cultural studies.

Despite her conversion to Christianity, Sekaquaptewa retained an intense
interest in Hopi ceremonialism, and as the matriarch of the Eagle Clan, she was
particularly involved in women's ceremonial life. In her later years she lived in
the village of Kikutsmovi on Third Mesa, and her home became a center for clan
and family activities. She credited the publication of her autobiography, *Me and
Mine*, as the critical factor gaining her a central place in Hopi society.

—Kathleen M. Sands

References

Bataille, Gretchen M., and Kathleen M. Sands. "Two Women in Transition." In *Native American Women Telling Their Lives*, 83–112. Lincoln: University of Nebraska Press, 1984.

"Iisaw: Hopi Coyote Stories," with Helen Sekaquaptewa. *Words and Place: Native Literature from the American Southwest.* Larry Evers, Project Director. New York: Clearwater Publishing, 1981. 18 min. Videotape.

Hopi: Songs of the Fourth World. Produced and directed by Pat Ferrero, 1983. Distributed by New Day Films. 58 min. Videotape.

Sands, Kathleen M., and Emory Sekaquaptewa. "Four Hopi Lullabies: Method and Meaning." *American Indian Quarterly* 4 (May 1978): 97–106.

Sekaquaptewa, Helen. *Me and Mine.* Edited by Louise Udall. Tucson: University of Arizona Press, 1969.

SHANLEY, KATHRYN [VANGEN] (b. 1947), born at Wolf Point, Montana, is assistant professor of English at the University of Washington in Seattle. She is a member of the Assiniboine tribe and grew up on the Fort Peck Reservation. She received a nursing degree from Metropolitan State University in Minneapolis in 1973. After pursuing nursing as a career, she returned to school to complete a BA degree in English (summa cum laude) at Moorhead State University in Minnesota. She then went on to graduate school at the University of Michigan, receiving her MA in English in 1982 and her PhD in 1987. Shanley received a Frances Allen Fellowship at the Newberry Library in Chicago to do research on Lakota written and oral traditions, and in 1985 she joined the faculty of the University of Washington.

Shanley has been a prolific literary critic. Her writings include analyses of contemporary American Indian authors, such as James Welch, N. Scott Momaday, and Leslie Silko, as well as traditional Lakota thinkers Black Elk and Lame Deer. She is completing a book on politics in the poetry and prose of James Welch and has also published her own poetry and short fiction. In 1988–89 Shanley received a Ford Foundation Minority Postdoctoral Fellowship.

She is also presently involved in a project that grew out of a November 1987 invitational conference at State University of New York at Stony Brook on the role of faculty in promoting the recruitment and retention of African American, Native American and Latino scholars, and she is a founding member of Open Mind, an organization established in 1991 which grew out of that conference and whose aim is to address the national need for minority scholars. She has developed a project on using American Indian autobiographies as primary source material in the teaching of American history and literature and led a workshop on this topic for the D'Arcy McNickle Center for the History of the American Indian at the Newberry Library in Chicago. Her work on American Indian literature is innovative, and she is strongly committed to the development of a unique American Indian pedagogy at the university level.

—Clara Sue Kidwell

Reference

Vangen, Kathryn Winona Shanley. "Only an Indian: The Prose and Poetry of James Welch." PhD diss., University of Michigan, 1987.

SHAW, ANNA MOORE [CHEHIA] (1898–1975)

was born on the Gila River Pima Reservation to a Christianized family headed by Red Arrow, later known as Josiah Moore, a leader in his tribe. After eagerly following her older brother to a missionary boarding school in Tucson, she attended the Phoenix Indian High School where she was a student leader. There she met her husband, Ross Shaw, who subsequently became a freight wagon driver for the Santa Fe Railroad. In 1918 they set up a household in a multi-ethnic neighborhood in Phoenix where they raised two children. She was not interested in returning to the Gila River Reservation, feeling that she and her husband had an obligation to use their educations in an urban setting and to assimilate into Anglo culture without losing Indian identity. Active in her local community and in church affairs, Shaw was determined to overcome bigotry; her advocacy for intercultural understanding was given strong impetus by a visit from Carlos Montezuma, a well-known Indian spokesman, just before his death in 1922.

As her children became older, she began to regret the loss of traditional Pima stories and to compile her own version of tales she remembered from her youth. Her collection, *Pima Legends*, was published in 1968. Though she was satisfied with life in Phoenix and her fifty-year role as a mediator of two cultures, when her husband retired, she agreed to move to the Salt River Pima Reservation. There she devoted her considerable energies to reviving traditional Piman skills, teaching basket weaving to younger women in the tribe during a time when the techniques had nearly died out. She also edited the reservation newspaper, was instrumental in setting up a museum of Pima culture, and continued her activities in the Presbyterian congregation.

During her later years she began to write down a series of episodic recollections about her life. Upon urging of family and friends, she submitted her work for publication. The autobiography, supplemented by interview material and edited into a chronological narrative, was published in 1974. Titled *A Pima Past*, it is characterized by her positive attitude toward life and her dedication to multicultural understanding.

In 1981 Shaw was posthumously inducted into the Arizona Hall of Fame for her work in advocating interracial harmony.

—Kathleen M. Sands

References

Bataille, Gretchen M., and Kathleen M. Sands. "Two Women in Transition." In *Native American Women Telling Their Lives*, 83–112. Lincoln: University of Nebraska Press, 1984.

Shaw, Anna Moore. *A Pima Past.* Tucson: University of Arizona Press, 1975.
———. *Pima Legends.* Tucson: University of Arizona Press, 1968.
Tsosie, Rebecca. "Changing Women: The Cross-Currents of American Indian Feminine Identity." *American Culture and Research Journal* 12 (1988): 1–37.

SILKO, LESLIE MARMON (b. 1948) was born in Albuquerque to Lee H. Marmon (Laguna) and Virginia (from a Plains tribe). Of Indian-white-Mexican ancestry, she grew up on the Laguna Pueblo Reservation, where she learned the rich cultural lore of the Lagunas through the stories told by her grandmother Lillie and "Aunt Susie" (her grandmother Hank Marmon's sister-in-law), whose influence was fundamental in shaping Silko's personality.

She attended a Catholic high school in Albuquerque, and in 1969 she received a BA in English from the University of New Mexico. The same year she published her first short story, "The Man to Send Rain Clouds," based on a real incident that happened at Laguna, and she was awarded a National Endowment for the Humanities Discovery Grant. She attended three semesters of law school at the University of New Mexico and then decided to devote herself to writing.

Later, she taught at Navajo Community College at Tsaile, Arizona, and then went during the mid-seventies to Ketchikan, Alaska, where she wrote her novel, *Ceremony*.

She has received numerous grants and awards, including a National Endowment for the Arts Fellowship and a MacArthur Foundation Award in 1981 to complete her second novel, *Almanac of the Dead*.

Her first book-length publication, a collection of poems, *Laguna Woman*, appeared in 1974, and seven short stories were published the same year in one of the first anthologies of contemporary Native American writing, *The Man to Send Rain Clouds*.

Ceremony, her first novel, received enthusiastic praise. It tells the story of a half-breed Laguna World War II alienated veteran who is gradually able to heal himself by reenacting a traditional and yet modified ceremony with the help of a powerful mixed-blood medicine man, who significantly changes the rituals to face a different reality after the coming of white people. Only these innovations make the ceremony grow and keep it strong. The cycle of restoration leads to the achievement of a sense of unity between the individual and the land; oral storytelling is seen as a link between past and present in a mythological concept of time. Myths and legends are interwoven with the main narrative, and they are in fact the mythological parallel of what is happening to the protagonist. The ceremonial nature of existence is reflected in the ritualistic use of the storytelling—both ancient and modern—and its healing power. Silko, at the beginning of the novel, in a kind of traditional formula, creates a persona of herself—the storyteller who tells a story called *Ceremony* that the Pueblo creatix Thought Woman is thinking. A miscellany of family stories and photographs, *Storyteller* (which includes some of the poems and short stories already appearing in *Laguna*

Woman and *The Man to Send Rain Clouds*) can be considered as an autobiography, a new version, in written form, of traditional oral storytelling

The recent *Almanac of the Dead*, whose composition covers a period of ten years, is an ambitious and complex novel, both for its time structure and special locations, a radical and revisionary view of the history of the West, of the conquest and the exploitation of the Americas through two continents and four centuries of Indian life and culture, violence and oppression. "A brilliant, haunting and tragic novel of ruin and resistance in the Americas," as Larry McMurtry has defined it, *Almanac of the Dead* is a grim and utterly bleak view of the contemporary world, in which Silko seems to find no hope to relieve evil and corruption surrounding our age.

—Laura Coltelli

References

Allen, Paula Gunn. "The Ceremonial Motion of Indian Time: Long Ago, So Far." In *The Sacred Hoop*, edited by Paul Gunn Allen, 147–54. Boston: Beacon Press, 1986.

———. "The Feminine Landscape of Leslie Marmon Silko's *Ceremony*." In *Studies in American Indian Literature*, edited by Paula Gunn Allen, 127–33. New York: MLA, 1983.

Coltelli, Laura. "Re-Enacting Myths and Stories: Tradition and Renewal in *Ceremony*." In *Native American Literatures*, edited by Laura Coltelli, 173–84. Pisa: Seu, 1989.

Hailey, David E., Jr. "The Visual Elegance of Ts'its'tsi'nako and the Other Invisible Characters in *Ceremony*." *Wicazo Sa Review* 4 (Fall 1990): 1–6.

Herzog, Kristin. "Thinking Woman and Feeling Man: Gender in Leslie Marmon Silko's *Ceremony*." *MELUS* 12 (Summer 1985): 25–36.

Hirsch, Bernard A. "The Telling Which Continues: Oral Tradition and the Written Word in Leslie Marmon Silko's *Storyteller*." *American Indian Quarterly* 4 (Winter 1988): 1–26.

Lincoln, Kenneth. "Grandmother Storyteller: Leslie Silko." In *Native American Renaissance*, edited by Kenneth Lincoln, 222–50. Berkeley: University of California Press, 1983.

Ruoff, LaVonne A. "Ritual and Research: Keres Traditions in the Short Fiction of Leslie Silko." *MELUS* 5 (1978): 3–17.

Sands, Kathleen M., ed. "A Special Symposium Issue on Leslie Marmon Silko's *Ceremony*." *American Indian Quarterly* 5 (February 1979): 1–75.

Seyersted, Per. *Leslie Marmon Silko*. Boise, ID: Boise State University, 1980.

Silko, Leslie Marmon. *Almanac of the Dead*. New York: Simon and Schuster, 1991.

———. *Ceremony*. New York: Viking Press, 1977.

———. *The Delicacy and the Strength of Lace: Letters Between Leslie Marmon Silko and James Wright*. Saint Paul, MN: Greywolf Press, 1986.

———. *Laguna Woman*. Greenfield Center, NY: Greenfield Review Press, 1974.

———. *Storyteller*. New York: Seaver, 1981.

Swann, Edith. "Laguna Symbolic Geography and Silko's *Ceremony.*" *American Indian Quarterly* 12 (Summer 1988): 229–49.

———. "Healing Via the Sunrise Cycle in Silko's *Ceremony.*" *American Indian Quarterly* 12 (Fall 1988): 313–28.

SISK-FRANCO, CALEEN A. (b. 1952) was born in Redding, a small town near Mount Shasta in northern California. A member of the Wintu tribe, Sisk-Franco is the seventh of eleven children. She graduated from Shasta Union High School in 1970 and earned her AA degree from Shasta College two years later. After earning her BA degree in physical education from California State University at Chico in 1975, she went on to obtain a teaching certificate the next year. Currently, while working full-time, she is completing an MA degree in physical education at CSU, Chico.

Since 1976 Sisk-Franco has been actively engaged in education. From 1976–77 she was the director of Title V Indian Education in Santa Rosa and Richmond, California. In 1977 Sisk-Franco devoted two years to teaching adults at the Indian Education Center in her hometown. In 1979 she returned to teaching kindergarten through twelfth grade, this time in Fort Hall, Idaho. In 1981 she returned to northern California and taught grades K-4 in Marysville for five years. Since 1986 she has worked as the American Indian recruiter and advisor at her alma mater, CSU, Chico.

Throughout her years of teaching, recruiting, and advising, Sisk-Franco has been actively engaged in working on behalf of all Native American people and for federal recognition of the Wintu. From 1985–90 she was the chair of Toyon Wintu Center, Inc., the main tribal organization for the Wintu people. She is a board member of Four Winds of Education, an Indian-organized community education program in Chico, as well as a participant on the CSU Chico Provost's Repatriation Committee. In addition, she is a member of the National Indian Education Association, the Northern California Indian Recruiters Consortium, and the California State Department Indian Education Advisory Board.

As part of her commitment to serving her people, Sisk-Franco has published several editorials calling attention to the Wintu struggle for federal re-recognition and land rights. In 1971 the Toyon Wintu Center was built on 61 acres northwest of Redding, California, but twelve years later (1983) the Bureau of Indian Affairs (BIA) revoked the Wintu's "indefinite use permit." Years of political and legal struggles ensued, but in 1985 the BIA declared the Wintus "unrecognized Indians." As a result the Wintu people became ineligible for any BIA health or educational services. In 1989 the Native people still living at Toyon were evicted and their buildings were bulldozed. On June 18, 1990, Sisk-Franco began a much publicized water-only fast to hasten the state and federal government's responses to the Wintu appeal for federal recognition and to transfer the Toyon Wintu Center land base to tribal control. Sisk-Franco ended her fast twenty-one days later (July 8, 1990) when she received a letter from US

Senator Daniel Inouye, chair of the Senate Select Committee on Indian Affairs, in which he promised to support the California Tribal Status Act of 1990.

In addition to educational and political activism, Sisk-Franco is committed to traditional Wintu spirituality and is raising her son, Michael, to follow Winnemem Wintu traditions. Her leadership provides an important model for other Indian people of how to combine traditional teachings and a university education.

—Hertha D. Wong

References

Aylworth, Roger. "Two Women Fast for Wintu Recognition." *Enterprise-Record* [Chico] 29 June 1990, 1st edition: 2A.

Budman, Matthew. "Going to the Top of the Mountain: A Chico State Administrator's Fast for Indian Life." *News and Review* [Chico] 28 June 1990: 15–16.

"CSUC Indian Adviser Ends Successful Fast." *News and Review* [Chico] 12 July 1990: 26.

Sisk-Franco, Caleen A. "Toyon Belongs to the Wintu." *News from Native California* 4 (Fall 1989): 10–12.

Wong, Hertha. Interview with Caleen Sisk-Franco, Oakland, CA, 20 March 1991.

———. Written personal communication with Caleen Sisk-Franco, 1 March 1991.

SKYE, FERIAL DEER (b. 1940) was born in Keshena, Wisconsin, on the Menominee Indian Reservation. She is the daughter of Joseph Deer, an enrolled Menominee, and Constance Wood Deer, of English-Scotch-Irish descent. After elementary education in Milwaukee and Shawano, Wisconsin, she graduated from high school in Shawano in 1958, third in a class of one hundred eighty-five students. She then attended the University of Wisconsin in Madison, graduating with honors with a BS in secondary education, with a major in dance and a minor in English in 1962.

She continued her education by attending the Dance Department of the Juilliard School of Music in 1962–63. She attended graduate school in dance at the University of Wisconsin from 1968–69 and 1978–79. She earned an MA in educational psychology and guidance from the University of South Dakota in Vermillion in 1975, and received her EdD from the University of South Dakota in educational psychology and counseling in 1988. Her dissertation is entitled, "A Study of the Effects of Dance Education on Stress in College-Age American Indian Women."

She is married to Clarence Skye, a Hunkpapa Sioux, and they are the parents of three children: Clifton born on February 5, 1965, Martin born on March 25, 1966, and daughter Wenonah born on September 8, 1967. Besides being a mother, she has had a busy life as a school counselor, dance instructor, and professional dancer. From 1977–78 she served as a school counselor at the Pierre Indian Learning Center in South Dakota. From August 1982 until January 1988, she was a special education counselor for South Dakota's Crow Creek and Lower Brule Sioux tribes.

Her dance career began in her undergraduate days. As a college senior in 1962, she was chosen as dance soloist in *Earth-Trapped*, a dance-opera based on a Sioux ghost legend, choreographed by Forrest Coggan of the University of Wisconsin–Madison faculty. This was repeated in 1971 in Kalamazoo, Michigan, and in 1972 at South Dakota State University in Brookings. She presented a dance-lecture demonstration at the South Dakota State Teachers's Convention in Rapid City in 1970 and was a dance participant in the Brookings, South Dakota, Fine Arts Festival in the summers of 1972 and 1973. In 1973 and 1974 she conducted an Indian student dance project called "Dakota Wicohan" sponsored by the South Dakota Arts Council. In 1976 she was a dance soloist in the South Dakota Bi-Centennial Program under Marjorie Weeks at the Kennedy Center in Washington, DC, performing a ritualistic modern dance which she choreographed to an interpretation of the Sioux national anthem by Curt Jurrens.

In 1987 she was appointed a member of the South Dakota Arts Council by Governor George S. Mickleson. She was re-appointed to a three-year term in 1988. She is a member of educational committees in South Dakota and Wisconsin. From 1989–91 she served as director of Multi-Cultural Affairs at St. Norbert College in DePere, Wisconsin. In the summer of 1991 she moved back to South Dakota.

—Jack Marken

References

"Keshena Native to Head SNC Minority Program." *Green Bay Press-Gazette* 22 December 1989: B2.

"Q & A: Skye sees aiding self-esteem as important in new SNC post." *Green Bay Press-Gazette* 14 January 1990: A16.

Skye, Ferial Deer, Orla J. Christensen, and Joan T. England. "A Study of the Effects of a Culturally-Based Dance Education Model on Identified Stress Factors in American Indian College Women." *Journal of American Indian Education* 29 (October 1989): 26–31.

SLIPPERJACK, RUBY (b. 1952) was born of Ojibway parents in northern Ontario (Whitewater Lake). Growing up on her father's trapline, her early childhood was full of stories being told to her by elders, and she developed a keen interest in storytelling. She remembers her mother making napkin dolls as props for stories the children had to invent. Later, while attending school in an isolated community, she started to write down little stories on any paper she could get her hands on, borrowing pencils from school. She was a very clandestine child-author

then because writing and reading were not esteemed useful occupations in a traditional hunting and trapping community. In her high school years, Ruby Slipperjack attended Shingwauk Residential School in Sault St. Marie and high school in Thunder Bay. She later enrolled at Lakehead University, graduating with BA and BEd degrees in 1989. She is currently working toward an MA degree in education.

Besides being an accomplished painter, her first novel, *Honour the Sun*, won her instant recognition as an outstandingly gifted and skilled writer, despite the book's limited circulation as a small press product. The central character is Owl, whose experiences from the age of ten until about sixteen are related with great atmospheric density and realism, based on careful observation of human nature and details concerning all beings that surround the girl. Social criticism is never addressed as such, but the realistic depictions of living conditions in the nameless northern "bush" village by the railroad tracks carry a convincing humanist message, speaking out strongly against the abuse of women and children by males, be they drunken bullies or "nice" blue-eyed teachers. Owl's toughness and optimism carry her through the tragedy of a one-parent family gradually slipping apart like the community that surrounds its members. There is no lament and no attack, but the book itself is rather a celebration of an indomitable will for survival and a creativity that is deeply rooted in a very traditional upbringing in the northern "bush," shared by many Native authors in Canada (Acco, Campbell, Deranger, Highway, Keeshig-Tobias). Often humorous and sometimes depressingly sad, *Honour the Sun* records an adolescent's curiosity about life's puzzles, reaching a large degree of psychological universality. Consequently, Owl's exact tribal or band identity is never disclosed, nor would such an ethnic label seem important in the community depicted. Her forthcoming second novel will deal with the experiences of a young boy in both a rural and an urban setting.

Ruby Slipperjack is married and has three children. She lives in Thunder Bay, Ontario.

—Hartmut Lutz

References

Petrone, Penny. *Native Literature in Canada*. Toronto: Oxford University Press, 1990.

Slipperjack, Ruby. "Coal Oil, Crayons and Schoolbooks." In *All My Relations: An Anthology of Contemporary Canadian Native Fiction*, edited by Thomas King, 27–37. Toronto: McClelland and Stewart, 1990.

———. *Honour the Sun*. Winnipeg: Pemmican Press, 1987.

———. "Ruby Slipperjack [Interview]." In *Contemporary Challenges: Conversations with Canadian Native Authors*, edited by Hartmut Lutz, 203–16. Saskatoon, SK: Fifth House, 1991.

SMITH, JAUNE QUICK-TO-SEE (b. 1940) was born in St. Ignatius on
the Flathead Indian Reservation in Montana. She is of French-Cree/Shoshone
descent. She received a BA degree in art education from Framingham State
College in 1976 and an MA in painting from the University of New Mexico in
1980. She is currently living in New Mexico.

Smith is a painter whose abstract, non-traditional paintings reflect influences
of de Kooning, Miro, Klee, and Picasso but find their power in traditional images
of landscape, animals, cave paintings, and rock art. She says that she "makes
parallels from the old world to contemporary art . . . like being able to speak two
languages and find the word that is common to both." She is so successful at
merging these disparate worlds, that her work is known for its excellence in both
contemporary New York and Native American art circles. Her work has been
shown and installed in permanent collections throughout the United States and
Europe. Gallery and museum shows include the Corcoran Art Gallery, Washington, DC; the Museum of Modern Art, San Francisco; and the Heard Museum,
Phoenix. She has had over twenty-five solo exhibits and has been included in
more than fifty group exhibits.

Her father, a horseman, horse trader, amateur artist, and collector of Charles
Russell prints, was very influential in Smith's becoming an artist. The earthy
colors of her paintings are inspired by the hues in the horse tack and bunkhouses
of her father's world. The horse images so frequently found in her paintings can
also be traced to her father's background, as well as to artistic depictions of her
own horse, Cheyenne.

Smith is an active lecturer and spokeswoman for traditional and contemporary
Native American artists. She founded two artists' cooperatives: Coup Marks, on
the Flathead Reservation, and Grey Canyon Artists in Albuquerque, which has
since become a national co-op. She is a supporter of art and education for the
Flathead Reservation, providing scholarships and speaking to help Salish-
Kootenai College on the reservation. She has served as a panel member on the
Washington State and Idaho State Arts Commissions and a board member for
ATLATL, an Indian organization for the arts. She co-curated an Indian
Women's Exhibit for AIR Gallery in New York and "Sweetgrass, Cedar, and
Sage" (with Harmony Hammond) at the Gallery of the American Indian
Community House, New York. She has also been involved in founding and
curating or jurying many other exhibits. Recent awards include: Honorary
Professor, Beaumont Chair, Washington University, St. Louis, 1989; Fellowship
Award, Western States Art Foundation, 1988; and Purchase Award of Arts and
Letters, New York, 1987.

—Julie A. Russ

References

American Indian Artists: Jaune Quick-To-See Smith, Shoshone French Cree Painter.
Distributed by Native American Public Broadcasting Consortium. Produced by
PBS Television, 1982. 30 min. Videocassette.

Bass, Ruth. "Jaune Quick-To-See Smith." *Art News* (March 1984): 224.

Cohen, Ronny. "Jaune Quick-To-See Smith at Kornblee." *Art in America* 68 (March 1980): 116–17.

Galligan, Gregory. "Jaune Quick-To-See Smith: Crossing the Great Divide." *Arts* (January 1986): 54–55.

———. "Jaune Quick-To-See Smith: Racing with the Moon." *Arts* (January 1987): 82–83.

Hammond, Harmony, and Jaune Quick-To-See Smith. *Women of Sweetgrass, Cedar and Sage*. New York: Gallery of the American Indian Community House, 1985.

Hurst, Tricia. "Crossing Bridges." *Southwest Art* 10 (April 1981): 82–89.

Smith, Katherine. "Outside the Pueblo." *Portfolio* (July 1982): 52–57.

Zwinger, Susan. "Viewpoint: An Interview with Artist Jaune Quick-To-See Smith." *El Palacio* 92 (Summer/Fall 1986): 51–54.

SMITH, KATHLEEN (b. 1939), tribal scholar, cultural consultant, artist, and writer, the daughter of Steven Smith, Jr., Olemitcha (Bodega) Miwok, and Lucyanna Lozinto Smith, Hihilakawna (Dry Creek) Pomo, was the sixth of eight children, the first to be born in a hospital (Sonoma County Hospital in Santa Rosa, California).

Smith earned a BFA from the San Francisco Art Institute in 1977 and has worked as a field hand, packing clerk, computer operator, and stockroom clerk. Advised as a teenager by her Uncle Manuel Cordova (Dry Creek Pomo) to "work for your people," and taught pride in her Indian heritage by her family, she has also been a Native American observer and archeology technician, cultural consultant and interpreter, administrative assistant to the Model Urban Indian Centers Project in Washington, DC, Sonoma County YMCA Native American outreach worker, and organizer of a Dry Creek Pomo language class.

Faced with an Army Corps of Engineers project which would flood the Warm Springs Valley, home to her ancestors for generations (Lake Sonoma was filled in 1985), Smith served as archeology technician and coordinator for the Native American Advisory Council of the Warm Springs Cultural Resources Study, which sought to preserve and record the traditions and tribal history of her Dry Creek people. Smith's maternal great-grandmother, Juana Cook, was the last family member to live on that land, being driven from it by US Army troops in an 1850s "Death March."

Smith has contributed to her community as a board member and vice-chair of the Sonoma County Indian Health Project, 1978–84; a board member of California Indian Rural Health, 1979–81; a commissioner on the Sonoma County Status of Women Commission, 1980–82; a board member of the California State Rural Services Advisory Committee, 1981–83; and a charter member of the Sonoma County Women's Support Network, 1981–87.

She designed the logo for the National Women's History Project, co-authored a biography of Indian health activist Annie Wauenka for the Second Grade Social Studies Curriculum, and is presently a columnist for *News from Native California*, a quarterly publication which provides an inside view of California Indian history and culture.

Smith received the Sonoma County YWCA's Women of Achievement Award in the Art Category in 1980 and a 1988–89 California Arts Council Traditional Folk Arts Master Apprentice Grant for Pomo basketmaking. She has been featured in several publications, and her art work has been commissioned and shown throughout central California.

Presently, Smith is devoting herself to her painting, which has roots in her cultural traditions, writing a book about her people's foods and history, and coordinating an effort to obtain federal acknowledgement for her Bodega Miwok people. In 1991 she was appointed to the Board of the Olompali People of Olompali State Park.

—Bev Ortiz

References

Eisenberg, Bonnie, and Marylynne Slayen. "An Interview with Kathleen Smith." *Women's Voices* 6 (March 1981): 16–17.

Fellman, Debbie. "Indian Tribes Seek Unity, Identity." *The Contra Costa Times* [Walnut Creek, CA] 22 August 1990: A4.

Ingle, Schuyler. "Secrets of the Earth." *New West* 6 (July 1981): 88–93, 126–29.

Johnson, Holly. "Artists Remain Loyal to Heritage." *The Sacramento Union* [Sacramento, CA] 25 August 1990: D1.

Ortiz, Bev. "The Art of Life: An Interview with Five Smith Artists." *News from Native California* 3 (May/June 1989): 8–11.

———. Oral and taped interviews with Kathleen Smith, 1987–90.

Wyss, Dennis. "Miwok Bands Mount Drive for Rights, Respect, Dignity." *Marin Independent Journal* [Novato, CA] 30 July 1990: A1, A7.

SNEVE, VIRGINIA DRIVING HAWK (b. 1933) authored several novels with Native American characters, including *Jimmy Yellow Hawk* (Holiday House, 1972) and *High Elk's Treasure* (Holiday House, 1972), received the Distinguished Alumnus Award from South Dakota State University, and was named 1975 Woman of Achievement by the National Federation of Press Women. She was born and raised on the Rosebud Reservation, is an enrolled member of the Rosebud Sioux tribe, attended Bureau of Indian Affairs day schools on the reservation, and graduated from St. Mary's High School for Indian Girls, Springfield, South Dakota, in 1950. She received a BS (1954) and MEd (1969) from South Dakota State University, Brookings, South Dakota.

She taught music and English at a white public high school and in a Pierre junior high; English, speech, and drama at the Flandreau Indian School and later served as a guidance counselor there. She has worked as a consultant producer-writer for South Dakota Public Broadcasting, creating television scripts stressing the ethnic pride and cultural traditions of Native Americans. She is presently the secondary Title V counselor for the Rapid City School District and a part-time instructor in English for Oglala Lakota College, Rapid City Extension Services.

Sneve (surname rhymes with "navy") is married to Vance M. Sneve, retired from the Bureau of Indian Affairs, who now owns an antique business, has three children, and four grandchildren.

Sneve has stated that, "In my writing, both fiction and nonfiction, I try to present an accurate portrayal of American Indian life as I have known it. I also attempt to interpret history from the viewpoint of the American Indian. In doing so, I hope to correct the many misconceptions and untruths which have been too long perpetrated by non-Indian authors who have written about us."

—Edith Blicksilver

References

Blicksilver, Edith, ed. *The Ethnic American Woman: Problems, Protests, Lifestyle.* Dubuque, IA: Kendall/Hunt, 1978.

Colonese, Tom, and Louise Owens. *American Indian Novelists: An Annotated Critical Bibliography.* New York: Garland, 1985.

Contemporary Authors. New Revision Series, vol. 3. Detroit, MI: Gale, 1981.

Sioux Falls Argus-Leader 5 August 1973: Sect. C, 8.

Sneve, Virginia Driving Hawk. Letter to Edith Blicksilver, 30 July 1990.

SOMERSAL, LAURA (1892–1990), tribal scholar, cultural consultant, Indian handgame player, and nationally and internationally renowned basketweaver, teacher, and lecturer, was born to Mary John Fish Eli (Alexander Valley Wappo) and Bill Fish (Dry Creek Pomo) on the Stone Ranch outside Geyserville, California, where her father was working. Baptized Dolores Ellen Fish in Healdsburg at age five, Somersal was the fifth of six children. She had two older brothers, Tony Jack and George, and a younger sister Josephine. Three other siblings died before she was born; she also had a half brother, Will Fish. Her first home was a brush house; her last was a trailer at the Dry Creek Rancheria.

Wappo was Somersal's first language. Fluent in several Indian dialects as different as English and Russian, she also understood Spanish and spoke English, learning her "alphabets" from a disabled boy she cared for as a teenager.

Somersal picked hops and fruits throughout her youth; in her teens she worked as a housekeeper at various ranches. Married for the first time at age sixteen and several times thereafter, Somersal had no children of her own, but raised several relatives and a foster son.

At about age eight or nine, she began learning to weave baskets from her uncle, Jack Woho (Wappo), later studying its intricacies under the tutelage of her sister-in-law Rosie, "Fernando's daughter." Lacking formal education (Indians weren't then allowed to attend public schools, and her blind mother kept her from being sent to Indian school), Somersal was able to devote herself to her culture. A respected tribal scholar, she taught and lectured about Pomo/Wappo basketry throughout California, including institutions of higher learning, and once travelled to Washington, DC, to identify baskets for the Smithsonian Institution.

Somersal was instrumental in preserving the Wappo language, overcoming the objections of some of her people to share that language with non-Indians; she collaborated with linguist Jesse O. Sawyer to publish a Wappo/English dictionary in 1965 and other smaller publications. She was featured in numerous articles as well as a film; and she was instrumental in a project to transplant basketry and other native plants from an area that the Army Corps planned to flood (now Lake Sonoma). Her mother Mary Eli and brother George were principal consultants for Harold E. Driver's 1936 *Wappo Ethnography*.

In 1978 Somersal was honored with the first ever Woman of Achievement Award by the Sonoma County Commission on the Status of Women and received recognition from Women of Color as a woman who had done the most for her community. Although she would have traded her world-wide fame for a child of her own, her contributions to preservation of Wappo culture were unparalleled. As anthropologist David Peri said of her in 1980: "She's a Picasso of Indian basketweaving, and an Einstein in terms of Indian culture."

—Bev Ortiz

References

Beard, Yolande S. *The Wappo: A Report*. Banning, CA: Malki Museum Press, 1979.

Ortiz, Bev. Personal Communication with Bette Holmes, 1990.

———. Oral and taped interviews with Laura Somersal, 1985–90.

———. "With Respect: Laura Fish Somersal." *News from Native California* 3 (November 1990/January 1991): 4–5.

Sawyer, Jesse O. "English-Wappo Vocabulary." *University of California Publications in Linguistics* 43 (August 1965): 1–128.

Smith, Ray. "Weaving a Future from the Past." *The Press Democrat* [Santa Rosa, CA] 23 October 1980: B1, 7.

STANLEY, DOROTHY AMORA (1924–1990), tribal scholar, cultural consultant, educator, tribal chair, and political activist, was born in Los Angeles, California, to Alice Carsoner Pruitt and Raymond Dudley. Her maternal grandparents and great-grandmother were descended from families of hereditary Northern Miwok leaders.

Stanley's youth was spent at Bald Rock (near Twain Harte) and the Tuolumne Mewuk Rancheria, where she was raised by her mother Alice Pruitt, stepfather Raymond Fuller, aunt and uncle Etta and Richard Fuller, and Raymond's mother Annie Jack Fuller, the wife of Chief William Fuller and Stanley's primary teacher of Northern Miwok culture.

Brought up speaking Northern and Central Miwok, Stanley learned English in public school and attended the Bureau of Indian Affair's Stewart, Nevada, boarding school as a teenager. Upon graduation, she worked at jobs which included cashier, strawberry picker, and candymaker, eventually becoming employed twenty-five years as an operator/supervisor for Pacific Telephone.

In the early 1970s Stanley and fourth husband Elmer Stanley (Southern Miwok), her teenage sweetheart, returned to the Sierra Nevada. There she chaired the Acorn Festival of the Tuolumne Mewuk Rancheria, 1973; was appointed to the Tuolumne County Commission on Aging, 1974–75; served on the business committee of the Tuolumne Mewuk Tribal Council, 1975–76; was Native American liaison for the Department of Interior Heritage Conservation and Recreation Services for the New Melones Dam Project, 1975–76; was appointed to the Advisory Council for Area Technical Agency for Aging, 1975–76; acted as project director for the Tuolumne Indian Rural Health Project, 1976–77; and was elected Tuolumne Mewuk Tribal Council Chair, 1980. Stanley also served on the boards of various employment, mental health, alcoholism, Indian housing, and Indian education agencies and commissions and was once vice-chair of the Advisory Board of the Bureau of Indian Affairs Central Agency. She also fought for years to preserve her people's archaeological sites.

Stanley was a consultant for linguists, ethnographers, archaeologists, and anthropologists, and demonstrated and lectured about her culture throughout the state and as far away as Washington, DC. In 1980 and 1981 she supervised the Miwok Indian Village at a West Side lumber company; from 1982 to 1985 she supervised the Indian Cultural Program at Yosemite National Park.

In her lifetime, Stanley raised seven children, made substantial contributions to the preservation and continuance of Miwok culture, and worked extensively on behalf of her community. As stated by ethnographer Craig Bates, "She was a link with a people and a past."

—Bev Ortiz

References

Bates, Craig. "With Respect: Dorothy Stanley." *News from Native California* 5 (November 1990/January 1991): 6–8.

Ortiz, Bev. Personal communication with Craig Bates, 1990.

———. Oral and taped interviews with Dorothy Stanley, 1988.

———. "Skills Remembered, Cherished, and Continued: Northern Sierra Miwok Food Preparation and Soaproot Brush Making." *News from Native California* 4 (Spring 1990): 16–19.

STEELE, LOIS FISTER (b. 1939), enrolled member of the Ft. Peck Assiniboine tribe, began her career as an educator teaching at public schools in various Indian communities in Montana between 1963 and 1969. Although her teaching experience ranges widely—from being an instructor and dean of women at Dawson College, Glendive, Montana (1970–73), to being assistant professor of family at the University of North Dakota Medical School (1984–85) and clinical lecturer at the University of Arizona, Department of Family and Medicine (1986–present)—Steele is most well known for her role as director (and consultant) of the Indians Into Medicine Program (INMED) at the University of North Dakota, between 1973 and 1985. INMED is a unique program that enables young American Indians to pursue undergraduate science degrees and to be placed in schools where they can successfully complete their training for careers in medicine and other health professions. During Steele's years at INMED, she expanded the budget from $50,000 to more than $1 million and instituted an outreach program to Indian youth on reservations, through INMED's Traveling Medicine Show, featuring puppets and a coloring book based on the traditional mythical figures, Coyote and Turtle. At the time INMED began, there were only sixteen Indian physicians in the nation; through INMED more than sixty Indians have received degrees in medicine and other allied health professions.

Born in Washington, DC, in 1939, the first daughter of Russell Fister, a Bureau of Indian Affairs official, and Winona Simons (Assiniboine), Steele grew up on the Ft. Peck Reservation, Poplar, Montana. She earned a BA from Colorado College, 1961; MS in science teaching from the University of Montana, 1969; and medical doctorate from the University of Minnesota, 1978.

After thirteen years of teaching in various capacities and her first tenure as director of INMED, Steele decided to pursue her lifelong goal of becoming a medical doctor; she entered the University of Minnesota Medical School at Duluth, a two-year program at the end of which she earned the Lampson Award as Most Valuable Woman Medical Student. She finished her studies on the Minneapolis campus in 1978 and fulfilled her residency requirements at Methodist Hospital in Minneapolis and at the University of North Dakota, Grand Forks, in 1984, the latter four years of which she also functioned again as director of INMED. She is a board-certified family medicine practitioner.

Currently serving as clinical director for the Pascua Yaqui tribe in Tucson, Arizona, Steele works to promote and develop a tribally controlled health delivery system, while conducting research on the American Indian health concerns. She has participated in numerous conferences and has presented papers on topics related to domestic abuse, AIDS, American Indian women's roles in the feminist movement, cancer prevention and control for American Indians and Alaskan Natives, American Indians in medical education, informed consent regarding sterilization of Indian people, stress and hypertension, and Indian women coping with stress.

In addition Steele is the recipient of many prestigious awards: Indian Health Service Award for Health Promotion Disease Prevention Work, 1989; American Indian Science and Engineering Society Ely Parker Award, 1989; Who's Who in North Dakota, 1984; Indian Health Service Award, Aberdeen Area, 1983; Distinguished Achievement Award, Rocky Mountain College Alumni Association, 1981; Outstanding Educator of America Award, 1970; and Honorary Sociology Fraternity, Pi Gamma Mu, Colorado Springs, Colorado, 1961.

—Kathryn W. Shanley

References

Steele, Lois F. "Cross-cultural Perspectives in Patient Education: Native Americans." In *Patient Education in the Primary Care Setting*, edited by Mary Nell Currie and Barbara Widmar, 95–99. Kansas City, MO: St. Mary's Hospital, 1985.

———, writer and ed. *Medicine Women*. Grand Forks: INMED, University of North Dakota, 1985.

STEWART, IRENE [GLINEZBAH, GOES TO WAR WITH] (b. 1907), politician and activist, was born in traditional Navajo fashion near Canyon de Chelly on the Navajo Reservation in northern Arizona to weaver Elenor Bancroft and medicine man Jake Watchman. After the death of her mother in 1911, Stewart went to live with her grandmother where she learned the responsibilities of Navajo womanhood.

With the insistence of government officials and the request of her father, Stewart was removed from her grandmother's home and was taken to the Fort Defiance Indian School from which she graduated in 1922. She continued her education at both the Haskell Institute in Lawrence, Kansas, and the Albuquerque Indian School, receiving her diploma in home economics from the latter in 1929. Later that year, Stewart enrolled in a nine-month Bible course in California designed to train assistant missionaries for the Presbyterian church, an education she continues to draw upon in her work with the Presbyterian Mission in Chinle, Arizona.

While in California, Stewart met and married a member of the Oneida tribe. This marriage produced four sons, but was later dissolved due to differences. In 1942, Stewart married Greyeyes, a Navajo medicine man who was much older than she and who practiced traditional Navajo customs; this union provided Stewart with the strength and confidence to run for Tribal Council in 1955. Although she lost this election by a narrow margin, Stewart went on to serve as council secretary for fifteen years.

In addition, Stewart has served the Navajo tribe as a warehouse supervisor, a member of the Children's Welfare Foundation, a district loan representative for the Navajo Tribal Council, and as a Chinle representative to the Navajo Nations'

Council on Aging. Today, Stewart is retired and spends most of her time at home with family and friends.

—Michelle Savoy

Reference

Stewart, Irene. *A Voice in Her Tribe: A Navajo Woman's Own Story.* Edited by Doris Ostrander Dawdy and Mary Shepardson. Socorro, NM: Ballena Press, 1980.

STROUD, VIRGINIA (b. 1949) was born in Madera, California, where she lived with a Kiowa family after the deaths of her parents. She went to Oklahoma where she attended Bacone Junior College (1969–79) and the University of Oklahoma (1971–76), where she majored in art education. During her college years she was named Miss Cherokee Tribal Princess (1969–70), Miss National Congress of American Indians (1970–71) and Miss Indian America (1971).

In spite of urging by an art professor to quit painting Indian subjects, Virginia Stroud has created a style of painting that depicts everyday life images from Indian America. Referring to herself as a "visual orator," Stroud's work knows no cultural or tribal boundaries. She paints scenes with Navajo dancers and weavers, Apache sunflower seed gatherers, and Cherokees in wagons. Regardless of the subject, Stroud's work is warm and carries a touch of whimsy, humor, and joy. Her painting "Where From Here," described as a self-portrait, illustrates the problem of identity faced by many Native Americans and Native American artists today. According to Stroud as she is quoted in Wade and Strickland: "Indians live in a world where they always have to explain themselves. . . . You work, you accomplish, and you improve your standard of living, and then non-Indians say you aren't Indian any more." For Stroud, art is the medium through which she deals with herself and the world she must live in: "[W]ithout anything to paint and record, we would be drifting, searching for where we fit in."

Stroud's work has drawn a loyal and enthusiastic following. In 1970 she won first place at the American Indian Artists Exhibition at the Philbrook Art Center; she was the youngest artist to receive that prize. Since then she has regularly won honors at the Heard Museum and the Philbrook and in 1982 was named Artist of the Year by the Indian Arts and Crafts Association. Her work is in the permanent collections at the Heard Museum in Phoenix, the Philbrook Art Center in Tulsa, and the Minneapolis Institute of Art. Her work is also collected by many individuals, either as originals or reproductions. She has served as visiting artist-in-residence for the Oklahoma Arts and Humanities Council and consulted with the Oklahoma Indian Education Association.

—Laura Graves

References

Jacka, Lois Essary, and Jerry Jacka. *Beyond Tradition: Contemporary Indian Art and Its Evolution.* Flagstaff, AZ: Northland Press, 1988.

Stroud, Virginia. Biographical file. McFarlin Library, University of Tulsa.

———. Biographical file. Philbrook Art Center and Special Collections Library, Tulsa, OK.

"Virginia Alice Stroud." In *Native American Art Sampler: A Patchwork of Contemporary Art,* edited by Paul and Rosemary Spedded Rock. Santa Fe: Wheelwright Museum of Indian Art, 1982.

"Virginia Stroud: Artist Profile." *Four Winds* (Winter 1980): 58–61.

Wade, Edwin L., and Rennard Strickland. *Magic Images: Contemporary Native American Art.* Norman: Philbrook Art Center and University of Oklahoma, 1981.

SWAN, MADONNA (b. 1928) [MADONNA MARY SWAN ABDALLA] was born on the Cheyenne River Reservation of the Lakota Sioux, spending most of her life in Cherry Creek. She went to mission school at Immaculate Conception School in Stephan, South Dakota. In 1944 she was diagnosed with tuberculosis and spent the next six years at the Sioux Sanitorium in Rapid City. Her autobiography is a testament to the courage and determination with which she faced both the disease and the stigma attached to it. Because of these virtues and the unending support and love of her family, she was able to find a cure. In September 1950, she was admitted to the Sanitor at Custer, the "white" TB sanitorium. At Sanitor, Swan received more advanced treatments. The tuberculosis was cured, although she has been susceptible to colds and pneumonia throughout her life.

Despite her weakened state, Swan finished her GED, got a certificate in horology (clock and watch repair), and completed approximately one hundred and thirty hours towards a bachelor's degree in education. When first leaving the sanitorium Swan held several clerical and jewelry repair positions. In 1966 she began to work as a teacher in the Head Start Program on the reservation, resigning in 1971 because of poor health. She again attempted to complete her bachelor's degree in 1974, taking classes at the University of South Dakota, but again her health failed her. Swan remained active, serving on the board of the Tri-Community Development Cooperative and tribal employee relations committees. In 1983, Swan received the North American Indian Woman of the Year award.

Madonna Swan's autobiography is an important historical document, chronicling Lakota world views and values, humanizing tuberculosis statistics, and documenting Lakota reservation life in the twentieth century.

—Pattiann Frinzi

Reference

St. Pierre, Mark, ed. *Madonna Swan, A Lakota Woman's Story.* Norman: University of Oklahoma Press, 1991.

SWENTZELL, RINA [RINA NARANJO] (b. 1939), architect and educator, was born in Santa Clara Pueblo, New Mexico, the third of eight children of Rose and Michael Naranjo, a Santa Clara (Tewa) family noted for its artistic achievements. After earning her BA in education from New Mexico Highlands University, she taught for several years in public schools and Pueblo day schools. Returning to graduate school at the University of New Mexico, she earned her MA in architecture in 1976 and, with the support of a Ford Foundation Fellowship, her PhD in American Studies in 1982.

The consistent theme uniting Swentzell's diverse areas of expertise is her focus on environmental communication: How physical structures embody ideological values, and how both influence human lives, particularly in bicultural situations. Her analysis of the disruptive effects of the institutional design of Indian schools led to involvement in the renovation of several Southwestern schools, encouraging student and community participation to make the schools more reflective of Native American traditions. As an architect, she also works with people building their own homes, assisting them in constructing their own ideas, rather than imposing her vision on their lifestyles. As an educator, she continues to work with design, both of school buildings and curricula emphasizing cultural values, and she is sought after nationwide as an instructor, guest lecturer, and speaker. She has served as a consultant on many projects, including museum exhibitions and televised documentaries, and she has published several articles on Pueblo Indian culture and architecture. Swentzell has also given generously of her time to serve on many planning committees and governing boards for the Pueblos, the state of New Mexico, and her profession of architecture. She has been honored as Alumni of the Year by the University of New Mexico Indian Alumni Chapter, and as 1989 International Woman by UNM's Women Studies Program.

Married, with three daughters and a son, and now eight grandchildren, Swentzell lives outside Santa Fe, New Mexico, in a house she and her family designed and built. In her life, as well as in her work, she consistently strives to embody traditional Pueblo values of connection, nurturing, and harmony. These qualities, together with her warmth, wisdom, and clarity of expression, have earned her widespread and sincere respect.

—Helen M. Bannan

References

Lichtenstein, Grace. "The Evolution of a Craft Tradition: Three Generations of Naranjo Women." *Ms.* 11 (April 1983): 59–60, 92.

Swentzell, Rina. "A Comparison of Basic Incompatibilities Between European/
   American and Traditional Pueblo World-View and Value System." PhD diss.,
   University of New Mexico, 1982.
———. "An Understated Sacredness." *Mass: Journal of the School of Architecture
   and Planning* [University of New Mexico] 3 (Fall 1985): 24–25.
———, and Tito Naranjo. "Nurturing: The Gia at Santa Clara Pueblo." *El Palacio*
   92 (Summer/Fall 1986): 35–39.

T

TALLMOUNTAIN, MARY (b. 1918) was born of Athabaskan/ Russian/ Irish lineage in the last year of World War I, one hundred miles south of the Arctic Circle and two hundred miles west of Fairbanks. On a clear day in Nulato she could see Siberia. TallMountain remembers "pure, wonderful snow" and the Yukon River going by "incessantly." Her mother contracted tuberculosis, and TallMountain was adopted "outside" at the age of six, psychically ripped from her Native family. It was fifty years before she could return. The cabins were still moss-covered, reindeer antlers tied to the eaves, a boardwalk through the village.

In the early 1970s Paula Gunn Allen found TallMountain working as a secretary in San Francisco, and a curious writerly adoption clicked into place. For one and a half years, TallMountain wrote sixteen hours a day on a Selectric typewriter; each Tuesday she brought her work to Allen for tutoring. It was a rebirth of gifted childhood, an elder writer's awakening. Paula Allen introduces *The Light on the Tent Wall: A Bridging* (1990): "Who is this woman, this survivor, this half-breed, this poet, this friend? If you know the land of her origins and the cadences of the People, if you recall the rhythm of Roman liturgy, the solemnity of the Mass, if you read this collection with care, hearing the eerie, powerful silences that surround the words, you will know who she is, what extinction is, and what survival engenders." With pointalist country diction and rattling tree-branch rhythms, TallMountain's voice could sweeten the pit of winter. She counterpoints loss with come-on lyrical lilts. This self-taught writer knows where her cadences lie, when the currents run deep, where the accents trip off the consonants:

> By the fires that night
> we feasted
> The Old Ones clucked,
> sucking and smacking,
> sopping the juices with sourdough bread.
> The grease would warm us
> when hungry winter howled.

TallMountain enjoys herself these days, clearly, this new found focus and status as a Native elder with words for the younger. She giggles and covers her mouth through bursts of wellspring laughter, a hilarity deep down inside, province of the wolf and wolverine, the fanged trickster warriors who have seen her through terrible losses—her childhood untimely torn from the Yukon, her mother's tragedy from tuberculosis, her brothers' deaths from the same (she never saw a second brother sent to live in another village), her father's disappearance

for sixty years until TallMountain found him in Phoenix, her sense of estrange-
ment on the "outside" of the West Coast, the financial ruin and death of her
adoptive physician father when she was a teenager in the Depression, her
adoptive mother's suicide not long after, joblessness and hard times and finally
legal secretarial work to try to stabilize her life, battles with depression and broken
hearts and alcoholism, two bouts with cancer, recently a quadruple heart bypass
. . . from which she awoke laughing, the doctors told her. "In her way
TallMountain is Coyote," Allen writes, "and like that quintessential old survivor,
she knows that if you're going to face death, and if you're to engage the sacred,
you'd better have your sense of humor intact."

That wolverine won't shut up; the wolf can't die. TallMountain has too much
to tell her cat, Emily Dickinson, about "good" grease and other things, about
humor and survival, about "positivity" in the face of devastation, about having a
good heart in a tough world, about accepting and caring and forgiving and putting
up with all of us in a wilderness of losses, a darkness of metal and dungeon of
concrete. Because TallMountain has learned the simplest and most difficult of
wisdoms, how to take each breath with joy, with care, with appreciation, with a
twinkle in her olive-brown eyes and an irrepressible hoot in her throat. "Gooood
grease!" She consoles the last wolf in her city,

> Yes, I said.
> I know what they have done.

—Kenneth Lincoln

References

Allen, Paula Gunn. Introduction to *The Light on the Tent Wall: A Bridging*, by
Mary TallMountain. Native American Series, no. 8. Los Angeles: UCLA
American Indian Studies Center, 1990.

———, ed. *Spider Woman's Granddaughters: Short Stories by American Indian
Women*. Boston: Beacon Press, 1989.

Brant, Beth, ed. *A Gathering of Spirit: Writing and Art by North American Indian
Woman*. Montpelier, VT: Sinister Wisdom, 1984.

Green, Rayna, ed. *That's What She Said: Contemporary Poetry and Fiction by Native
American Women*. Bloomington: Indiana University Press, 1984.

Lincoln, Kenneth. *Indi'n Humor: Bicultural Play in Native America*. New York:
Oxford University Press, 1991.

Nelson, Richard K. *Make Prayers to the Raven: A Koyukon View of the Northern
Forest*. Chicago: University of Chicago Press, 1983.

TallMountain, Mary. *Continuum*. Marvin, SD: Blue Cloud Press, 1988.

———. *There Is No Word for Goodbye*. Marvin SD: Blue Cloud Press, 1982.

———. "You Can Go Home Again: A Sequence." In *I Tell You Now: Autobiographical Essays by Native American Writers*, edited by Brian Swan and Arnold
Krupat, 1–13. Lincoln: University of Nebraska Press, 1987.

TANTAQUIDGEON, GLADYS (b. 1899), Mohegan scholar of Algonquian Indian cultures and descendent of the seventeenth-century sachem Uncas and the eighteenth-century preacher Samson Occom, was selected by her great-aunt Fidelia Fielding (1827–1908), the last speaker of the Mohegan-Pequot language, and two other elders of the Connecticut Mohegan community, to be the bearer of tribal medicinal and other lore. Educated as an anthropologist by Frank Speck at the University of Pennsylvania, she conducted field research on other Algonquian peoples, including the Montagnais-Naskapi of Quebec, the Wampanoag of Gay Head and Mashpee, Massachusetts, the Nanticoke of Delaware, and the Delaware of Oklahoma and Ontario, resulting in published articles on their crafts, medicines, and folklore. Her Mohegan identity aided her as an anthropologist in recording the rapidly disappearing traditional knowledge of Eastern Algonquians.

In 1934 she began work for the Bureau of Indian Affairs as a community worker and later became a specialist in Indian arts for the Indian Arts and Crafts Board on reservations in the Dakotas, Montana, and Wyoming. She returned to her home community in 1947 to assist in the operations of the family-run Tantaquidgeon Indian Museum, which serves as a cultural and educational resource center for and about New England's Native peoples. In 1986 the Women's Studies Program of the University of Connecticut established the annual Gladys Tantaquidgeon Award in her honor.

—John D. Nichols

References

Fawcett, Melissa. "The Role of Gladys Tantaquidgeon." In *Papers of the Fifteenth Algonquian Conference*, edited by William Cowan, 135–45. Ottawa: Carleton University, 1984.

Simmons, William S. *Spirit of the New England Tribes: Indian History and Folklore, 1620–1984*. Hanover, NH: University Press of New England, 1986.

Tantaquidgeon, Gladys. *Folk Medicine of the Delaware and Related Algonkian Indians*. Rev. ed. Pennsylvania Historical and Museum Commission Anthropological Series 3. Harrisburg, 1972.

———. "Newly Discovered Straw Basketry of the Wampanoag Indians." *Indian Notes* 7 (1930): 475–83.

———. "Notes on the Gay Head Indians of Massachusetts." *Indian Notes* 7 (1930): 1–26.

———. "Notes on the Origin and Uses of Plants of the Lake St. John Montagnais." *Journal of American Folklore* 54 (1932): 265–67.

TAPAHONSO, LUCI (b. 1951), Navajo mother of two daughters, was born at Shiprock, New Mexico. She has published three volumes of poetry: *One More Shiprock Night*, *Seasonal Woman* (illustrated by the Navajo painter R.C. Gorman and introduced by John Nichols), and *A Breeze Swept Through* (with Klee-like drawings by the Flathead artist Jaune Quick-to-See Smith). During the 1980s, Tapahonso taught as an assistant professor of literature at the University of New Mexico, Albuquerque. She now lives in Lawrence, Kansas, with her Acoma husband and daughters, Misty Dawn and Lori Tazbah Ortiz.

Tapahonso's poetry meshes naturally shifting voices, a kind of code-switching poetics with bifocal, transcultural perspectives. The lines are occasionally sprinkled with an insider's Navajo, her own first tongue of family privacies and Southwest regional commitments. The voice switches to a poetically truncated brand of bicultural Red English ("Joe Babe," some *Diné* say) in pan-tribal spoken dialect: "It does it good for me." The effect is one of finely modulated, feminist humor—a woman's oblique, slant-rhymed, nurturing sense of comic survival, of children that embody the future, of a sense of home to swing from, of a generational past of elders, land, tribal history, and communal culture (including food). Most consistently, the poetry resonates to the tuning flute of her own aesthetic voice, filtering through a naturalistically visual imagination—careful, everyday selections from the common languages of both cultures in her life.

Tapahonso's daughters step in and out of the poems; her subjects retain consistently a sense of family, home, and extended kin—that is, who, and among whom, and where she belongs. She writes of earthen births, children, siblings, uncles and aunts, parents and grandparents, lovers and husband, girlfriends, rivals, cowboys, coyotes, sheep, and horses. Hers is a gynocratic or woman-empowered tribal strength. Tapahonso's grandmother broke wild broncos, according to one poem, and her mother baked incomparable bread. The poet speaks often of tribal food—husked corn, deepfat frybread, mutton and chili, Spam, Diet Pepsi, Hills Brothers Coffee. Luci serves a hot brewed cup to her mother's brother, Tom Jim, as they talk things over:

> I sit down again and he tells me
>   some coffee has no kick but
>   this one is the one.
>   It does it good for me.

The Southwest animates her verse landscape—arroyos, buttes, mesas, mesquite, chamisa, sagebrush, greasewood, piñons, desert chaparral, and the alluring Lukachukai Mountains. Powwows, rodeos, dance competitions, sudden deaths, desert highways into the sky, Chinle and Albuquerque and Dulce and Gallup locate her poems among real events in Indian places today. The voice is quick, and quick to shift with a woman's sharp wit in nurturings, teasings, gossipings, prayings, hurtings, carings, disciplinings, midnight writings, and dawn pollen blessings. Hers is the humor of a people who delight in going on adventures, assured of traditional home—a Navajo people who love and forgive and care for their own over vast journeys, wrenching acculturations, and odd accommodations that prove positive in the long view. She writes of "REALLY HOT CHILI!!" on feast days with her husband's Acoma people:

> Myself, I don't eat it straight.
> It's better mixed with beans or the kid's stew,
> which is plain without chili.
> They tease me about it but it's okay.
>
> I'm Navajo: fry bread and mutton are my specialty.
> Like my brother said I get along on sheep thrills.
>
> Some Pueblos just don't understand.

This poet is happy to be alive, to be Navajo, to be woman. She will not be embarrassed by elemental delights in a good laugh, unquestioned love for children, her husband's workday return, or her grandfather's quiet song at a dawn birth. She is disarmingly up-front about the goodnesses all around her, above the historical losses: "I drink a lot of coffee/and it sure does it for me." It is this sophisticated innocence, this lyric naturalism, that makes the poems singularly enjoyable, especially Navajo, and specially womanist.

—Kenneth Lincoln

References

Allen, Paula Gunn. *The Sacred Hoop: Recovering the Feminine in American Indian Traditions.* Boston: Beacon Press, 1986.

Balassi, William, John F. Crawford, and Annie O. Eysturoy, eds. *This Is about Vision: Interviews with Southwestern Writers.* Albuquerque: University of New Mexico Press, 1990.

Brant, Beth, ed. *A Gathering of Spirit: Writing and Art by North American Indian Women.* Montpelier, VT: Sinister Wisdom, 1984.

Bruchac, Joseph. "A *MELUS* Interview: Luci Tapalonso." *MELUS* 11 (Spring 1984): 88–91.

Kluckhohn, Clyde, and Dorothea Leighton. *The Navajo.* Garden City: Doubleday, 1962.

Lincoln, Kenneth. *Indi'n Humor: Bicultural Play in Native America.* New York: Oxford, 1991.

Tapahonso, Luci. *A Breeze Swept Through.* Albuquerque: West End Press, 1987.

———. *One More Shiprock Night.* San Antonio: Tejas Art, 1981.

———. *Seasonal Woman.* Santa Fe: Tooth of Time, 1982.

Witherspoon, Gary. *Language and Art in the Navajo Universe.* Ann Arbor: University of Michigan, 1977.

TEKAKWITHA, KATERI [TEKAKOUITHA, TAGASKOUITA KATHERINE] (1656–1680) was the first North American Indian to be beatified by the Roman Catholic church. Tekakwitha's mother is believed to have been a Christian Algonquin who was captured by Mohawks about 1653. Married to a non-Christian Mohawk, she gave birth to Tekakwitha in 1656. Both parents died in a smallpox epidemic in 1660, which left Tekakwitha's face scarred and eyesight damaged. The uncle who raised her after this time was strongly anti-Christian; nevertheless, Tekakwitha greatly admired several Jesuits who passed through her village in 1667 and desired to become a Christian.

One of the hallmarks of Tekakwitha's character is the importance she placed on virginity. When she came of age, Tekakwitha refused her family's suggestions that she marry. This conviction probably stemmed from a fascination with the behavior of Ursuline nuns at Montreal, of which she had been told by Christian members of her village. Her refusal to marry and her desire to refrain from working on the Sabbath greatly angered her family; they accused her of not helping to support them and withheld food from her. This persecution increased after her baptism, which occurred at Easter 1676, following an unusually short but intense period of instruction with a Jesuit who was impressed with her preparedness. Following the Jesuit practice at the time of isolating converts when possible from their non-Christian relatives, and after a threat on her life by her family, the resident priest persuaded Tekakwitha to escape to the mission village of St. Francis Xavier, on the St. Lawrence River, in the fall of 1677.

At the mission, Tekakwitha received intense instruction in Christianity. She was seen as an extraordinarily gifted pupil and was admitted to Communion within a few months. Anastasia Tegonhatsiongo, a former friend of her mother's, treated Tekakwitha like a daughter and assisted her in her spiritual development, and in this environment Tekakwitha's spirituality thrived. Tekakwitha manifested a spirit of great humility and charity and practiced continual mortifications of the body—burning herself, standing in the snow, whipping herself with branches—to show her love of Christ. This self-torture may have had additional meanings for Tekakwitha, who lived in an age when prisoners were still tortured. One was expected to remain brave and impassive during torture, enduring pain for personal and family honor; Tekakwitha gave Christian meanings to this traditional behavior. Some of these self-imposed penances were considered extreme, and she was ordered by the Jesuits to modify them. Tekakwitha wished to found a community of Native religious women, but this was considered premature by the priests, and she was dissuaded from it. She was allowed to pronounce a vow of virginity on the Feast of the Annunciation, March 25, 1679.

Tekakwitha's mortifications of her body weakened her always frail health, and she died on April 17, 1680, at only twenty-four years of age. At her death, her smallpox-scarred face suddenly became beautiful, and shortly afterwards a series of apparitions, healings, and other intercessions attributed to her began. In 1744 Charlevoix described her as being "universally regarded as the Protectress of

Canada"; devotion to her has increased steadily since then, and hundreds of thousands of men and women have made pilgrimages to her shrine at the mission of St. Francis Xavier at Caughnawaga, where her relics are kept, and to her natal village at Auriesville, New York. After intensive lobbying, she was declared Venerable by the Church in 1943 and was Beatified in 1980, the first two steps on the path to sainthood. She has also become the focus of the international Kateri Tekakwitha Movement, which fosters the development of a distinctively Native American Catholicism.

Kateri Tekakwitha's life has been closely documented by Catholic clergy, who saw in her intense devotion a symbol of the potential success of their missionary endeavors. She has likewise become a symbol for Native Catholics, to whom she represents acceptance of Native American peoples by the Catholic church and the possibility of a Native American Catholicism. Despite the growth of this Native Catholic movement and the recent change in attitudes by the Church towards Native peoples, biographies of Tekakwitha have not yet dealt adequately with her Native identity and the manner in which she reconciled her new faith with her Native world view. That she might have been able to truly join aspects of both traditions makes her an even more meaningful figure for contemporary Native peoples.

—Laura Peers

References

Allen, Christine. "Women in Colonial French America." In *Women and Religion in America*. Vol. 2. Edited by Rosemary Radford Ruether and Rosemary Skinner Keller, 79–131. San Francisco: Harper and Row, 1983.

Bechard, Henri S.J. "Tekakwitha." *Dictionary of Canadian Biography*. Vol. 1. Toronto: University of Toronto Press, 1966.

Blanchard, David. "To the Other Side of the Sky: Catholicism at Kahnawake, 1667–1700." *Anthropologica* 24 (1982): 77–102.

Mathes, Valerie Sherer. "American Indian Women and the Catholic Church." *North Dakota History* 47 (Fall 1980): 20–25.

Peterson, Jacqueline, and Mary Druke. "American Indian Women and Religion." In *Women and Religion in America*. Vol. 2. Edited by Rosemary Radford Ruether and Rosemary Skinner Keller, 1–41. San Francisco: Harper and Row, 1983.

The Position of the Historical Section of the Sacred Congregation of Rites on the Introduction of the Cause for Beatification and Canonization and on the Virtues of the Servant of God Katherine Tekakwitha, the Lily of the Mohawks. New York: Fordham University Press, 1940.

TELLES, LUCY PARKER (1870?-1956) was the daughter of Louisa Sam, of Yosemite Valley Miwok descent, and Mack "Bridgeport" Tom, a Mono Lake Paiute. She married Jack Parker, a Paiute from the Mono Lake area, who died shortly after a son, Lloyd, was born in 1902. She married John Telles, a Mexican-

American from Texas, in 1914, and they had a son, John Telles, Jr., in 1922. When John Telles became ill, Lucy Telles turned to basket making to support her family.

As a small girl, she learned the art of basketry, an essential part of traditional life among the Miwok and Paiute people. Due to the demand for Native basketry by early white tourists to the Yosemite Valley region, Telles (and others) began developing baskets that were not utilitarian, but art. She is responsible for being the first weaver to use many new and different weaving techniques, including using red and black together in the same design unit, realistic floral, butterfly, and hummingbird motifs, lids for baskets that snap into place, and flattened top, high-shouldered baskets. By 1912 she had gained a reputation as the best weaver in the region, and by the 1920s other weavers were copying her innovations in design and weaving techniques. In 1929 she began a basket that would take her four years to complete. It reached thirty-six inches in diameter and twenty inches in height, for which she won first prize at the Panama-Pacific Exposition in San Francisco in 1939. From 1947 on, she began to demonstrate weaving for the National Park Service at Yosemite Valley, and at the time of her death, she had been working on a basket that, judging from the size of the base, would have been larger than any basket ever produced in the Yosemite region. Lucy Telles produced hundreds of baskets in her lifetime that reflected the perfection of the three-rod basketry technique, innovation in two and three color designs, and designs never used before by the Miwok-Paiute people.

—Julie A. Russ

References

Bates, Craig D. "Lucy Telles, Outstanding Weaver of the Yosemite Miwok-Paiute." *Pacific Historian* 24 (1980): 396–403.
———. "Lucy Telles, A Supreme Weaver of the Yosemite Miwok Paiute." *American Indian Basketry* 2 (1982): 23–29.
Ross, George. "Lucy Telles, Basket Maker." *Yosemite Nature Notes* 26 (1948): 67–68.

THE-OTHER-MAGPIE [MARY BUOYER, MAGPIE OUTSIDE] (1849?-?),

The-Other-Magpie was known for her warrior-like skill and bravery while riding with Crow wolves (army scouts) during the Battle of the Rosebud in 1876. Although both Magpie Outside and The-Other-Magpie can be placed in the same vicinity during the Battle of the Rosebud, it is doubtful they are the same woman. Pretty-shield says that The-Other-Magpie "had no man of her own," and yet Magpie Outside was married to Mitch Buoyer. Magpie Outside is also described by Thomas H. Leforge, her second husband, as a calm woman, whereas The-Other-Magpie is called "a wild one . . . both bad and brave" by Pretty-shield.

Pretty-shield saw the battle where The-Other-Magpie exhibited her bravery. "I saw the two women, Finds-Them-And-Kills-Them, and The-Other-Magpie, riding and singing with them [the wolves]. . . . The-Other-Magpie [had] a long coup-stick, with one breath-feather on its small end." She circled the Lakota, singing her war-song and waving her coup-stick. When the Lakota closed in on a grounded wolf, The-Other-Magpie rode straight at them, waving her coup-stick. "See," she called out, "my spit is my arrows." Then she struck the Lakota with her coup-stick, and saved her companion. That day she took a scalp and cut it into many pieces, so that the men might have more scalps to dance with when they returned from battle. Her appearance as a warrior was formidable. She wore a stuffed woodpecker on her head, and her forehead was painted yellow.

Magpie Outside, also known as Mary Buoyer, was born in May 1849 into the Burnt Mouth Clan of Mountain Crows. She married four times: Mitch Buoyer, or Two-Bodies, a half-breed Sioux who interpreted for Custer and died with him; Thomas H. Leforge, or Horse-Rider, a white who lived with the Crows; Jack, a white who was employed by the Crow Indian Agency on the reservation; Cold Wind, a full blooded Crow Indian, born in 1865. Her children were Jim and Mary Buoyer; and Tom (Born-in-Another-Place), Phoebe, and Rosa Leforge.

Unlike The-Other-Magpie, Leforge describes Magpie Outside as "a true and good wife," "calm," "benignant," with "goodness of heart," one who loved "all human beings," "a special friend of every orphan and decrepit old person in the tribe," and one who exhibited "benevolence, generosity, magnanimity."

She saw that each of her children were educated, and later she became a medicine woman. She died on the Crow Reservation sometime after 1900.

—Audrey M. Godfrey

References

Ewers, John C. "Deadlier Than the Male." *American Heritage* 16 (June 1965): 10–13.

Mathes, Valerie Sherer. "Native American Women in Medicine and the Military." *Journal of the West* 21 (April 1982): 41–48.

Leforge, Thomas H. As told by Thomas B. Marquis. *Memoirs of a White Crow Indian*. Lincoln: University of Nebraska Press, 1974.

Liberty, Margot. "Hell Came with Horses: Plains Indian Women in the Equestrian Era." *Montana: The Magazine of Western History* 32 (Summer 1982): 10–19.

Linderman, Frank B. *Pretty-Shield, Medicine Woman of the Crows*. Lincoln: University of Nebraska Press, 1972.

U.S. Bureau of the Census. 1900. Crow Agency, Custer County, Montana. Indian Population.

THORPE, GRACE (b. 1921) was born in Yale, Oklahoma, growing up in the same community and attending the same Indian boarding schools as her father, Jim Thorpe. She is a member of the Sauk-Fox tribe and a descendant of the chieftain Blackhawk. Her degrees include a paralegal certification from Antioch

School of Law in 1974 and a BA from the University of Tennessee, Knoxville, in 1980.

Thorpe joined the Women's Army Corps during World War II and was stationed in New Guinea for more than two years before being selected as a member of the staff for General McArthur's headquarters command in Japan. During her tour in Japan she married Fred Seeley and gave birth to a son, Thorpe, and daughter, Dagmar. The couple were later divorced. In 1950 she returned to the US, took up residence in Pearl River, New York, and sold Yellow Page ads to businesses in the New York area.

In the mid-1960s, Thorpe decided to redirect her talents toward helping the Native American community, and she became quite active in the areas of land re-acquisition, government and public relations, and community organization. In 1966 Thorpe helped to secure the property for Deganawidah-Quetzalcoatl University, an institution designed to meet the specific needs of Native American and Chicano students. She spent a year with the National Congress of American Indians working to interest private companies in the idea of locating plants on reservations where Indians would be both trained and employed. During the first two months of 1970 she participated in the successful takeover of Alcatraz and the Ft. Lawton Museum in Washington state, handling much of the public relations work on both occasions. While working with various women's clubs in 1971, she helped start the National Indian Women's Action Corps. Thorpe served as a legislative assistant to the US Senate Sub-Committee on Indian Affairs and then spent two years with the American Indian Policy Review Board sponsored by the US House of Representatives. In 1980 she returned to Oklahoma where she now serves as a part-time district court judge for the Five Tribes in Stroud, Oklahoma.

Grace Thorpe is vice-president of the Jim Thorpe Foundation and together with her sister Charlotte has worked for the return of their father's Olympic medals. She wrote "Jim Thorpe Family History: 1750–1904," published in *Chronicles of Oklahoma*.

—Arlon Benson

References

Anderson, Owanah, ed. *Ohoyo One Thousand: A Resource Guide of American Indian/Alaska Native Women, 1982.* Wichita Falls, TX: Ohoyo Resource Center, 1982.

Benson, Arlon. Personal communication with Grace Thorpe, 17 March 1992.

Berman, Susan. "Working for My People: Thorpe's Daughter Indian Activist." *Akwesasne Notes* 3 (March 1971): 27.

Thorpe, Grace. "Jim Thorpe Family History: From Wisconsin to Indian Territory, Part I." *Chronicles of Oklahoma* 59 (Spring 1981): 91–105. Part II. 59 (Summer 1981): 179–201.

TIGER, WINIFRED (b. 1924) is an enrolled member of the Eastern Band of Cherokees, having grown up in the Paint Town community of rural North Carolina. She was sent to the Cherokee Indian School to complete her secondary education and graduated in 1943. At Cherokee she met a handsome young Seminole Indian boy from Florida, Howard Tiger, an outstanding athlete and leader, who was attending school, along with his sister, Betty Mae, and several members of their tribe. After World War II began, Howard left school and volunteered for the Marine Corps, where he saw combat action in the Pacific on Guam and Iwo Jima. In 1946 Howard returned to North Carolina and he and Winifred were married; the couple had three sons and a daughter.

In 1957 the family returned to Florida, where Howard became a leading political figure in the newly organized Seminole Tribe of Florida, which had just received a federal constitution and corporate charter. He served as a member of the Tribal Council and as president of the board of directors, which supervised tribal business affairs. He was also an avid promoter of sports and recreation activities on the reservations. When Howard died in a heavy equipment accident in 1967, he was so highly respected that the Tribal Council named an annual sports tournament and the first reservation athletic facilities in his honor.

Winifred Tiger was not a member of the Seminole tribe and thus ineligible to vote or hold office. Nevertheless, she was one of the best educated and most respected women in the Seminole community and played an important role in improving tribal relations with the local education authorities. From 1966–72 she was employed by the Broward County (Florida) School Board as liaison with the Seminole tribe, checking Seminole school attendance, solving health and social needs, and finding children who were hiding in the woods or their homes to avoid attending school. When the Seminole tribe contracted its education programs from the Bureau of Indian Affairs, Tiger was selected as the education counselor. In 1985 she was named Director of Education for the Seminole Tribe of Florida, charged with supervising an expanding staff and new reservation school programs. Among her accomplishments have been achieving full academic accreditation for the Afachkee Day School—an elementary school operated by the tribe on the Big Cypress Reservation—improving the drop-out rate for Seminole youngsters attending public schools, and recently initiating plans for a residential secondary school on the Seminole Reservation. She has also served as an advisor to the Broward County School Board and was a member of the school board for the Intertribal School at Intermountain, Utah. Among the honors that she has received are a Certificate of Recognition from the Broward County School Board, the Human Relations Award of the Broward County Teachers Association, and the Broward County Pioneers Award. Winifred Tiger is currently recognized as a leading spokesperson for Indian educational issues in south Florida.

—Harry A. Kersey, Jr.

References

Harrington, V.N. to T.M. Reed. *BIA Central Office Files*, File 13671–1957–
    Seminole 055. Washington, DC: The National Archives, 15 September 1959.
Kersey, Harry. Personal Communication with Winifred Tiger, 3 December 1990.
Seminole Tribe of Florida and Seminole Tribe of Florida, Inc. 1977. *20th Anniver-
    sary of Seminole Tribal Organization 1957–1977, Saturday, August 20, 1977.*
    Hollywood, FL: Seminole Tribe. Mimeo.

TOHE, LAURA (b. 1952), born in Fort Defiance, Arizona, of the Sleepy Rock People for the Bitterwater Clan, grew up as Crystal, near the Chuska Mountains on the eastern edge of the Navajo Reservation. Her Navajo name translates roughly to Woman Among Warriors. Baptized into the Mormon religion, she became disillusioned when a Mormon church member told her that if she kept Mormon law, when she died, she would become white. Her Navajo father and Navajo/Laguna mother spoke both English and Navajo at home, and as a young child in boarding school (she lived at Albuquerque Indian School but attended public school), she helped friends bridge Navajo and Anglo culture by translating for them. She remembers children being punished for speaking Navajo, but she was raised to value her heritage, and she is committed to its preservation.

Tohe's poetry moves between the world views of two cultures whose languages offer no natural cognates. This is not to say that every poem's intent is to merge the irreconcilable. In "At Mexican Springs," for example, Gallup, the notorious off-reservation strip of bars and motels, becomes the symbol of soul-robbery, but the land which stretches "across these eternal sandstones" ensures that she "will live to tell her children" the ancient stories that carry meaning down through time. Her book, *Making Friends with Water*, was published by Nosila Press in 1986. Her poems and stories continue to appear in a variety of literary magazines and anthologies.

Tohe is completing her PhD at the University of Nebraska. Her creative dissertation area is poetry and storytelling, and she plans to examine the relationship between Native American creation myths and the roles of Native American women. She holds an MA in English from the University of Nebraska and a BA in psychology from the University of New Mexico. She teaches composition, literature, reading, and creative writing at the University of Nebraska and has served as a guest speaker, panel member, and resource person for conferences and presentations on Native culture. Recently, she has given poetry readings for the Modern Language Association and for the Center for Great Plains Studies.

Tohe lives with her husband and two sons in Omaha, Nebraska. It is the family, she believes, that must instill in children a reverence for Navajo thought, traditions, and values. Seasons, for example, have strong associations on the

reservation; in fall, it was gathering piñon nuts. In urban Omaha, connection to the land is diminished, and it becomes more difficult to ask children to revere what they cannot experience. In the same way that Navajos do not believe in bringing live flowers to graves because life is for the living, Tohe is not so much nostalgic about the historical past as grateful for the present. She enjoys her family and her work despite the magnetic pull of the Dinetáh. She takes the advice of her mother and grandmother (who is remembered in "To Shimá sání"): "Celebrate what you have. You can create your own happiness and health."
—Rhoda Carroll

References

Bruchac, Joseph, ed. *Songs from this Earth on Turtle's Back: Contemporary American Indian Poetry.* Greenfield Center, NY: Greenfield Review Press, 1983.
Cochran, Jo, et al., eds. "Bearing Witness/Sobreviviendo: An Anthology of Native American/Latina Art and Literature." *Calyx: A Journal of Art and Literature by Women* 8 (1984).
Tohe, Laura. *Making Friends with Water.* Omaha, NE: Nosila Press, 1986.

TOMASSA [TOMASSE] (c. 1840–1900) was born in a respectable, wealthy family in the Republic of Mexico and taken captive by a band of Carissa Comanche while she was a small child, along with her cousin, a boy a year or so older. After living with the Comanches for ten years, they were ransomed by the US government and sent back to Mexico. For some unknown reason, neither she nor her cousin were claimed, so they were left with a wealthy Mexican family that treated them as servants.

After staying in Mexico for about a year, she and her cousin decided to return to the Comanches. The two children hid food sufficient to chance the journey hundreds of miles north. They took one horse, and the North Star was their only guide. When their food gave out, they killed the horse, dried the meat, and took the hide along to use in making moccasins. Miraculously, when the last of the dried meat was gone, they stumbled into a Comanche camp which proved to be the very band with whom they had formerly lived.

When she was around fourteen, her Comanche mother told her she was to marry Blue Leggings. Tomassa broke Comanche custom and refused to go with Blue Leggings. She stated she wished to marry Joseph Chandler (1823–73), a half-Cherokee, half-white farmer who owned a farm near what would become Fort Sill, Oklahoma. Chandler bought her from Blue Leggings for three dollars and a crowing chicken. During the Civil War (1861–65) renegades sacked and burned the area, and the Chandlers were forced to flee to Texas. They returned in 1868 to their land in Oklahoma.

In 1871 Tomassa became employed as an interpreter for the first school at Fort Sill. She spoke Spanish, English, Comanche, and Caddo and was of great service to the officials at Fort Sill. Due to their close friendship with the Comanches, Tomassa and her husband were able to warn the Indian Agency of impending Indian raids.

Tomassa was respected by the Indian agents and the Comanches because of her humanity. Once, when two Comanche captives escaped, they went to Tomassa's home for protection. She treated them kindly and was later able to secure their freedom.

Chandler died in 1873, making Tomassa a widow with three sons and one daughter. Some years later Tomassa married George Conover, a retired army man. She had several more children by him. In 1887 Tomassa was converted to Christianity and joined the Methodist church. She died in 1900 and was buried on her ranch at the extreme western edge of Grady County, Oklahoma.

—Joyce Ann Kievit

References

Butler, Josiah. "Pioneer School Teaching at the Comanche-Kiowa Agency School, 1870–1873." *Chronicles of Oklahoma* 6 (December 1928): 483–528.

Corwin, Hugh D. *Comanche and Kiowa Captives in Oklahoma and Texas.* Lawton, OK: By the author, 1959.

———. *The Kiowa Indians.* Lawton, OK: By the author, 1958.

Methvin, J.J. *In the Limelight.* Anadarko, OK: By the author, c. 1925.

Waltrip, Lela, and Rufus Waltrip. *Indian Women.* New York: David McKay, 1964.

TREMBLAY, GAIL (b. 1945), of Onondaga, Micmac, and French Canadian descent, was born in Buffalo, New York. A well-known poet and visual artist, Tremblay holds a BA in drama from the University of New Hampshire and an MFA in creative writing from the University of Oregon.

The author of two collections of poetry, *Talking to the Grandfathers* and *Indian Singing in Twentieth Century America,* Tremblay has earned a significant reputation as one of the most striking voices in contemporary American poetry. Her work has appeared in a number of well-known journals, including *Denver Quarterly, Northwest Review, Calyx,* and *Maize* and has been anthologized in a number of volumes, including *New Voices from the Longhouse, Harper's Anthology of 20th Century Native American Poetry,* and *Dancing on the Rim of the World: An Anthology of Contemporary Northwest Native American Writing.* Tremblay has received numerous awards for her writing and has given poetry readings across the country.

Tremblay has also earned a substantial national reputation as a visual artist, particularly in fiber works and weaving. She is best known for her wall hangings, masks, tapestries, and mixed media weavings of wood, fiber, and metal. The recipient of numerous awards, Tremblay has exhibited her work in both group and individual shows nationally and internationally. Her work was a highly acclaimed addition to *Women of Sweetgrass, Cedar, and Sage,* a national exhibition which toured North America. Her work has also been exhibited in Japan and Switzerland.

Both her poetry and her visual art draw upon the traditional culture of her ancestry. Images and symbols of traditional Native American motifs find a home in her work juxtaposed and yet in complement with the most contemporary artistic training and modes of expression.

Tremblay is also a vital force in the Northwest educational network. Since 1981 she has been on the faculty of Evergreen State College in Olympia, Washington, where she has been a leader in programs in Native American studies, multicultural studies, and fine arts. Tremblay gives frequent presentations across the country on the development of multicultural programs. A dynamic educator and nationally acclaimed artist and poet, Gail Tremblay has found a number of mediums in which to articulate her profoundly spiritual and highly artistic vision.

—Andrea Lerner

References

Lerner, Andrea, ed. *Dancing on the Rim of the World: An Anthology of Contemporary Northwest Native American Writing.* Tucson: University of Arizona Press, 1990.

Tremblay, Gail. "Artist's Statement." In *Contemporary Native American Art.* Exhibit Catalog. Stillwater: Oklahoma State University, 1983.

———. "Artist's Statement." In *Women of Sweetgrass, Cedar, and Sage.* Exhibit Catalog. Phoenix: ATLATL, 1984.

———. "Carrier of Culture" and "Artist's Statement." In *New Directions Northwest: Contemporary Native American Art.* Exhibit Catalog. 1987.

———. *Indian Singing in North America.* Corvallis, OR: Calyx, 1990.

———. *Talking to the Grandfathers.* American Poetry Series, Annex 21, no. 3. Omaha: University of Nebraska, 1981.

TSUPU (c. 1815–1890) was born near Petaluma, California. Little is known about either her mother, Tcupi Yomi, a Coast Miwok Indian from the Olum (Bodega) band or her father, Tsutcuk, a Coast Miwok Indian from the Petaluma band. Nor is much known about the seven brothers and sisters she is reputed to have had. Tsupu survived both the Spanish and Mexican invasions of Coast Miwok territory and single-handedly passed her knowledge of Coast Miwok language and culture to her children, particularly to her sons, Tom and Bill Smith, and their families.

Tsupu spoke both Olum (Bodega Miwok) and Kashaya Pomo. Undoubtedly, she knew other Coast Miwok languages as well. She first married Tintic (Tomas Comtechal, or Kom-sha-tal), a Kashaya Pomo from Fort Ross. They had four children. Their son, Thomas Comtechal (later called Tom Smith), became the last prominent Coast Miwok doctor and spiritual leader. Later, Tsupu moved to Bodega Bay where she became maid/mistress of Captain Steven Smith, a Quaker settler from Massachusetts with a Peruvian wife. Smith claimed a large tract of Bodega Miwok land as his own. With Smith, Tsupu had a son, Bill, who established an important and prosperous fishing business with his sons at Bodega Bay.

Tsupu's survival and tenacious memory assured both the survival of a people and their culture. Her granddaughter, Sarah Smith Ballard, who died in the early 1970s at nearly one hundred years of age, was the last fluent speaker of Olum (Bodega Miwok). Sara, in turn, passed much of her knowledge to her grandson, David Peri, Coast Miwok tribal scholar and professor of anthropology at Sonoma State University. Today over one thousand Indians can trace their ancestry to Tsupu. And because of Tsupu, these Indians can know something about their Coast Miwok history and culture.

Among Tsupu's descendants are many Indian scholars, including David Peri, professor of anthropology, Sonoma State University; Bill Smith, former professor and director of American Indian Studies, Sonoma State University; Kathleen Smith, artist, writer, and tribal scholar; and Greg Sarris, assistant professor of English, University of California, Los Angeles.

—Greg Sarris

References

Kelly, Isabel. *Ethnographic Notes on the Coast Miwok Indians.* Miwok Archeological Preserve of Marin, 1991.

Sarris, Greg. Personal communication with David Peri. Berkeley, California, June 1990.

———. Personal communication with Kathleen Smith. Berkeley, California, June 1990.

V

VELARDE, PABLITA [TSE TSAN, GOLDEN DAWN] (b. 1918), a famous Tewa Indian painter from Santa Clara Pueblo, New Mexico, is the third daughter of Herman and Marianita Velarde, who died of tuberculosis in 1921. In 1924 Velarde and her two older sisters were enrolled in St. Catherine's Indian School in Santa Fe. In their summers in the Pueblo, they frequently stayed with their grandmother, medicine woman, Qualupita, from whom Velarde learned traditional customs and arts. From her father, a respected storyteller, she learned traditional myths and legends, and from the petroglyphs at Puye Ruins, ancestral designs. In 1932 Velarde began attending the Santa Fe Indian School run by the BIA, where she was one of many students encouraged by art teacher Dorothy Dunn to paint from their tribal experience. In 1933 she was selected to work with artist Olive Rush on murals for the Chicago "Century of Progress" World's Fair, and in 1934, she again worked with Rush on WPA art projects. After graduating from the Indian School in 1936, Velarde taught arts and crafts at the Santa Clara Day School, and worked again with Rush in 1938 on a mural for the Maisel Trading Post in Albuquerque. In 1939 she was employed by the Park Service to paint archaeological and ethnological murals, which reconstructed the life of her ancestors in Frijoles Canyon at the Bandelier National Monument Visitors' Center. Velarde married an Anglo man, Herbert Hardin, in 1942, and in 1943 gave birth to daughter Helen, who became an artist in her own right, and in 1944 gave birth to son Herby. The conflict between her Indian heritage and life in the Anglo world and the conflict between their respective careers proved too great. They divorced in 1959.

Whether in her "memory paintings" done in tempera or oil or in her "earth paintings," and whether realistic or abstract, Velarde's art re-presents designs, images, and ceremonial and mythic scenes from Pueblo life. What she has remembered and created from her own experience has been supplemented by both historical scholarship and ethnographic research, which has at times been criticized or opposed by tribal members. In 1948 she won her first important prize at the Philbrook Art Center's Annual Indian Art Show, and in 1954 she was awarded the Palmes Academiques from the French government. She won all the top prizes at the Inter-Tribal Indian Ceremonial in Gallup in 1955, including Grand Prize for her painting, "Old Father, the Storyteller." In 1956 she finished "The Green Corn Dance," a twenty-one foot mural for the Foote Cafeteria in Houston. During this time, Velarde also returned frequently to Santa Clara Pueblo and spent time with her father listening to and recording his stories. The result of their collaboration was *Old Father, the Storyteller*, an illustrated book of Tewa legends selected as one of the best Western books of the year in 1960. Since then, she has received countless honors and awards, including the New Mexico

Governor's Award and an Honor Award from the National Women's Caucus for Art. Her paintings and murals are on permanent display at the Indian Pueblo Cultural Center in Albuquerque and countless Indian artists, especially women artists, have been inspired and enabled by her example.

—Barbara A. Babcock

References

Dunn, Dorothy. "Pablita Velarde, Painter of Pueblo Life." *El Palacio* 59 (1952): 335–41.
Gridley, Marion E. "Pablita Velarde, Artist of the Pueblos." In *American Indian Women*, 94–104. New York: Hawthorn Books, 1974.
Nelson, Mary Carroll. *Pablita Velarde*. Minneapolis: Dillon Press, 1971.
———. "Pablita Velarde." *American Indian Art* 3 (1978): 50–57, 90.
Velarde, Pablita. *Old Father, the Storyteller*. Globe, AZ: D. S. King, 1960.

VENEGAS, HILDRETH MARIE TWOSTARS (b. 1919) has spent her life in community service. The daughter of Jemima and David Twostars, born in Sisseton, South Dakota, Venegas has spent most of her life there.

After early schooling in Sisseton, she attended Flandreau Indian School for her final three high school years, graduating in 1938. She then attended Haskell Institute and earned her diploma for a two-year course in business. In 1977 she was selected by Haskell for their Outstanding Alumni Award.

Over her lifetime she continued her education at regional colleges and universities. In 1949 she attended the Phoenix Academy of Beauty Culture in Arizona. On graduation, she passed the state board exam and received her license to practice as a beautician. She is still licensed in Arizona and South Dakota. In 1985 she received an associate degree in general studies from the Sisseton-Wahpeton Community College. She has nearly finished the hours necessary for a BS degree from the University of Minnesota at Morris.

For almost forty years she has worked in government service, primarily in the Indian Health Service. Twenty of these years were spent as an administrative officer in the Indian Hospital in Sisseton. For most of these years she was either the hospital director or health systems administrator. She is one of the few Indian women to have held such positions in the Indian Health Service.

Her life has been filled with honors and awards. In 1970 she was the first Indian woman to be selected South Dakota Merit Mother, an honor repeated in 1981. Also in 1970 she received the title "Mrs. Indian Seminar" at the first national meeting of American Indian women at Fort Collins, Colorado. Later she was selected national president of the North American Indian Women's Association at their meeting in Chilocco, Oklahoma, in June 1977.

In 1978 she was given special recognition and a letter from President Carter, who invited her to participate in the White House Conference on Balanced

National Growth and Economic Development. On March 31, 1980, she received the Jefferson Award in recognition of outstanding public service and active involvement in community affairs and continual effort to improve the image of the Indian. In October 1983, she received a certificate and plaque at the first Indian Women's Recognition Ceremony during the annual convention of the National Congress of American Indians held in Green Bay, Wisconsin. It is fitting that her efforts to establish Indian-white harmony should be honored by both races.

In retirement her community work continues. She serves on three city committees and is president-elect of the South Dakota Lung Association. She also spends time talking to school children and to adult groups about improving the image of the Indian by bettering the communications, understanding, and attitudes between Indians and non-Indians.

—Jack Marken

References

"Hildreth Venegas." *The University of South Dakota Bulletin.* Vermillion, SD: The Institute of Indian Studies, 1988.

North American Indian Women's Association. "Message from the President." *Highlights* 1 (June 1977/March 1978): 1.

"Venegas Outstanding Alumna." *The Indian Leader* [Haskell Junior College, Lawrence, KS] 13 May 1977: 1.

VOLBORTH, JUDITH MOUNTAIN LEAF [IVALOO] (b. 1955) is an Apache-Comanche poet born in New York City. She studied at the University of California at Los Angeles, where she honed her skills in prose, poetry, and particularly, in haiku, a Japanese form of impressionistic free verse. Tribal themes dominate her work, and the trickster figure of Coyote is a frequent subject. While traditional motifs are common in her work, so are images of strong, modern Native women and their unique struggles.

Volborth's synthesis of ancient forms with more contemporary works, *Thunder Root: Traditional and Contemporary Native American Verse,* was published by the American Indian Studies Center at her alma mater, UCLA. In addition to her creative writing, Volborth is an adept writer on the mechanics and styles employed in contemporary Indian literature. Her analysis of the power of sound and language in Native literature appeared in *Native American Literature: Forum* 7, a special publication of Serrizo Editoriale Universitario of Pisa, Italy.

A current resident of Santa Monica, California, Judith Volborth is very interested in the performance of her own works and in the meaning of dramatic readings for the preservation of Native culture.

—Cynthia Kasee

References

Coltelli, Laura, ed. *Native American Literature: Forum 7, 1989*. Pisa, Italy: Serrizo Editoriale Universitario, 1989.

Green, Rayna, ed. *That's What She Said*. Bloomington: Indiana University Press, 1984.

Swan, Brian, ed. Special Issue on Native American literature of *Shantih* (1979).

Volborth, Judith Mountain Leaf. *Thunder Root: Traditional and Contemporary Native American Verse*. Los Angeles: UCLA American Indian Studies Center, 1978.

W

WALSH, MARNIE

WALSH, MARNIE [M. M. B. WALSH] is a Sioux writer and Dakota native who prefers that her work speak for itself. She avoids releasing personal information, which she once called "biographical garbage." Walsh earned BA degrees in history and English from Pennsylvania State University and an MA in creative writing from the University of New Mexico. During her graduate studies, she was awarded a fellowship by the National Endowment for the Arts.

In 1975, Walsh published her first novel, *Dolly Purdo* (Putnam's). In 1976, she produced another novel, *The Four Colored Hoop* (Putnam's), and a collection of poetry called *Taste of the Knife*. Her poetry has appeared in numerous publications, including *From the Belly of the Shark* (Vintage Books), *Voices from Wah'Kon-Tah* (International Publishers), *Dacotah Territory, Scree, South Dakota Review, Best of the Small Presses* (Pushcart Press), *The Third Woman: Minority Writers of the US* (Houghton Mifflin), and *Women Poets of the World* (Macmillan). Her poetry is noted for its starkly realistic depictions of life on Sioux reservations in North and South Dakota.

—Lois Griffitts

References

Hobson, Geary, ed. *The Remembered Earth*. Albuquerque: University of New Mexico Press, 1979.
Locher, Frances, ed. *Contemporary Authors* 101 (1981): 540.
Walsh, Marnie. *Taste of the Knife*. Boise, ID: Ahsahta Press, 1976.

WALTERS, ANNA LEE

WALTERS, ANNA LEE (b. 1946), a Pawnee/Otoe-Missouria, is a writer of poems, short stories, novels, and essays. She was born on September 9, 1946, in Pawnee, Oklahoma, the daughter of Luther and Juanita M. (Taylor) McGlaslin. Walters attended the College of Santa Fe from 1972 to 1974. Her career includes positions as a library technician for the Institute of American Indian Arts in Santa Fe, New Mexico (1968–74); a technical writer for Dineh Cooperatives in Chinle, Arizona (1975); and a technical writer for curriculum development for the Navajo Community College in Tsaile, Arizona (1976–84). She also worked for a short time in the National Anthropological Archives at the Smithsonian.

A prolific writer, Walters has co-authored a textbook, *The Sacred: Ways of Knowledge, Sources of Life*, and has contributed work to many anthologies, including *The Man to Send Rainclouds* (Viking, 1974), *Warriors of the Rainbow* (Viking, 1975), and *The Third Woman* (Houghton, 1978). In an interview published in *Wildfire*, Walters says that one of her primary reasons for writing is to demonstrate to contemporary audiences the Native American tribal perspective of histories and philosophies. She stresses that the tribal view of the world is unique and that Native Americans adhere to and live according to that non-mainstream view that needs to be understood. This serves as one of the major premises of her novel, *Ghost Singer*. In her essay, "Odyssey of Indian Time," Walters emphasizes the spiritual, continual, and intangible sense of time in tribal cultures. Her award-winning collection of short stories, *The Sun Is Not Merciful*, chronicles a people—triumphant, not defeated—who come to terms with time, life, and place. Walters, in short, writes in many genres about the people and culture she knows, with a full understanding of what it is to be Native American in contemporary society.

Walters is married to Harry Walters, a Navajo and museum curator. They live on the Navajo Reservation in Arizona, where she is director of the Navajo Community College Press. She is the mother of two sons.

—Laurie Lisa

References

Beck, Peggy V., and Anna Lee Walters. *The Sacred: Ways of Knowledge, Sources of Life*. Tsaile, AZ: Navajo Community College, 1977.

Hogan, Linda, ed. *Frontiers: Special Issue on Native American Women* 6 (1981).

Ortiz, Simon H., ed. *Earth Power Coming: Short Fiction in Native American Literature*. Tsaile, AZ: Navajo Community College Press, 1983.

Ryan, Matthew. "Interview with Anna Lee Walters." *Wildfire* 4 (Summer 1989): 16–21.

Walters, Anna Lee. "American Indian Thought and Identity in American Fiction." In *Coyote was Here: Essays on Contemporary Native American Literary and Political Mobilization*, edited by Bo Scholer, 35–39. Aarhus, Denmark: University of Aarhus, 1984.

———. *Ghost Singer*. Menomonie, WI: Northland, 1988.

———. "Odyssey of Indian Time." *Book Forum* 5 (1981): 396–99.

———. *The Spirit of Native America: Beauty and Mysticism in American Indian Art*. San Francisco: Chronicle Books, 1989.

———. *The Sun Is Not Merciful*. Ithaca, NY: Firebrand Books, 1985.

WARD, NANCY [NANYE-HI, ONE WHO GOES ABOUT] (c. 1738–1824), the last "Beloved Woman" of the Cherokees, was born at Chota, the sacred "Mother Town" of the Cherokees. She was born into the Wolf Clan and was the niece of Attakullakulla, a prudent chief who allowed Moravian missionaries into the Cherokee country, only after exacting a promise that they would build schools to teach his people about the ways of the whites. Ward, sometimes called "Wild Rose," is first noted at the Battle of Taliwa in 1755. She was married to Kingfisher, a warrior who was killed in this skirmish with the Creeks. Fighting alongside him, Ward became enraged at the Creeks for his

death, and she rallied the Cherokee forces to a decisive victory. For her heroism, she was named "Beloved Woman," a title reserved for wise women who have distinguished themselves in battle or who have been the wives or mothers of great warriors.

In her role as Beloved Woman, Ward performed such duties as sitting in General Council (where she had full voice and vote), heading the Women's Council, preparing the Black Drink for the Green Corn (busk) ceremony, and acting as a negotiator in treaty parlays. It is noted that in meeting with John Sevier to strike peace terms with the Americans (Little Pigeon River, Tennessee, 1781), she was appalled that he had no women negotiators. He was as appalled that she was trusted with such an important task. It has been recorded that she admonished him to return to his people and explain the terms to the women, saying, "Let your women hear our words."

As a Beloved Woman, Nancy Ward also had the right to save a captive already condemned to death. In 1780 she saved the life of a Mrs. Bean, a white woman captive about to be immolated. Ward nursed her back to health and then set her free, but not before Mrs. Bean had introduced Ward to the art of weaving in the manner of the whites and to raising cattle for dairying. While these innovations are attached to the name of Nancy Ward with great honor, there is at least one other that calls forth great shame, for Nancy Ward was the first Cherokee to have black slaves.

Many years of broken promises on the part of the Americans eventually took their toll on Ward's credulity, and by the Cherokee Council of 1817, she was no longer advising peace. She told the younger people not to cede any more land because already the talk of Indian removal west of the Mississippi was being heard and believed. Fearing removal in her lifetime, Ward took to the trade of innkeeping and married a white man, Bryan (Briant) Ward. They kept a small inn on the Ocowee River's Womankiller Ford. She bore three children and became prosperous before her death in 1824. Her son, Fivekiller, was with his mother at her death and reported that a white light ascended from her body and flew into the sacred mound at Chota, the same mound destroyed by the Tennessee Valley Authority's Tellico Dam Project of the 1970s and 1980s. Nancy Ward is buried somewhere near present-day Vonore, Tennessee. Many honors have been bestowed in her name since her death. Among these, the Nashville, Tennessee, chapter of the Daughters of the American Revolution is named for her.

—Cynthia Kasee

References

Dockstader, Frederick J., ed. *Great North American Indians: Profiles in Life and Leadership.* New York: Van Nostrand Reinhold, 1977.

Felton, Harold W. *Nancy Ward: Cherokee.* New York: Dodd Mead, 1975.

McClary, Ben Harris. "The Last Beloved Woman of the Cherokees." *Tennessee Historical Society Quarterly* 21 (1962): 352–64.

Tucker, Norma. "Nancy Ward, Ghighau of the Cherokees." *Georgia Historical Quarterly* 53 (June 1969): 192–200.

Woodward, Grace Steele. *The Cherokees.* Norman: University of Oklahoma Press, 1963.

WAUNEKA, ANNIE DODGE (b. 1910), a public health activist and politician, was born in the Navajo Nation near Sawmill, Arizona. She was the privileged daughter of Henry Chee Dodge, the first elected chairman of the Navajo Tribal Council, after the tribe adopted a constitutional form of government in 1923. Although Henry Dodge was a wealthy rancher and an influential politician, he believed that his children should learn Navajo traditions and values. From an early age, Wauneka had chores such as sheepherding, as well as her lessons at the Albuquerque Indian School.

An advantage in Wauneka's life was growing up fully bilingual. She was equally comfortable in Navajo and English and was able to act as a cultural translator between the conservative and liberal elements of the tribe. Soon Wauneka realized that the way her unique talents could best serve the Navajo was through improving the health of the more traditional segment. Wary of the ways of Indian Health Service physicians, ways which many thought were witchcraft, many conservatives refused to receive injections or to have their children or grandchildren inoculated. Diseases such as tuberculosis ran rampant, both because of this cultural misunderstanding and poor sanitation. For several years, many while also serving in tribal office, Wauneka dedicated her life to finding common ground for Navajo patients and non-Navajo health professionals. She made home visits to isolated hogans to discuss the importance of inoculating children, wrote a lexicon of terms in Navajo to be used by doctors and nurses to explain procedures, and acted in films promoting improved sanitation which were shown throughout the reservation.

Her selfless work on behalf of the Navajo erased any doubts about this daughter of a wealthy liberal politician. Wauneka's brother, Thomas Dodge, had won the tribal chairmanship in 1933, continuing the Dodge family tradition of political service. In 1951 Wauneka decided to join the family ranks and won a position as tribal council representative from the Klagetoh District. Annie Dodge, now Mrs. George Wauneka, became the first woman elected to Tribal Council. Her work in public health made her the obvious choice to head the Council's Health Committee. Her successes garnered her two more terms in Council (1955, 1959). She felt so certain that her talents were needed by the Navajo people that she risked her marriage to continue her work. In 1953 her husband was running for the position Wauneka had been holding, but she felt he was not a good candidate, so she ran against him and easily defeated him.

As she continued her grassroots work with the Navajo Tribal Council Health Committee, Annie Dodge Wauneka went to college, eventually earning the credentials to back up her work. She graduated with her BS in public health from the University of Arizona in the mid-1950s. In 1959 she received the Arizona State Public Health Association's Outstanding Worker in Public Health Award, as well as the Indian Achievement Award from the Indian Council Fire of Chicago. In 1960 Wauneka began hosting a biweekly radio show from KGAK radio in Gallup. The program, done completely in Navajo, covered topics of interest to the Navajo Nation, as well as health improvement information. A tireless worker, Wauneka was eventually appointed to the Surgeon General's Advisory Board and served as a board member of the National Tuberculosis Association.

In 1963 Annie Dodge Wauneka received the Presidential Medal of Freedom, given to her at the White House by John Kennedy. In recent years, Wauneka has received an honorary doctorate in public health from the University of Arizona and has continued to be among the most influential woman in the Navajo Nation.

—Cynthia Kasee

References

Anderson, Owanah, ed. *Ohoyo One Thousand: Resource Guide of American Indian/ Alaska Native Women, 1982*. Wichita Falls, TX: Ohoyo Resource Center, 1982.
Gridley, Marion, ed. and comp. *Indians of Today*. 4th ed. Chicago: ICFP, 1971.
Nelson, Mary Caroll. *Annie Wauneka*. Minneapolis: Dillon, 1972.
Steiner, Stan. *The New Indians*. New York: Harper and Row, 1968.
Witt, Shirley Hill. "An Interview with Dr. Annie Dodge Wauneka." *Frontiers* 6 (Fall 1981): 64–67.

WETAMOO [NAMUMPAM, TATATANUM, TATAPANUM, SQUAW SACHEM OF THE POCASSET, WETEMOO, WETAMOU, WETAMOE, WEETAMOO, WEETAMOU, WEETAMOE, WEETAMMO, WEETAMORE, QUEEN WETAMOO] (1635? 1650?-1676) was born near the Fall River in present day Rhode Island and was an Algonquin leader during King Philip's War. Available information about her life is very contradictory. Her father (Corbitant?) was a sachem of the Pocasset village of the Wampanoag confederacy. When he died, Wetamoo succeeded her father as sachem. Wetamoo was married several times, most notably to Alexander (Wamsutta), grand sachem of the Wampanoag confederacy and brother of King Philip (Metacom). When Alexander died she married Quequequamanchet (Petonowowett, Peter Nunnuit, "Ben") whom she left because he sided with the colonists at the beginning of King Philip's War. She then married Quinnapin (Quinapin, Quequequamanchet), a Narraganset. During King Philip's War, allied with King Philip, Wetamoo and Quinnapin captured a white woman, Mary Rowlandson, who in her memoirs described Wetamoo's leadership role and regal stature.

During the King Philip conflicts Wetamoo and her people were hunted by the Plymouth colonists, and in 1876, as she was escaping down the Fall River, she drowned. The colonists cut off her head and displayed it on a rod in Taunton (Plymouth?).

—Pattiann Frinzi

References

Biographical Dictionary of Indians of the Americas. Vol. 2. Newport Beach, CA: American Indian Publishers, 1983.

Bourne, Russell. *The Red King's Rebellion: Racial Politics in New England, 1675–1678.* New York: Atheneun, 1990.

Church, Colonel Benjamin. *Diary of King Philip's War, 1675–1676.* Edited by Alan and Mary Simpson. Riverton, RI: Lockwood Publications, 1975.

Horowitz, David. *The First Frontier: The Indian Wars and America's Origins, 1607–1776.* New York: Random House, 1978.

Mathes, Valerie Shirer. "Native American Women in Medicine and the Military." *Journal of the West* 21 (April 1982): 41–48.

———. "A New Look at the Role of Women in Indian Society." *American Indian Quarterly* 2 (1975): 131–39.

Rowlandson, Mary. *The Sovereignty and Goodness of God, Together With The Faithfulness of His Promises Displayed; Being a Narrative of the Captivity and Restoration of Mrs. Mary Rowlandson, A Minister's Wife in New England.* London: Joseph Poole, 1682.

WHITE, ELIZABETH Q. [POLINGAYSI QOYAWAYMA] (c. 1892–1990) was a Hopi woman born at Old Oraibi, Arizona, to Sevenka and Qoyawayma (called Fred by the Mennonite missionaries in the area). She was a member of her mother's Coyote Clan and a child of her father's Kachina Clan. As a child she was raised in the traditional Hopi way, but in her teens certain feelings of restlessness prompted her parents to allow her to leave home to attend school in the white world. She attended Sherman Institute in Riverside, California, and graduated from Bethel College, a Mennonite school in Newton, Kansas. Most of her white education conflicted with the lifeways of her home, and this conflict caused her much unhappiness. She worked in German-owned homes to pay her way through school and was surprised at the hard work, equating the Hopi women slaving at their grindstones to the German women slaving at their washboards. She made friends with Elizabeth Schmidt who, upon finding out that Polingaysi did not know her exact birthday, only that it was in the spring, offered to share her birthdate with her—April 9. At Bethel she trained to be a Mennonite missionary; and when she returned to Oraibi, she built a house from

which to do missionary work, but she soon began to feel troubled about her calling among the Hopi.

In 1924 she took a job as a housekeeper at the government day school at Hotevilla, then began to teach first grade and soon became officially certified to teach in the Indian Service system. In 1941 she was chosen from all the Indian Service teachers to conduct a workshop at Chemawa, Oregon, for teachers and supervisors from the United States and Alaska. She continued to teach until 1954, with more than thirty years of teaching in the Indian Service. She was given the United States Department of the Interior's Distinguished Service Award for her long career in Indian education.

While she was teaching she married Lloyd White, part Cherokee, in 1931 at Bloomfield Trading Post near Toadlena, but they soon separated. When she retired from teaching, she turned to music, writing, and pottery making. Her pottery has been displayed in private collections and in major museums, such as the Museum of Northern Arizona and the Heard Museum in Phoenix. She has written several books describing traditional Hopi life and the difficult transitions between cultures. She lived in Flagstaff and founded the Hopi Student Scholarship Fund at Northern Arizona University. She died at the Phoenix Indian Hospital and was buried at Kykotsmovi Cemetery. Chief Tawaquaptewa once called her "the little one who wanted to be a white man."

—Gretchen Ronnow

References

Qoyawayma, Polingaysi. *No Turning Back: A Hopi Indian Woman's Struggle to Live in Two Worlds.* Albuquerque: University of New Mexico Press, 1964.
———. *The Sun Girl: A True Story about Dawamana.* Flagstaff: Museum of Northern Arizona Press, 1978.
———, and Vada Carlson. *Broken Pattern: Sunlight and Shadows of Hopi History.* Happy Camp, CA: Naturegraph, 1985.
Sweitzer, Paul. "Hopi Authoress, White is Dean." *The Sun* [Flagstaff] 8 December 1990: 7.

WHITE, MADELINE MELBA (b. 1944) is a prolific artist who is represented by over fifty paintings in the collection of the Tekakwitha Fine Arts Center in Sisseton, South Dakota, and who produced over seven hundred paintings from 1968–82. Born in a log cabin at Long Hollow near Sisseton, she is the daughter of Indian ranchers who raised horses, cows, and chickens and grew vegetables for sale in town. Her father died when she was five years old, and because her mother was unable to support the family, White was sent to the Tekakwitha Orphanage.

She attended Wahpeton Indian School for her elementary education, then went to Flandreau Indian School for her high school education. She received no formal art training and began painting in 1968 as a result of an argument with her brother, Cliff, who said he was a better artist than she was. She was befriended by Tino Walkingbull and Paul WarCloud, two notable Sisseton artists, who taught her technique and gave her confidence. She was influenced by the paintings of George Catlin and Frederic Remington.

She says she paints to keep the culture of her people alive. She hopes that people will look at her paintings and like them. She does not mind adverse criticism from Indian people, but she dislikes criticism from non-Indians who do not try to understand Indian culture. To her, historical accuracy is important. Her paintings are created not just to be looked at, but to be studied. They are expressions of her cultural heritage. The range of her work is very wide. In addition to Indian culture, she paints scenes from Biblical literature and portraits of contemporaries. She is an excellent portrait painter, with an outstanding ability to perceive and include details that bring her subjects to life. Her paintings have a striking boldness of line and color.

White lives with members of her family in Indian housing north of Sisseton. After a three-year vacation from work as a result of illness, she has begun painting again, working often in the artists' studio at the Tekakwitha Fine Arts Center. Her paintings are in private and public collections in the Upper Plains states.

—Jack Marken

Reference

Marken, Jack. Personal communication with Madeline Melba White, 1990.

WHITEMAN, ROBERTA HILL (b. 1947) is a Wisconsin Oneida mother of three children, Jacob, Heather, and Melissa, married since 1980 to the Arapaho artist Ernest Whiteman. Roberta studied for a BA at the University of Wisconsin and an MFA at the University of Montana in 1973. She taught for Poets-in-the-Schools Programs in Minnesota, Arizona, Wyoming, South Dakota (Rosebud Sioux Reservation), Oklahoma, Montana, and Wisconsin. Whiteman teaches American literature at the University of Wisconsin, Eau Claire, and presently is on leave completing a doctorate in American Studies at the University of Minnesota. Holy Cow! Press published her poems, *Star Quilt* (illustrated by her husband). "I work as hard (consciously, unconsciously) as I can to hear the music of the voice that speaks through me," Whiteman says in *The Third Woman*. She also states: "I sense that I am trying to regain an image of wholeness. Before that can occur, I feel one must be aware of what is left."

The Iroquois word *Oneida* comes from *oneyote a ka* or "people of the erected stone" in upstate New York. Transplanted from Native lands, this poet and mother has learned the Coyote's peace-making patience, ironically composite. In *Star Quilt* she writes iambic verse with a vision courageously decentered, still stable in personal commitments to her children, husband, and life work. Her logic skitters, her lines search, her images dissociate. There is lightning in her star quiltings, thunder in Oneida stone origins. Whiteman fingers the jagged edges of pain with blues candor and chanted courage. The Coyotess takes her "Leap in the Dark":

> Truth waits in the creek, cutting the winter brown hills.
> It sings with needles of ice, sings because of its scars.

Whiteman's tutor at the University of Montana, Richard Hugo, taught her to trust the strange tongues, the startled insights, Coyote's yellow eyes and yips toward the losses that bond. "More than land's between us," she paid tribute in "Blue Mountain" to the middle-aged Anglo poet who asked that their common losses be chanted as collaborative gain. "Chant to me in your poems/of our loss and let the poem itself be our gain," Hugo counseled in *31 Poems and 13 Dreams*. "You're gaining/the hurt world worth having. Friend, let me be Indian." As with her Montana peer, James Welch, Whiteman learned by Hugo's example and tutoring the patterned natural rhythms of the blank verse line, the essentially iambic foot of Euro-American traditional verse—and she plays off this Western form in much of her poetry.

The Dakota painter, Oscar Howe, also served as Whiteman's teacher, no stranger to surreal and cubist visions. For half a century in South Dakota, he taught and painted a wildly beautiful, visionary cosmos, where inner structures and tonal surfaces shared a modernist play with form on the canvas. Whiteman wrote a poem about Howe's painting, "Woman Seed Player": "you said no one had ever gone full circle, /from passion through pattern and back again/toward pebbles moist with moonlight." From all these mentors, lost mother and alcoholic father, children and husbands, Anglo poet and Dakota painter, sea's fire and grey stone's blood, Whiteman asks the contrary's humor to heal her wounds: "Teach me/your crisscross answer/to the crackling of gulls." This poet-mother writes for her son, Jacob, "Son, we've little time and much to learn." Love is "the final healer," and Indians,

> stand on the edge of words, hugging canned meat
> waiting for owls to come grind
> nightsmell in our ears.

"One finds in this work," Carolyn Forché writes in the foreword to *Star Quilt*, "a map of the journey each of us must complete, wittingly or not, as children and exiles of the Americas." Mothers and children reform new families and "dream of rebirth" from "this slow hunger, /this midnight swollen four hundred years":

Some will anoint the graves with pollen
Some of us may wake unashamed.
Some will rise that clear morning like the swallows.

—Kenneth Lincoln

References

Bruchac, Joseph. "Massaging the Earth: An Interview with Roberta Hill Whiteman." In *Survival This Way: Interviews with Native American Poets*, edited by Joseph Bruchac, 323–35. Tucson: University of Arizona Press, 1987.

Campis, Jack. "Oneida." In *Handbook of North American Indians*. Vol. 15. Edited by Bruce G. Trigger. Washington, DC: Smithsonian, 1978.

Fisher, Dexter, ed. *The Third Woman: Minority Women Writers of the United States*. Boston: Houghton Mifflin, 1980.

Lincoln, Kenneth. *Indi'n Humor: Bicultural Play in Native America*. New York: Oxford University Press, 1991.

McCullough, Ken. "*Star Quilt* as Mandala: An Assessment of the Poetry of Roberta Hill Whiteman." *North Dakota Quarterly* 53 (Spring 1985): 194–203.

Niatum, Duane, ed. *Carriers of the Dream Wheel: Contemporary Native American Poetry*. New York: Harper and Row, 1975.

———. *Harper's Anthology of 20th Century Native American Poetry*. San Francisco: Harper and Row, 1988.

Whiteman, Roberta Hill. *Star Quilt*. Minneapolis: Holy Cow! Press, 1984.

WILLIAMS, ALICE CLING (b. 1953) began a renaissance in Navajo

pottery about 1976. Previously, Navajo pottery was strictly utilitarian. Pots had bullet-shaped bottoms, which made them functional as cooking vessels but unmarketable to non-Navajos. The vessel's surface was scraped with a corncob, which produced a rough surface and the only decoration was a filet around the rim. This was the style of pottery Alice Williams learned to make from her mother, Rose Williams. Alice Williams took her traditional Navajo pots to Bill Beaver, a trader at Sacred Mountain Trading Post. He was the only trader at the time who bought Navajo pottery. Even though he offered the pots at a very low price, Williams's pots were not very popular. Alice Williams says that the reason her pots did not sell was because they were ugly.

It was because of this that Alice Williams began polishing her unfired vessels with a smooth stone, rather than the traditional corncob, and paying closer attention to the manner in which the piñon pitch was applied after the pot was fired. She also paid closer attention to vessel shape and overall design. Today Alice Williams's pots are very popular and command among the highest prices paid for Navajo pots. Her vessels are highly polished and have only the thinnest veneer of piñon pitch, which combines to make the vessels seem as if they are carved from highly polished wood. Her work has won numerous awards at the Museum of Northern Arizona and Heard Museum. Because of her success, and because Bill Beaver continued to encourage her and a few Navajo potters as they experimented with their craft, Navajo pottery did not vanish. Indeed, it is a vital craft. Today the largest collection of Alice Williams's work is held at the Arizona State Museum. Alice Cling Williams and her husband live at Shonto, Arizona, on the Navajo Reservation where she works as a teacher's aide.

—Laura Graves

References

Bernstein, Bruce D., and Susan Brown McGreevy. *Anii Anaadaalyaa'igii: Continuity and Innovation in Recent Navajo Art*. Santa Fe, NM: Wheelwright Museum of Indian Art, 1988.
Graves, Laura. Field Notes. 1980–90.
Hartman, Russell P. *Navajo Pottery*. Flagstaff, AZ: Northland Press, 1989.
Wright, H. Diane. "Navajo Pottery." *American Indian Art* 12 (1987): 26–35.
———, and Jan Bell. "Potters and Their Work." *Plateau* 58 (1987): 24–31.

WINNIE, LUCILLE JERRY [SAH-GAN-DE-OH] (b. 1905) provides an account of her life story in *Sah-Gan-De-Oh, The Chief's Daughter*. Winnie, a Seneca/Cayuga woman, was born in Oklahoma and raised on reservations in both Oklahoma and Montana. Her father, a teacher whom she lovingly calls "Chief," worked to improve the Indians' education and living conditions on these reservations, and although "The Chief" died when Winnie was only twelve, his belief in the need to acculturate the Indian people into modern society became the most influential factor in her life. Her autobiography is of her acculturation into modern white society.

Shortly before her father's death, Winnie left her family to attend her father's alma mater, Haskell Institute, a government school for Indians in Lawrence, Kansas. After seven years at the Institute, she left to follow her father's profession and became a teacher for the US Indian Service. However, she soon abandoned teaching for a series of jobs in various government agencies and private businesses. The greater part of Winnie's autobiography is devoted to her life as a single career woman in a society that was increasingly adopting women into its work force.

Winnie ends her autobiography with her return to a reservation, thus framing her life story with accounts of reservation life. In 1963 she became the director of arts and crafts on the Northern Cheyenne Reservation in Montana. Here she worked to help the Cheyenne people become more economically independent by teaching them how to produce and market authentic Indian products. Through her work with the Cheyenne, Winnie knew she had helped accomplished "The Chief's" mission: the integration of the Indian into the American way of life without the loss of individual heritage.

—Jeanne Olson

References

Bataille, Gretchen M., and Kathleen M. Sands, eds. *American Indian Women: A Guide to Research*. New York: Garland, 1991.

Brumble, David H., ed. *An Annotated Bibliography of American Indian and Eskimo Autobiographies*. Lincoln: University of Nebraska Press, 1981.

Green, Rayna, ed. *Native American Women: A Contextual Bibliography*. Bloomington: Indiana University Press, 1983.

Winnie, Lucille. *Sah-Gan-De-Oh, The Chief's Daughter*. New York: Vantage, 1969.

WITT, SHIRLEY HILL (b. 1941), Mohawk academic and public servant, was born and raised on St. Regis Reservation in New York. She became involved in Indian affairs while still an undergraduate student at the University of New Mexico (UNM). In 1961 Witt and nine other Indian students began meeting at the Gallup Indian Center and discussing what role young Indians should play in the emergent Indian rights movement. From those meetings, the National Indian Youth Council was born, and Shirley Hill Witt was its first vice-president. A charter member of the organization, Witt and another founder, Herbert Blatchford, continued to work together on Indian rights concerns throughout Witt's years at UNM. Together they became protestors at the fledgling fish-ins starting at Quillayute River near Puget Sound. They went on to salvage the Gallup Indian Center during its low point in the late 1960s with such programs as the Workshops for Leaders, a youth training program.

A religious traditionalist, Shirley Hill Witt also related to the common experience of peoples of Catholic culture. For many years, she has worked to forge ties between Indians and Chicanos in the Southwest, calling on them to see the similarities of their ethnic experiences. She served as a conduit between the two groups when Chicano politician Reies Tijerina sought the Indian vote in statewide elections in the late 1960s.

Keeping up with her schoolwork while staying active in community organizing and raising two children as a single parent, she received her BA, MA, and PhD in anthropology from UNM. She moved into the national arena of Indian issues when she served as an assistant researcher for the Indian Claims Commission in the 1970s. In recent years, Shirley Hill Witt has been the director of Natural Resources for the State of New Mexico. In addition to her more famous exploits as an organizer and speaker, Witt is also an active feminist (noting in a Women of All Red Nations (WARN) publication that the sexism of the US government in not prosecuting women activists after Wounded Knee II was what allowed the Indian rights movement to remain intact with national leaders in litigation and in jail), has been a member of the US Civil Rights Commission, and is a published author.

—Cynthia Kasee

References

Green, Rayna, ed. *That's What She Said*. Bloomington: Indiana University Press, 1984.

Witt, Shirley Hill. "The Brave-Hearted Women: The Struggle at Wounded Knee." *Civil Rights Digest* 8 (1976): 38–45.

———. "Native Women Today: Sexism and the Indian Woman." *Civil Rights Digest* 6 (Spring 1974): 29–35.

WITTSTOCK, LAURA WATERMAN was born on the Cattaraugus
Indian Reservation and is a member of the Seneca Nation of New York, Heron clan. She is a political activist for Native American peoples. She is a journalist, writer, and education and programs consultant. She was the founder, developer, and president of MIGIZI Communications, a radio news service providing weekly radio shows on seventeen stations for Native peoples in the Midwest Great Lakes area.

Wittstock has been active in women's advocacy including work for the Women's Educational Equity Act (WEEA) advisory board and Harriet Tubman Battered Women's Center. In 1975, she served as a panelist for the United Nations International Women's Year World Conference for Women in Development held in Mexico City. She has also been active in Native alcoholism programs, including the Juel Fairbanks Aftercare in St. Paul (an alcohol treatment program), and the National Commission on Alcoholism and Alcohol Related Problems.

She is presently the manager for Native American Research Institute in the Center V Satellite Office. Her responsibilities there include training and providing technical assistance to recipients of Title IV Indian Education Grants in several of the north Midwestern states.

She has been the director of the American Indian Press Association as well as editor for the *Legislative Review*. She has published in *Media Bulletin*, *Civil Rights Digest*, *Indian Voice*, and *Akwesasne Notes*.

—Lucy Leriche

References

Anderson, Owanah, ed. *Ohoyo One Thousand: A Resource Guide to American Indian/Alaska Native Women, 1982*. Wichita Falls, TX: Ohoyo Resource Center, 1982.

Wittstock, Laura Waterman. "Native American Women: Twilight of a Long Maidenhood." In *Comparative Perspectives of Third World Women: The Import of Race, Sex and Class*, edited by Beverly Lindsey, 207–27. New York: Praeger, 1980.

———. "Native American Women in the Feminist Milieu." In *Contemporary Native American Addresses*, edited by John Maestas, 373–76. Provo, UT: Brigham Young University, 1976.

WOMAN CHIEF [THE ABSAROKA AMAZON] (c. 1806–1858) was born

into the Gros Ventre of the Prairie and captured by the Crow around the age of ten. Unlike the Crow males who practiced female behaviors and cross-dressing, Woman Chief dressed as a woman but pursued male activities. As a young woman, she was known for her marksmanship and her ability to kill and butcher buffalo in the field. Her foster father seems to have encouraged this behavior, since his own sons had died or been captured in the ongoing hostilities with the Blackfoot. When he died in battle, she became the head of his lodge and family.

Woman Chief (her Gros Ventre and childhood Crow names are unknown) achieved the status of warrior during a Blackfoot raid, when she is reported to have single-handedly turned an ambush and protected a fort that sheltered both Crow and white families. Her reputation made, Woman Chief gathered a group of young men and led guerilla-style raids on the Blackfoot with great success, measured in horses and human scalps. Soon she was elevated to the Council of Chiefs and given the title by which we know her. Her rank was third in a band of one-hundred sixty lodges. After the Treaty of Laramie in 1851, she was involved in peacemaking efforts with the tribes of the upper Missouri and visited the tribe of her birth, the Gros Ventre of the Prairie. Although a peace lasted for three or four years, ultimately Woman Chief died in ambush at the hands of the tribe of her parents.

Woman Chief fascinated the contemporary white men who encountered her. Because of her rejection of the doctrine of separate spheres of activity for men and women, which whites perceived in the Crow camps along the fur routes, she seemed an exotic and revolutionary figure. These informants compare her to European images of the Amazon, crediting her lack of a husband to her ferocity and tribal status, and making much of the fact that Woman Chief took up to four "wives" to manage the domestic work of her lodge. Many of these assessments must be seen as biased by white doctrines of gender, labor, and domesticity in the nineteenth century, yet they suggest possibilities for a re-examination of this nearly mythic figure.

—Jennifer L. Jenkins

References

Capps, Benjamin. *Woman Chief*. Garden City, NJ: Doubleday, 1979.
Denig, Edwin Thompson. In *Indian Tribes of the Upper Missouri*, edited by J.N.B. Hewitt. Bureau of American Ethnology Forty-sixth Annual Report (1928–29). Washington, DC: Bureau of American Ethnology, 1930.

———. "Biography of Woman Chief." In *Five Indian Tribes of the Upper Missouri*, edited by John C. Ewers, 195–200. Norman: University of Oklahoma Press, 1961.

Kurz, Rudolph J. *Journal of Rudolph Friedrich Kurz: An Account of his Experiences Among Fur Traders and American Indians on the Mississippi and Missouri Rivers During the Years 1846–1852*. Edited by J.N.B. Hewitt. Bureau of American Ethnology Bulletin 115. Washington, DC: Bureau of American Ethnology, 1937.

WOODY, ELIZABETH (b. 1959) was born in Ganado, Arizona, of Warm Springs, Wasco, and Navajo heritage. Woody studied creative writing at the Institute of American Indian Arts in Santa Fe, New Mexico. There her talent was fostered by teachers including Joy Harjo and Phil Foss, as well as fellow students including Phillip Minthorn and Joe Dale Tate Nevaquaya. Later, Woody studied at Portland State University with Primus St. John, as well as Henry Carlile, and at Evergreen State College. Although Woody credits much of her growth as a writer to her teachers, she also points to the influence of her family, as well as to a long oral legacy which predominates not only her work but her vision.

While readers of Northwest literature have long recognized Portland-based Elizabeth Woody as a prominent presence in the literary community, with the publication of her first book, *Hand Into Stone*, Woody's writing achieved national recognition. Awarded the American Book Award and lauded by Simon Ortiz, Barry Lopez, and Joy Harjo, the book offers to its readers a stunning range of emotion and concern. Clearly political in its embrace of the fishing rights issue that concerns so many of the Northwest's Native people, the book also details the destruction of the environment, and the hazards of nuclear energy and offers a compelling renunciation of the ways in which Native people continue to be victimized by the forces of oppression. Yet Woody's poetry is also profoundly spiritual and ultimately hopeful. With her visions of the ways in which people come together, the power of the earth and its creatures to heal, her words finally become themselves a kind of healing, a kind of song.

Woody's poems have appeared in a number of journals, including *Wooster Review*, *Mr. Cognito*, *Contact II*, and *Akwekon*; her work is also featured in a number of anthologies, including *Dancing on the Rim of the World*, *Sur le Dos de la Torte: revue billingue de litterature amerindienne*, *Bearing Witness/Sobreviviendo*, *The Clouds Threw This Light*, and *Songs from this Earth on Turtle's Back*.

Woody has also earned a substantial reputation as a visual artist and a photographer. Her art has been featured in a number of Northwest shows, as well as exhibits in San Francisco, Minneapolis, New York, and Washington, DC. She has worked closely with Lillian Pitt, one of the most renowned artists in the Northwest today. Woody's photographs were featured in a number of texts, including *Faces of a Reservation*, *Songs from this Earth on Turtle's Back*, and *Dancing on the Rim of the World*.

Woody is active in a number of arts, political, and community organizations. An enrolled member of the Confederated Tribes of Warm Springs (Oregon), she is also active in the Native American Arts Council, the Metropolitan Arts Commission, and ATLATL, a national Native American Arts organization. In 1988 Woody was a founding member of the Northwest Native American Writer's Association. The organization has sought to bring together the region's writers and to foster increased opportunities for publication, readings, and collaboration.

—Andrea Lerner

References

Bruchac, Joseph, ed. *Songs From this Earth on Turtle's Back: Contemporary American Indian Poetry*. Greenfield Center, NY: Greenfield Review Press, 1983.

Cochran, Jo, J.T. Stewart, and Mayumi Tsutakawa, eds. *Bearing Witness/ Sobreviviendo: An Anthology of Native American/Latina Art and Literature*. *Calyx: A Journal of Art and Literature by Women* 8 (Spring 1984).

Lerner, Andrea, ed. *Dancing on the Rim of the World: Contemporary Northwest Native American Writing*. Tucson: University of Arizona Press, 1990.

Van Thienen, trans. *Sur le Dos de la Torte: revue billingue de litterature amerindienne*. Rillieux, France: N.p., 1989.

Woody, Elizabeth. *Hand Into Stone*. New York: Contact II Press, 1988.

WRIGHT, MURIEL HAZEL (1889–1975), well known as a historian and an editor, began her career as a teacher and administrator in elementary and secondary schools in southern Oklahoma. Born at Lehigh, Choctaw Nation, into an economically affluent Choctaw family, she received a sound education in the schools of the Choctaw Nation, at Wheaton College, and at East Central State Normal School in Oklahoma. From 1912 to 1924 she held various teaching and administrative posts, except for one year spent in graduate studies at Barnard College of Columbia University.

In the 1920s Wright began a writing career that extended to the end of her life. Her first major effort was *Oklahoma: A History of the State and Its People* (Lewis Historical Publishing, 1929), a four-volume work which she wrote with Joseph B. Thoburn. That same year she published *The Story of Oklahoma*, a public school textbook. From 1929 to 1931 she was employed by the Oklahoma Historical Society to conduct research for the history of the Five Civilized Tribes, and during the next decade, she devoted herself to writing. From the 1920s to the early 1970s, she produced seven books, including the standard *A Guide to the Indian Tribes of Oklahoma* (University of Oklahoma Press, 1951) and dozens of articles, nearly one hundred of which appeared in *Chronicles of Oklahoma*, the journal of the Oklahoma Historical Society.

Throughout her writing career, Wright held significant positions. First, she was active in the affairs of the Choctaw Nation. From 1922 to 1928 she was secretary of the Choctaw Committee, which conducted Choctaw business affairs. She worked to restore and preserve the Choctaw Council House at Tuskahoma. In 1934 she helped to organize the Choctaw Advisory Council and served as secretary until 1944. Second, she assumed editorial responsibilities for *Chronicles of Oklahoma* in 1943. Though officially associate editor until 1955, when she was named editor, she performed all editorial duties from her appointment until retirement in 1973. A persistent and exacting editor, she exerted a strong influence on the historiography of the Indian tribes of Oklahoma. In recognition of her writings on the American Indian, Oklahoma City University awarded her an honorary Doctor of Humanities degree in 1964, and in 1971 the North American Indian Women's Association recognized her as the outstanding Indian woman of the twentieth century.

—Daniel F. Littlefield, Jr.

References

Arrington, Ruth. "Muriel Hazel Wright." In *Notable American Women, The Modern Period: A Biographical Dictionary*, edited by Barbara Sicheman and Carol Hurd Green, 751–52. Cambridge: The Belknap Press of Harvard University, 1980.

Fischer, LeRoy H. "Muriel H. Wright, Historian of Oklahoma." *Chronicles of Oklahoma* 52 (Spring 1974): 3–29.

Z

ZEPEDA, OFELIA (b. 1952), a Tohono O'odham and professor of linguistics and former director of the American Indian Studies Program at the University of Arizona, is also a poet and one of the foremost scholars in Tohono O'odham language and literature. Raised in Stanfield, near Casa Grande, Arizona, and close to both the Tohono O'odham and Pima Reservations, Zepeda enrolled and took three degrees in linguistics (BA, MA, and PhD) at the University of Arizona after graduation from public schools. She was the first Tohono O'odham to receive a doctorate in linguistics and has regularly taught that language at the University since 1979, and since 1978 in the Papago Reservation Teacher Training Program. She has been instrumental in establishing centers for undergraduate and graduate Native American students and in developing a cross-disciplinary, cross-cultural degree program.

In addition to her university service, Zepeda has worked with her tribe to improve literacy in both English and Tohono O'odham. In 1983 she developed *A Papago Grammar* from tapes of Native speakers because no textbook existed for the classes she taught. Her participation with the reservation committee for Tohono O'odham Language Policy yielded an official policy that encourages the speaking of the Native language in all grade levels. She also regularly participates in the summer American Indian Language Development Institute, which encourages Native Americans to complete their teaching certification.

Zepeda also writes poetry that blends English with Tohono O'odham oral tradition. Zepeda is a frequent recipient of grants and fellowships for linguistics, education, and humanities projects on her tribe's language and literature, which will promote literacy in both English and Tohono O'odham into the twenty-first century.

—Jay Ann Cox

References

Alvarez, Manuel, Ofelia Zepeda, et al. *The Tohono O'odham Language Policy.* Tohono O'odham Nation, 1988.

Evers, Larry, ed., with Ofelia Zepeda, et al. *The South Corner of Time.* Tucson: University of Arizona, 1983.

Zepeda, Ofelia. *A Papago Grammar.* Tucson: University of Arizona Press, 1983.

———, comp. and trans. *Sand Papago Oral History Project.* Limited copies available from Tucson, AZ: Western Archeological and Conservation Center, 1985.

———, ed. *Mat Hekid o ju: When It Rains. Papago and Pima Poetry.* Sun Tracks, vol. 7. Tucson: University of Arizona Press, 1982.

ZUNI, FLORA (1897–1983)

ZUNI, FLORA (1897–1983) was born into the Badger Clan on July 1 and was the third child of her parents. Her father was a member of the Bear Clan and an accomplished artist and her mother, Lina, an accomplished potter. She received her education at the boarding school at Black Rock and became one of the few Zuni of her time who could speak English. Later, this skill allowed her to become an interpreter for several different groups, including anthropologists, Bureau of Indian Affairs employees, Public Health Service employees, missionaries and teachers. In 1915 she married a man from the Sun Clan, and in 1918, she went to work as a teacher at the Zuni Day School. Her first husband died in 1939 and two years later she married a man from the Deer Clan. Zuni had six children, two of whom died.

Noted as an interpreter and storyteller of great skill, Zuni worked with anthropologists such as A.L. Kroeber, Ruth Benedict, Ruth Bunzel, and Elsie Clews Parsons in collecting Zuni folk tales, prayers, and linguistic material. Bunzel said of Zuni, "Flora had excellent command of English and translated her own texts and interpreted for her father, mother, and sisters and helped with the revision and analysis of all texts." Zuni also became an entrepreneur and saleswoman who lodged boarders and sold turquoise on commission to help support her family.

Zuni remained a traditional Zuni throughout her lifetime, sponsoring several initiations into the *kachina* society and her medicine society and attending summer and winter dances. She strongly believed in the importance of carrying traditions from one generation to the next.

—Joni Adamson Clarke

References

Bunzel, Ruth. "Anthropologists at Zuni." *Proceedings of the American Philosophical Society* 116 (August 1972): 323.

———. *Zuni Texts*. Publications of the American Ethnological Society, vol. 15, edited by Franz Boaz. New York: G.E. Stechert, 1933.

Pandey, Triloki Nath. "Flora Zuni—A Portrait." In *American Indian Intellectuals: 1976 Proceedings of the American Ethnological Society*, edited by Margot Liberty, 217–25. St. Paul: West Publishing, 1976.

Contributors

JULIE LAMAY ABNER is a graduate student in English composition at California State University, San Bernardino, whose thesis is "A Rhetorical Study of Three Contemporary American Indian Novels: *House Made of Dawn, Ceremony,* and *Love Medicine.*" She is also the research and editorial assistant for the American Indian Studies Series from Peter Lang Publishing.

BARBARA BABCOCK is a professor of English and Comparative Cultural and Library Studies at the University of Arizona. She received her PhD from the University of Chicago. Her major publications include *Pueblo Mothers and Children: Essays by Elsie Clews Parsons, 1915–1924; Daughters of the Desert: Woman Anthropologists and the Native American Southwest, 1880–1980* (with Nancy Parezo); and *The Pueblo Storyteller: Development of a Figurative Ceramic Tradition* (with Guy and Doris Monthan).

HELEN M. BANNAN is director of the Women's Studies Center and associate professor of history at Florida Atlantic University. She received her PhD in American Studies from Syracuse University. Her published articles include "Newcomers to Navajoland: Transculturation in the Memoirs of Anglo Women, 1900–1945" in *New Mexico Historical Review;* "Spider Woman's Web: Mothers and Daughters in Southwestern Native American Literature" in *The Lost Tradition: Mothers and Daughters in Literature;* and "'True Womanhood' on the Reservation: Field Matrons in United States Indian Service," a SIROW working paper.

GRETCHEN M. BATAILLE is Associate Dean in the College of Liberal Arts and Sciences and a professor of English and Women's Studies at Arizona State University. Her publications include *American Indian Women Telling Their Lives* and *American Indian Women: A Guide to Research,* both co-authored with Kathleen M. Sands.

DAWN BATES, an assistant professor at Arizona State University, received her PhD from the University of Washington. She is currently preparing a dictionary of Lushootseed with Vi Hilbert and Thom Hess.

ARLON BENSON earned his BA in English from Arizona State University in 1989. He is currently pursuing an MA in English and working as a tutor and counselor at the Educational Support Program at Arizona State University. He served as a research assistant on *American Indian Women: A Guide to Research* published in 1991 by Garland.

EDITH BLICKSILVER is an associate professor of English at Georgia Institute of Technology. Her activities include a position on the book review staff of the Atlanta *Journal-Constitution,* an organizer and first secretary of MELUS, and president of the Georgia/South Carolina College English Association. Her book, *The Ethnic American Woman: Problems, Protests, Lifestyle,* was cited as "The Best Non-Fiction Book of the Year" in 1979 and in 1989 came out in an expanded edition, which includes two new units and twenty additional works.

RENAE BREDIN is a doctoral candidate at the University of Arizona. She received her BA from the University of Utah and her MA from Rutgers University.

RHODA CARROLL is an associate professor of English at Vermont College of Norwich University. Her poems and stories have appeared in a variety of literary magazines and anthologies; she has review essays and interviews in *Studies in American Indian Literatures* and in *American Indian Quarterly*. She holds an MA in English and an MFA in creative writing from the University of Arizona.

DEXTER FISHER CIRILLO received her PhD in English from the City University of New York and is currently a private art dealer in American Indian art in New York. She has served as director of Gallery 10 of Arizona in New York City and as coordinator of art exhibitions and special events at various museums and sites throughout the country. In addition to numerous articles and book reviews on art, education, and literature, Cirillo's publications include (under the name Dexter Fisher) critical introductions to *American Indian Stories* by Zitkala Ša/Gertrude Bonnin and *Co-Ge-We-A* by Mourning Dove. She is also the editor of *The Third Woman: Minority Women Writers of the United States* and *Minority Language and Literature—Retrospective and Perspective*, and she is co-editor (with Robert B. Stepto) of *Afro-American Literature: The Reconstruction of Instruction*. Her book, *Southwestern Indian Jewelry*, was published in 1992.

JONI ADAMSON CLARKE is working on her PhD in English and is a graduate teaching associate at the University of Arizona. She received her MA degree from Brigham Young University. Her article, "Why Bears are Good to Think and Theory Doesn't Have to Be Murder: Transformation and Oral Tradition in the Work of Louise Erdrich," is forthcoming in *Studies in American Indian Literatures*.

LAURA COLTELLI is an associate professor of American literature at the University of Pisa. Her publications on Native American literature include two studies on Leslie Marmon Silko's fiction, *Winged Words: Native American Writers Speak*, and the Italian edition of N. Scott Momaday's *The Names*. She is co-general editor of a series devoted to contemporary Native American writers. A former Fulbright Visiting Professor at the University of Boston and UCLA, she has also been the recipient of a postdoctoral fellowship from the Institute of American Cultures and American Indian Studies Center of the University of California at Los Angeles. She has received the Faculty Enrichment Award (1988/89) from the International Council for Canadian Studies.

JAY ANN COX is a PhD candidate in Comparative Cultural and Literary Studies at the University of Arizona and is also a teaching and research assistant in English, Spanish, and Comparative Cultural and Literary Studies. Her publications include "Dangerous Definitions: Female Tricksters in Contemporary Native American Fiction" in *Wicazo Sa* and "The Native American Trickster" (with Barbara Babcock) in *Dictionary of Native American Literature*, forthcoming from Greenwood Press.

KATHLEEN McNERNEY DONOVAN is a doctoral candidate at the University of Arizona. She is studying American literature, with an emphasis on Native American literature. She received her MA from the University of Nebraska.

PATTIANN FRINZI is a graduate student in the Interdisciplinary Humanities Program at Arizona State University. She is also pursuing a certificate in Scholarly Editing and Publishing. She received her bachelor's degree in music with an emphasis in ethnomusicology from Florida State University.

AUDREY M. GODFREY earned a BS and MS from Utah State University. Her publications include *Women's Voices: An Untold History of the Latter-day Saints, 1830–1900* with Kenneth W. Godfrey and Jill Mulvay Derr; "Uncle Sam's Most Foolish Expedition" in *This People*; and "Housewives, Hussies, and Heroines, or the Women of Johnston's Army" in *Utah Historical Quarterly*.

LAURA GRAVES is a part-time instructor in the Department of History at Sacramento City College (Folsom Prison) and at California State University, Sacramento. Her publications include *Contemporary Hopi Pottery*, and "Navajo Rugs: A Marketing Success." She received her PhD from Northern Arizona University.

LOIS GRIFFITTS received her BA in English literature from the University of Idaho, and she is an MA literature candidate at Arizona State University. She is currently a teaching assistant at Arizona State University.

GRETCHEN G. HARVEY is a PhD candidate in the Department of History at Arizona State University, currently instructor of history at North Dakota State University, Fargo. Her dissertation in progress is a biography of Ruth Muskrat Bronson, 1897–1982.

HELEN JASKOSKI received her PhD from Stanford University. Currently, she is a professor of English and comparative literature at California State University, Fullerton. Jaskoski is editor of the quarterly, *Studies in American Indian Literatures*, and is the author of "From the Time Immemorial: Native American Traditions in Contemporary Short Fiction."

JENNIFER L. JENKINS is assistant editor of *Arizona Quarterly* and a PhD candidate at the University of Arizona. She received her AM degree from the University of Chicago. Jenkins has published in *Intertextuality and Contemporary American Fiction* and *ESQ*.

CYNTHIA KASEE is a professor of American Indian Studies at the Union Institute in Cincinnati, Ohio. She is also the ethnologist for the North American Indian Council of Greater Cincinnati. She has contributed to the Garland Publishing's *Encyclopedia of the American Wars* and the *Anthology of Contemporary Cherokee Prose*. Her poetry has appeared in *The Eagle*. Kasee received her PhD in American Indian Studies from the Union Institute.

HARRY A. KERSEY, JR., is a professor of history at Florida Atlantic University. He received BA and MA degrees from the University of Florida and a PhD from the University of Illinois. His publications include: *Pelts, Plumes and Hides: White Traders Among the Seminole Indians, 1870–1930; The Florida Seminoles and the New Deal, 1933–1942;* and *The Seminole and Miccosukee Tribes: A Critical Bibliography.* Kersey served as a member of the Florida Governor's Council on Indian Affairs for ten years.

CLARA SUE KIDWELL is an associate professor of Native American Studies at the University of California at Berkeley. She received her MA and PhD degrees from the University of Oklahoma. Kidwell has been the recipient of numerous pre- and post-doctoral fellowships, including the Smithsonian Institution Fellowship, the Newberry Library Summer Fellowship, and the University of California Humanities Fellowship. Kidwell is on the board of trustees for the National Museum of the American Indian and a member of the American Historical Association and American Society for Ethnohistory.

JOYCE ANN KIEVIT received her BA from Hope College in Holland, Michigan. Currently, she is working on her graduate degree and as a research assistant at the University of Houston, Clear Lake.

LUCY LERICHE is a graduate student at Arizona State University in the Interdisciplinary Humanities Program. She received her BA from Johnson State College in Vermont.

ANDREA LERNER is currently completing her PhD in English at the University of Arizona and received an MA in creative writing from Stanford University. She is the editor of *Dancing on the Rim of the World: Contemporary Northwest Native American Writing.*

KENNETH LINCOLN is a professor of English and American Indian Studies at UCLA, where he has taught since 1969. He received his MA and PhD degrees from Indiana University. Lincoln has directed the UCLA American Indian Studies graduate program, edited *The American Indian Culture and Research Journal,* and chaired the Faculty Advisory Committee to the UCLA American Indian Studies Center. He has gathered, edited, and prefaced eight volumes of poetry in UCLA's Native American Series. In addition, he has published *Native American Literatures: "old like hills, like stars"; Native American Renaissance; The Good Red Road: Passages into Native America* (with Al Logan Slagle); and *Indi'n Humor: Bicultural Play in Native America.*

LAURIE LISA is in the doctoral program in American literature at Arizona State University. She received her BS degree from the University of Illinois at Champaign and her MA degree from Arizona State University.

DANIEL F. LITTLEFIELD, JR., is a professor of English and director of the American Native Press Archives at the University of Arkansas at Little Rock. His latest work is *Alex Posey: Creek Poet, Journalist, and Humorist.* In association with James W. Parins, Littlefield has published numerous books, including: *American Indian and Alaska Native Newspapers and Periodicals, 1826–1924* (and two more volumes covering the years 1925–1970 and

1971–1985) and a *A Biobibliography of Native American Writers, 1772–1924* (with a supplement published in 1985). He received his PhD from Oklahoma State University.

K. TSIANINA LOMAWAIMA is an assistant professor of anthropology at the University of Washington. Her Stanford University doctoral dissertation was entitled "They Called it Prairie Light: Oral Histories from Chilocco Indian Agricultural School, 1920–1940." Her articles have appeared in *American Indian Quarterly*, and she also worked on the 1986 script annotations, chapter VIII of the *Resource Handbook*, for the film *Hopi: Songs of the Fourth World*. She was named for Tsianina Blackstone, her great aunt.

HARTMUT LUTZ holds two PhD degrees from the Universität Tübingen and the Universität Osnabrück. He has been the recipient of a fellowship from the American Council of Learned Societies, a Fulbright Fellowship, and a Faculty Enrichment Award and Faculty Research Award from Canadian International Affairs. From 1989–90, he was a visiting professor at Saskatchewan Indian Federated College in Regina, Saskatchewan, supported by the German Academic Exchange Service. His publications include *D-Q University: Self-Determination in Native American Higher Education; "Indianer"*; and *"Native Americans": Zur sozial- und literarhistorischen Vermittlung eines Stereotypes*. He is also editor of *Achte Deines Bruders Traum! Gespräche mit nordamerikanischen Indianern*. He is a professor of North American Studies at the University of Osnabrück, Germany, and has published *Contemporary Challenges: Conversations With Canadian Native Authors*.

ELIZABETH A. McNEIL received her MFA degree in the Creative Writing Program at Arizona State University, and is currently in the PhD program, where she teaches composition and creative writing. McNeil has published "The New and Golden Harvest: Margaret Fuller's Call for an 'American Literature' Fulfilled" in *Critically Speaking*, and she has published reviews of *Annie John* by Jamaica Kincaid and *Skokie: Rights or Wrong* (a documentary film) by Sheila Chamovitz, both in *Explorations in Sights and Sounds*.

JACK MARKEN is a professor of English, *emeritus*, at South Dakota State University. He received his BA from the University of Akron and his MA and PhD from Indiana University. Among his publications are *The American Indian: Language and Literature* and *Bibliography of the Sioux*, written with Herbert T. Hoover. His essay, "Literature and Legends of South Dakota," appears in *Centennial Planning Project of the South Dakota Committee on the Humanities*, and "The Lore of South Dakota" appears in *South Dakota: Changing, Changeless 1889–1989*. He currently serves as general editor for the Native American Bibliography Series and the Native American Bibliography Series published by Scarecrow Press.

DEVON A. MIHESUAH is an assistant professor of Native American history at Northern Arizona University. She received her PhD from Texas Christian University, writing her dissertation on "History of the Cherokee Female Seminary: 1851–1910," and is a former Ford Foundation Dissertation Fellow. Her journal articles and chapters in books include the following: "Too Dark to be Angels: The Class System Among the Cherokees at Female Seminary" in *American Indian Culture and Research Journal*; "'Commendable

Progress': Acculturation at the Cherokee Female Seminary" in *American Indian Quarterly*; "Indians in Arizona" in *Politics and Public Policy in Arizona*; and "Despoiling and Desecretation of American Indian Property and Possessions" in *National Forum*. In addition to writing book reviews and serving as an editorial consultant for journals, Mihesuah is currently working on *Cultivating the Rose Buds: History of the Cherokee Female Seminary, 1851–1909*.

JOHN D. NICHOLS is a professor of Native studies and linguistics at the University of Manitoba. He received his PhD from Harvard University. Nichols is the editor of the quarterly *Algonquian and Iroquoian Linguistics*. He has also edited *An Ojibwe Text Anthology*, *Statement Made by the Indians: A Bilingual Petition of the Chippewas of Lake Superior, 1864*; Leonard Bloomfield's edition of *The Dog's Children: Anishinaabe Texts Told by Angeline Williams*; Maude Kegg's *Nookomis Gaainaajimotawid/What My Grandmother Told Me*; and *Portage Lake*.

JAMES H. O'DONNELL III is a professor of history at Marietta College and author of numerous books, articles, and monographs, including *The Southern Indians in the American Revolution*; *The Georgia Frontier, 1773–1783*; *The Cherokees and the American Revolution in North Carolina*; and *Southeastern Frontiers, 1540–1840*. In addition, he is the recipient of many grants and fellowships, such as the American Philosophical Society Research Grant and the Huntington Library Fellowship. He has also served as both a media consultant and a bibliographical consultant. His work in progress is entitled *The Noise and Miseries of War: The Northern Indians, 1774–1783*. O'Donnell received his PhD from Duke University.

JEANNE OLSON received her BA from Eastern Montana College and her MA at Arizona State University. She is currently a teaching associate in the Department of English at Arizona State University.

BEV ORTIZ currently holds positions as an ethnographic consultant under the auspices of Cabrillo College, California Polytechnic State University, Domican College, and San Jose State University, and as a naturalist for the Easy Bay Regional Park District. In addition, Ortiz is a skills and technology columnist for *News from Native California*. She has published *It Will Live Forever: Yosemite Indian Acorn Preparation* and "Mount Diablo as Myth and Reality: An Indian History Convoluted" in *American Indian Quarterly*. She has also served as a board member on Oyate (Indian Education), on the executive committee and as president of the Miwok Archaeological Preserve of Marin, and as chair and commissioner for the Walnut Creek Park and Recreation Commission.

JAMES W. PARINS is a professor of English at the University of Arkansas, Little Rock. His publications include *John Rollin Ridge: His Life and Works*; and *American Indian and Alaska Native Newspapers and Periodicals, 1826–1984* (in three volumes) and *A Biobibliography of Native American Writers, 1772–1924*, both in collaboration with Daniel F. Littlefield, Jr. Parins received his PhD from the University of Wisconsin.

JAMES ROBERT PAYNE is an associate professor of English at New Mexico State University. He received his PhD from the University of California at Davis. He is the editor of and contributor to *Multicultural Autobiography: American Lives* and is the editor of *Joseph Seamon Cotter, Jr.: Complete Poems*. Payne has also published "Hamlin Garland" in *Heath Anthology of American Literature*; "Perceptions of Multicultural America in Personal Narratives of Hamlin Garland" in *A/B: Auto/Biography Studies*; and "Griggs and Corrothers: Historical Reality and Black Fiction" in *Explorations in Ethnic Studies*.

LAURA L. PEERS is an ethnohistorian and curator currently working as a research and curatorial associate for the De Smet Project in the Department of History at Washington State University. She received her MS in Canadian history from the Universities of Winnipeg and Manitoba. Publications include "Secondary Sources, Subsistence, and Gender Bias: The Saulteaux" in *Proceedings of the National Symposium on Aboriginal Women* and "The Western Ojibwa, 1821–1870" in *Proceedings of Conference on Aboriginal Resource Use in Canada*. She is currently writing *An Ethnohistory of the Canadian Saulteaux, 1780–1870* and working as a research and curatorial associate on an exhibition and catalogue: *Sacred Encounters: Jesuit Missionaries and the Indians of the Rocky Mountain West*.

JANET L. PETERSON received her BA in English literature from the University of Colorado at Denver. She is currently working on an MA at Arizona State University, with an emphasis on twentieth century American literature and ethnic and women's studies. She is currently a teaching assistant at Arizona State University.

BERND PEYER received his PhD in American Studies from Johann Wolfgang Goethe Universitat, Frankfurt. He is currently a lecturer for the Institut fur England- und Amerikastudien at the same university. Peyer has published several articles and monographs on the subject of Indian literature and art, and he was editor of *The Singing Spirit*, published by the University of Arizona Press.

STEVEN R. PRICE is a graduate student in the English MA program at Arizona State University. He received his undergraduate degree from the University of Wisconsin, Oshkosh.

KENNETH M. ROEMER is a professor of English and a graduate advisor at the University of Texas at Arlington. He received his PhD in American Civilization from the University of Pennsylvania. He is the author/editor of *Approaches to Teaching Momaday's "The Way to Rainy Mountain"* and three books on utopian literature. In addition, Roemer has published articles and reviews on Native American literatures in collections such as *Smoothing the Ground*, and in publications such as *The Chronicle of Higher Education*, *College English*, SAIL, *American Indian Quarterly*, and *American Indian Culture and Research Journal*.

GRETCHEN RONNOW teaches at Northern Arizona University in Flagstaff, Arizona. Her publications include "John Milton Oskison" in *The Dictionary of Native American Literature*; "Tayo, Death, and Desire: A Lacanian Reading of Leslie Silko's *Ceremony*" in *Narrative Chance: Postmodern Discourse on Native American Indian Literatures*; and "John Milton Oskison, Cherokee Journalist: A Singer of the Semiotics of Power" in *Native Press Research Journal*. Ronnow is working on her PhD at the University of Arizona.

JULIE RUSS received her undergraduate degree from Ohio State University. She is enrolled in the MA program in English at Arizona State University.

KATHLEEN MULLEN SANDS is a professor in the Department of English and affiliated faculty in the Department of Anthropology at Arizona State University where she teaches folklore, American Indian literatures, and interdisciplinary courses. She is the co-author (with Gretchen Bataille) of *American Indian Women Telling Their Lives* and *American Indian Women: A Guide to Research*. She is the editor of *Circle of Motion: Arizona Anthology of Contemporary Indian Literature*, senior editor of *People of Pascua* by Edward H. Spicer, and editor-interpreter of *Autobiography of a Yaqui Poet* by Refugio Savala. She has also published numerous articles on American Indian literatures and folklore.

GREG SARRIS received his PhD in Modern Thought and Literature from Stanford University. His essays and articles have appeared in numerous journals and magazines, including *College English, MELUS, American Indian Quarterly, Studies in American Indian Literatures, National Women's Studies Association, De/Colonizing the Subject: Race, Gender, and Class in Women's Autobiography, The Ethnography of Reading, In Writing,* and *News from Native California*. Currently, he is assistant professor of English at the University of California, Los Angeles.

MICHELLE SAVOY received her BA in English from the University of Wisconsin, Milwaukee. She is currently enrolled in the graduate program in English at Arizona State University.

ERIC SEVERSON received his BA from Pennsylvania State University and his MA in American literature from Arizona State University. He currently teaches English composition at Arizona State University.

KATHRYN W. SHANLEY is an enrolled member of the Assiniboine. Her graduate degrees were earned at the University of Michigan, and she currently teaches American and American Indian literature in the English Department at the University of Washington, where she is also an adjunct to American Ethnic Studies, American Indian Studies, and Women's Studies. She has a forthcoming book on the work of James Welch, a Blackfeet/Gros Ventre writer from Montana.

THELMA J. SHINN is a professor of English and Women's Studies at Arizona State University. She received her MA and PhD degrees from Purdue University. In addition to many articles and chapters in books, Shinn has published *Worlds Within Women* and *Radiant Daughters: Fictional American Women*.

RODNEY SIMARD, who received his PhD from the University of Alabama, is assistant professor of English at California State University, San Bernardino. Author of *Postmodern Drama: Contemporary Playwrights in America and Britain* and *The Whole Writer's Catalog: An Introduction to Advanced Composition*, he has published widely on a variety of topics in various journals and collections. A Cherokee, he is also general editor of the American Indian Studies Series from Peter Lang Publishing.

FAREN R. SIMINOFF has a JD degree from Syracuse University College of Law. Currently, Siminoff is a candidate for an MA degree in history from New York University.

WINONA STEVENSON received her MA from the University of British Columbia and is completing her doctoral studies at the University of California, Berkeley. She has published "Rebirth of Women Warriors" and "Dreamers who Inspire" in *Saskatchewan Indian*. Her other articles include "SUNTEP Students and Universal Education: The Global Experience of Mixed Blood Peoples" in *New Breed*.

MARK G. THIEL is an assistant archivist for the Native American Catholic Collections at Marquette University in Milwaukee, Wisconsin. He received his BS degree in sociology/anthropology and his MAT in history from the University of Wisconsin, Stevens Point. He is a certified archivist from the Academy of Certified Archivists, co-author of *Guide to Catholic Indian Mission and School Records in Midwest Repositories*, and author of "The Powwow: A Celebration of Tradition" published in *Wisconsin Academy Review*.

CLIFFORD E. TRAFZER is a professor and chair of Ethnic Studies and the director of American Indian Studies at the University of California, Riverside. He received his PhD in history from Oklahoma State University. Trafzer has been awarded the Washington Governor's Book Award for *Renegade Tribe*. He has also received numerous teaching and research awards. His published work is prolific and includes *The Chinook, California's Indians and the Gold Rush*, and *A Trip to a Pow Wow* (authored under the pen name of Richard Red Hawk).

CATHERINE UDALL is managing editor of the National Association for Ethnic Studies publications and assistant editor for *Native Peoples* magazine in Phoenix, Arizona. She received her BA in English and history from Brigham Young University and MA in history from Arizona State University.

NORMA C. WILSON, a professor of English at the University of South Dakota, received her PhD from the University of Oklahoma. She has published a collection of poems, *Wild Iris*. Wilson has also published essays on the work of N. Scott Momaday, Leslie Marmon Silko, Linda Hogan, Lance Henson, and other writers in publications such as the *Denver Quarterly*, *Mickle Street Review*, and *A: A Journal of Contemporary Literature*. In addition, she was a contributing editor to the *Heath Anthology of American Literature* and has essays published in *The Dictionary of Native American Literature* and *Approaches to Teaching Momaday's "The Way to Rainy Mountain."*

HERTHA D. WONG is an assistant professor in the Department of English at the University of California, Berkeley. She received her MA and PhD degrees from the University of Iowa. Her articles include "Pictographs as Autobiography: Plains Indian Sketchbooks of the Late Nineteenth and Early Twentieth Centuries" in *American Literary History* and "N. Scott Momaday's *The Way to Rainy Mountain*: Contemporary Native American Autobiography" in *American Indian Culture and Research Journal*. Two articles are forthcoming in anthologies: "Adoptive Mothers and Thrown Away Children in the Novels of Louise Erdrich" in *Narrating Mothers: Theorizing Maternal Subjectivities* and

"Plains Indian Names and the 'Autobiographical Act'" in *Autobiography and Postmodernism*. Her book, *Sending My Heart Back Across the Years: Tradition and Innovation in Native American Autobiography*, was published by Oxford University Press.

Appendix One

Entries by Primary Areas of Specialization

ACTIVISM

Allen, Paula Gunn
Aquash, Anna Mae Pictou
Armstrong, Jeannette
Blackgoat, Roberta
Bonnin, Gertrude Simmons
Brant, Beth
Brass, Eleanor
Chrystos
Crow Dog, Mary
Deer, Ada
Gould, Janet
Hailstone, Vivian
Harris, LaDonna
Hogan, Linda
Horn, Kahn-Tineta
Jemison, Alice Lee
Keeshig-Tobias, Lenore
LaDuke, Winona
Lavell, Jeannette
Maracle, Lee
McCloud, Janet
Neakok, Sadie Brower
Nunez, Bonita Wa Wa Calachaw
Pease-Windy Boy, Jeanine
Stanley, Dorothy Amora
Thorpe, Grace
Wauneka, Annie Dodge
Witt, Shirley Hill
Wittstock, Laura Waterman

ANTHROPOLOGY

Archambault, JoAllyn
Deloria, Ella Cara
Medicine, Beatrice A.
Rose, Wendy
Tantaquidgeon, Gladys
Witt, Shirley Hill

ARCHITECTURE

Swentzell, Rina

ARTS

Ackerman, Maria Joseph
Allen, Elsie
Archambault, JoAllyn
Ashevak, Kenojuak
Ashoona, Pitseolak
Bahe, Liz Sohappy
Bennett, Kay Curley
Bighorse, Tiana
Bird, Gloria
Bird, JoAnne
Blue Legs
Burns, Diane M.
Burton, Jimalee Chitwood
Carius, Helen Slwooko
Chouteau, Yvonne
Chrystos
Cordero, Helen Quintana
Dat-So-La-Lee
Dick, Lena Frank
Dietz, Angel DeCora

Endrezze, Anita
Folwell, Jody
Gonzales, Rose
Hailstone, Vivien
Hardin, Helen Bagshaw
Hill, Joan
Isom, Joan Shaddox
Kegg, Maude Mitchell
Lewis, Lucy
Loloma, Otellie
Martinez, Maria Montoya
Mayo, Sarah Jim
McKay, Mabel
Medicine Flower, Grace
Medicine Snake Woman
Morez, Mary
Nampeyo
Nampeyo, Daisy Hooee
Naranjo-Morse, Nora
Nunez, Bonita Wa Wa Calachaw
Owen, Angie Reano
Parker, Julia F.
Parrish, Essie
Pavatea, Garnet
Peña, Tonita
Roessel, Ruth W.
Rose, Wendy
Saila, Pitaloosie
Sakiestewa, Ramona
Sanchez, Carol Lee
Slipperjack, Ruby
Smith, Jaune Quick-To-See
Smith, Kathleen
Somersal, Laura
Stroud, Virginia
Telles, Lucy Parker
Tremblay, Gail
Velarde, Pablita
White, Elizabeth Q.
White, Madeline Melba
Williams, Alice Cling
Woody, Elizabeth

BUSINESS

Big Eyes
Bordeaux, Shirley

CAPTIVE

Parker, Cynthia Ann
Tomassa

CHRISTIAN LEADERSHIP

Sacred White Buffalo, Mother Mary
    Catherine
Tekakwitha, Kateri

COSMETOLOGY

Venegas, Hildreth Marie Twostars

CULTURAL INTERPRETATION

Allen, Elsie
Brant, Molly
Buffalo Bird Woman
Cuero, Delfina
Davidson, Florence Edenshaw
Dorion Woman
Green, Rayna Diane
Highwalking, Belle
Juneau, Josette
Kegg, Maude Mitchell
Kellogg, Laura Cornelius
Lowry, Annie
Medicine Snake Woman
Mountain Wolf Woman
Owl Woman
Parker, Julia F.
Pocahontas
Pretty-shield
Sacagawea
Sekaquaptewa, Helen
Smith, Kathleen
Somersal, Laura
Stanley, Dorothy Amora
Tomassa
Tsupu
Zuni, Flora

EDUCATION

Ahenakew, Freda
Alberty, Eliza Missouri Bushyhead
Allen, Minerva
Anderson, Mabel Washbourne

Archambault, JoAllyn
Armstrong, Jeannette
Ayoungman, Vivian
Broker, Ignatia
Bronson, Ruth Muskrat
Brown, Catharine
Brown, Emily Ivanoff
Callahan, Sophia Alice
Cleghorn, Mildred Imoch
Cobb, Isabelle
Cochran, Jo Whitehorse
Cook-Lynn, Elizabeth
Cuny, Sister Genevieve
Dauenhauer, Nora Marks
Deer, Ada
Dietz, Angel DeCora
Erdrich, Louise
Francisco, Nia
Hailstone, Vivien
Hale, Janet Campbell
Hampton, Carol Cussen
Harjo, Joy
Harnar, Nellie Shaw
Heth, Charlotte Anne Wilson
Hilbert, Vi
Hogan, Linda
Hungry Wolf, Beverly
Isom, Joan Shaddox
John, Mary
Kidwell, Clara S.
Kilpatrick, Anna Gritts
Kirkness, Verna J.
Krepps, Ethel C.
LaFlesche Picotte Diddock, Marguerite
LaFlesche Tibbles, Susette
LaRoque, Emma
Loloma, Otellie
Mann, Henri
Medicine, Beatrice A.
Momaday, Natachee Scott
Neakok, Sadie Brower
Nelson, Margaret F.
Parker, Julia F.
Paul, Alice S.
Pease-Windy Boy, Jeanine
Peterson, Helen
Picotte, Agnes

Potts, Marie
Roe Cloud, Elizabeth Bender
Roessel, Ruth W.
Rose, Wendy
Ross, Agnes Allen
Sanchez, Carol Lee
Saubel, Katherine Siva
Shanley, Kathryn
Silko, Leslie Marmon
Sisk-Franco, Caleen A.
Sneve, Virginia Driving Hawk
Somersal, Laura
Stanley, Dorothy Amora
Steele, Lois Fister
Swan, Madonna
Swentzell, Rina
Tiger, Winifred
Velarde, Pablita
White, Elizabeth Q.
Witt, Shirley Hill
Wright, Muriel Hazel
Zepeda, Ofelia

FUR TRADE

Ainse, Sally
Netnokwa

HISTORIAN

Eaton, Rachel Caroline
Parker, Julia F.
Wright, Muriel Hazel

LAW

Arthur, Claudeen Bates
Krepps, Ethel C.
Neakok, Sadie Brower
Pinkerman-Uri, Connie Redbird
Thorpe, Grace

LIBRARY

Salabiye, Velma S.

LINGUISTICS

Ahenakew, Freda
Brink, Jeanne

Deloria, Ella Cara
Hilbert, Vi
Zepeda, Ofelia

LITERATURE/CRITICISM

Abeita, Louise
Allen, Minerva
Allen, Paula Gunn
Anauta
Anderson, Mabel Washbourne
Anderson, Owanah
Armstrong, Jeannette
Awiakta, Marilou
Bahe, Liz Sohappy
Bennett, Kay Curley
Bighorse, Tiana
Bonnin, Gertrude Simmons
Brant, Beth
Brass, Eleanor
Brigham, Besmilr Moore
Brown, Emily Ivanoff
Burns, Diane M.
Burton, Jimalee Chitwood
Callahan, Sophia Alice
Campbell, Maria
Cardiff, Gladys
Carlo, Poldine Demoski
Chrystos
Cochran, Jo Whitehorse
Cook-Lynn, Elizabeth
Crying Wind
Culleton, Beatrice
Dauenhauer, Nora Marks
De Clue, Charlotte
Dietz, Angel DeCora
Endrezze, Anita
Erdrich, Louise
Evans, Mary Augusta Tappage
Francisco, Nia
Fry, Maggie Ann Culver
Glancy, Diane
Goose, Mary
Gould, Janice May
Green, Rayna Diane
Hail, Raven
Hale, Janet Campbell
Harjo, Joy

Henry, Jeannette
Hogan, Linda
Hungry Wolf, Beverly
Isom, Joan Shaddox
Joe, Rita
Johnson, Emily Pauline
Johnston, Verna Patronella
Keams, Geraldine
Keeshig-Tobias, Lenore
LaDuke, Winona
LaFlesche Tibbles, Susette
LaRoque, Emma
Lone Dog, Louise
Mann, Henri
Maracle, Lee
McDaniel, Wilma Elizabeth
Medicine, Beatrice A.
Mourning Dove
Naranjo-Morse, Nora
Rose, Wendy
Sanchez, Carol Lee
Shanley, Kathryn
Shaw, Anna Moore
Silko, Leslie Marmon
Slipperjack, Ruby
Smith, Kathleen
Sneve, Virginia Driving Hawk
Stewart, Irene
TallMountain, Mary
Tapahonso, Luci
Tohe, Laura
Tremblay, Gail
Volborth, Judith Mountain Leaf
Walsh, Marnie
Walters, Anna Lee
White, Elizabeth Q.
Whiteman, Roberta Hill
Winnie, Lucille Jerry
Wittstock, Laura Waterman
Woody, Elizabeth
Wright, Muriel Hazel
Zepeda, Ofelia

MEDICINE (WESTERN)

Bronson, Ruth Muskrat
Cobb, Isabelle
Ignacio, Carmella

Jumper, Betty Mae
Krepps, Ethel C.
LaFlesche Picotte, Susan
Parrish, Essie
Pinkerman-Uri, Connie Redbird
Shanley, Kathryn
Steele, Lois Fister
Wauneka, Annie Dodge

MEDICINE (TRADITIONAL)

Billie, Susie
Chona, Maria
Coocoochee
Jarvis, Rosie
Lozen
McKay, Mabel
Modesto, Ruby
Sanapia
The-Other-Magpie

MISSIONARY WORK

Brown, Catharine
Cuny, Sister Genevieve
LaFlesche Picotte, Susan
Stewart, Irene
White, Elizabeth Q.

MUSIC

Gould, Janice May
Hail, Raven
Heth, Charlotte Anne Wilson
Kilpatrick, Anna Gritts
Lawson, Roberta Campbell
White, Elizabeth Q.

PERFORMANCE

Blackstone, Tsianina Redfeather
Keams, Geraldine
Horn, Kahn-Tineta
Sainte-Marie, Buffy
Skye, Ferial Deer

PHOTOGRAPHY

Woody, Elizabeth

SOCIAL WORK

Deer, Ada

STORYTELLING

Hilbert, Vi
Keeshig-Tobias, Lenore
Slipperjack, Ruby
Tohe, Laura
Zuni, Flora

TRIBAL LEADERSHIP

Awashonks
Hopkins, Sarah Winnemucca
Jimulla, Viola Pelhame
Jumper, Betty Mae
LaFlesche Farley, Rosalie
Mankiller, Wilma
Musgrove, Mary
Osceola, Laura Mae
Queen Anne of Pamunkey
Tiger, Winifred
Ward, Nancy
Wauneka, Annie Dodge
Wetamoo

WARRIOR

Dahteste
Lozen
Running Eagle
The-Other-Magpie
Woman Chief

Appendix Two

Entries by Decades of Birth

Before 1840

Ainse, Sally
Alberty, Eliza Missouri Bushyhead
Awashonks
Big Eyes
Brant, Molly
Brown, Catharine
Buffalo Bird Woman
Coocoochee
Dat-So-La-Lee
Dorion Woman
Juana Maria
Juneau, Josette
Lozen
Medicine Snake Woman
Musgrove, Mary
Netnokwa
Owl Woman
Parker, Cynthia Ann
Pocahontas
Running Eagle
Sacagawea
Tekakwitha, Kateri
Tomassa
Tsupu
Ward, Nancy
Wetamoo
Woman Chief

1841–1860

Chona, Maria
Cobb, Isabelle
Hopkins, Sarah Winnemucca

Indian Emily
Jarvis, Rosie
LaFlesche Tibbles, Susette
Mayo, Sarah Jim
Nampeyo
Pretty-shield
The-Other-Magpie

1861–1880

Anderson, Mabel Washbourne
Bonnin, Gertrude Simmons
Dahteste
Dietz, Angel DeCora
Eaton, Rachel Caroline
Jimulla, Viola Pelhame
Johnson, Emily Pauline
Kellogg, Laura Cornelius
LaFlesche Farley, Rosalie
LaFlesche Picotte Diddock, Marguerite
LaFlesche Picotte, Susan
Lawson, Roberta Campbell
Lowry, Annie
Running Eagle
Sacred White Buffalo, Mother Mary
    Catherine
Telles, Lucy Parker

1881–1900

Allen, Elsie
Billie, Susie
Blackstone, Tsianina Redfeather
Bronson, Ruth Muskrat
Cuero, Delfina

Davidson, Florence Edenshaw
Deloria, Ella Cara
Dick, Lena Frank
Evans, Mary Augusta Tappage
Fry, Maggie Ann Culver
Highwalking, Belle
Lewis, Lucy
Martinez, Maria Montoya
Mountain Wolf Woman
Mourning Dove
Nunez, Bonita Wa Wa Calachaw
Peña, Tonita
Potts, Marie
Roe Cloud, Elizabeth Bender
Sanapia
Sekaquaptewa, Helen
Shaw, Anna Moore
Somersal, Laura
Tantaquidgeon, Gladys
White, Elizabeth Q.
Wright, Muriel Hazel
Zuni, Flora

1901–1920

Ashoona, Pitseolak
Bighorse, Tiana
Blackgoat, Roberta
Brass, Eleanor
Brigham, Besmilr Moore
Broker, Ignatia
Brown, Emily Ivanoff
Burton, Jimalee Chitwood
Carlo, Poldine Demoski
Cleghorn, Mildred Imoch
Cordero, Helen Quintana
Hailstone, Vivien
Harnar, Nellie Shaw
Henry, Jeannette
Hilbert, Vi
Jemison, Alice Lee
John, Mary
Johnston, Verna Patronella
Kegg, Maude Mitchell
Kilpatrick, Anna Gritts
McDaniel, Wilma Elizabeth
McKay, Mabel
Modesto, Ruby

Momaday, Natachee Scott
Nampeyo, Daisy Hooee
Neakok, Sadie Brower
Parrish, Essie
Pavatea, Garnet
Peterson, Helen
Ross, Agnes Allen
Saubel, Katherine Siva
Stewart, Irene
TallMountain, Mary
Velarde, Pablita
Venegas, Hildreth Marie Twostars
Wauneka, Annie Dodge
Winnie, Lucille Jerry

1921–1940

Abeita, Louise
Ackerman, Maria Joseph
Ahenakew, Freda
Allen, Paula Gunn
Anderson, Owanah
Ashevak, Kenojuak
Awiakta, Marilou
Bennett, Kay Curley
Blue Legs
Campbell, Maria
Carius, Helen Slwooko
Chouteau, Yvonne
Cook-Lynn, Elizabeth
Cuny, Sister Genevieve
Dauenhauer, Nora Marks
Deer, Ada
Hail, Raven
Hampton, Carol Cussen
Hardin, Helen Bagshaw
Harris, LaDonna
Heth, Charlotte Anne Wilson
Horn, Kahn-Tineta
Isom, Joan Shaddox
Joe, Rita
Jumper, Betty Mae
Kirkness, Verna J.
Loloma, Otellie
Mann, Henri
McCloud, Janet
Medicine, Beatrice A.
Medicine Flower, Grace

Nelson, Margaret F.
Osceola, Laura Mae
Parker, Julia F.
Picotte, Agnes
Pinkerman-Uri, Connie Redbird
Roessel, Ruth W.
Sainte-Marie, Buffy
Sanchez, Carol Lee
Skye, Ferial Deer
Smith, Jaune Quick-To-See
Smith, Kathleen
Sneve, Virginia Driving Hawk
Stanley, Dorothy Amora
Steele, Lois Fister
Swan, Madonna
Swentzell, Rina
Thorpe, Grace
Tiger, Winifred

1941–1960

Allen, Minerva
Aquash, Anna Mae Pictou
Archambault, JoAllyn
Armstrong, Jeannette
Arthur, Claudeen Bates
Ayoungman, Vivian
Bahe, Liz Sohappy
Bird, Gloria
Bird, JoAnne
Bordeaux, Shirley
Brant, Beth
Brink, Jeanne
Burns, Diane M.
Callahan, Sophia Alice
Cardiff, Gladys
Chrystos
Cochran, Jo Whitehorse
Crow Dog, Mary
Crying Wind
Culleton, Beatrice
De Clue, Charlotte
Endrezze, Anita
Erdrich, Louise

Folwell, Jody
Francisco, Nia
Glancy, Diane
Goose, Mary
Gould, Janice May
Green, Rayna Diane
Hale, Janet Campbell
Harjo, Joy
Hogan, Linda
Hungry Wolf, Beverly
Ignacio, Carmella
Keams, Geraldine
Keeshig-Tobias, Lenore
Kidwell, Clara S.
LaDuke, Winona
LaRoque, Emma
Mankiller, Wilma
Maracle, Lee
Morez, Mary
Naranjo-Morse, Nora
Owen, Angie Reano
Pease-Windy Boy, Jeanine
Rose, Wendy
Saila, Pitaloosie
Sakiestewa, Ramona
Salabiye, Velma S.
Shanley, Kathryn
Silko, Leslie Marmon
Sisk-Franco, Caleen A.
Slipperjack, Ruby
Stroud, Virginia
Tapahonso, Luci
Tohe, Laura
Tremblay, Gail
Volborth, Judith Mountain Leaf
Walters, Anna Lee
White, Madeline Melba
Whiteman, Roberta Hill
Williams, Alice Cling
Witt, Shirley Hill
Woody, Elizabeth
Zepeda, Ofelia

Appendix Three

Entries by State/Province of Birth

ALASKA

Ackerman, Maria Joseph
Brown, Emily Ivanoff
Carius, Helen Slwooko
Carlo, Poldine Demoski
Dauenhauer, Nora Marks
Neakok, Sadie Brower

ALBERTA

Ayoungman, Vivian
LaRoque, Emma

APACHERIA

Dahteste
Lozen

ARCTIC

Ashevak, Kenojuak
Ashoona, Pitseolak
Saila, Pitaloosie
TallMountain, Mary

ARIZONA

Arthur, Claudeen Bates
Bighorse, Tiana
Blackgoat, Roberta
Chona, Maria
Francisco, Nia
Ignacio, Carmella
Jimulla, Viola Pelhame
Keams, Geraldine

Loloma, Otellie
Morez, Mary
Nampeyo
Nampeyo, Daisy Hooee
Paul, Alice S.
Pavatea, Garnet
Roessel, Ruth W.
Salabiye, Velma S.
Sekaquaptewa, Helen
Shaw, Anna Moore
Stewart, Irene
Tohe, Laura
Wauneka, Annie Dodge
White, Elizabeth Q.
Williams, Alice Cling
Woody, Elizabeth
Zepeda, Ofelia

ARKANSAS

Alberty, Eliza Missouri Bushyhead
Anderson, Mabel Washbourne

BAFFIN ISLAND

Anauta

BRITISH COLUMBIA

Armstrong, Jeannette
Davidson, Florence Edenshaw
Evans, Mary Augusta Tappage
John, Mary
Maracle, Lee

CALIFORNIA

Allen, Elsie
Bird, Gloria
Bird, JoAnne
Burns, Diane M.
Chrystos
Cuero, Delfina
Dat-So-La-Lee
Dick, Lena Frank
Endrezze, Anita
Gould, Janice May
Hailstone, Vivien
Hale, Janet Campbell
Jarvis, Rosie
Juana Maria
McKay, Mabel
Modesto, Ruby
Nunez, Bonita Wa Wa Calachaw
Parker, Julia F.
Parrish, Essie
Pinkerman-Uri, Connie Redbird
Potts, Marie
Rose, Wendy
Saubel, Katherine Siva
Sisk-Franco, Caleen A.
Smith, Kathleen
Somersal, Laura
Stanley, Dorothy Amora
Stroud, Virginia
Telles, Lucy Parker
Tiger, Winifred
Tsupu

CHEROKEE NATION

Brown, Catharine

COLORADO

Hogan, Linda

CONNECTICUT

Tantaquidgeon, Gladys

FLORIDA

Billie, Susie
Jumper, Betty Mae

Osceola, Laura Mae

GEORGIA

Musgrove, Mary

IDAHO

Mourning Dove
Sacagawea

ILLINOIS

Parker, Cynthia Ann

IOWA

Goose, Mary

KENTUCKY

Momaday, Natachee Scott

MANITOBA

Culleton, Beatrice
Kirkness, Verna J.

MEXICO

Tomassa

MICHIGAN

Brant, Beth

MINNESOTA

Broker, Ignatia
Erdrich, Louise
Kegg, Maude Mitchell
LaDuke, Winona
Roe Cloud, Elizabeth Bender

MISSISSIPPI

Brigham, Besmilr Moore

MISSOURI

Glancy, Diane

MONTANA

Allen, Minerva
Cardiff, Gladys
Highwalking, Belle
Medicine Snake Woman
Pretty-shield
Shanley, Kathryn
Smith, Jaune Quick-To-See
Steele, Lois Fister

NEBRASKA

Bordeaux, Shirley
Dietz, Angel DeCora
LaFlesche Farley, Rosalie
LaFlesche Picotte, Susan
LaFlesche Picotte Diddock, Marguerite
LaFlesche Tibbles, Susette

NEVADA

Harnar, Nellie Shaw
Hopkins, Sarah Winnemucca
Lowry, Annie
Mayo, Sarah Jim

NEW MEXICO

Abeita, Louise
Allen, Paula Gunn
Bennett, Kay Curley
Cordero, Helen Quintana
Folwell, Jody
Gonzales, Rose
Hardin, Helen Bagshaw
Lewis, Lucy
Martinez, Maria Montoya
Medicine Flower, Grace
Naranjo-Morse, Nora
Owen, Angie Reano
Peña, Tonita
Sakiestewa, Ramona
Sanchez, Carol Lee
Silko, Leslie Marmon
Swentzell, Rina
Tapahonso, Luci
Velarde, Pablita
Zuni, Flora

NEW YORK

Ainse, Sally
Brant, Molly
Horn, Kahn-Tineta
Jemison, Alice Lee
Tekakwitha, Kateri
Tremblay, Gail
Volborth, Judith Mountain Leaf
Witt, Shirley Hill
Wittstock, Laura Waterman

NORTH CAROLINA

Henry, Jeannette

NORTH DAKOTA

Buffalo Bird Woman
Sacred White Buffalo, Mother Mary
 Catherine

NOVA SCOTIA

Aquash, Anna Mae Pictou
Joe, Rita

OKLAHOMA

Anderson, Owanah
Archambault, JoAllyn
Blackstone, Tsianina Redfeather
Bronson, Ruth Muskrat
Burton, Jimalee Chitwood
Callahan, Sophia Alice
Cleghorn, Mildred Imoch
De Clue, Charlotte
Eaton, Rachel Caroline
Fry, Maggie Ann Culver
Hail, Raven
Hampton, Carol Cussen
Harjo, Joy
Harris, LaDonna
Heth, Charlotte Anne Wilson
Hill, Joan
Isom, Joan Shaddox
Kidwell, Clara S.
Kilpatrick, Anna Gritts
Krepps, Ethel C.
Mankiller, Wilma

Mann, Henri
McDaniel, Wilma Elizabeth
Nelson, Margaret F.
Sanapia
Thorpe, Grace
Walters, Anna Lee
Winnie, Lucille Jerry
Wright, Muriel Hazel

ONTARIO

Johnson, Emily Pauline
Johnston, Verna Patronella
Keeshig-Tobias, Lenore
Lavell, Jeannette
Slipperjack, Ruby

QUEBEC

Coocoochee

RHODE ISLAND

Awashonks
Wetamoo

SASKATCHEWAN

Ahenakew, Freda
Brass, Eleanor
Campbell, Maria

SOUTH DAKOTA

Blue Legs
Bonnin, Gertrude Simmons
Cook-Lynn, Elizabeth
Crow Dog, Mary
Cuny, Sister Genevieve
Deloria, Ella Cara
Medicine, Beatrice A.
Peterson, Helen
Picotte, Agnes

Ross, Agnes Allen
Sneve, Virginia Driving Hawk
Swan, Madonna
Venegas, Hildreth Marie Twostars
White, Madeline Melba

TENNESSEE

Awiakta, Marilou
Cobb, Isabelle

TEXAS

Big Eyes
Chouteau, Yvonne
Green, Rayna Diane
Indian Emily

VERMONT

Brink, Jeanne

VIRGINIA

Pocahontas
Queen Anne

WASHINGTON

Bahe, Liz Sohappy
Cochran, Jo Whitehorse
Hilbert, Vi
McCloud, Janet
Pease-Windy Boy, Jeanine

WISCONSIN

Deer, Ada
Juneau, Josette
Kellogg, Laura Cornelius
Mountain Wolf Woman
Skye, Ferial Deer
Whiteman, Roberta Hill

Appendix Four

Entries by Tribal Affiliation

ABENAKI

Brink, Jeanne

ACOMA

Lewis, Lucy

ALGONQUIN

Tekakwitha, Kateri
Wetamoo

APACHE

Dahteste
Indian Emily

APACHE/COMANCHE

Volborth, Judith Mountain Leaf

ASSINIBOINE

Allen, Minerva
Shanley, Kathryn
Steele, Lois Fister

ATHABASKAN

TallMountain, Mary

BLACKFOOT

Ayoungman, Vivian

BLOOD

Hungry Wolf, Beverly
Medicine Snake Woman

CADDO

Hampton, Carol Cussen

CAHUILLA

Modesto, Ruby
Saubel, Katherine Siva

CARRIER

John, Mary

CHEMEHUEVI/OJIBWA

Burns, Diane M.

CHEROKEE

Alberty, Eliza Missouri Bushyhead
Anderson, Mabel Washbourne
Awiakta, Marilou
Bronson, Ruth Muskrat
Brown, Catharine
Burton, Jimalee Chitwood
Cardiff, Gladys
Chouteau, Yvonne
Cobb, Isabelle
Eaton, Rachel Caroline
Fry, Maggie Ann Culver
Glancy, Diane
Green, Rayna Diane
Hail, Raven
Henry, Jeannette
Heth, Charlotte Anne Wilson
Isom, Joan Shaddox
Kilpatrick, Anna Gritts

Mankiller, Wilma
McDaniel, Wilma Elizabeth
Momaday, Natachee Scott
Nelson, Margaret F.
Stroud, Virginia
Tiger, Winifred
Ward, Nancy

CHEROKEE/CREEK

Hill, Joan

CHEROKEE/DELAWARE

Lawson, Roberta Campbell

CHEYENNE

Highwalking, Belle
Mann, Henri
Owl Woman

CHICKSAW

Hogan, Linda

CHIRICAHUA APACHE

Lozen

CHOCTAW

Anderson, Owanah
Brigham, Besmilr Moore
Wright, Muriel Hazel

CHOCTAW/CHEROKEE

Pinkerman-Uri, Connie Redbird

CHOCTAW/CHIPPEWA

Kidwell, Clara S.

CHOCTAW/SICANGU

Bordeaux, Shirley

COCHITI

Cordero, Helen Quintana

COEUR d'ALENE

Hale, Janet Campbell

COMANCHE

Harris, LaDonna
Sanapia
Tomassa

CREE

Ahenakew, Freda
Sainte-Marie, Buffy

CREE/MÉTIS

LaRoque, Emma

CREE/SAULTAUX

Brass, Eleanor

CREE/SHOSHONE

Smith, Jaune Quick-To-See

CREEK

Blackstone, Tsianina Redfeather
Callahan, Sophia Alice
Harjo, Joy
Musgrove, Mary

CROW

Pease-Windy Boy, Jeanine
Pretty-shield
The-Other-Magpie

DIEGUEÑO

Cuero, Delfina

FORT SILL APACHE

Cleghorn, Mildred Imoch

GROS VENTRE

Woman Chief

HAIDA

Davidson, Florence Edenshaw

HIDATSA

Buffalo Bird Woman

HOPI

Loloma, Otellie
Nampeyo
Nampeyo, Daisy Hooee
Sakiestewa, Ramona
Sekaquaptewa, Helen
White, Elizabeth Q.

INUIT

Anauta
Ashevak, Kenojuak
Ashoona, Pitseolak
Carius, Helen Slwooko
Saila, Pitaloosie

INUPIAT

Neakok, Sadie Brower

IOWA

Dorion Woman

IROQUOIS

Brant, Molly

ISLETA

Abeita, Louise

KICKAPOO

Crying Wind

KIOWA

Krepps, Ethel C.

LAGUNA

Silko, Leslie Marmon

LAGUNA/SIOUX

Allen, Paula Gunn
Sanchez, Carol Lee

LAGUNA/ SANTO DOMINGO

Bird, Gloria

LUISENO

Nunez, Bonita Wa Wa Calachaw

MAIDU

Gould, Janice May
Potts, Marie

MENOMINEE

Chrystos
Deer, Ada
Juneau, Josette
Skye, Ferial Deer

MESQUAKIE/CHIPPEWA

Goose, Mary

MÉTIS

Campbell, Maria
Culleton, Beatrice
Maracle, Lee

MICMAC

Aquash, Anna Mae Pictou
Joe, Rita

MIWOK

Stanley, Dorothy Amora
Telles, Lucy Parker
Tsupu

MIWOK/HOPI

Rose, Wendy

MIWOK/POMO

Smith, Kathleen

MOHAWK

Brant, Beth
Coocoochee
Horn, Kahn-Tineta
Johnson, Emily Pauline
Witt, Shirley Hill

MOHAWK/DELAWARE

Lone Dog, Louise

MOHEGAN

Tantaquidgeon, Gladys

NAVAJO

Arthur, Claudeen Bates
Bennett, Kay Curley
Bighorse, Tiana
Blackgoat, Roberta
Francisco, Nia
Keams, Geraldine
Morez, Mary
Roessel, Ruth W.
Salabiye, Velma S.
Stewart, Irene
Tapahonso, Luci
Wauneka, Annie Dodge
Williams, Alice Cling

NAVAJO/LAGUNA

Tohe, Laura

NICOLEÑO

Juana Maria

OJIBWA (CHIPPEWA)

Broker, Ignatia
Erdrich, Louise
Johnston, Verna Patronella
Kegg, Maude Mitchell
LaDuke, Winona
Lavell, Jeannette
Roe Cloud, Elizabeth Bender
Slipperjack, Ruby

OJIBWAY/POTTAWATOMI

Keeshig-Tobias, Lenore

OKANAGAN

Armstrong, Jeannette

OKANOGAN/COLVILLE

Mourning Dove

ONEIDA

Ainse, Sally
Kellogg, Laura Cornelius
Whiteman, Roberta Hill

ONONDAGA/ MICMAC

Tremblay, Gail

OSAGE

De Clue, Charlotte

OTTAWA

Netnokwa

PAIUTE

Harnar, Nellie Shaw
Hopkins, Sarah Winnemucca
Lowrey, Anne

PAMUNKEY

Queen Anne

PAWNEE/OTOE- MISSOURIA

Walters, Anna Lee

PIEGAN

Running Eagle

PIMA

Shaw, Anna Moore

POMO

Allen, Elsie
Jarvis, Rosie
McKay, Mabel
Parker, Julia F.
Parrish, Essie

PONCA/OMAHA

LaFlesche Picotte Diddock, Marguerite
LaFlesche Farley, Rosalie
LaFlesche Picotte, Susan
LaFlesche Tibbles, Susette

POWHATEN

Pocahontas

SAN ILDEFONSO

Peña, Tonita

SAN JUAN

Gonzales, Rose

SANTA CLARA

Folwell, Jody
Medicine Flower, Grace
Hardin, Helen Bagshaw
Swentzell, Rina

SANTO DOMINGO

Owen, Angie Reano

SAUK-FOX

Thorpe, Grace

SEMINOLE

Billie, Susie
Jumper, Betty Mae
Osceola, Laura Mae

SENECA

Wittstock, Laura Waterman

SENECA/CAYUGA

Winnie, Lucille Jerry

SENECA/CHEROKEE

Jemison, Alice Lee

SHOSHONE

Sacagawea

SIOUX

Archambault, JoAllyn
Bird, JoAnne
Blue Legs
Bonnin, Gertrude Simmons
Cochran, Jo Whitehorse
Cook-Lynn, Elizabeth
Crow Dog, Mary
Cuny, Sister Genevieve
Deloria, Ella Cara
Medicine, Beatrice A.
Peterson, Helen
Picotte, Agnes
Ross, Agnes Allen
Sacred White Buffalo, Mother Mary
  Catherine
Sneve, Virginia Driving Hawk
Swan, Madonna
Venegas, Hildreth Marie Twostars
Walsh, Marnie
White, Madeline Melba

SODA CREEK

Evans, Mary Augusta Tappage

SWAMPY CREE

Kirkness, Verna J.

TEWA

Martinez, Maria Montoya
Naranjo-Morse, Nora
Velarde, Pablita

TEWA/HOPI

Pavatea, Garnet

TLINGIT

Ackerman, Maria Joseph
Dauenhauer, Nora Marks

TOHONO O'ODHAM (PAPAGO)

Chona, Maria
Ignacio, Carmella
Paul, Alice S.
Zepeda, Ofelia

TULALIP

McCloud, Janet

UPPER SKAGIT

Hilbert, Vi

WAMPANOAG

Awashonks

WAPPO/POMO

Somersal, Laura

WARM SPRINGS/ WASCO/ NAVAJO

Woody, Elizabeth

WASHO

Dat-So-La-Lee
Dick, Lena Frank
Mayo, Sarah Jim

WICHITAS

Big Eyes

WINNEBAGO

Dietz, Angel DeCora
Mountain Wolf Woman

WINTU

Sisk-Franco, Caleen A.

YAKIMA

Bahe, Liz Sohappy

YAQUI

Endrezze, Anita

YAVAPAI

Jimulla, Viola Pelhame

YUKON ATHABASCAN

Carlo, Poldine Demoski

YUPIK

Brown, Emily Ivanoff

YUROK/KAROK

Hailstone, Vivien

ZUNI

Zuni, Flora

Index